THE POETIC EDDA

BY

HENRY ADAMS BELLOWS

THE POETIC EDDA

TRANSLATED FROM THE ICELANDIC WITH AN INTRODUCTION AND NOTES

BY

HENRY ADAMS BELLOWS

TWO VOLUMES IN ONE

1936

PRINCETON UNIVERSITY PRESS: PRINCETON

AMERICAN SCANDINAVIAN FOUNDATION

NEW YORK

CONTENTS

ACKNOWLEDGEMENT

The General Introduction mentions many of the scholars to whose work this translation owes a special debt. Particular reference, however, should here be made to the late William Henry Schofield, Professor of Comparative Literature in Harvard University and President of The American-Scandinavian Foundation, under whose guidance this translation was begun; to Henry Goddard Leach, for many years Secretary of The American-Scandinavian Foundation, and to William Witherle Lawrence, Professor of English in Columbia University and Chairman of the Foundation's Committee on Publications, for their assistance with the manuscript and the proofs; and to Hanna Astrup Larsen, the Foundation's literary secretary, for her efficient management of the complex details of publication.

GENERAL INTRODUCTION

THERE is scarcely any literary work of great importance which has been less readily available for the general reader, or even for the serious student of literature, than the Poetic Edda. Translations have been far from numerous, and only in Germany has the complete work of translation been done in the full light of recent scholarship. In English the only versions were long the conspicuously inadequate one made by Thorpe, and published about half a century ago, and the unsatisfactory prose translations in Vigfusson and Powell's *Corpus Poeticum Boreale*, reprinted in the Norrœna collection. An excellent translation of the poems dealing with the gods, in verse and with critical and explanatory notes, made by Olive Bray, was, however, published by the Viking Club of London in 1908. In French there exist only partial translations, chief among them being those made by Bergmann many years ago. Among the seven or eight German versions, those by the Brothers Grimm and by Karl Simrock, which had considerable historical importance because of their influence on nineteenth century German literature and art, and particularly on the work of Richard Wagner, have been largely superseded by Hugo Gering's admirable translation, published in 1892, and by the recent two volume rendering by Genzmer, with excellent notes by Andreas Heusler, 194-1920. There are competent translations in both Norwegian and Swedish. The lack of any complete and adequately annotated English rendering in metrical form, based on a critical text, and profiting by the cumulative labors of such scholars as Mogk, Vigfusson, Finnur Jonsson, Grundtvig, Bugge, Gislason, Hildebrand, Lüning, Sweet, Niedner, Ettmüller, Müllenhoff, Edzardi, B. M. Olsen, Sievers, Sijmons, Detter, Heinzel, Falk, Neckel, Heusler, and Gering, has kept this extraordinary work practically out of the reach of those who have had neither time nor inclination to master the intricacies of the original Old Norse.

On the importance of the material contained in the *Poetic Edda* it is here needless to dwell at any length. We have inherited the Germanic traditions in our very speech, and the *Poetic Edda* is the original storehouse of Germanic mythology. It is, indeed, in many ways the greatest literary monument preserved to us out of the antiquity of the kindred races which we call Germanic. Moreover, it has a literary value altogether apart from its historical significance. The mythological poems include, in the *Voluspo*, one of the vastest conceptions of the creation and ultimate destruction of the world ever crystallized in literary form; in parts of the *Hovamol*, a collection of wise counsels that can bear comparison with most of the Biblical Book of Proverbs; in the *Lokasenna*, a comedy none the less full of vivid characterization because its humor is often broad; and in the *Thrymskvitha*, one of the finest ballads in the world. The hero poems give us, in its oldest and most vivid extant form, the story of Sigurth, Brynhild, and Atli, the Norse parallel to the German *Nibelungenlied*. The Poetic Edda is not only of great interest to the student of antiquity; it is a collection including some of the most remark able poems which have been preserved to us from the period before the pen and the printing-press. replaced the poet-singer and oral tradition. It is above all else the desire to make better known the dramatic force, the vivid and often tremendous imagery, and the superb conceptions embodied in these poems which has called forth the present translation.

WHAT IS THE POETIC EDDA?

Even if the poems of the so-called Edda were not so significant and intrinsically so valuable, the long series of scholarly struggles which have been going on over them for the better part of three centuries would in itself give them a peculiar interest. Their history is strangely mysterious. We do not know who composed them, or when or where they were composed; we are by no means sure who collected them or when he did so; finally, we are not absolutely certain as to what an "Edda" is, and the best guess at the meaning of the word renders its application to this collection of poems more or less misleading.

A brief review of the chief facts in the history of the *Poetic Edda* will explain why this uncertainty has persisted. Preserved in various manuscripts of the thirteenth and early fourteenth centuries is a prose work consisting of a very extensive collection of mythological stories, an explanation of the important figures and tropes of Norse poetic diction,--the poetry of the Icelandic and Norwegian skalds was appallingly complex in this respect,--and a treatise on metrics. This work, clearly a handbook for poets, was commonly known as the "Edda" of Snorri Sturluson, for at the head of the copy of it in the *Uppsalabok*, a manuscript written presumably some fifty or sixty years after Snorri's death, which was in 1241, we find: "This book is called Edda, which Snorri Sturluson composed." This work, well known as the *Prose Edda*, Snorri's *Edda* or the *Younger Edda*, has recently been made available to readers of English in the admirable translation by Arthur G. Brodeur, published by the American-Scandinavian Foundation in 1916.

Icelandic tradition, however, persisted in ascribing either this *Edda* or one resembling it to Snorri's much earlier compatriot, Sæmund the Wise (1056-1133). When, early in the seventeenth century, the learned Arngrimur Jonsson proved to everyone's satisfaction that Snorri and nobody else must have been responsible for the work in question, the next thing to determine was what, if anything, Sæmund had done of the same kind. The nature of Snorri's book gave a clue. In the mythological stories related a number of poems were quoted, and as these and other poems were to all appearances Snorri's chief sources of information, it was assumed that Sæmund must have written or compiled a verse *Edda*--whatever an "Edda" might be--on which Snorri's work was largely based.

So matters stood when, in 1643, Brynjolfur Sveinsson, Bishop of Skalholt, discovered a manuscript, clearly written as early as 1300, containing twenty-nine poems, complete or fragmentary, and some of them with the very lines and stanzas used by Snorri. Great was the joy of the scholars, for here, of course, must be at least a part of the long-sought *Edda* of Sæmund the Wise. Thus the good bishop promptly labeled his find, and as Sæmund's *Edda*, the *Elder Edda* or the *Poetic Edda* it has been known to this day.

This precious manuscript, now in the Royal Library in Copenhagen, and known as the *Codex Regius* (R2365), has been the basis for all published editions of the Eddic poems. A few poems of similar character found elsewhere have subsequently been added to the collection, until now most editions include, as in this translation, a total of thirty-four. A shorter manuscript now in the Arnamagnæan collection in Copenhagen (AM748), contains fragmentary or complete versions of six of the poems in the *Codex Regius*, and one other, *Baldrs Draumar*, not found in that collection. Four other poems (*Rigsthula, Hyndluljoth, Grougaldr* and *Fjolsvinnsmol*, the last two here combined under the title of Svipdagsmol), from various manuscripts, so closely resemble in subject-matter and style the poems in the *Codex Regius* that they have been included by most editors in the collection. Finally, Snorri's *Edda* contains one complete poem, the *Grottasongr*, which many editors have added to the poetic collection; it is, however, not included in this translation, as an admirable English version of it is available in Mr. Brodeur's rendering of Snorri's work.

iv

From all this it is evident that the *Poetic Edda*, as we now know it, is no definite and plainly limited work, but rather a more or less haphazard collection of separate poems, dealing either with Norse mythology or with hero-cycles unrelated to the traditional history of greater Scandinavia or Iceland. How many other similar poems, now lost, may have existed in such collections as were current in Iceland in the later twelfth and thirteenth centuries we cannot know, though it is evident that some poems of this type are missing. We can say only that thirty-four poems have been preserved, twenty-nine of them in a single manuscript collection, which differ considerably in subject-matter and style from all the rest of extant Old Norse poetry, and these we group together as the *Poetic Edda*. But what does the word "Edda" mean? Various guesses have been made. An early assumption was that the word somehow meant "Poetics," which fitted Snorri's treatise to a nicety, but which, in addition to the lack of philological evidence to support this interpretation, could by no stretch of scholarly subtlety be made appropriate to the collection of poems. Jacob Grimm ingeniously identified the word with the word "edda" used in one of the poems, the *Rigsthula*, where, rather conjecturally, it means "great-grand mother." The word exists in this sense no where else in Norse literature, and Grimm's suggestion of "Tales of a Grandmother," though at one time it found wide acceptance, was grotesquely. inappropriate to either the prose or the verse work.

At last Eirikr Magnusson hit on what appears the likeliest solution of the puzzle: that "Edda" is simply the genitive form of the proper name "Oddi." Oddi was a settlement in the southwest of Iceland, certainly the home of Snorri Sturluson for many years, and, traditionally at least, also the home of Sæmund the Wise. That Snorri's work should have been called "The Book of Oddi" is altogether reasonable, for such a method of naming books was common--witness the "Book of the Flat Island" and other early manuscripts. That Sæmund may also have written or compiled another "Oddi-Book" is perfectly possible, and that tradition should have said he did so is entirely natural.

It is, however, an open question whether or not Sæmund had anything to do with making the collection, or any part of it, now known as the Poetic Edda, for of course the seventeenth-century assignment of the work to him is negligible. p. xvii We can say only that he may have made some such compilation, for he was a diligent student of Icelandic tradition and history, and was famed throughout the North for his learning. But otherwise no trace of his works survives, and as he was educated in Paris, it is probable that he wrote rather in Latin than in the vernacular.

All that is reasonably certain is that by the middle or last of the twelfth century there existed in Iceland one or more written collections of Old Norse mythological and heroic poems, that the *Codex Regius*, a copy made a hundred years or so later, represents at least a considerable part of one of these, and that the collection of thirty-four poems which we now know as the*Poetic* or *Elder Edda* is practically all that has come down to us of Old Norse poetry of this type. Anything more is largely guesswork, and both the name of the compiler and the meaning of the title "Edda" are conjectural.

THE ORIGIN OF THE EDDIC POEMS

There is even less agreement about the birthplace, authorship and date of the Eddic poems themselves than about the nature of the existing collection. Clearly the poems were the work of many different men, living in different periods; clearly, too, most of them existed in oral tradition for generations before they were committed to writing. In general, the mythological poems seem strongly marked by pagan sincerity, although efforts have been made to prove them the results of deliberate archaizing; and as Christianity became generally accepted throughout the Norse world early in the eleventh century, it seems altogether likely that most of the poems dealing with the gods definitely antedate the year 1000. The earlier terminus is still a matter of dispute. The general weight of critical opinion, based chiefly on the linguistic evidence presented by Hoffory, Finnur Jonsson and others, has indicated that the poems did not assume anything closely analogous to their present forms prior to the ninth century. On the other hand, Magnus Olsen's interpretation of the inscriptions on the Eggjum Stone, which he places as early as the seventh century, have led so competent a scholar as Birger Nerman to say that "we may be warranted in concluding that some of the Eddic poems may have originated, wholly or partially, in the second part of the seventh century." As for the poems belonging to the hero cycles, one or two of them appear to be as late as 1100, but most of them probably date back at least to the century and a half following 900. It is a reasonable guess that the years between 850 and 1050 saw the majority of the Eddic poems worked into definite shape, but it must be remembered that many changes took place during the long subsequent period of oral transmission, and also that many of the legends, both mythological and heroic, on which the poems were based certainly existed in the Norse regions, and quite possibly in verse form, long before the year 900.

As to the origin of the legends on which the poems are based, the whole question, at least so far as the stories of the gods are concerned, is much too complex for discussion here. How much of the actual narrative material of the mythological lays is properly to be called Scandinavian is a matter for students of comparative mythology to guess at. The tales underlying the heroic lays are clearly of foreign origin: the Helgi story comes from Denmark, and that of Völund from Germany, as also the great mass of traditions centering around Sigurth (Siegfried), Brynhild, the sons of Gjuki, Atli (Attila), and Jormunrek (Ermanarich). The introductory notes to the various poems deal with the more important of these questions of origin. of the men who composed these poems,--'wrote" is obviously the wrong word--we know absolutely nothing, save that some of them must have been literary artists with a high degree of conscious skill. The Eddic poems are "folk-poetry,"--whatever that may be,--only in the sense that some of them strongly reflect racial feelings and beliefs; they are anything but crude or primitive in workmanship, and they show that not only the poets themselves, but also many of their hearers, must have made a careful study of the art of poetry.

Where the poems were shaped is equally uncertain. Any date prior to 875 would normally imply an origin on the mainland, but the necessarily fluid state of oral tradition made it possible for a poem to be "composed" many times over, and in various and far-separated places, without altogether losing its identity. Thus, even if a poem first assumed something approximating its present form in Iceland in the tenth century, it may none the less embody language characteristic of Norway two centuries earlier. Oral poetry has always had an amazing preservative power over language, and in considering the origins of such poems as these, we must cease thinking in terms of the printing-press, or even in those of the scribe. The claims of Norway as the birthplace of most of the Eddic poems have been extensively advanced, but the great literary activity of Iceland after the settlement of the island by Norwegian emigrants late in the ninth century makes the theory of an Icelandic home for many of the poems appear plausible. The two Atli lays, with what authority we do not know, bear in the *Codex Regius* the superscription "the Greenland poem," and internal evidence suggests that this statement may be correct. Certainly in one poem, the *Rigsthula*, and probably in several others, there are marks of Celtic influence. During a considerable part of the ninth and tenth centuries, Scandinavians were active in Ireland and in most of the western islands inhabited by branches of the Celtic race. Some scholars have, indeed, claimed nearly all the Eddic poems for these "Western Isles." However, as Iceland early came to be the true cultural center of this Scandinavian island world, it may be said that the preponderant evidence concerning the development of the Eddic poems in anything like their present form points in that direction, and certainly it was in Iceland that they were chiefly preserved.

THE EDDA AND OLD NORSE LITERATURE

Within the proper limits of an introduction it would be impossible to give any adequate summary of the history and literature with which the Eddic poems are indissolubly connected, but a mere mention of a few of the salient facts may be of some service to those who are unfamiliar with the subject. Old Norse literature covers approximately the period between 850 and 1300. During the first part of that period occurred the great wanderings of the Scandinavian peoples, and particularly the Norwegians. A convenient date to remember is that of the sea-fight of Hafrsfjord, 872, when Harald the Fair-Haired broke the power of the independent Norwegian nobles, and made himself overlord of nearly all the country. Many of the defeated nobles fled overseas, where inviting refuges had been found for them by earlier wanderers and plunder-seeking raiders. This was the time of the inroads of the dreaded Northmen in France, and in 885 Hrolf Gangr (Rollo) laid siege to Paris itself. Many Norwegians went to Ireland, where their compatriots had already built Dublin, and where they remained in control of most of the island till Brian Boru shattered their power at the battle of Clontarf in 1014.

Of all the migrations, however, the most important were those to Iceland. Here grew up an active civilization, fostered by absolute independence and by remoteness from the wars which wracked Norway, yet kept from degenerating into provincialism by the roving life of the people, which brought them constantly in contact with the culture of the South. Christianity, introduced throughout the Norse world about the year 1000, brought with it the stability of learning, and the Icelanders became not only the makers but also the students and recorders of history. The years between 875 and 1100 were the great spontaneous period of oral literature. Most of the military and political leaders were also poets, and they composed a mass of lyric poetry concerning the authorship of which we know a good deal, and much of which has been preserved. Narrative prose also flourished, for the Icelander had a passion for story-telling and story-hearing. After 1100 came the day of the writers. These sagamen collected the material that for generations had passed from mouth to mouth, and gave it permanent form in writing. The greatest bulk of what we now have of Old Norse literature,--and the published part of it makes a formidable library,--originated thus in the earlier period before the introduction of writing, and was put into final shape by the scholars, most of them Icelanders, of the hundred years following 1150.

After 1250 came a rapid and tragic decline. Iceland lost its independence, becoming a Norwegian province. Later Norway too fell under alien rule, a Swede ascending the Norwegian throne in 1320. Pestilence and famine laid waste the whole North; volcanic disturbances worked havoc in Iceland. Literature did not quite die, but it fell upon evil days; for the vigorous native narratives and heroic poems of the older period were substituted translations of French romances. The poets wrote mostly doggerel; the prose writers were devoid of national or racial inspiration.

The mass of literature thus collected and written down largely between 1150 and 1250 maybe roughly divided into four groups. The greatest in volume is made up of the sagas: narratives mainly in prose, ranging all the way from authentic history of the Norwegian kings and the early Icelandic settlements to fairy-tales. Embodied in the sagas is found the material composing the second group: the skaldic poetry, a vast collection of songs of praise, triumph, love, lamentation, and so on, almost uniformly characterized by an appalling complexity of figurative language. There is no absolute line to be drawn between the poetry of the skalds and the poems of the *Edda*, which we may call the third group; but in addition to the remarkable artificiality of style which marks the skaldic poetry, and which is seldom found in the poems of the *Edda*, the skalds dealt almost exclusively with their own emotions, whereas the Eddic poems are quite impersonal. Finally, there is the fourth group, made up of didactic works, religious and legal treatises, and so on, studies which originated chiefly in the later period of learned activity.

PRESERVATION OF THE EDDIC POEMS

Most of the poems of the *Poetic Edda* have unquestionably reached us in rather bad shape. During the long period of oral transmission they suffered all sorts of interpolations, omissions and changes, and some of them, as they now stand, are a bewildering hodge-podge of little related fragments. To some extent the diligent twelfth century compiler to whom we owe the*Codex Regius*--Sæmund or another-- was himself doubtless responsible for the patchwork process, often supplemented by narrative prose notes of his own; but in the days before written records existed, it was easy to lose stanzas and longer passages from their context, and equally easy to interpolate them where they did not by any means belong. Some few of the poems, however, appear to be virtually complete and unified as we now have them.

Under such circumstances it is clear that the establishment of a satisfactory text is a matter of the utmost difficulty. As the basis for this translation I have used the text prepared by Karl Hildebrand (1876) and revised by Hugo Gering (1904). Textual emendation has, however, been so extensive in every edition of the *Edda*, and has depended so much on the theories of the editor, that I have also made extensive use of many other editions, notably those by Finnur Jonsson, Neckel, Sijmons, and Detter and Heinzel, together with numerous commentaries. The condition of the text in both the principal codices is such that no great reliance can be placed on the accuracy of the copyists, and frequently two editions will differ fundamentally as to their readings of a given passage or even of an entire-poem. For this reason, and because guesswork necessarily plays so large a part in any edition or translation of the Eddic poems, I have risked overloading the pages with textual notes in order to show, as nearly as possible, the exact state of the original together with all the more significant emendations. I have done this particularly in the case of transpositions, many of which appear absolutely necessary, and in the indication of passages which appear to be interpolations.

THE VERSE-FORMS OF THE EDDIC POEMS

The many problems connected with the verse-forms found in the Eddic poems have been analyzed in great detail by Sievers, Neckel, and others. The three verse-forms exemplified in the poems need only a brief comment here, however, in order to make clear the method used in this translation. All of these forms group the lines normally in four-line stanzas. In the so-called Fornyrthislag ("Old Verse"), for convenience sometimes referred to in the notes as four-four measure, these lines have all the same structure, each line being sharply divided by a cæsural pause into two half-lines, and each half-line having two accented syllables and two (sometimes three) unaccented ones. The two half-lines forming a complete line are bound together by the alliteration, or more properly initial-rhyme, of three (or two) of the accented syllables. The following is an example of the Fornyrthislag stanza, the accented syllables being in italics:

VreiÞr vas *VingÞ*órr, | es *vakna*Þi
ok *síns ham*ars | of *sakna*Þi;
skegg nam *hris*ta, | *skor* nam *dý*ja,
ré*Þ JarÞ*ar *burr* | *umb* at *Þreif*ask.

In the second form, the Ljothahattr ("Song Measure"), the first and third line of each stanza are as just described, but the second and fourth are shorter, have no cæsural pause, have three accented syllables, and regularly two initial-rhymed accented syllables, for which reason I have occasionally referred to Ljothahattr as four-three measure. The following is an example:

Ar skal *rí*sa | sás *an*nars *vill*
  fé eÞa *fior haf*a;
*ligg*jandi *ulfr* | sjaldan *láer* of *getr*
  né *sof*andi *maÞr sigr.*

In the third and least commonly used form, the Malahattr ("Speech Measure"), a younger verse-form than either of the other two, each line of the four-line stanza is divided into two half-lines by a cæsural pause, each half line having two accented syllables and three (sometimes four) unaccented ones; the initial rhyme is as in the Fornyrthislag. The following is an example:

Horsk vas *hús*freyja, | *hug*Þi at *mann*viti,
lag heyrÞi *òr*Þa, | hvat á *laun máel*tu;
Þá vas *vant vit*ri, | *vil*di Þeim *hjal*Þa:
skyldu of *sáe sig*la, | en *sjolf* né *kvamsk*at.

A poem in Fornyrthislag is normally entitled - *kvitha* (*Thrymskvitha, Guthrunarkvitha,* etc.), which for convenience I have rendered as "lay," while a poem in Ljothahattr is entitled - *mol* (*Grimnismol, Skirnismol,* etc.), which I have rendered as "ballad." It is difficult to find any distinction other than metrical between the two terms, although it is clear that one originally existed.

Variations frequently appear in all three kinds of verse, and these I have attempted to indicate through the rhythm of the translation. In order to preserve so far as possible the effect of the Eddic verse, I have adhered, in making the English version, to certain of the fundamental rules governing the Norse line and stanza formations. The number of lines to each stanza conforms to what seems the best guess as to the original, and I have consistently retained the number of accented syllables. in translating from a highly inflected language into one depending largely on the use of subsidiary words, it has, however, been necessary to employ considerable freedom as to the number of unaccented syllables in a line. The initial-rhyme is

xliii

generally confined to two accented syllables in each line. As in the original, all initial vowels are allowed to rhyme interchangeably, but I have disregarded the rule which lets certain groups of consonants rhyme only with themselves (*e.g.*, I have allowed initial *s* or *st* to rhyme with *sk* or *sl*). In general, I have sought to preserve the effect of the original form whenever possible without an undue sacrifice of accuracy. For purposes of comparison, the translations of the three stanzas just given are here included:

Fornyrthislag:

Wild was *Ving*thor | *when* he *awoke*,
And *when* his *mighty* | *ham*mer he *missed*;
He *shook* his *beard*, | his *hair* was *brist*ling,
To *grop*ing *set* | the *son* of *Jorth*.

Ljothahattr:

He must *ear*ly go *forth* | who *fain* the *blood*
Or the *goods* of an*other* would *get*;
The *wolf* that lies *id*le | shall *win* little *meat*,
Or the *sleep*ing man suc*cess*.

Malahattr:

Wise was the *wom*an, | she *fain* would use *wis*dom,
She *saw* well what *meant* | all they *said* in *sec*ret; . .
From her *heart* it was *hid* | how *help* she might *ren*der,
The *sea* they should *sail*, | while her*self* she should *go* not.

PROPER NAMES

The forms in which the proper names appear in this translation will undoubtedly perplex and annoy those who have become accustomed to one or another of the current methods of anglicising Old Norse names. The nominative ending -r it has seemed best to, omit after consonants, although it has been retained after vowels; in Baldr the final -r is a part of the stem and is of course retained. I have rendered the Norse Þ by "th" throughout, instead of spasmodically by "d," as in many texts: *e.g.*, Othin instead of Odin. For the Norse ø I have used its equivalent, "ö," *e.g.*, Völund; for the o I have used "o" and not "a," *e.g.*, Voluspo, not Valuspa or Voluspa. To avoid confusion with accents the long vowel marks of the Icelandic are consistently omitted, as likewise in modern Icelandic proper names. The index at the end of the book indicates the pronunciation in each case.

CONCLUSION

That this translation may be of some value to those who can read the poems of the *Edda* in the original language I earnestly hope. Still more do I wish that it may lead a few who hitherto have given little thought to the Old Norse language and literature to master the tongue for themselves. But far above either of these I place the hope that this English version may give to some, who have known little of the ancient traditions of what is after all their own race, a clearer insight into the glories of that extraordinary past, and that I may through this medium be able to bring to others a small part of the delight which I myself have found in the poems of the *Poetic Edda*.

THE POETIC EDDA

VOLUME I

LAYS OF THE GODS

VOLUSPO

The Wise-Woman's Prophecy

INTRODUCTORY NOTE

At the beginning of the collection in the *Codex Regius* stands the Voluspo, the most famous and important, as it is likewise the most debated, of all the Eddic poems. Another version of it is found in a huge miscellaneous compilation of about the year 1300, the *Hauksbok*, and many stanzas are included in the *Prose Edda* of Snorri Sturluson. The order of the stanzas in the *Hauksbok* version differs materially from that in the *Codex Regius*, and in the published editions many experiments have been attempted in further rearrangements. On the whole, how ever, and allowing for certain interpolations, the order of the stanzas in the *Codex Regius* seems more logical than any of the wholesale "improvements" which have been undertaken.

The general plan of the *Voluspo* is fairly clear. Othin, chief of the gods, always conscious of impending disaster and eager for knowledge, calls on a certain "Volva," or wise-woman, presumably bidding her rise from the grave. She first tells him of the past, of the creation of the world, the beginning of years, the origin of the dwarfs (at this point there is a clearly interpolated catalogue of dwarfs' names, stanzas 10-16), of the first man and woman, of the world-ash Yggdrasil, and of the first war, between the gods and the Vanir, or, in Anglicized form, the Wanes. Then, in stanzas 27-29, as

1

a further proof of her wisdom, she discloses some of Othin's own secrets and the details of his search for knowledge. Rewarded by Othin for what she has thus far told (stanza 30), she then turns to the real prophesy, the disclosure of the final destruction of the gods. This final battle, in which fire and flood overwhelm heaven and earth as the gods fight with their enemies, is the great fact in Norse mythology; the phrase describing it, *ragna rök*, "the fate of the gods," has become familiar, by confusion with the word rökkr, "twilight," in the German *Göterdämmerung*. The wise-woman tells of the Valkyries who bring the slain warriors to support Othin and the other gods in the battle, of the slaying of Baldr, best and fairest of the gods, through the wiles of Loki, of the enemies of the gods, of the summons to battle on both sides, and of the mighty struggle, till Othin is slain, and "fire leaps high about heaven itself" (stanzas 31-58). But this is not all. A new and beautiful world is to rise on the ruins of the old; Baldr comes back, and "fields unsowed bear ripened fruit" (stanzas 59-66).

This final passage, in particular, has caused wide differences of opinion as to the date and character of the poem. That the poet was heathen and not Christian seems almost beyond dispute; there is an intensity and vividness in almost every stanza which no archaizing Christian could possibly have achieved. On the other hand, the evidences of Christian influence are sufficiently striking to outweigh the arguments of Finnur Jonsson, Müllenhoff and others who maintain that the *Voluspo* is purely a product of heathendom. The roving Norsemen of the tenth century, very few of whom had as yet accepted Christianity, were nevertheless in close contact with Celtic races which had already been converted, and in many ways the Celtic influence was strongly felt. It seems likely, then, that the *Voluspo* was the work of a poet living chiefly in Iceland, though possibly in the "Western Isles," in the middle of the tenth century, a vigorous believer in the old gods, and yet with an imagination active enough to be touched by the vague tales of a different religion emanating from his neighbor Celts.

How much the poem was altered during the two hundred years between its composition and its first being committed to writing is largely a matter of guesswork, but, allowing for such an obvious interpolation as the catalogue of dwarfs, and for occasional lesser errors, it seems quite needless to assume such great changes as many editors do. The poem was certainly not composed to tell a story with which its early hearers were quite familiar; the lack of continuity which baffles modern readers presumably did not trouble them in the least. It is, in effect, a series of gigantic pictures, put into words with a directness and sureness which bespeak the poet of genius. It is only after the reader, with the help of the many notes, has-- familiarized him self with the names and incidents involved that he can begin to understand the effect which this magnificent poem must have produced on those who not only understood but believed it.

1. Hearing I ask | from the holy races,
From Heimdall's sons, | both high and low;
Thou wilt, Valfather, | that well I relate
Old tales I remember | of men long ago.

2. I remember yet | the giants of yore,
Who gave me bread | in the days gone by;
Nine worlds I knew, | the nine in the tree
With mighty roots | beneath the mold.

3. Of old was the age | when Ymir lived;
Sea nor cool waves | nor sand there were;
Earth had not been, | nor heaven above,
But a yawning gap, | and grass nowhere.

4. Then Bur's sons lifted | the level land,
Mithgarth the mighty | there they made;
The sun from the south | warmed the stones of earth,
And green was the ground | with growing leeks.

5. The sun, the sister | of the moon, from the south
Her right hand cast | over heaven's rim;
No knowledge she had | where her home should be,
The moon knew not | what might was his,
The stars knew not | where their stations were.

6. Then sought the gods | their assembly-seats,
The holy ones, | and council held;
Names then gave they | to noon and twilight,
Morning they named, | and the waning moon,
Night and evening, | the years to number.

7. At Ithavoll met | the mighty gods,
Shrines and temples | they timbered high;
Forges they set, and | they smithied ore,
Tongs they wrought, | and tools they fashioned.

8. In their dwellings at peace | they played at tables,
Of gold no lack | did the gods then know,--
Till thither came | up giant-maids three,
Huge of might, | out of Jotunheim.

9. Then sought the gods | their assembly-seats,
The holy ones, | and council held,
To find who should raise | the race of dwarfs
Out of Brimir's blood | and the legs of Blain.

10. There was Motsognir | the mightiest made
Of all the dwarfs, | and Durin next;
Many a likeness | of men they made,
The dwarfs in the earth, | as Durin said.

11. Nyi and Nithi, | Northri and Suthri,
Austri and Vestri, | Althjof, Dvalin,
Nar and Nain, | Niping, Dain,

Bifur, Bofur, | Bombur, Nori,
An and Onar, | Ai, Mjothvitnir.

12. Vigg and Gandalf) | Vindalf, Thrain,
Thekk and Thorin, | Thror, Vit and Lit,
Nyr and Nyrath,-- | now have I told--
Regin and Rathsvith-- | the list aright.

13. Fili, Kili, | Fundin, Nali,
Heptifili, | Hannar, Sviur,
Frar, Hornbori, | Fræg and Loni,
Aurvang, Jari, | Eikinskjaldi.

14. The race of the dwarfs | in Dvalin's throng
Down to Lofar | the list must I tell;
The rocks they left, | and through wet lands
They sought a home | in the fields of sand.

15. There were Draupnir | and Dolgthrasir,
Hor, Haugspori, | Hlevang, Gloin,

Dori, Ori, | Duf, Andvari,
Skirfir, Virfir, | Skafith, Ai.

16. Alf and Yngvi, | Eikinskjaldi,
Fjalar and Frosti, | Fith and Ginnar;
So for all time | shall the tale be known,
The list of all | the forbears of Lofar.

17. Then from the throng | did three come forth,
From the home of the gods, | the mighty and gracious;
Two without fate | on the land they found,
Ask and Embla, | empty of might.

18. Soul they had not, | sense they had not,
Heat nor motion, | nor goodly hue;

Soul gave Othin, | sense gave Hönir,
Heat gave Lothur | and goodly hue.

19. An ash I know, | Yggdrasil its name,
With water white | is the great tree wet;
Thence come the dews | that fall in the dales,
Green by Urth's well | does it ever grow.

20. Thence come the maidens | mighty in wisdom,
Three from the dwelling | down 'neath the tree;
Urth is one named, | Verthandi the next,--
On the wood they scored,-- | and Skuld the third.
Laws they made there, | and life allotted
To the sons of men, and set their fates.

21. The war I remember, | the first in the world,
When the gods with spears | had smitten Gollveig,
And in the hall | of Hor had burned her,
Three times burned, | and three times born,
Oft and again, | yet ever she lives.

22. Heith they named her | who sought their home,
The wide-seeing witch, | in magic wise;
Minds she bewitched | that were moved by her magic,
To evil women | a joy she was.

23. On the host his spear | did Othin hurl,
Then in the world | did war first come;
The wall that girdled | the gods was broken,
And the field by the warlike | Wanes was trodden.

24. Then sought the gods | their assembly-seats,
The holy ones, | and council held,
Whether the gods | should tribute give,
Or to all alike | should worship belong.

25. Then sought the gods | their assembly-seats,
The holy ones, | and council held,
To find who with venom | the air had filled,
Or had given Oth's bride | to the giants' brood.

26. In swelling rage | then rose up Thor,--
Seldom he sits | when he such things hears,--
And the oaths were broken, | the words and bonds,
The mighty pledges | between them made.

27. I know of the horn | of Heimdall, hidden
Under the high-reaching | holy tree;
On it there pours | from Valfather's pledge
A mighty stream: | would you know yet more?

28. Alone I sat | when the Old One sought me,
The terror of gods, | and gazed in mine eyes:
"What hast thou to ask? | why comest thou hither?
Othin, I know | where thine eye is hidden."

29. I know where Othin's | eye is hidden,
Deep in the wide-famed | well of Mimir;
Mead from the pledge | of Othin each mom
Does Mimir drink: | would you know yet more?

30. Necklaces had I | and rings from Heerfather,
Wise was my speech | and my magic wisdom;
.   .   .   .
Widely I saw | over all the worlds.

31. On all sides saw I | Valkyries assemble,
Ready to ride | to the ranks of the gods;
Skuld bore the shield, | and Skogul rode next,
Guth, Hild, Gondul, | and Geirskogul.
Of Herjan's maidens | the list have ye heard,
Valkyries ready | to ride o'er the earth.

32. I saw for Baldr, | the bleeding god,
The son of Othin, | his destiny set:

Famous and fair | in the lofty fields,
Full grown in strength | the mistletoe stood.

33. From the branch which seemed | so slender and fair
Came a harmful shaft | that Hoth should hurl;
But the brother of Baldr | was born ere long,
And one night old | fought Othin's son.

34. His hands he washed not, | his hair he combed not,
Till he bore to the bale-blaze | Baldr's foe.
But in Fensalir | did Frigg weep sore
For Valhall's need: | would you know yet more?

35. One did I see | in the wet woods bound,
A lover of ill, | and to Loki like;
By his side does Sigyn | sit, nor is glad
To see her mate: | would you know yet more?

36. From the east there pours | through poisoned vales
With swords and daggers | the river Slith.
.   .   .   .
.   .   .   .

37. Northward a hall | in Nithavellir
Of gold there rose | for Sindri's race,
And in Okolnir | another stood,
Where the giant Brimir | his beer-hall had.

38. A hall I saw, | far from the sun,
On Nastrond it stands, | and the doors face north,
Venom drops | through the smoke-vent down,
For around the walls | do serpents wind.

39. I saw there wading | through rivers wild
Treacherous men | and murderers too,
And workers of ill | with the wives of men;
There Nithhogg sucked | the blood of the slain,
And the wolf tore men; | would you know yet more?

40. The giantess old | in Ironwood sat,
In the east, and bore | the brood of Fenrir;
Among these one | in monster's guise
Was soon to steal | the sun from the sky.

41. There feeds he full | on the flesh of the dead,
And the home of the gods | he reddens with gore;
Dark grows the sun, | and in summer soon
Come mighty storms: | would you know yet more?

42. On a hill there sat, | and smote on his harp,
Eggther the joyous, | the giants' warder;
Above him the cock | in the bird-wood crowed,
Fair and red | did Fjalar stand.

43. Then to the gods | crowed Gollinkambi,
He wakes the heroes | in Othin's hall;
And beneath the earth | does another crow,
The rust-red bird | at the bars of Hel.

44. Now Garm howls loud | before Gnipahellir,
The fetters will burst, | and the wolf run free;
Much do I know, | and more can see
Of the fate of the gods, | the mighty in fight.

45. Brothers shall fight | and fell each other,
And sisters' sons | shall kinship stain;

Hard is it on earth, | with mighty whoredom;
Axe-time, sword-time, | shields are sundered,

Wind-time, wolf-time, | ere the world falls;
Nor ever shall men | each other spare.

46. Fast move the sons | of Mim, and fate
Is heard in the note | of the Gjallarhorn;
Loud blows Heimdall, | the horn is aloft,
In fear quake all | who on Hel-roads are.

47. Yggdrasil shakes, | and shiver on high
The ancient limbs, | and the giant is loose;
To the head of Mim | does Othin give heed,
But the kinsman of Surt | shall slay him soon.

48. How fare the gods? | how fare the elves?
All Jotunheim groans, | the gods are at council;
Loud roar the dwarfs | by the doors of stone,
The masters of the rocks: | would you know yet more?

49. Now Garm howls loud | before Gnipahellir,
The fetters will burst, | and the wolf run free
Much do I know, | and more can see
Of the fate of the gods, | the mighty in fight.

50. From the east comes Hrym | with shield held high;
In giant-wrath | does the serpent writhe;
O'er the waves he twists, | and the tawny eagle
Gnaws corpses screaming; | Naglfar is loose.

51. O'er the sea from the north | there sails a ship
With the people of Hel, | at the helm stands Loki;
After the wolf | do wild men follow,
And with them the brother | of Byleist goes

52. Surt fares from the south | with the scourge of branches,
The sun of the battle-gods | shone from his sword;

The crags are sundered, | the giant-women sink,
The dead throng Hel-way, | and heaven is cloven.

53. Now comes to Hlin | yet another hurt,
When Othin fares | to fight with the wolf,
And Beli's fair slayer | seeks out Surt,
For there must fall | the joy of Frigg.

54. Then comes Sigfather's | mighty son,
Vithar, to fight | with the foaming wolf;
In the giant's son | does he thrust his sword
Full to the heart: | his father is avenged.

55. Hither there comes | the son of Hlothyn,
The bright snake gapes | to heaven above;
. . . .
Against the serpent | goes Othin's son.

56. In anger smites | the warder of earth,--
Forth from their homes | must all men flee;-
Nine paces fares | the son of Fjorgyn,
And, slain by the serpent, | fearless he sinks.

57. The sun turns black, | earth sinks in the sea,
The hot stars down | from heaven are whirled;
Fierce grows the steam | and the life-feeding flame,
Till fire leaps high | about heaven itself.

58. Now Garm howls loud | before Gnipahellir,
The fetters will burst, | and the wolf run free;
Much do I know, | and more can see
Of the fate of the gods, | the mighty in fight.

59. Now do I see | the earth anew
Rise all green | from the waves again;

The cataracts fall, | and the eagle flies,
And fish he catches | beneath the cliffs.

60. The gods in Ithavoll | meet together,
Of the terrible girdler | of earth they talk,

And the mighty past | they call to mind,
And the ancient runes | of the Ruler of Gods.

61. In wondrous beauty | once again
Shall the golden tables | stand mid the grass,
Which the gods had owned | in the days of old,

. . . .

62. Then fields unsowed | bear ripened fruit,
All ills grow better, | and Baldr comes back;
Baldr and Hoth dwell | in Hropt's battle-hall,
And the mighty gods: | would you know yet more?

63. Then Hönir wins | the prophetic wand,

. . . .

And the sons of the brothers | of Tveggi abide
In Vindheim now: | would you know yet more?

64. More fair than the sun, | a hall I see,
Roofed with gold, | on Gimle it stands;
There shall the righteous | rulers dwell,
And happiness ever | there shall they have.

65. There comes on high, | all power to hold,
A mighty lord, | all lands he rules.

. . . .

. . . .

66. From below the dragon | dark comes forth,
Nithhogg flying | from Nithafjoll;

The bodies of men on | his wings he bears,
The serpent bright: | but now must I sink.

[1. A few editors, following Bugge, in an effort to clarify the poem, place stanzas 22, 28 and 30 before stanzas 1-20, but the arrangement in both manuscripts, followed here, seems logical. In stanza I the Volva, or wise-woman, called upon by Othin, answers him and demands a hearing. Evidently she be longs to the race of the giants (cf. stanza 2), and thus speaks to Othin unwillingly, being compelled to do so by his magic power. Holy: omitted in *Regius*; the phrase "holy races" probably means little more than mankind in general. Heimdall: the watchman of the gods; cf. stanza 46 and note. Why mankind should be referred to as Heimdall's sons is uncertain, and the phrase has caused much perplexity. Heimdall seems to have had various at tributes, and in the Rigsthula, wherein a certain Rig appears as the ancestor of the three great classes of men, a fourteenth century annotator identifies Rig with Heimdall, on what authority we do not know, for the Rig of the poem seems much more like Othin (cf. Rigsthula, introductory prose and note). Valfather ("Father of the Slain"): Othin, chief of the gods, so called because the slain warriors were brought to him at Valhall ("Hall of the Slain") by the Valkyries ("Choosers of the Slain").

2. Nine worlds: the worlds of the gods (Asgarth), of the Wanes (Vanaheim, cf. stanza 21 and note), of the elves (Alfheim), of men (Mithgarth), of the giants (Jotunheim), of fire (Muspellsheim, cf. stanza 47 and note), of the dark elves (Svartalfaheim), of the dead (Niflheim), and presumably of the dwarfs (perhaps Nithavellir, cf. stanza 37 and note, but the ninth world is uncertain). The tree: the world-ash Yggdrasil, [fp. 4] symbolizing the universe; cf. *Grimnismol*, 29-35 and notes, wherein Yggdrasil is described at length.]

[3. *Ymir*: the giant out of whose body the gods made the world; cf. *Vafthruthnismol*, 21. in this stanza as quoted in Snorri's Edda the first line runs: "Of old was the age ere aught there was." *Yawning gap*: this phrase, "Ginnunga-gap," is sometimes used as a proper name.

4. Bur's sons: Othin, Vili, and Ve. Of Bur we know only that his wife was Bestla, daughter of Bolthorn; cf. *Hovamol*, 141. Vili and Ve are mentioned by name in the Eddic poems only in *Lokasenna*, 26. *Mithgarth* ("Middle Dwelling"): the world of men. *Leeks*: the leek was often used as the symbol of fine growth (cf. *Guthrunarkvitha* I, 17), and it was also supposed to have magic power (cf. *Sigrdrifumol*, 7).

5. Various editors have regarded this stanza as interpolated; Hoffory thinks it describes the northern summer night in which the sun does not set. Lines 3-5 are quoted by Snorri. In the manuscripts line 4 follows line 5. Regarding the sun and moon [fp. 5] as daughter and son of Mundilferi, cf. *Vafthruthnismol*, 23 and note, and *Grimnismol*, 37 and note.]

[6. Possibly an interpolation, but there seems no strong reason for assuming this. Lines 1-2 are identical with lines 1-2 of stanza 9, and line 2 may have been inserted here from that later stanza.

7. *Ithavoll* ("Field of Deeds"?): mentioned only here and in stanza 60 as the meeting-place of the gods; it appears in no other connection.

8. *Tables*: the exact nature of this game, and whether it more closely resembled chess or checkers, has been made the subject of a 400-page treatise, Willard Fiske's "Chess in Iceland." *Giant-maids*: perhaps the three great Norns, corresponding to the three fates; cf. stanza 20, and note. Possibly, however, something has been lost after this stanza, and the missing passage, replaced by the catalogue of the dwarfs (stanzas 9-16), may have explained the "giant-maids" otherwise than as Norns. In *Vafthruthnismol*, 49, the Norns (this time "three throngs" in stead of simply "three") are spoken of as giant-maidens; [fp. 6] *Fafnismol*, 13, indicates the existence of many lesser Norns, belonging to various races. *Jotunheim*: the world of the giants.]

[9. Here apparently begins the interpolated catalogue of the dwarfs, running through stanza 16; possibly, however, the interpolated section does not begin before stanza 11. Snorri quotes practically the entire section, the names appearing in a some what changed order. *Brimir* and *Blain*: nothing is known of these two giants, and it has been suggested that both are names for Ymir (cf. stanza 3). Brimir, however, appears in stanza 37 in connection with the home of the dwarfs. Some editors treat the words as common rather than proper nouns, Brimir meaning "the bloody moisture" and Blain being of uncertain significance

10. Very few of the dwarfs named in this and the following stanzas are mentioned elsewhere. It is not clear why Durin should have been singled out as authority for the list. The occasional repetitions suggest that not all the stanzas of the catalogue came from the same source. Most of the names presumably had some definite significance, as Northri, Suthri, Austri, and Vestri ("North," "South", "East," and "West"), [fp. 7] Althjof ("Mighty Thief"), Mjothvitnir ("Mead-Wolf"), Gandalf ("Magic Elf"), Vindalf ("Wind Elf"), Rathwith ("Swift in Counsel"), Eikinskjaldi ("Oak Shield"), etc., but in many cases the interpretations are sheer guesswork.]

[12. The order of the lines in this and the succeeding four stanzas varies greatly in the manuscripts and editions, and the names likewise appear in many forms. *Regin*: probably not identical with Regin the son of Hreithmar, who plays an important part in the *Reginsmol* and *Fafnismol*, but cf. note on *Reginsmol*, introductory prose.

14. *Dvalin*: in Hovamol, 144, Dvalin seems to have given magic runes to the dwarfs, probably accounting for their skill in craftsmanship, while in *Fafnismol*, 13, he is mentioned as the father of some of the lesser Norns. The story that some of the dwarfs left the rocks and mountains to find a new home on the sands is mentioned, but unexplained, in Snorri's Edda; of *Lofar* we know only that he was descended from these wanderers.]

[15. *Andvari*: this dwarf appears prominently in the *Reginsmol*, which tells how the god Loki treacherously robbed him of his wealth; the curse which he laid on his treasure brought about the deaths of Sigurth, Gunnar, Atli, and many others.

17. Here the poem resumes its course after the interpolated section. Probably, however, something has been lost, for there is no apparent connection between the three giant-maids of stanza 8 and the three gods, Othin, Hönir and Lothur, who in stanza 17 go forth to create man and woman. The word "three" in stanzas 9 and 17 very likely confused some early reciter, or perhaps the compiler himself. *Ask* and *Embla*: ash and elm; Snorri gives them simply as the names of the first man and woman, but says that the gods made this pair out of trees.

18. *Hönir*: little is known of this god, save that he occasion ally appears in the poems in company with Othin and Loki, and [fp. 9] that he survives the destruction, assuming in the new age the gift of prophesy (cf. stanza 63). He was given by the gods as a hostage to the Wanes after their war, in exchange for Njorth (cf. stanza 21 and note). *Lothur*: apparently an older name for Loki, the treacherous but ingenious son of Laufey, whose divinity Snorri regards as somewhat doubtful. He was adopted by Othin, who subsequently had good reason to regret it. Loki probably represents the blending of two originally distinct figures, one of them an old fire-god, hence his gift of heat to the newly created pair.]

[19. *Yggdrasil*: cf. stanza 2 and note, and *Grimnismol*, 29-35 and notes. Urth ("The Past"): one of the three great Norns. The world-ash is kept green by being sprinkled with the marvelous healing water from her well.

20. *The maidens*: the three Norns; possibly this stanza should follow stanza 8. *Dwelling: Regius* has "sæ" (sea) instead of "sal" (hall, home), and many editors

have followed this reading, although Snorri's prose paraphrase indicates "sal." *Urth, Verthandi and Skuld*: "Past," "Present" and "Future." *Wood*, etc.: the magic signs (runes) controlling the destinies of men were cut on pieces of wood. Lines 3-4 are probably interpolations from some other account of the Norns.]

[21. This follows stanza 20 in *Regius*; in the *Hauksbok* version stanzas 25, 26, 27, 40, and 41 come between stanzas 20 and 21. Editors have attempted all sorts of rearrangements. *The war*: the first war was that between the gods and the Wanes. The cult of the Wanes (Vanir) seems to have originated among the seafaring folk of the Baltic and the southern shores of the North Sea, and to have spread thence into Norway in opposition to the worship of the older gods; hence the "war." Finally the two types of divinities were worshipped in common; hence the treaty which ended the war with the exchange of hostages. Chief among the Wanes were Njorth and his children, Freyr and Freyja, all of whom became conspicuous among the gods. Beyond this we know little of the Wanes, who seem originally to have been water-deities. *I remember*: the manuscripts have "she remembers," but the Volva is apparently still speaking of her own memories, as in stanza 2. *Gollveig* ("Gold-Might"): apparently the first of the Wanes to come among the gods, her ill treatment being the immediate cause of the war. Müllenhoff maintains that Gollveig is another name for Freyja. Lines 5-6, one or both of them probably interpolated, seem to symbolize the refining of gold by fire. *Hor* ("The High One"): Othin.

22. *Heith* ("Shining One"?): a name often applied to wise women and prophetesses. The application of this stanza to Gollveig is far from clear, though the reference may be to the [fp. 11] magic and destructive power of gold. It is also possible that the stanza is an interpolation. Bugge maintains that it applies to the Volva who is reciting the poem, and makes it the opening stanza, following it with stanzas 28 and 30, and then going on with stanzas I ff. The text of line 2 is obscure, and has been variously emended.]

[23. This stanza and stanza 24 have been transposed from the order in the manuscripts, for the former describes the battle and the victory of the Wanes, after which the gods took council, debating whether to pay tribute to the victors, or to admit them, as was finally done, to equal rights of worship.

25. Possibly, as Finn Magnusen long ago suggested, there is something lost after stanza 24, but it was not the custom of the Eddic poets to supply transitions which their hearers could generally be counted on to understand. The story referred to in stanzas 25-26 (both quoted by Snorri) is that of the rebuilding of Asgarth after its destruction by the Wanes. The gods employed a giant as builder, who demanded as his reward the sun and moon, and the goddess Freyja for his wife. The gods,

terrified by the rapid progress of the work, forced Loki, who had advised the bargain, to delay the giant by a trick, so that the [fp. 12] work was not finished in the stipulated time (cf. *Grimnismol*, 44, note). The enraged giant then threatened the gods, whereupon Thor slew him. *Oth's bride*: Freyja; of Oth little is known beyond the fact that Snorri refers to him as a man who "went away on long journeys."]

[26. *Thor*: the thunder-god, son of Othin and Jorth (Earth) cf. particularly Harbarthsljoth and Thrymskvitha, passim. *Oaths*, etc.: the gods, by violating their oaths to the giant who rebuilt Asgarth, aroused the undying hatred of the giants' race, and thus the giants were among their enemies in the final battle.

27. Here the Volva turns from her memories of the past to a statement of some of Othin's own secrets in his eternal search for knowledge (stanzas 27-29). Bugge puts this stanza after stanza 29. *The horn of Heimdall*: the Gjallarhorn ("Shrieking Horn"), with which Heimdall, watchman of the gods, will summon them to the last battle. Till that time the horn is buried under Yggdrasil. *Valfather's pledge*: Othin's eye (the sun?), which he gave to the water-spirit Mimir (or Mim) in exchange for the latter's wisdom. It appears here and in stanza 29 as a drinking-vessel, from which Mimir drinks the magic mead, and from which he pours water on the ash Yggdrasil. Othin's sacrifice of his eye in order to gain knowledge of his final doom is one of the series of disasters leading up to the destruction of the gods. There were several differing versions of the story of Othin's relations with Mimir; another one, quite incompatible with this, appears in stanza 47. In the manuscripts *I know* and *I see* appear as "she knows" and "she sees" (cf. note on 21).]

[28. The *Hauksbok* version omits all of stanzas 28-34, stanza 27 being there followed by stanzas 40 and 41. *Regius* indicates stanzas 28 and 29 as a single stanza. Bugge puts stanza 28 after stanza 22, as the second stanza of his reconstructed poem. The Volva here addresses Othin directly, intimating that, although he has not told her, she knows why he has come to her, and what he has already suffered in his search for knowledge regarding his doom. Her reiterated "would you know yet more?" seems to mean: "I have proved my wisdom by telling of the past and of your own secrets; is it your will that I tell likewise of the fate in store for you?" *The Old One*: Othin.

29. The first line, not in either manuscript, is a conjectural emendation based on Snorri's paraphrase. Bugge puts this stanza after stanza 20.

30. This is apparently the transitional stanza, in which the Volva, rewarded by Othin for her knowledge of the past (stanzas 1-29), is induced to proceed with her

real prophecy (stanzas 31-66). Some editors turn the stanza into the third person, making it a narrative link. Bugge, on the other hand, puts it [fp. 14] after stanza 28 as the third stanza of the poem. No lacuna is indicated in the manuscripts, and editors have attempted various emendations. *Heerfather* ("Father of the Host"): Othin.]

[31. *Valkyries*: these "Choosers of the Slain" (cf. stanza I, note) bring the bravest warriors killed in battle to Valhall, in order to re-enforce the gods for their final struggle. They are also called "Wish-Maidens," as the fulfillers of Othin's wishes. The conception of the supernatural warrior-maiden was presumably brought to Scandinavia in very early times from the South-Germanic races, and later it was interwoven with the likewise South-Germanic tradition of the swan-maiden. A third complication developed when the originally quite human women of the hero-legends were endowed with the qualities of both Valkyries and swan-maidens, as in the cases of Brynhild (cf. *Gripisspo*, introductory note),*Svava* (cf. *Helgakvitha HJorvarthssonar*, prose after stanza 5 and note) and Sigrun (cf. *Helgakvitha Hundingsbana* I, 17 and note). The list of names here given may be an interpolation; a quite different list is given in *Grimnismol*, 36. *Ranks of the gods*: some editors regard the word thus translated as a specific place name. *Herjan* ("Leader of Hosts"): Othin. It is worth noting that the name *Hild* ("Warrior") is the basis of Bryn-hild ("Warrior in Mail Coat").

32. Baldr: The death of Baldr, the son of Othin and Frigg, was the first of the great disasters to the gods. The story is fully told by Snorri. Frigg had demanded of all created things, saving only the mistletoe, which she thought too weak to be worth troubling [fp. 15] about, an oath that they would not harm Baldr. Thus it came to he a sport for the gods to hurl weapons at Baldr, who, of course, was totally unharmed thereby. Loki, the trouble-maker, brought the mistletoe to Baldr's blind brother, Hoth, and guided his hand in hurling the twig. Baldr was slain, and grief came upon all the gods. Cf. *Baldrs Draumar*.]

[33. The lines in this and the following stanza have been combined in various ways by editors, lacunae having been freely conjectured, but the manuscript version seems clear enough. *The brother of Baldr*: Vali, whom Othin begot expressly to avenge Baldr's death. The day after his birth he fought and slew Hoth.

34. *Frigg*: Othin's wife. Some scholars have regarded her as a solar myth, calling her the sun-goddess, and pointing out that her home in*Fensalir* ("the sea-halls") symbolizes the daily setting of the sun beneath the ocean horizon.

35. The translation here follows the *Regius* version. The *Hauksbok* has the same final two lines, but in place of the first [fp. 16] pair has, "I know that Vali | his

brother gnawed, / With his bowels then | was Loki bound." Many editors have followed this version of the whole stanza or have included these two lines, often marking them as doubtful, with the four from *Regius*. After the murder of Baldr, the gods took Loki and bound him to a rock with the bowels of his son Narfi, who had just been torn to pieces by Loki's other son, Vali. A serpent was fastened above Loki's head, and the venom fell upon his face. Loki's wife, *Sigyn*, sat by him with a basin to catch the venom, but whenever the basin was full, and she went away to empty it, then the venom fell on Loki again, till the earth shook with his struggles. "And there he lies bound till the end." Cf. *Lokasenna*, concluding prose.]

[36. Stanzas 36-39 describe the homes of the enemies of the gods: the giants (36), the dwarfs (37), and the dead in the land of the goddess Hel (38-39).
The *Hauksbok* version omits stanzas 36 and 37. *Regius* unites 36 with 37, but most editors have assumed a lacuna. *Slith* ("the Fearful"): a river in the giants' home. The "swords and daggers" may represent the icy cold.

37. *Nithavellir* ("the Dark Fields"): a home of the dwarfs. Perhaps the word should be "Nithafjoll" ("the Dark Crags"). *Sindri*: the great worker in gold among the dwarfs. *Okolnir* [fp. 17] ("the Not Cold"): possibly a volcano. *Brimir*: the giant (possibly Ymir) out of whose blood, according to stanza 9, the dwarfs were made; the name here appears to mean simply the leader of the dwarfs.]

[38. Stanzas 38 and 39 follow stanza 43 in the *Hauksbok* version. Snorri quotes stanzas 39, 39, 40 and 41, though not consecutively. *Nastrond*("Corpse-Strand"): the land of the dead, ruled by the goddess Hel. Here the wicked undergo tortures. *Smoke vent*: the phrase gives a picture of the Icelandic house, with its opening in the roof serving instead of a chimney.

39. The stanza is almost certainly in corrupt form. The third line is presumably an interpolation, and is lacking in most of the late, paper manuscripts. Some editors, however, have called lines 1-3 the remains of a full. stanza, with the fourth line lacking, and lines 4-5 the remains of another. The stanza depicts the torments of the two worst classes of criminals known to Old Norse morality--oath-breakers and murderers.*Nithhogg* ("the Dread Biter"): the dragon that lies beneath the ash Yggdrasil and gnaws at its roots, thus symbolizing the destructive elements in the universe; cf. *Grimnismol*, 32, 35. *The wolf*: presumably the wolf Fenrir, one of the children of Loki and the giantess Angrbotha (the others being Mithgarthsorm and the goddess Hel), who was chained by the gods with the marvelous chain Gleipnir, fashioned by a dwarf "out of six things: the [fp. 18] noise of a cat's step, the beards of women, the roots of mountains, the nerves of bears, the breath of

fishes, and the spittle of birds." The chaining of Fenrir cost the god Tyr his right hand; cf. stanza 44.]

[40. The *Hauksbok* version inserts after stanza 39 the refrain stanza (44), and puts stanzas 40 and 41 between 27 and 21. With this stanza begins the account of the final struggle itself. *The giantess*: her name is nowhere stated, and the only other reference to Ironwood is in*Grimnismol*, 39, in this same connection. The children of this giantess and the wolf Fenrir are the wolves Skoll and Hati, the first of whom steals the sun, the second the moon. Some scholars naturally see here an eclipse myth.

41. In the third line many editors omit the comma after "sun," and put one after "soon," making the two lines run: "Dark grows the sun | in summer soon, / Mighty storms--" etc. Either phenomenon in summer would be sufficiently striking.

42. In the *Hauksbok* version stanzas 42 and 43 stand between stanzas 44 and 38. *Eggther*: this giant, who seems to be the watchman of the giants, as Heimdall is that of the gods and Surt of the dwellers in the fire-world, is not mentioned elsewhere in [fp. 19] the poems. *Fjalar*, the cock whose crowing wakes the giants for the final struggle.]

[43. *Gollinkambi* ("Gold-Comb"): the cock who wakes the gods and heroes, as Fjalar does the giants. *The rust-red bird*: the name of this bird, who wakes the people of Hel's domain, is nowhere stated.

44. This is a refrain-stanza. In *Regius* it appears in full only at this point, but is repeated in abbreviated form before stanzas 50 and 59. In the*Hauksbok* version the full stanza comes first between stanzas 35 and 42, then, in abbreviated form, it occurs four times: before stanzas 45, 50, 55, and 59. In the *Hauksbok* line 3 runs: "Farther I see and more can say." *Garm*: the dog who guards the gates of Hel's kingdom; cf. Baldrs Draumar, 2 ff., and *Grimnismol*, 44. *Gniparhellir* ("the Cliff-Cave"): the entrance to the world of the dead. *The wolf*: Fenrir; cf. stanza 39 and note.

45. From this point on through stanza 57 the poem is quoted by Snorri, stanza 49 alone being omitted. There has been much discussion as to the status of stanza 45. Lines 4 and 5 look like an interpolation. After line 5 the *Hauksbok* has a line running: "The world resounds, the witch is flying." Editors have arranged these seven lines in various ways, with lacunae freely indicated. *Sisters' sons*: in all Germanic countries the relations between uncle and nephew were felt to be particularly close.]

[46. *Regius* combines the first three lines of this stanza with lines 3, 2, and I of stanza 47 as a single stanza. Line 4, not found in *Regius*, is introduced from the *Hauksbok* version, where it follows line 2 of stanza 47. *The sons of Mim*: the spirits of the water. On Mini (or Mimir) cf. stanza 27 and note. Gjallarhorn: the "Shrieking Horn" with which Heimdall, the watchman of the gods, calls them to the last battle.

47. In *Regius* lines 3, 2, and I, in that order, follow stanza 46 without separation. Line 4 is not found in *Regius*, but is introduced from the*Hauksbok* version. *Yggdrasil*: cf. stanza 19 and note, and *Grimnismol*, 29-35. *The giant*: Fenrir. *The head of Mim*: various myths were current about Mimir. This stanza refers to the story that he was sent by the gods with Hönir as a hostage to the Wanes after their war (cf. stanza 21 and note), and that the Wanes cut off his head and returned it to the gods. Othin embalmed the head, and by magic gave it the power of speech, thus making Mimir's noted wisdom always available. of course this story does not fit with that underlying the references to Mimir in stanzas 27 and 29. *The kinsman of Surt*: the wolf [fp. 21] Fenrir, who slays Othin in the final struggle; cf. stanza 53. Surt is the giant who rules the fire-world, Muspellsheim; cf. stanza 52.]

[48. This stanza in *Regius* follows stanza 51; in the *Hauksbok* it stands, as here, after 47. *Jotunheim*: the land of the giants.

49. Identical with stanza 44. In the manuscripts it is here abbreviated.

50. *Hrym*: the leader of the giants, who comes as the helmsman of the ship Naglfar (line 4). *The serpent*: Mithgarthsorm, one of the children of Loki and Angrbotha (cf. stanza 39, note). The serpent was cast into the sea, where he completely encircles the land; cf. especially *Hymiskvitha,passim. The eagle*: the giant Hræsvelg, who sits at the edge of heaven in the form of an eagle, and makes the winds with his wings; cf.*Vafthruthnismol*, 37, and *Skirnismol*, 27. *Naglfar*: the ship which was made out of dead men's nails to carry the giants to battle.]

[51. *North*: a guess; the manuscripts have "east," but there seems to be a confusion with stanza 50, line 1. *People of Hel*: the manuscripts have "people of Muspell," but these came over the bridge Bifrost (the rainbow), which broke beneath them, whereas the people of Hel came in a ship steered by Loki. *The wolf*: Fenrir. *The brother of Byleist*: Loki. Of Byleist (or Byleipt) no more is known.

52. *Surt*: the ruler of the fire-world. *The scourge of branches*: fire. This is one of the relatively rare instances in the Eddic poems of the type of poetic diction which characterizes the skaldic verse.

53. *Hlin*: apparently another name for Frigg, Othin's wife. After losing her son Baldr, she is fated now to see Othin slain by the wolf Fenrir. *Beli's slayer*: the god Freyr, who killed the giant Beli with his fist; cf. *Skirnismol*, 16 and note. On Freyr, who belonged to the race of the Wanes, and was the brother of Freyja, see especially *Skirnismol, passim. The Joy of Frigg*: Othin.]

[54. As quoted by Snorri the first line of this stanza runs: "Fares Othin's son | to fight with the wolf." *Sigfather* ("Father of Victory"): Othin. His son, Vithar, is the silent god, famed chiefly for his great shield, and his strength, which is little less than Thor's. He survives the destruction. *The giant's son*: Fenrir.

55. This and the following stanza are clearly in bad shape. In *Regius* only lines I and 4 are found, combined with stanza 56 as a single stanza. Line I does not appear in the *Hauksbok* version, the stanza there beginning with line 2. Snorri, in quoting these two stanzas, omits 55, 2-4, and 56, 3, making a single stanza out of 55, I, and 56, 4, 2, I, in that order. Moreover, the *Hauksbok* manuscript at this point is practically illegible. The lacuna (line 3) is, of course, purely conjectural, and all sorts of arrangements of the lines have been attempted by editors, *Hlothyn*: another name for Jorth ("Earth"), Thor's mother; his father was Othin. *The snake*: Mithgarthsorm; cf. stanza 5c and note. *Othin's son*: Thor. The fourth line in *Regius* reads "against the wolf," but if this line refers to Thor at all, and not to Vithar, the *Hauksbok* reading, "serpent," is correct.

56. *The warder of earth·* Thor *The son of Fjorgyn*: again [fp. 24] Thor, who, after slaying the serpent, is overcome by his venomous breath, and dies. Fjorgyn appears in both a masculine and a feminine form. in the masculine 1t is a name for Othin; in the feminine, as here and in *Harbarthsljoth*, 56, it apparently refers to Jorth.]

[57. With this stanza ends the account of the destruction.

58. Again the refrain-stanza (cf. stanza 44 and note), abbreviated in both manuscripts, as in the case of stanza 49. It is probably misplaced here.

59. Here begins the description of the new world which is to rise out of the wreck of the old one. It is on this passage that a few critics have sought to base their argument that the poem is later than the introduction of Christianity (circa 1000), but this theory has never seemed convincing (cf. introductory note).

60. The third line of this stanza is not found in *Regius*. *Ithavoll*: cf. stanza 7 and note. *The girdler of earth*: *Mithgarthsorm*: [fp. 25], who, lying in the sea,

22

surrounded the land. *The Ruler of Gods*: Othin. The runes were both magic signs, generally carved on wood, and sung or spoken charms.]

[61. The *Hauksbok* version of the first two lines runs:

"The gods shall find there, | wondrous fair,
The golden tables | amid the grass."

No lacuna (line 4) is indicated in the manuscripts. *Golden tables*: cf. stanza 8 and note.

62. *Baldr*: cf. stanza 32 and note. Baldr and his brother, Hoth, who unwittingly slew him at Loki's instigation, return together, their union being a symbol of the new age of peace. *Hropt*: another name for Othin. His "battle-hall" is Valhall.

63. No lacuna (line 2) indicated in the manuscripts. *Hönir*: cf. stanza 18 and note. In this new age he has the gift of foretelling the future. *Tveggi*("The Twofold"): another name for [fp. 26] Othin. His brothers are Vili and Ve (cf. *Lokasenna*, 26, and note). Little is known of them, and nothing, beyond this reference, of their sons. *Vindheim* ("Home of the Wind"): heaven.]

[64. This stanza is quoted by Snorri. *Gimle*: Snorri makes this the name of the hall itself, while here it appears to refer to a mountain on which the hall stands. It is the home of the happy, as opposed to another hall, not here mentioned, for the dead. Snorri's description of this second hall is based on *Voluspo*, 38, which he quotes, and perhaps that stanza properly belongs after 64.

65. This stanza is not found in *Regius*, and is probably spurious. No lacuna is indicated in the *Hauksbok* version, but late paper manuscripts add two lines, running:

"Rule he orders, | and rights he fixes,
Laws he ordains | that ever shall live."

The name of this new ruler is nowhere given, and of course the suggestion of Christianity is unavoidable. It is not certain, how ever, that even this stanza refers to Christianity, and if it does, it may have been interpolated long after the rest of the poem was composed.

66. This stanza, which fits so badly with the preceding ones, [fp. 27] may well have been interpolated. It has been suggested that the dragon, making a last attempt to rise, is destroyed, this event marking the end of evil in the world. But in both manuscripts the final half-line does not refer to the dragon, but, as the gender shows, to the Volva herself, who sinks into the earth; a sort of conclusion to the entire prophecy. Presumably the stanza (barring the last half-line, which was probably intended as the conclusion of the poem) belongs somewhere in the description of the great struggle. *Nithhogg*: the dragon at the roots of Yggdrasil; cf. stanza 39 and note. *Nithafjoll* ("the Dark Crags"); nowhere else mentioned. *Must I*: the manuscripts have "must she."]

HOVAMOL

The Ballad of the High One

INTRODUCTORY NOTE

This poem follows the *Voluspo* in the *Codex Regius*, but is preserved in no other manuscript. The first stanza is quoted by Snorri, and two lines of stanza 84 appear in one of the sagas.

In its present shape it involves the critic of the text in more puzzles than any other of the Eddic poems. Without going in detail into the various theories, what happened seems to have been somewhat as follows. There existed from very early times a collection of proverbs and wise counsels, which were attributed to Othin just as the Biblical proverbs were to Solomon. This collection, which presumably was always elastic in extent, was known as "The High One's Words," and forms the basis of the present poem. To it, however, were added other poems and fragments dealing with wisdom which seemed by their nature to imply that the speaker was Othin. Thus a catalogue of runes, or charms, was tacked on, and also a set of proverbs, differing essentially in form from those comprising the main collection. Here and there bits of verse more nearly narrative crept in; and of course the loose structure of the poem made it easy for any reciter to insert new stanzas almost at will. This curious miscellany is what we now have as the *Hovamol*.

Five separate elements are pretty clearly recognizable: (1) the *Hovamol* proper (stanzas 1-80), a collection of proverbs and counsels for the conduct of life; (2) the *Loddfafnismol* (stanzas 111-138), a collection somewhat similar to the first, but specific ally addressed to a certain Loddfafnir; (3) the *Ljothatal* (stanzas 147-165), a collection of charms; (4) the love-story of Othin and Billing's daughter (stanzas 96-102), with an introductory dissertation on the faithlessness of women in general (stanzas 81-95), which probably

25

crept into the poem first, and then pulled the story, as an apt illustration, after it; (5) the story of how Othin got the mead of poetry--the draught which gave him the gift of tongues--from the maiden Gunnloth (stanzas 103-110). There is also a brief passage (stanzas 139 146) telling how Othin won the runes, this passage being a natural introduction to the *Ljothatal*, and doubtless brought into the poem for that reason.

It is idle to discuss the authorship or date of such a series of accretions as this. Parts of it are doubtless among the oldest relics of ancient Germanic poetry; parts of it may have originated at a relatively late period. Probably, however, most of its component elements go pretty far back, although we have no way of telling how or when they first became associated.

It seems all but meaningless to talk about "interpolations" in a poem which has developed almost solely through the process of piecing together originally unrelated odds and ends. The notes, therefore, make only such suggestions as are needed to keep the main divisions of the poem distinct.

Few gnomic collections in the world's literary history present sounder wisdom more tersely expressed than the Hovamol. Like the Book of Proverbs it occasionally rises to lofty heights of poetry. If it presents the worldly wisdom of a violent race, it also shows noble ideals of loyalty, truth, and unfaltering courage.

1. Within the gates | ere a man shall go,
(Full warily let him watch,)
Full long let him look about him;
For little he knows | where a foe may lurk,
And sit in the seats within.

2. Hail to the giver! | a guest has come;
Where shall the stranger sit?

Swift shall he be who, | with swords shall try
The proof of his might to make.

3. Fire he needs | who with frozen knees
Has come from the cold without;
Food and clothes | must the farer have,
The man from the mountains come.

4. Water and towels | and welcoming speech
Should he find who comes, to the feast;
If renown he would get, | and again be greeted,
Wisely and well must he act.

5. Wits must he have | who wanders wide,
But all is easy at home;
At the witless man | the wise shall wink
When among such men he sits.

6. A man shall not boast | of his keenness of mind,
But keep it close in his breast;
To the silent and wise | does ill come seldom
When he goes as guest to a house;
(For a faster friend | one never finds
Than wisdom tried and true.)

7. The knowing guest | who goes to the feast,
In silent attention sits;
With his ears he hears, | with his eyes he watches,
Thus wary are wise men all.

8. Happy the one | who wins for himself
Favor and praises fair;
Less safe by far | is the wisdom found
That is hid in another's heart.

9. Happy the man | who has while he lives
Wisdom and praise as well,
For evil counsel | a man full oft
Has from another's heart.

10. A better burden | may no man bear
For wanderings wide than wisdom;
It is better than wealth | on unknown ways,
And in grief a refuge it gives.

11. A better burden | may no man bear
For wanderings wide than wisdom;
Worse food for the journey | he brings not afield
Than an over-drinking of ale.

12. Less good there lies | than most believe
In ale for mortal men;
For the more he drinks | the less does man
Of his mind the mastery hold.

13. Over beer the bird | of forgetfulness broods,
And steals the minds of men;
With the heron's feathers | fettered I lay
And in Gunnloth's house was held.

14. Drunk I was, | I was dead-drunk,
When with Fjalar wise I was;
'Tis the best of drinking | if back one brings
His wisdom with him home.

15. The son of a king | shall be silent and wise,
And bold in battle as well;
Bravely and gladly | a man shall go,
Till the day of his death is come.

16. The sluggard believes | he shall live forever,
If the fight he faces not;
But age shall not grant him | the gift of peace,
Though spears may spare his life.

17. The fool is agape | when he comes to the feast,
He stammers or else is still;
But soon if he gets | a drink is it seen
What the mind of the man is like.

18. He alone is aware | who has wandered wide,
And far abroad has fared,
How great a mind | is guided by him
That wealth of wisdom has.

19. Shun not the mead, | but drink in measure;
Speak to the point or be still;
For rudeness none | shall rightly blame thee
If soon thy bed thou seekest.

20. The greedy man, | if his mind be vague,
Will eat till sick he is;
The vulgar man, | when among the wise,
To scorn by his belly is brought.

21. The herds know well | when home they shall fare,
And then from the grass they go;
But the foolish man | his belly's measure
Shall never know aright.

22. A paltry man | and poor of mind
At all things ever mocks;
For never he knows, | what he ought to know,
That he is not free from faults.

23. The witless man | is awake all night,
Thinking of many things;
Care-worn he is | when the morning comes,
And his woe is just as it was.

24. The foolish man | for friends all those
Who laugh at him will hold;
When among the wise | he marks it not
Though hatred of him they speak.

25. The foolish man | for friends all those
Who laugh at him will hold;
But the truth when he comes | to the council he learns,
That few in his favor will speak.

26. An ignorant man | thinks that all he knows,
When he sits by himself in a corner;
But never what answer | to make he knows,
When others with questions come.

27. A witless man, | when he meets with men,
Had best in silence abide;
For no one shall find | that nothing he knows,
If his mouth is not open too much.
(But a man knows not, | if nothing he knows,
When his mouth has been open too much.)

28. Wise shall he seem | who well can question,
And also answer well;
Nought is concealed | that men may say
Among the sons of men.

29. Often he speaks | who never is still
With words that win no faith;
The babbling tongue, | if a bridle it find not,
Oft for itself sings ill.

30. In mockery no one | a man shall hold,
Although he fare to the feast;
Wise seems one oft, | if nought he is asked,
And safely he sits dry-skinned.

31. Wise a guest holds it | to take to his heels,
When mock of another he makes;
But little he knows | who laughs at the feast,
Though he mocks in the midst of his foes.

32. Friendly of mind | are many men,
Till feasting they mock at their friends;
To mankind a bane | must it ever be
When guests together strive.

33. Oft should one make | an early meal,
Nor fasting come to the feast;
Else he sits and chews | as if he would choke,
And little is able to ask.

34. Crooked and far | is the road to a foe,
Though his house on the highway be;
But wide and straight | is the way to a friend,
Though far away he fare.

35. Forth shall one go, | nor stay as a guest
In a single spot forever;
Love becomes loathing | if long one sits
By the hearth in another's home.

36. Better a house, | though a hut it be,
A man is master at home;
A pair of goats | and a patched-up roof
Are better far than begging.

37. Better a house, | though a hut it be,
A man is master at home;
His heart is bleeding | who needs must beg
When food he fain would have.

38. Away from his arms | in the open field
A man should fare not a foot;
For never he knows | when the need for a spear
Shall arise on the distant road.

39. If wealth a man | has won for himself,
Let him never suffer in need;
Oft he saves for a foe | what he plans for a friend,
For much goes worse than we wish.

40. None so free with gifts | or food have I found
That gladly he took not a gift,
Nor one who so widely | scattered his wealth
That of recompense hatred he had.

41. Friends shall gladden each other | with arms and garments,
As each for himself can see;
Gift-givers' friendships | are longest found,
If fair their fates may be.

42. To his friend a man | a friend shall prove,
And gifts with gifts requite;
But men shall mocking | with mockery answer,
And fraud with falsehood meet.

43. To his friend a man | a friend shall prove,
To him and the friend of his friend;
But never a man | shall friendship make
With one of his foeman's friends.

44. If a friend thou hast | whom thou fully wilt trust,
And good from him wouldst get,
Thy thoughts with his mingle, | and gifts shalt thou make,
And fare to find him oft.

45. If another thou hast | whom thou hardly wilt trust,
Yet good from him wouldst get,
Thou shalt speak him fair, | but falsely think,
And fraud with falsehood requite.

46. So is it with him | whom thou hardly wilt trust,
And whose mind thou mayst not know;
Laugh with him mayst thou, | but speak not thy mind,
Like gifts to his shalt thou give.

47. Young was I once, | and wandered alone,
And nought of the road I knew;
Rich did I feel | when a comrade I found,
For man is man's delight.

48. The lives of the brave | and noble are best,
Sorrows they seldom feed;
But the coward fear | of all things feels,
And not gladly the niggard gives.

49. My garments once | in a field I gave
To a pair of carven poles;
Heroes they seemed | when clothes they had,
But the naked man is nought.

50. On the hillside drear | the fir-tree dies,
All bootless its needles and bark;
It is like a man | whom no one loves,--
Why should his life be long?

51. Hotter than fire | between false friends
Does friendship five days burn;
When the sixth day comes | the fire cools,
And ended is all the love.

52. No great thing needs | a man to give,
Oft little will purchase praise;
With half a loaf | and a half-filled cup
A friend full fast I made.

53. A little sand | has a little sea,
And small are the minds of men;
Though all men are not | equal in wisdom,
Yet half-wise only are all.

54. A measure of wisdom | each man shall have,
But never too much let him know;
The fairest lives | do those men live
Whose wisdom wide has grown.

55. A measure of wisdom | each man shall have,
But never too much let him know;
For the wise man's heart | is seldom happy,
If wisdom too great he has won.

56. A measure of wisdom | each man shall have,
But never too much let him know;
Let no man the fate | before him see,
For so is he freest from sorrow.

57. A brand from a brand | is kindled and burned,
And fire from fire begotten;
And man by his speech | is known to men,
And the stupid by their stillness.

58. He must early go forth | who fain the blood
Or the goods of another would get;
The wolf that lies idle | shall win little meat,
Or the sleeping man success.

59. He must early go forth | whose workers are few,
Himself his work to seek;
Much remains undone | for the morning-sleeper,
For the swift is wealth half won.

60. Of seasoned shingles | and strips of bark
For the thatch let one know his need,
And how much of wood | he must have for a month,
Or in half a year he will use.

61. Washed and fed | to the council fare,
But care not too much for thy clothes;
Let none be ashamed | of his shoes and hose,
Less still of the steed he rides,
(Though poor be the horse he has.)

62. When the eagle comes | to the ancient sea,
He snaps and hangs his head;
So is a man | in the midst of a throng,
Who few to speak for him finds.

63. To question and answer | must all be ready
Who wish to be known as wise;
Tell one thy thoughts, | but beware of two,--
All know what is known to three.

64. The man who is prudent | a measured use
Of the might he has will make;
He finds when among | the brave he fares
That the boldest he may not be.

65. .   .   .   .
. .   .   .
Oft for the words | that to others one speaks
He will get but an evil gift.

66. Too early to many | a meeting I came,
And some too late have I sought;
The beer was all drunk, | or not yet brewed;
Little the loathed man finds.

67. To their homes men would bid | me hither and yon,
If at meal-time I needed no meat,
Or would hang two hams | in my true friend's house,
Where only one I had eaten.

68. Fire for men | is the fairest gift,
And power to see the sun;
Health as well, | if a man may have it,
And a life not stained with sin.

69. All wretched is no man, | though never so sick;
Some from their sons have joy,
Some win it from kinsmen, | and some from their wealth,
And some from worthy works.

70. It is better to live | than to lie a corpse,
The live man catches the cow;
I saw flames rise | for the rich man's pyre,
And before his door he lay dead.

71. The lame rides a horse, | the handless is herdsman,
The deaf in battle is bold;
The blind man is better | than one that is burned,
No good can come of a corpse.

72. A son is better, | though late he be born,
And his father to death have fared;
Memory-stones | seldom stand by the road
Save when kinsman honors his kin.

73. Two make a battle, | the tongue slays the head;
In each furry coat | a fist I look for.

74. He welcomes the night | whose fare is enough,
(Short are the yards of a ship,)
Uneasy are autumn nights;
Full oft does the weather | change in a week,
And more in a month's time.

75. A man knows not, | if nothing he knows,
That gold oft apes begets;
One man is wealthy | and one is poor,
Yet scorn for him none should know.

76. Among Fitjung's sons | saw I well-stocked folds,--
Now bear they the beggar's staff;
Wealth is as swift | as a winking eye,
Of friends the falsest it is.

77. Cattle die, | and kinsmen die,
And so one dies one's self;
But a noble name | will never die,
If good renown one gets.

78. Cattle die, | and kinsmen die,
And so one dies one's self;
One thing now | that never dies,
The fame of a dead man's deeds.

79. Certain is that | which is sought from runes,
That the gods so great have made,

And the Master-Poet painted;

. . . .

. . . . . of the race of gods:
Silence is safest and best.

80. An unwise man, | if a maiden's love
Or wealth he chances to win,
His pride will wax, but his wisdom never,
Straight forward he fares in conceit.

* * *

81. Give praise to the day at evening, | to a woman on her pyre,
To a weapon which is tried, | to a maid at wed lock,
To ice when it is crossed, | to ale that is drunk.

82. When the gale blows hew wood, | in fair winds seek the water;
Sport with maidens at dusk, | for day's eyes are many;
From the ship seek swiftness, | from the shield protection,
Cuts from the sword, | from the maiden kisses.

83. By the fire drink ale, | over ice go on skates;
Buy a steed that is lean, | and a sword when tarnished,
The horse at home fatten, | the hound in thy dwelling.

* * *

84. A man shall trust not | the oath of a maid,
Nor the word a woman speaks;
For their hearts on a whirling | wheel were fashioned,
And fickle their breasts were formed.

85. In a breaking bow | or a burning flame,
A ravening wolf | or a croaking raven,
In a grunting boar, | a tree with roots broken,
In billowy seas | or a bubbling kettle,

86. In a flying arrow | or falling waters,
In ice new formed | or the serpent's folds,
In a bride's bed-speech | or a broken sword,
In the sport of bears | or in sons of kings,

87. In a calf that is sick | or a stubborn thrall,
A flattering witch | or a foe new slain.

88. In a brother's slayer, | if thou meet him abroad,
In a half-burned house, | in a horse full swift--
One leg is hurt | and the horse is useless--
None had ever such faith | as to trust in them all.

89. Hope not too surely | for early harvest,
Nor trust too soon in thy son;
The field needs good weather, | the son needs wisdom,
And oft is either denied.

*   *   *

90. The love of women | fickle of will
Is like starting o'er ice | with a steed unshod,
A two-year-old restive | and little tamed,
Or steering a rudderless | ship in a storm,
Or, lame, hunting reindeer | on slippery rocks.

*   *   *

91. Clear now will I speak, | for I know them both,
Men false to women are found;
When fairest we speak, | then falsest we think,
Against wisdom we work with deceit.

92. Soft words shall he speak | and wealth shall he offer
Who longs for a maiden's love,

And the beauty praise | of the maiden bright;
He wins whose wooing is best.

93. Fault for loving | let no man find
Ever with any other;
Oft the wise are fettered, | where fools go free,
By beauty that breeds desire.

94. Fault with another | let no man find
For what touches many a man;
Wise men oft | into witless fools
Are made by mighty love.

95. The head alone knows | what dwells near the heart,
A man knows his mind alone;
No sickness is worse | to one who is wise
Than to lack the longed-for joy.

96. This found I myself, | when I sat in the reeds,
And long my love awaited;
As my life the maiden | wise I loved,
Yet her I never had.

97. Billing's daughter | I found on her bed,
In slumber bright as the sun;
Empty appeared | an earl's estate
Without that form so fair.

98. "Othin, again | at evening come,
If a woman thou wouldst win;
Evil it were | if others than we
Should know of such a sin."

99. Away I hastened, | hoping for joy,
And careless of counsel wise;

Well I believed | that soon I should win
Measureless joy with the maid.

100. So came I next | when night it was,
The warriors all were awake;
With burning lights | and waving brands
I learned my luckess way.

101. At morning then, | when once more I came,
And all were sleeping still,
A dog found | in the fair one's place,
Bound there upon her bed.

102. Many fair maids, | if a man but tries them,
False to a lover are found;
That did I learn | when I longed to gain
With wiles the maiden wise;
Foul scorn was my meed | from the crafty maid,
And nought from the woman I won.

*   *   *

103. Though glad at home, | and merry with guests,
A man shall be wary and wise;
The sage and shrewd, | wide wisdom seeking,
Must see that his speech be fair;
A fool is he named | who nought can say,
For such is the way of the witless.

104. I found the old giant, | now back have I fared,
Small gain from silence I got;
Full many a word, | my will to get,
I spoke in Suttung's hall.

105. The mouth of Rati | made room for my passage,
And space in the stone he gnawed;

Above and below | the giants' paths lay,
So rashly I risked my head.

106. Gunnloth gave | on a golden stool
A drink of the marvelous mead;
A harsh reward | did I let her have
For her heroic heart,
And her spirit troubled sore.

107. The well-earned beauty | well I enjoyed,
Little the wise man lacks;
So Othrörir now | has up been brought
To the midst of the men of earth.

108. Hardly, methinks, | would I home have come,
And left the giants' land,
Had not Gunnloth helped me, | the maiden good,
Whose arms about me had been.

109. The day that followed, | the frost-giants came,
Some word of Hor to win,
(And into the hall of Hor;)
Of Bolverk they asked, | were he back midst the gods,
Or had Suttung slain him there?

110. On his ring swore Othin | the oath, methinks;
Who now his troth shall trust?
Suttung's betrayal | he sought with drink,
And Gunnloth to grief he left.

* * *

111. It is time to chant | from the chanter's stool;
By the wells of Urth I was,
I saw and was silent, | I saw and thought,
And heard the speech of Hor.

(Of runes heard I words, | nor were counsels wanting,
At the hall of Hor,
In the hall of Hor;
Such was the speech I heard.)

112. I rede thee, Loddfafnir! | and hear thou my rede,---
Profit thou hast if thou hearest,
Great thy gain if thou learnest:
Rise not at night, | save if news thou seekest,
Or fain to the outhouse wouldst fare.

113. I rede thee, Loddfafnir! | and hear thou my rede,--
Profit thou hast if thou hearest,
Great thy gain if thou learnest:
Beware of sleep | on a witch's bosom,
Nor let her limbs ensnare thee.

114. Such is her might | that thou hast no mind
For the council or meeting of men;
Meat thou hatest, | joy thou hast not,
And sadly to slumber thou farest.

115. I rede thee, Loddfafnir! | and hear thou my rede,--
Profit thou hast if thou hearest,
Great thy gain if thou learnest:
Seek never to win | the wife of another,
Or long for her secret love.

116. I rede thee, Loddfafnir! | and hear thou my rede,--
Profit thou hast if thou hearest,
Great thy gain if thou learnest:
If o'er mountains or gulfs | thou fain wouldst go,
Look well to thy food for the way.

117. I rede thee, Loddfafnir! | and hear thou my rede,--
Profit thou hast if thou hearest,

Great thy gain if thou learnest:
An evil man | thou must not let
Bring aught of ill to thee;
For an evil man | will never make
Reward for a worthy thought.

118. I saw a man | who was wounded sore
By an evil woman's word;
A lying tongue | his death-blow launched,
And no word of truth there was.

119. I rede thee, Loddfafnir! | and hear thou my rede,--
Profit thou hast if thou hearest,
Great thy gain if thou learnest:
If a friend thou hast | whom thou fully wilt trust,
Then fare to find him oft;
For brambles grow | and waving grass
On the rarely trodden road.
120. I rede thee, Loddfafnir! | and hear thou my rede,--
Profit thou hast if thou hearest,
Great thy gain if thou learnest:
A good man find | to hold in friendship,
And give heed to his healing charms.

121. I rede thee, Loddfafnir! | and hear thou my rede,-
Profit thou hast if thou hearest,
Great thy gain if thou learnest:
Be never the first | to break with thy friend
The bond that holds you both;
Care eats the heart | if thou canst not speak
To another all thy thought.

122. I rede thee, Loddfafnir! | and hear thou my rede,--
Profit thou hast if thou hearest,
Great thy gain if thou learnest:

Exchange of words | with a witless ape
Thou must not ever make.

123. For never thou mayst | from an evil man
A good requital get;
But a good man oft | the greatest love
Through words of praise will win thee.

124. Mingled is love | when a man can speak
To another all his thought;
Nought is so bad | as false to be,
No friend speaks only fair.

125. I rede thee, Loddfafnir! | and hear thou my rede,--
Profit thou hast if thou hearest,
Great thy gain if thou learnest:
With a worse man speak not | three words in dispute,
Ill fares the better oft
When the worse man wields a sword.

126. I rede thee, Loddfafnir! | and hear thou my rede,-
Profit thou hast if thou hearest,
Great thy gain if thou learnest:
A shoemaker be, | or a maker of shafts,
For only thy single self;
If the shoe is ill made, | or the shaft prove false,
Then evil of thee men think.

127. I rede thee, Loddfafnir! | and hear thou my rede,--
Profit thou hast if thou hearest,
Great thy gain if thou learnest:
If evil thou knowest, | as evil proclaim it,
And make no friendship with foes.

128. I rede thee, Loddfafnir! | and hear thou my rede,--
Profit thou hast if thou hearest,

Great thy gain if thou learnest:
In evil never | joy shalt thou know,
But glad the good shall make thee.

129. I rede thee, Loddfafnir! | and hear thou my rede,--
Profit thou hast if thou hearest,
Great thy gain if thou learnest:
Look not up | when the battle is on,--
(Like madmen the sons | of men become,--)
Lest men bewitch thy wits.

130. I rede thee, Loddfafnir! | and hear thou my rede,-
Profit thou hast if thou hearest,
Great thy gain if thou learnest:
If thou fain wouldst win | a woman's love,
And gladness get from her,
Fair be thy promise | and well fulfilled;
None loathes what good he gets.

131. I rede thee, Loddfafnir! | and hear thou my rede,-
Profit thou hast if thou hearest,
Great thy gain if thou learnest:
I bid thee be wary, | but be not fearful;
(Beware most with ale or another's wife,
And third beware | lest a thief outwit thee.)

132. I rede thee, Loddfafnir! | and hear thou my rede,-
Profit thou hast if thou hearest,
Great thy gain if thou learnest:
Scorn or mocking | ne'er shalt thou make
Of a guest or a journey-goer.

133. Oft scarcely he knows | who sits in the house
What kind is the man who comes;
None so good is found | that faults he has not,
Nor so wicked that nought he is worth.

134. I rede thee, Loddfafnir! | and hear thou my rede,--
Profit thou hast if thou hearest,
Great thy gain if thou learnest:
Scorn not ever | the gray-haired singer,
Oft do the old speak good;
(Oft from shrivelled skin | come skillful counsels,
Though it hang with the hides,
And flap with the pelts,
And is blown with the bellies.)

135. I rede thee, Loddfafnir! | and hear thou my rede,--
Profit thou hast if thou hearest,
Great thy gain if thou learnest:
Curse not thy guest, | nor show him thy gate,
Deal well with a man in want.

136. Strong is the beam | that raised must be
To give an entrance to all;
Give it a ring, | or grim will be
The wish it would work on thee.

137. I rede thee, Loddfafnir! | and hear thou my rede,--
Profit thou hast if thou hearest,
Great thy gain if thou learnest:
When ale thou drinkest) | seek might of earth,
(For earth cures drink, | and fire cures ills,
The oak cures tightness, | the ear cures magic,
Rye cures rupture, | the moon cures rage,
Grass cures the scab, | and runes the sword-cut;)
The field absorbs the flood.

138. Now are Hor's words | spoken in the hall,
Kind for the kindred of men,
Cursed for the kindred of giants:
Hail to the speaker, | and to him who learns!

Profit be his who has them!
Hail to them who hearken!

* * *

139. I ween that I hung | on the windy tree,
Hung there for nights full nine;
With the spear I was wounded, | and offered I was
To Othin, myself to myself,
On the tree that none | may ever know
What root beneath it runs.

140. None made me happy | with loaf or horn,
And there below I looked;
I took up the runes, | shrieking I took them,
And forthwith back I fell.

141. Nine mighty songs | I got from the son
Of Bolthorn, Bestla's father;
And a drink I got | of the goodly mead
Poured out from Othrörir.

142. Then began I to thrive, | and wisdom to get,
I grew and well I was;
Each word led me on | to another word,
Each deed to another deed.

143. Runes shalt thou find, | and fateful signs,
That the king of singers colored,
And the mighty gods have made;
Full strong the signs, | full mighty the signs
That the ruler of gods doth write.

144. Othin for the gods, | Dain for the elves,
And Dvalin for the dwarfs,

Alsvith for giants | and all mankind,
And some myself I wrote.

145. Knowest how one shall write, | knowest how one shall rede?
Knowest how one shall tint, | knowest how one makes trial?
Knowest how one shall ask, | knowest how one shall offer?
Knowest how one shall send, | knowest how one shall sacrifice?

146. Better no prayer | than too big an offering,
By thy getting measure thy gift;
Better is none | than too big a sacrifice,
. . . .
So Thund of old wrote | ere man's race began,
Where he rose on high | when home he came.

* * *

147. The songs I know | that king's wives know not,
Nor men that are sons of men;
The first is called help, | and help it can bring thee
In sorrow and pain and sickness.

148. A second I know, | that men shall need
Who leechcraft long to use;
. . . .
. . . .

149. A third I know, | if great is my need
Of fetters to hold my foe;
Blunt do I make | mine enemy's blade,
Nor bites his sword or staff.

150. A fourth I know, | if men shall fasten
Bonds on my bended legs;
So great is the charm | that forth I may go,

The fetters spring from my feet,
Broken the bonds from my hands.

152. A fifth I know, | if I see from afar
An arrow fly 'gainst the folk;
It flies not so swift | that I stop it not,
If ever my eyes behold it.

152. A sixth I know, | if harm one seeks
With a sapling's roots to send me;
The hero himself | who wreaks his hate
Shall taste the ill ere I.

153. A seventh I know, | if I see in flames
The hall o'er my comrades' heads;
It burns not so wide | that I will not quench it,
I know that song to sing.

154. An eighth I know, | that is to all
Of greatest good to learn;
When hatred grows | among heroes' sons,
I soon can set it right.

155. A ninth I know, | if need there comes
To shelter my ship on the flood;
The wind I calm | upon the waves,
And the sea I put to sleep.

156. A tenth I know, | what time I see
House-riders flying on high;
So can I work | that wildly they go,
Showing their true shapes,
Hence to their own homes.

157. An eleventh I know, | if needs I must lead
To the fight my long-loved friends;

I sing in the shields, | and in strength they go
Whole to the field of fight,
Whole from the field of fight,
And whole they come thence home.

158. A twelfth I know, | if high on a tree
I see a hanged man swing;
So do I write | and color the runes
That forth he fares,
And to me talks.

159. A thirteenth I know, | if a thane full young
With water I sprinkle well;
He shall not fall, | though he fares mid the host,
Nor sink beneath the swords.

160. A fourteenth I know, | if fain I would name
To men the mighty gods;
All know I well | of the gods and elves,
Few be the fools know this.

161. A fifteenth I know, | that before the doors
Of Delling sang Thjothrörir the dwarf;
Might he sang for the gods, | and glory for elves,
And wisdom for Hroptatyr wise.

162. A sixteenth I know, | if I seek delight
To win from a maiden wise;
The mind I turn | of the white-armed maid,
And thus change all her thoughts.

163. A seventeenth I know, | so that seldom shall go
A maiden young from me;
.   .   .   .
.   .   .   .

164. Long these songs | thou shalt, Loddfafnir,
Seek in vain to sing;
Yet good it were | if thou mightest get them,
Well, if thou wouldst them learn,
Help, if thou hadst them.

165. An eighteenth I know, | that ne'er will I tell
To maiden or wife of man,--
The best is what none | but one's self doth know,
So comes the end of the songs,--
Save only to her | in whose arms I lie,
Or who else my sister is.

[1. This stanza is quoted by Snorri, the second line being omitted in most of the *Prose Edda* manuscripts.

2. Probably the first and second lines had originally nothing to do with the third and fourth, the last two not referring to host or guest, but to the general danger of backing one's views with the sword.]

[6. Lines 5 and 6 appear to have been added to the stanza.]

[12. Some editors have combined this stanza in various ways with the last two lines of stanza it, as in the manuscript the first two lines of the latter are abbreviated, and, if they belong there at all, are presumably identical with the first two lines of stanza 10.]

[13. *The heron*: the bird of forgetfulness, referred to in line 1. *Gunnloth*: the daughter of the giant Suttung, from whom Othin won the mead of poetry. For this episode see stanzas 104-110.

14. *Fjalar*: apparently another name for Suttung. This stanza, and probably 13, seem to have been inserted as illustrative.]

[25. The first two lines are abbreviated in the manuscript, but are doubtless identical with the first two lines of stanza 24.

27. The last two lines were probably added as a commentary on lines 3 and 4.]

[36. The manuscript has "little" in place of "a hut" in line I, but this involves an error in the initial-rhymes, and the emendation has been generally accepted.

37. Lines I and 2 are abbreviated in the manuscript, but are doubtless identical with the first two lines of stanza 56.

39. In the manuscript this stanza follows stanza 40.]

[40. The key-word in line 3 is missing in the manuscript, but editors have agreed in inserting a word meaning "generous."

41. In line 3 the manuscript adds "givers again" to "gift-givers."]

[55-56. The first pairs of lines are abbreviated in the manuscript.]

[61. The fifth line is probably a spurious addition.]

[62. This stanza follows stanza 63 in the manuscript, but there are marks therein indicating the transposition.

65. The manuscript indicates no lacuna (lines I and 2). Many editors have filled out the stanza with two lines from late paper manuscripts, the passage running:

"A man must be watchful | and wary as well,
And fearful of trusting a friend."

]

[70. The manuscript has "and a worthy life" in place of "than to lie a corpse" in line I, but Rask suggested the emendation as early as 1818, and most editors have followed him.]

[73-74. These seven lines are obviously a jumble. The two lines of stanza 73 not only appear out of place, but the verse form is unlike that of the surrounding stanzas. In 74, the second line is clearly interpolated, and line I has little enough connection with lines 3, 4 and 5. It looks as though some compiler (or copyist) had inserted here various odds and ends for which he could find no better place.

75. The word "gold" in line 2 is more or less conjectural, the manuscript being obscure. The reading in line 4 is also doubtful.]

[76. in the manuscript this stanza follows 79, the order being: 77, 78, 76, 80, 79, 81. *Fitjung* ("the Nourisher"): Earth.

79. This stanza is certainly in bad shape, and probably out of place here. Its reference to runes as magic signs suggests that it properly belongs in some list of charms like the *Ljothatal* (stanzas 147-165). The stanza-form is so irregular as to show either that something has been lost or that there have been interpolations. The manuscript indicates no lacuna; Gering fills out the assumed gap as follows:

"Certain is that which is sought from runes,
The runes--," etc.

]

[81. With this stanza the verse-form, as indicated in the translation, abruptly changes to Malahattr. What has happened seems to have been something like this. Stanza 80 introduces the idea of man's love for woman. Consequently some reciter or compiler (or possibly even a copyist) took occasion to insert at this point certain stanzas concerning the ways of women. Thus stanza 80 would account for the introduction of stanzas 81 and 82, which, in turn, apparently drew stanza 83 in with them. Stanza 84 suggests the fickleness of women, and is immediately followed--again with a change of verse-form--by a list of things equally untrustworthy (stanzas 85-90). Then, after a few more stanzas on love in the regular measure of the *Hovamol* (stanza 91-9s), is introduced, by way of illustration, Othin's story of his [fp. 46] adventure with Billing's daughter (stanzas 96-102). Some such process of growth, whatever its specific stages may have been, must be assumed to account for the curious chaos of the whole passage from stanza 81 to stanza 102.]

[84. Lines 3 and 4 are quoted in the *Fostbrœthrasaga*.

85. Stanzas 85-88 and 90 are in Fornyrthislag, and clearly come from a different source from the rest of the *Hovamol*.

87. The stanza is doubtless incomplete. Some editors add from a late paper manuscript two lines running:

"In a light, clear sky | or a laughing throng,
In the bowl of a dog | or a harlot's grief!"

]

[89. This stanza follows stanza 89 in the manuscript. Many editors have changed the order, for while stanza 89 is pretty clearly an interpolation wherever it stands, it seriously interferes with the sense if it breaks in between 87 and 88.]

[96. Here begins the passage (stanzas 96-102) illustrating the falseness of woman by the story of Othin's unsuccessful love affair with Billing's daughter. Of this person we know nothing beyond what is here told, but the story needs little comment.]

[102. Rask adds at the beginning of this stanza two lines from a late paper manuscript, running:

"Few are so good | that false they are never
To cheat the mind of a man."

He makes these two lines plus lines I and 2 a full stanza, and line 3, 4, 5, and 6 a second stanza.]

[103. With this stanza the subject changes abruptly, and apparently the virtues of fair speech, mentioned in the last three lines, account for the introduction, from what source cannot be known, of the story of Othin and the mead of song (stanzas 104-110).

104. The giant *Suttung* ("the old giant") possessed the magic mead, a draught of which conferred the gift of poetry. Othin, desiring to obtain it, changed himself into a snake, bored his way through a mountain into Suttung's home, made love to the giant's daughter, Gunnloth, and by her connivance drank up all the mead. Then he flew away in the form of an eagle, leaving Gunnloth to her fate. While with Suttung he assumed the name of Bolverk ("the Evil-Doer").

105. *Rati* ("the Traveller"): the gimlet with which Othin bored through the mountain to reach Suttung's home.]

[106. Probably either the fourth or the fifth line is a spurious addition.

107. *Othrörir*: here the name of the magic mead itself, whereas in stanza 141 it is the name of the vessel containing it. Othin had no intention of bestowing any of the precious mead upon men, but as he was flying over the earth, hotly pursued by Suttung, he spilled some of it out of his mouth, and in this way mankind also won the gift of poetry.

108. *Hor*: Othin ("the High One"). The frost-giants, Suttung's kinsmen, appear not to have suspected Othin of being [fp. 52] identical with Bolverk, possibly because the oath referred to in stanza I to was an oath made by Othin to Suttung that there was no such person as Bolverk among the gods. The giants, of course, fail to get from Othin the information they seek concerning Bolverk, but Othin is keenly conscious of having violated the most sacred of oaths, that sworn on his ring.]

[111. With this stanza begins the Loddfafnismol (stanzas 111-138). Loddfafnir is apparently a wandering singer, who, from his "chanter's stool," recites the verses which he claims to have received from Othin. *Wells of Urth*: cf. *Voluspo*, 19 and note. Urth ("the Past") is one of the three Norns. This stanza is apparently in corrupt form, and editors have tried many experiments with it, both in rejecting lines as spurious and in rear ranging the words and punctuation. It looks rather as though the first four lines formed a complete stanza, and the last four had crept in later. The phrase translated "the specch of Hor" is "Hova mol," later used as the title for the entire poem.]

[112. Lines 1-3 are the formula, repeated (abbreviated in the manuscript) in most of the stanzas, with which Othin prefaces his counsels to Loddfafnir, and throughout this section, except in stanzas 111 and 138, Loddfafnir represents himself as simply quoting Othin's words. The material is closely analogous to that contained in the first eighty stanzas of the poem. In some cases (e. g., stanzas 117, 119, 121, 126 and 130) the formula precedes a full four-line stanza instead of two (or three) lines.]

[129. Line 5 is apparently interpolated.

131. Lines 5-6 probably were inserted from a different poem.]

[133. Many editors reject the last two lines of this stanza as spurious, putting the first two lines at the end of the preceding stanza. Others, attaching lines 3 and 4 to stanza 132, insert as the first two lines of stanza 133 two lines from a late paper manuscript, running:

"Evil and good | do men's sons ever
"Mingled bear in their breasts."

134. Presumably the last four lines have been added to this stanza, for the parallelism in the last three makes it probable that they belong together. The wrinkled skin of the old man is [fp. 59] compared with the dried skins and bellies of animals kept for various purposes hanging in an Icelandic house.]

[136. This stanza suggests the dangers of too much hospitality. The beam (bolt) which is ever being raised to admit guests becomes weak thereby. It needs a ring to help it in keeping the door closed, and without the ability at times to ward off guests a man becomes the victim of his own generosity.

137. The list of "household remedies" in this stanza is doubtless interpolated. Their nature needs no comment here.]

[138. In the manuscript this stanza comes at the end of the entire poem, following stanza 165. Most recent editors have followed Müllenhoff in shifting it to this position, as it appears to conclude the passage introduced by the somewhat similar stanza 111.

139. With this stanza begins the most confusing part of the *Hovamol*: the group of eight stanzas leading up to the Ljothatal, or list of charms. Certain paper manuscripts have before this stanza a title: "Othin's Tale of the Runes." Apparently stanzas 139, 140 and 142 are fragments of an account of how Othin obtained the runes; 141 is erroneously inserted from some version of the magic mead story (cf. stanzas 104-110); and stanzas 143, 144, 145, and 146 are from miscellaneous sources, all, however, dealing with the general subject of runes. With stanza 147 a clearly continuous passage begins once more. *The windy tree*: the ash Yggdrasil (literally "the Horse of Othin," so called be cause of this story), on which Othin, in order to win the magic runes, hanged himself as an offering to himself, and wounded himself with his own spear. Lines 5 and 6 have presumably been borrowed from *Svipdagsmol*, 30.]

[141. This stanza, interrupting as it does the account of Othin's winning the runes, appears to be an interpolation. The meaning of the stanza is most obscure. Bolthorn was Othin's grandfather, and Bestla his mother. We do not know the name of the uncle here mentioned, but it has been suggested that this son of Bolthorn was Mimir (cf. *Voluspo*, 27 and note, and 47 and note). In any case, the nine magic songs which he learned from his uncle seem to have enabled him to win the magic mead (cf. stanzas 104-110). Concerning *Othrörir*, here used as the name of the vessel containing the mead, cf. stanza 107 and note.

143. This and the following stanza belong together, and in many editions appear as a single stanza. They presumably come from some lost poem on the authorship of the runes. Lines 2 and 3 follow line 4 in the manuscript; the transposition was suggested by Bugge. *The king of singers*: Othin. The magic signs (runes) were commonly carved in wood, then colored red.]

[144. *Dain* and *Dvalin*: dwarfs; cf. *Voluspo*, 14, and note. Dain, however, may here be one of the elves rather than the dwarf of. that name. The two names also appear together in *Grimnismol*, 33, where they are applied to two of the four harts that nibble at the topmost twigs of Yggdrasil. *Alsvith* ("the All Wise") appears nowhere else as a giant's name. *Myself*: Othin. We have no further information concerning the list of those who wrote the runes for the various races, and these four lines seem like a confusion of names in the rather hazy mind of some reciter.

145. This Malahattr stanza appears to be a regular religious formula, concerned less with the runes which one "writes" and "tints" (cf. stanza 79) than with the prayers which one "asks" and the sacrifices which one "offers" and "sends." Its origin is wholly uncertain, but it is clearly an interpolation here. In the manuscript the phrase "knowest?" is abbreviated after the first line.]

[146. This stanza as translated here follows the manuscript reading, except in assuming a gap between lines 3 and 5. In Vigfusson and Powell's *Corpus Poeticum Boreale* the first three lines have somehow been expanded into eight. The last two lines are almost certainly misplaced; Bugge suggests that they belong at the end of stanza 144. *Thund*: another name for Othin. *When home he came*: presumably after obtaining the runes as described in stanzas 139 and 140.

147. With this stanza begins the *Ljothatal*, or list of charms. The magic songs themselves are not given, but in each case the peculiar application of the charm is explained. The passage, which is certainly approximately complete as far as it goes, runs to the end of the poem. In the manuscript and in most editions line 4 falls into two half-lines, running:

"In sickness and pain | and every sorrow."

]

[148. *Second*, etc., appear in the manuscript as Roman numerals. The manuscript indicates no gap after line 2.

152. The sending of a root with runes written thereon was an excellent way of causing death. So died the Icelandic hero Grettir the Strong.]

[156. *House-riders*: witches, who ride by night on the roofs of houses, generally in the form of wild beasts. Possibly one of the last two lines is spurious.

157. The last line looks like an unwarranted addition, and line 4 may likewise be spurious.

158. Lines 4-5 are probably expanded from a single line.]

[159. The sprinkling of a child with water was an established custom long before Christianity brought its conception of baptism.

161. This stanza, according to Müllenhoff, was the original conclusion of the poem, the phrase "a fifteenth" being inserted only after stanzas 162-165 had crept in. *Delling*: a seldom mentioned god who married Not (Night). Their son was Dag (Day). *Thjothrörir*: not mentioned elsewhere. *Hroptatyr*: Othin.]

[163. Some editors have combined these two lines with stanza 164. Others have assumed that the gap follows the first half-line, making "so that-from me" the end of the stanza.

164. This stanza is almost certainly an interpolation, and seems to have been introduced after the list of charms and the *Loddfafnismol* (stanzas 111-138) were combined in a single poem, for there is no other apparent excuse for the reference to Loddfafnir at this point. The words "if thou mightest get them" are a conjectural emendation.

165. This stanza is almost totally obscure. The third and fourth lines look like interpolations.]

VAFTHRUTHNISMOL

The Ballad of Vafthruthnir

INTRODUCTORY NOTE

The Vafthruthnismol follows the Hovamol in the *Codex Regius*. From stanza 20 on it is also included in the *Arnamagnæan Codex*, the first part evidently having appeared on leaf now lost. Snorri quotes eight stanzas of it in the *Prose Edda*, and in his prose text closely paraphrases many others.

The poem is wholly in dialogue form except for a single narrative stanza (stanza 5). After a brief introductory discussion between Othin and his wife, Frigg, concerning the reputed wisdom of the giant Vafthruthnir, Othin, always in quest of wisdom, seeks out the giant, calling himself Gagnrath. The giant immediately insists that they shall demonstrate which is the wiser of the two, and propounds four questions (stanzas 11, 13, 15, and 17), each of which Othin answers. It is then the god's turn to ask, and he begins with a series of twelve numbered questions regarding the origins and past history of life. These Vafthruthnir answers, and Othin asks five more questions, this time referring to what is to follow the destruction of the gods, the last one asking the name of his own slayer. Again Vafthruthnir answers, and Othin finally propounds the unanswerable question: "What spake Othin himself in the ears of his son, ere in the bale-fire he burned?" Vafthruthnir, recognizing his questioner as Othin himself, admits his inferiority in wisdom, and so the contest ends.

The whole poem is essentially encyclopædic in character, and thus was particularly useful to Snorri in his preparation of the *Prose Edda*. The encyclopædic poem with a slight narrative outline seems to have been exceedingly popular; the *Grimnismol* and the much later *Alvissmol* represent different phases of the same type.

60

The *Vafthruthnismol* and *Grimnismol* together, in deed, constitute a fairly complete dictionary of Norse mythology. There has been much discussion as to the probable date of the *Vafthruthnismol*, but it appears to belong to about the same period as the *Voluspo*: in other words, the middle of the tenth century. While there may be a few interpolated passages in the poem as we now have it, it is clearly a united whole, and evidently in relatively good condition.

Othin spake:
1, "Counsel me, Frigg, for I long to fare,
And Vafthruthnir fain would find;
fit wisdom old with the giant wise
Myself would I seek to match."

Frigg spake:
2. "Heerfather here at home would I keep,
Where the gods together dwell;
Amid all the giants an equal in might
To Vafthruthnir know I none."

Othin spake:
3. "Much have I fared, much have I found.
Much have I got from the gods;
And fain would I know how Vafthruthnir now
Lives in his lofty hall."

Frigg spake:
4. "Safe mayst thou go, safe come again,
And safe be the way thou wendest!
Father of men, let thy mind be keen
When speech with the giant thou seekest."

5. The wisdom then of the giant wise

Forth did he fare to try;
He found the hall | of the father of Im,
And in forthwith went Ygg.

Othin spake:
6. "Vafthruthnir, hail! | to thy hall am I come,
For thyself I fain would see;
And first would I ask | if wise thou art,
Or, giant, all wisdom hast won."

Vafthruthnir spake:
7. "Who is the man | that speaks to me,
Here in my lofty hall?
Forth from our dwelling | thou never shalt fare,
Unless wiser than I thou art."

Othin spake:
8. "Gagnrath they call me, | and thirsty I come
From a journey hard to thy hall;
Welcome I look for, | for long have I fared,
And gentle greeting, giant."

Vafthruthnir spake:
9. "Why standest thou there | on the floor whilst thou speakest?
A seat shalt thou have in my hall;

Then soon shall we know | whose knowledge is more,
The guest's or the sage's gray."

Othin spake:
10. "If a poor man reaches | the home of the rich,
Let him wisely speak or be still;
For to him who speaks | with the hard of heart
Will chattering ever work ill."

Vafthruthnir spake:
11. "Speak forth now, Gagnrath, | if there from the floor
Thou wouldst thy wisdom make known:
What name has the steed | that each morn anew
The day for mankind doth draw?"

Othin spake:
12. "Skinfaxi is he, | the steed who for men
The glittering day doth draw;
The best of horses | to heroes he seems,
And brightly his mane doth burn."

Vafthruthnir spake:
13. "Speak forth now, Gagnrath, | if there from the floor

Thou wouldst thy wisdom make known:
What name has the steed | that from East anew
Brings night for the noble gods?"

Othin spake:
14. "Hrimfaxi name they | the steed that anew
Brings night for the noble gods;
Each morning foam | from his bit there falls,
And thence come the dews in the dales."

Vafthruthnir spake:
15. "Speak forth now, Gagnrath, | if there from the floor
Thou wouldst thy wisdom make known:
What name has the river | that 'twixt the realms
Of the gods and the giants goes?"

Othin spoke:
16. "Ifing is the river | that 'twixt the realms
Of the gods and the giants goes;
For all time ever | open it flows,
No ice on the river there is."

Vafthruthnir spake:
17. "Speak forth now, Gagnrath, | if there from the floor

Thou wouldst thy wisdom make known:
What name has the field | where in fight shall meet
Surt and the gracious gods?"

Othin spake:
18. "Vigrith is the field | where in fight shall meet
Surt and the gracious gods;
A hundred miles | each way does it measure.
And so are its boundaries set."

Vafthruthnir spake:
19. "Wise art thou, guest! | To my bench shalt thou go,
In our seats let us speak together;
Here in the hall | our heads, O guest,
Shall we wager our wisdom upon."

Othin spake:
20. "First answer me well, | if thy wisdom avails,
And thou knowest it, Vafthruthnir, now:
In earliest time | whence came the earth,
Or the sky, thou giant sage?"

Vafthruthnir spake:
21. "Out of Ymir's flesh | was fashioned the earth,
And the mountains were made of his bones;
The sky from the frost-cold | giant's skull,
And the ocean out of his blood."

Othin spake:
22. "Next answer me well, | if thy wisdom avails,
And thou knowest it, Vafthruthnir, now:
Whence came the moon, | o'er the world of men
That fares, and the flaming sun?"

Vafthruthnir spake:
23. "Mundilferi is he | who begat the moon,
And fathered the flaming sun;
The round of heaven | each day they run,
To tell the time for men."

Othin spake:
24. "Third answer me well, | if wise thou art called,
If thou knowest it, Vafthruthnir, now:
Whence came the day, | o'er mankind that fares,
Or night with the narrowing moon?"

Vafthruthnir spake:
25. "The father of day | is Delling called,
And the night was begotten by Nor;
Full moon and old | by the gods were fashioned,
To tell the time for men."

Othin spake:
26. "Fourth answer me well, | if wise thou art called,
If thou knowest it, Vafthruthnir, now:
Whence did winter come, | or the summer warm,
First with the gracious gods?"

Vafthruthnir spake:
27. "Vindsval he was | who was winter's father,
And Svosuth summer begat;"

.   .   .   .
.   .   .   .

Othin spake:
28. "Fifth answer me well, | if wise thou art called,
If thou knowest it, Vafthruthnir, now:
What giant first | was fashioned of old,
And the eldest of Ymir's kin?"

Vafthruthnir spake:
29. "Winters unmeasured | ere earth was made
Was the birth of Bergelmir;
Thruthgelmir's son | was the giant strong,
And Aurgelmir's grandson of old."

Othin spake:
30. "Sixth answer me well, | if wise thou art called,
If thou knowest it, Vafthruthnir, now:
Whence did Aurgelmir come | with the giants' kin,
Long since, thou giant sage?"

Vafthruthnir spake:
31. "Down from Elivagar | did venom drop,
And waxed till a giant it was;

And thence arose | our giants' race,
And thus so fierce are we found."

Othin spake:
32. "Seventh answer me well, | if wise thou art called,
If thou knowest it, Vafthruthnir, now:
How begat he children, | the giant grim,
Who never a giantess knew?"

Vafthruthnir spake:
33. "They say 'neath the arms | of the giant of ice
Grew man child and maid together;
And foot with foot | did the wise one fashion
A son that six heads bore."

Othin spake:
34. "Eighth answer me well, | if wise thou art called,
If thou knowest it, Vafthruthnir, now:
What farthest back | dost thou bear in mind?
For wide is thy wisdom, giant!"

Vafthruthnir spake:
35. "Winters unmeasured | ere earth was made
Was the birth of Bergelmir;
This first knew I well, | when the giant wise
In a boat of old was borne."

Othin spake:
36. "Ninth answer me well, | if wise thou art called
If thou knowest it, Vafthruthnir, now:
Whence comes the wind | that fares o'er the waves
Yet never itself is seen?"

Vafthruthnir spake:
37. "In an eagle's guise | at the end of heaven
Hræsvelg sits, they say;
And from his wings | does the wind come forth
To move o'er the world of men."

Othin spake:
38. "Tenth answer me now, | if thou knowest all
The fate that is fixed for the gods:
Whence came up Njorth | to the kin of the gods,--
(Rich in temples | and shrines he rules,--)
Though of gods he was never begot?"

Vafthruthnir spake:
39. "In the home of the Wanes | did the wise ones create him,
And gave him as pledge to the gods;
At the fall of the world | shall he fare once more
Home to the Wanes so wise."

Othin spake:
40. "Eleventh answer me well, | . . . .
. . . .
What men . . . . . . | in . . . . . . home
Each day to fight go forth?"

Vafthruthnir spake:
41. "The heroes all | in Othin's hall
Each day to fight go forth;
They fell each other, | and fare from the fight
All healed full soon to sit."

Othin spake:
42. "Twelfth answer me now | how all thou knowest
Of the fate that is fixed for the gods;
Of the runes of the gods | and the giants' race
The truth indeed dost thou tell,
(And wide is thy wisdom, giant!)"

Vafthruthnir spake:
43. "Of the runes of the gods | and the giants' race
The truth indeed can I tell,
(For to every world have I won;)
To nine worlds came I, | to Niflhel beneath,
The home where dead men dwell."

Othin spake:
44. "Much have I fared, | much have I found,
Much have I got of the gods:
What shall live of mankind | when at last there comes
The mighty winter to men?"

Vafthruthnir spake:
45. "In Hoddmimir's wood | shall hide themselves
Lif and Lifthrasir then;
The morning dews | for meat shall they have,
Such food shall men then find."

Othin spake:
46. "Much have I fared, | much have I found,
Much have I got of the gods:

Whence comes the sun | to the smooth sky back,
When Fenrir has snatched it forth?"

Vafthruthnir spake:
47. "A daughter bright | Alfrothul bears
Ere Fenrir snatches her forth;
Her mother's paths | shall the maiden tread
When the gods to death have gone."

Othin spake:
48. "Much have I fared, | much have I found,
Much have I got of the gods:
What maidens are they, | so wise of mind.
That forth o'er the sea shall fare?"

Vafthruthnir spake:
49. "O'er Mogthrasir's hill | shall the maidens pass,
And three are their throngs that come;
They all shall protect | the dwellers on earth,
Though they come of the giants' kin."

Othin spake:
50. "Much have I fared, | much have I found,
Much have I got of the gods:
Who then shall rule | the realm of the gods,
When the fires of Surt have sunk?"

Vafthruthnir spake:
51. "In the gods' home Vithar | and Vali shall dwell,
When the fires of Surt have sunk;
Mothi and Magni | shall Mjollnir have
When Vingnir falls in fight."

Othin spake:
52. "Much have I fared, | much have I found,
Much have I got of the gods:

What shall bring the doom | of death to Othin,
When the gods to destruction go?"

Vafthruthnir spake:
53. "The wolf shall fell | the father of men,
And this shall Vithar avenge;
The terrible jaws | shall he tear apart,
And so the wolf shall he slay."

Othin spake:
54. "Much have I fared, | much have I found,
Much have I got from the gods:
What spake Othin himself | in the ears of his son,
Ere in the bale-fire he burned?"

Vafthruthnir spake:
55. "No man can tell | what in olden time
Thou spak'st in the ears of thy son;
With fated mouth | the fall of the gods
And mine olden tales have I told;
With Othin in knowledge | now have I striven,
And ever the wiser thou art."

[1. The phrases "Othin spake," "Frigg spake," etc., appear in abbreviated form in both manuscripts. *Frigg*: Othin's wife; cf. *Voluspo*, 34 and note. *Vafthruthnir* ("the Mighty in Riddles"): nothing is known of this giant beyond what is told in this poem.

2. *Heerfather* ("Father of the Host"): Othin.

3. This single narrative stanza is presumably a later [fp. 70] interpolation. *Im*: the name appears to be corrupt, but we know nothing of any son of Vafthruthnir. *Ygg* ("the Terrible"): Othin.]

[8. *Gagnrath* ("the Gain-Counsellor"): Othin on his travels always assumes a name other than his own.]

[10. This stanza sounds very much like many of those in the first part of the *Hovamol*, and may have been introduced here from some such source.

12. *Skinfaxi*: "Shining-Mane."]

[13. Here, and in general throughout the poem, the two-line introductory formulæ are abbreviated in the manuscripts.

14. *Hrimfaxi*: "Frosty-Mane."

16. *Ifing*: there is no other reference to this river, which never freezes, so that the giants cannot cross it.]

[17. *Surt*: the ruler of the fire-world (Muspellsheim), who comes to attack the gods in the last battle; cf. Voluspo, 52.

18. *Vigrith*: "the Field of Battle." Snorri quotes this stanza. A hundred miles: a general phrase for a vast distance.

19. With this stanza Vafthruthnir, sufficiently impressed with his guest's wisdom to invite him to share his own seat, resigns the questioning to Othin.

20. The fragmentary version of this poem in the *Arnamagnœan Codex* begins in the middle of the first line of this stanza.]

[21. Ymir: the giant out of whose body the gods made the world; cf. Voluspo, 3 and note.

22. In this and in Othin's following questions, both manuscripts replace the words "next," "third," "fourth," etc., by Roman numerals.

23. *Mundilferi* ("the Turner"?): known only as the father of Mani (the Moon) and Sol (the Sun). Note that, curiously [fp. 75] enough, Mani is the boy and Sol the girl. According to Snorri, Sol drove the horses of the sun, and Mani those of the moon, for the gods, indignant that they should have been given such imposing names, took them from their father to perform these tasks. Cf. *Grimnismol*, 37.]

[25. *Delling* ("the Dayspring"? Probably another form of the name, Dogling, meaning "Son of the Dew" is more correct): the husband of Not (Night); their son was Dag (Day); cf. Hovamol, 161. Nor: Snorri calls the father of Night Norvi or Narfi, and puts him among the giants. Lines 3-4: cf. Voluspo, 6.

71

27. Neither the *Regius* nor the *Arnamagnœan Codex* indicates a lacuna. Most editors have filled out the stanza with two lines from late paper manuscripts: "And both of these shall ever be, / Till the gods to destruction go." Bugge ingeniously paraphrases Snorri's prose: "Vindsval's father was Vosuth called, / And rough is all his race." *Vindsval*: "the Wind-Cold," also called Vindljoni, "the Wind-Man." *Svosuth*: "the Gentle."]

[28. *Ymir's kin*: the giants.

29. *Bergelmir*: when the gods slew Ymir in order to make the world out of his body, so much blood flowed from him that all the frost-giants were drowned except Bergelmir and his wife, who escaped in a boat; cf. stanza 35.
Of *Thruthgelmir* ("the Mightily Burning") we know nothing, but Aurgelmir was the frost-giants' name for Ymir himself. Thus Ymir was the first of the giants, and so Othin's question is answered.

31. Snorri quotes this stanza, and the last two lines are taken from his version, as both of the manuscripts omit them. *Elivagar* ("Stormy Waves"): Mogk suggests that this river may have been the Milky Way. At any rate, the venom carried in its waters [fp. 77] froze into ice-banks over Ginnunga-gap (the "yawning gap" referred to in *Voluspo*, 3), and then dripped down to make the giant Ymir.]

[33. Snorri gives, without materially elaborating on it, the same account of how Ymir's son and daughter were born under his left arm, and how his feet together created a son. That this offspring should have had six heads is nothing out of the ordinary, for various giants had more than the normal number, and Ymir's mother is credited with a little matter of nine hundred heads; cf. *Hymiskvitha*, 8. Of the career of Ymir's six headed son we know nothing; he may have been the Thruthgelmir of stanza 29.]

[35. Snorri quotes this stanza. *Bergelmir*: on him and his boat cf. stanza 29 and note.

37. Snorri quotes this stanza. *Hræsvelg* ("the Corpse-Eater") on this giant in eagle's form cf. Voluspo, So, and Skirnismol, 27.

38. With this stanza the question-formula changes, and Othin's questions from this point on concern more or less directly the great final struggle. Line 4 is presumably spurious. *Njorth*: on Njorth and the Wanes, who gave him as a hostage to the gods at the end of their war, cf.*Voluspo*, 21 and note.]

[40. In both manuscripts, apparently through the carelessness of some older copyist, stanzas 40 and 41 are run together: "Eleventh answer me well, what men in the home mightily battle each day? They fell each other, and fare from the fight all healed full soon to sit." Luckily Snorri quotes stanza 41 in full, and the translation is from his version. Stanza 40 should probably run something like this: "Eleventh answer me well, if thou knowest all / The fate that is fixed for the gods: / What men are they who in Othin's home / Each day to fight go forth?"

41. *The heroes*: those brought to Valhall by the Valkyries. After the day's fighting they are healed of their wounds and all feast together.]

[43. Nine worlds: cf. *Voluspo*, 2. *Niflhel*: "Dark-Hell."

44. The mighty winter: Before the final destruction three winters follow one another with no intervening summers.

45. Snorri quotes this stanza. Hoddmimir's wood: probably [fp. 81] this is the ash-tree Yggdrasil, which is sometimes referred to as "Mimir's Tree," because Mimir waters it from his well; cf. *Voluspo*, 27 and note, and *Svipdagsmol*, 30 and note. *Hoddmimir* is presumably another name for Mimir. *Lif* ("Life") and *Lifthrasir* ("Sturdy of Life"?): nothing further is known of this pair, from whom the new race of men is to spring.]

[46. *Fenrir*: there appears to be a confusion between the wolf Fenrir (cf. *Voluspo*, 39 and note) and his son, the wolf Skoll, who steals the sun (cf. *Voluspo*, 40 and note).

47. Snorri quotes this stanza. *Alfrothul* ("the Elf-Beam") the sun.]

[49. *Mogthrasir* ("Desiring Sons"): not mentioned elsewhere in the Eddic poems, or by Snorri. *The maidens*: apparently Norns, like the "giant-maids" in *Voluspo*, 8. These Norns, how ever, are kindly to men.

50. *Surt*: cf. *Voluspo*, 52 and note.

51. *Vithar*: a son of Othin, who slays the wolf Fenrir; cf. *Voluspo*, 54 and note. *Vali*: the son whom Othin begot to avenge Baldr's death; cf.*Voluspo*, 33 and note. *Mothi* ("Wrath") and *Magni* ("Might"): the sons of the god Thor, who after his death inherit his famous hammer,*Mjollnir*. Concerning this hammer cf. especially *Thrymskvitha*, *passim*. *Vingnir* ("the [fp. 83] Hurler"): Thor. Concerning his death cf. *Voluspo*, 56. This stanza is quoted by Snorri.]

[53. *The wolf*: Fenrir; cf. *Voluspo*, 53 and 54.

54. *His son*: Baldr. Bugge changes lines 3-4 to run: "What did Othin speak | in the ear of Baldr, / When to the bale-fire they bore him?" For Baldr's death cf. *Voluspo*, 3a and note. The question is, of course, unanswerable save by Othin himself, and so the giant at last recognizes his guest.

55. *Fated*: in stanza 19 Vafthruthnir was rash enough to wager his head against his guest's on the outcome of the contest of wisdom, so he knows that his defeat means his death.]

GRIMNISMOL

The Ballad of Grimnir

INTRODUCTORY NOTE

The *Grimnismol* follows the *Vafthruthnismol* in the *Codex Regius* and is also found complete in the *Arnamagnæan Codex*, where also it follows the *Vafthruthnismol*. Snorri quotes over twenty of its stanzas.

Like the preceding poem, the *Grimnismol* is largely encyclopedic in nature, and consists chiefly of proper names, the last forty-seven stanzas containing no less than two hundred and twenty-five of these. It is not, however, in dialogue form. As Müllenhoff pointed out, there is underneath the catalogue of mythological names a consecutive and thoroughly dramatic story. Othin, concealed under the name of Grimnir, is through an error tortured by King Geirröth. Bound between two blazing fires, he begins to display his wisdom for the benefit of the king's little son, Agnar, who has been kind to him. Gradually he works up to the great final moment, when he declares his true name, or rather names, to the terrified Geirröth, and the latter falls on his sward and is killed.

For much of this story we do not have to depend on guesswork, for in both manuscripts the poem itself is preceded by a prose narrative of considerable length, and concluded by a brief prose statement of the manner of Geirröth's death. These prose notes, of which there are many in the Eddic manuscripts, are of considerable interest to the student of early literary forms. Presumably they were written by the compiler to whom we owe the Eddic collection, who felt that the poems needed such annotation in order to be clear. Linguistic evidence shows that they were written in the twelfth or thirteenth century, for they preserve none of the older word-forms which help us to date many of the poems two or three hundred years earlier.

Without discussing in detail the problems suggested by these prose passages, it is worth noting, first, that the Eddic poems contain relatively few stanzas of truly narrative verse; and second, that all of them are based on narratives which must have been more or less familiar to the hearers of the poems. In other words, the poems seldom aimed to tell stories, although most of them followed a narrative sequence of ideas. The stories themselves appear to have lived in oral prose tradition, just as in the case of the sagas; and the prose notes of the manuscripts, in so far as they contain material not simply drawn from the poems themselves, are relics of this tradition. The early Norse poets rarely conceived verse as a suitable means for direct story telling, and in some of the poems even the simplest action is told in prose "links" between dialogue stanzas.

The applications of this fact, which has been too often over looked, are almost limitless, for it suggests a still unwritten chapter in the history of ballad poetry and the so-called "popular" epic. It implies that narrative among early peoples may frequently have had a period of prose existence before it was made into verse, and thus puts, for example, a long series of transitional stages before such a poem as the *Iliad*. In any case, the prose notes accompanying the Eddic poems prove that in addition to the poems themselves there existed in the twelfth century a considerable amount of narrative tradition, presumably in prose form, on which these notes were based by the compiler.

Interpolations in such a poem as the *Grimnismol* could have been made easily enough, and many stanzas have undoubtedly crept in from other poems, but the beginning and end of the poem are clearly marked, and presumably it has come down to us with the same essential outline it had when it was composed, probably in the first half of the tenth century.

King Hrauthung had two sons: one was called Agnar, and the other Geirröth. Agnar was ten winters old, and Geirröth eight. Once they both rowed in a boat with their fishing-gear to catch little fish; and the wind drove them out into the sea. In the darkness of the night they were wrecked on the shore; and going up, they found a poor peasant, with whom they stayed through the winter. The housewife took care of Agnar, and the peasant cared for Geirröth, and taught him wisdom. In the spring the peasant gave him a boat; and when the couple led them to the shore, the peasant spoke secretly with Geirröth. They had a fair wind, and came to their father's landing-place. Geirröth was forward in the boat; he leaped up on land, but pushed out the boat and said, "Go thou now where evil may have thee!" The boat drifted out to sea. Geirröth, however, went up to the house, and was well received, but his father was dead. Then Geirröth was made king, and became a renowned man.

Othin and Frigg sat in Hlithskjolf and looked over all the worlds. Othin said: "Seest thou Agnar, thy foster ling, how he begets children with a giantess in the cave? But Geirröth, my fosterling, is a king, and now rules over his land." Frigg said: "He is so miserly that he tortures his guests if he thinks that too many of them come to him." Othin replied that this was the greatest of lies; and they made a wager about this matter. Frigg sent her maid-servant, Fulla, to Geirröth. She bade the king beware lest a magician who was come thither to his land should bewitch him, and told this sign concerning him, that no dog was so fierce as to leap at him. Now it was a very great slander that King Geirröth was not hospitable; but nevertheless he had them take the man whom the dogs would not attack. He wore a dark-blue mantle and called himself Grimnir, but said no more about himself, though he was questioned. The king had him tortured to make him speak, and set him between two fires, and he sat there eight nights. King Geirröth had a son ten winters old, and called Agnar after his father's brother. Agnar went to Grimnir, and gave him a full horn to drink from, and said that the king did ill in letting him be tormented without cause. Grimnir drank from the horn; the fire had come so near that the mantle burned on Grimnir's back. He spake:

1. Hot art thou, fire! | too fierce by far;
Get ye now gone, ye flames!
The mantle is burnt, | though I bear it aloft,
And the fire scorches the fur.

2. 'Twixt the fires now | eight nights have I sat,
And no man brought meat to me,
Save Agnar alone, | and alone shall rule
Geirröth's son o'er the Goths.

3. Hail to thee, Agnar! | for hailed thou art
By the voice of Veratyr;
For a single drink | shalt thou never receive
A greater gift as reward.

4. The land is holy | that lies hard by
The gods and the elves together;
And Thor shall ever | in Thruthheim dwell,
Till the gods to destruction go.

5. Ydalir call they | the place where Ull
A hall for himself hath set;
And Alfheim the gods | to Freyr once gave
As a tooth-gift in ancient times.

6. A third home is there, | with silver thatched
By the hands of the gracious gods:
Valaskjolf is it, | in days of old
Set by a god for himself.

7. Sökkvabekk is the fourth, | where cool waves flow,
And amid their murmur it stands;
There daily do Othin | and Saga drink
In gladness from cups of gold.

8. The fifth is Glathsheim, | and gold-bright there
Stands Valhall stretching wide;
And there does Othin | each day choose
The men who have fallen in fight.

9. Easy is it to know | for him who to Othin
Comes and beholds the hall;
Its rafters are spears, | with shields is it roofed,
On its benches are breastplates strewn.

10. Easy is it to know | for him who to Othin
Comes and beholds the hall;
There hangs a wolf | by the western door,
And o'er it an eagle hovers.

11. The sixth is Thrymheim, | where Thjazi dwelt,
The giant of marvelous might;
Now Skathi abides, | the god's fair bride,
In the home that her father had.

12. The seventh is Breithablik; | Baldr has there
For himself a dwelling set,
In the land I know | that lies so fair,
And from evil fate is free.

13. Himinbjorg is the eighth, | and Heimdall there
O'er men holds sway, it is said;
In his well-built house | does the warder of heaven
The good mead gladly drink.

14. The ninth is Folkvang, | where Freyja decrees
Who shall have seats in the hall;
The half of the dead | each day does she choose,
And half does Othin have.

15. The tenth is Glitnir; | its pillars are gold,
And its roof with silver is set;
There most of his days | does Forseti dwell,
And sets all strife at end.

16. The eleventh is Noatun; | there has Njorth
For himself a dwelling set;
The sinless ruler | of men there sits
In his temple timbered high.

17. Filled with growing trees | and high-standing grass
Is Vithi, Vithar's land;
But there did the son | from his steed leap down,
When his father he fain would avenge.

18. In Eldhrimnir | Andhrimnir cooks
Sæhrimnir's seething flesh,--
The best of food, | but few men know
On what fare the warriors feast.

19. Freki and Geri | does Heerfather feed,
The far-famed fighter of old:
But on wine alone | does the weapon-decked god,
Othin, forever live.

20. O'er Mithgarth Hugin | and Munin both
Each day set forth to fly;
For Hugin I fear | lest he come not home,
But for Munin my care is more.

21. Loud roars Thund, | and Thjothvitnir's fish
joyously fares in the flood,
Hard does it seem | to the host of the slain
To wade the torrent wild.

22. There Valgrind stands, | the sacred gate,
And behind are the holy doors;
Old is the gate, | but few there are
Who can tell how it tightly is locked.

23. Five hundred doors | and forty there are,
I ween, in Valhall's walls;
Eight hundred fighters | through one door fare
When to war with the wolf they go.

24. Five hundred rooms | and forty there are
I ween, in Bilskirnir built;

Of all the homes | whose roofs I beheld,
My son's the greatest meseemed.

25. Heithrun is the goat | who stands by Heerfather's hall,
And the branches of Lærath she bites;
The pitcher she fills | with the fair, clear mead,
Ne'er fails the foaming drink.

26. Eikthyrnir is the hart | who stands by Heerfather's hall
And the branches of Lærath he bites;
From his horns a stream | into Hvergelmir drops,
Thence all the rivers run.

27. Sith and Vith, | Sækin and Ækin,
Svol and Fimbulthul, | Gunnthro, and Fjorm,
Rin and Rinnandi,
Gipul and Gopul, | Gomul and Geirvimul,
That flow through the fields of the gods;
Thyn and Vin, | Thol and Hol,
Groth and Gunnthorin.

28. Vino is one, | Vegsvin another,
And Thjothnuma a third;

Nyt and Not, | Non and Hron,
Slith and Hrith, | Sylg and Ylg,
Vith and Von, | Vond and Strond,
Gjol and Leipt, | that go among men,
And hence they fall to Hel.

29. Kormt and Ormt | and the Kerlaugs twain
Shall Thor each day wade through,
(When dooms to give | he forth shall go
To the ash-tree Yggdrasil;)
For heaven's bridge | burns all in flame,
And the sacred waters seethe.

30. Glath and Gyllir, | Gler and Skeithbrimir,
Silfrintopp and Sinir,
Gisl and Falhofnir, | Golltopp and Lettfeti,
On these steeds the gods shall go
When dooms to give | each day they ride
To the ash-tree Yggdrasil.

31. Three roots there are | that three ways run
'Neath the ash-tree Yggdrasil;
'Neath the first lives Hel, | 'neath the second the frost-giants,
'Neath the last are the lands of men.

32. Ratatosk is the squirrel | who there shall run
On the ash-tree Yggdrasil;
From above the words | of the eagle he bears,
And tells them to Nithhogg beneath.

33. Four harts there are, | that the highest twigs

Nibble with necks bent back;
Dain and Dvalin, | . . . . . .
Duneyr and Dyrathror.

34. More serpents there are | beneath the ash
Than an unwise ape would think;
Goin and Moin, | Grafvitnir's sons,
Grabak and Grafvolluth,
Ofnir and Svafnir | shall ever, methinks,
Gnaw at the twigs of the tree.

35. Yggdrasil's ash | great evil suffers,
Far more than men do know;

The hart bites its top, | its trunk is rotting,
And Nithhogg gnaws beneath.

36. Hrist and Mist | bring the horn at my will,
Skeggjold and Skogul;
Hild and Thruth, | Hlok and Herfjotur,
Gol and Geironul,
Randgrith and Rathgrith | and Reginleif
Beer to the warriors bring.

37. Arvak and Alsvith | up shall drag
Weary the weight of the sun;
But an iron cool | have the kindly gods
Of yore set under their yokes.

38. In front of the sun | does Svalin stand,
The shield for the shining god;
Mountains and sea | would be set in flames
If it fell from before the sun.

39. Skoll is the wolf | that to Ironwood
Follows the glittering god,
And the son of Hrothvitnir, | Hati, awaits
The burning bride of heaven.

40. Out of Ymir's flesh | was fashioned the earth,
And the ocean out of his blood;
Of his bones the hills, | of his hair the trees,
Of his skull the heavens high.

41. Mithgarth the gods | from his eyebrows made,
And set for the sons of men;
And out of his brain | the baleful clouds
They made to move on high.

42. His the favor of Ull | and of all the gods
Who first in the flames will reach;
For the house can be seen | by the sons of the gods
If the kettle aside were cast.

43. In days of old | did Ivaldi's sons
Skithblathnir fashion fair,
The best of ships | for the bright god Freyr,
The noble son of Njorth.

44. The best of trees | must Yggdrasil be,
Skithblathnir best of boats;
Of all the gods | is Othin the greatest,
And Sleipnir the best of steeds;
Bifrost of bridges, | Bragi of skalds,
Hobrok of hawks, | and Garm of hounds.

45. To the race of the gods | my face have I raised,
And the wished-for aid have I waked;
For to all the gods | has the message gone
That sit in Ægir's seats,
That drink within Ægir's doors.

46. Grim is my name, | Gangleri am 1,
Herjan and Hjalmberi,

Thekk and Thrithi, | Thuth and Uth,
Helblindi and Hor;

47. Sath and Svipal | and Sanngetal,
Herteit and Hnikar,
Bileyg, Baleyg, | Bolverk, Fjolnir,
Grim and Grimnir, | Glapsvith, Fjolsvith.

48. Sithhott, Sithskegg, | Sigfather, Hnikuth,
Allfather, Valfather, | Atrith, Farmatyr:
A single name | have I never had
Since first among men I fared.

49. Grimnir they call me | in Geirröth's hall,
With Asmund Jalk am I;
Kjalar I was | when I went in a sledge,
At the council Thror am I called,
As Vithur I fare to the fight;
Oski, Biflindi, | Jafnhor and Omi,
Gondlir and Harbarth midst gods.
So. I deceived the giant | Sokkmimir old
As Svithur and Svithrir of yore;
Of Mithvitnir's son | the slayer I was
When the famed one found his doom.

51. Drunk art thou, Geirröth, | too much didst thou drink,
. . . .
Much hast thou lost, | for help no more
From me or my heroes thou hast.

52. Small heed didst thou take | to all that I told,
And false were the words of thy friends;
For now the sword | of my friend I see,
That waits all wet with blood.

53. Thy sword-pierced body | shall Ygg have soon,
For thy life is ended at last;
The maids are hostile; | now Othin behold!
Now come to me if thou canst!

54. Now am I Othin, | Ygg was I once,
Ere that did they call me Thund;
Vak and Skilfing, | Vofuth and Hroptatyr,
Gaut and Jalk midst the gods;
Ofnir and Svafnir, | and all, methinks,
Are names for none but me.

King Geirröth sat and had his sword on his knee, half drawn from its sheath. But when he heard that Othin was come thither, then he rose up and sought to take Othin from the fire. The sword slipped from his hand, and fell with the hilt down. The king stumbled and fell forward, and the sword pierced him through, and slew him. Then Othin vanished, but Agnar long ruled there as king.

[Prose. The texts of the two manuscripts differ in many minor details. *Hrauthung*: this mythical king is not mentioned elsewhere. *Geirröth*: the manuscripts spell his name in various ways [fp. 86] *Frigg*: Othin's wife. She and Othin nearly always disagreed in some such way as the one outlined in this story. *Hlithskjolf* ("Gate-Shelf"): Othin's watch-tower in heaven, whence he can overlook all the nine worlds; cf. *Skirnismol*, introductory prose. *Grimnir*: "the Hooded One."]

[2. In the original lines 2 and 4 are both too long for the meter, and thus the true form of the stanza is doubtful. For line 4 both manuscripts have "the land of the Goths" instead of simply "the Goths." The word "Goths" apparently was applied indiscriminately to any South-Germanic people, including the Burgundians as well as the actual Goths, and thus here has no specific application; cf. *Gripisspo*, 35 and note.]

[3. *Veratyr* ("Lord of Men"): Othin. The "gift" which Agnar receives is Othin's mythological lore.

4. *Thruthheim* ("the Place of Might"): the place where Thor, the strongest of the gods, has his hall, Bilskirnir, described in stanza 24.

5. *Ydalir* ("Yew-Dales"): the home of Ulf, the archer among the gods, a son of Thor's wife, Sif, by another marriage. The wood of the yew-tree was used for bows in the North just as it was long afterwards in England. *Alfheim*: the home of the elves. *Freyr*: cf. Skirnismol, introductory prose and note. *Tooth-gift*: the custom of making a present to a child when it cuts its first tooth is, according to Vigfusson, still in vogue in Iceland.

6. *Valaskjolf* ("the Shelf of the Slain"): Othin's home, in which is his watch-tower, Hlithskjolf. Gering identifies this with Valhall, and as that is mentioned in stanza 8, he believes stanza 6 to be an interpolation.]

[7. *Sökkvabekk* ("the Sinking Stream"): of this spot and of Saga, who is said to live there, little is known. Saga may be an hypostasis of Frigg, but Snorri calls her a distinct goddess, and the name suggests some relation to history or story-telling.

8. *Glathsheim* ("the Place of Joy"): Othin's home, the greatest and most beautiful hall in the world. *Valhall* ("Hall of the Slain"): cf. *Voluspo*, V and note. Valhall is not only the hall whither the slain heroes are brought by the Valkyries, but also a favorite home of Othin.

10. The opening formula is abbreviated in both manuscripts. *A wolf*: probably the wolf and the eagle were carved figures above the door.]

[11. *Thrymheim* ("the Home of Clamor"): on this mountain the giant Thjazi built his home. The god, or rather Wane, Njorth (cf. *Voluspo*, 21, note) married Thjazi's daughter, Skathi. She wished to live in her father's hall among the mountains, while Njorth loved his home, Noatun, by the sea. They agreed to compromise by spending nine nights at Thrymheim and then three at Noatun, but neither could endure the surroundings of the other's home, so Skathi returned to Thrymheim, while Njorth stayed at Noatun. Snorri quotes stanzas 11-15.

12. *Breithablik* ("Wide-Shining"): the house in heaven, free from everything unclean, in which Baldr (cf. *Voluspo*, 32, note), the fairest and best of the gods, lived.

13. *Himinbjorg* ("Heaven's Cliffs"): the dwelling at the end of the bridge Bifrost (the rainbow), where Heimdall (cf. *Voluspo*, 27) keeps watch against the coming of the giants. In this stanza the two functions of Heimdall--as father of mankind (cf. *Voluspo*, 1 and note, and *Rigsthula*, introductory prose and note) and as

warder of the gods--seem both to be mentioned, but the second line in the manuscripts is apparently in bad shape, and in the editions is more or less conjectural.

14. *Folkvang* ("Field of the Folk): here is situated Freyja's [fp. 91] hall, Sessrymnir ("Rich in Seats"). Freyja, the sister of Freyr, is the fairest of the goddesses, and the most kindly disposed to mankind, especially to lovers. *Half of the dead*: Mogk has made it clear that Freyja represents a confusion between two originally distinct divinities: the wife of Othin (Frigg) and the northern goddess of love. This passage appears to have in mind her attributes as Othin's wife. Snorri has this same confusion, but there is no reason why the Freyja who was Freyr's sister should share the slain with Othin.]

[15. *Glitnir* ("the Shining"): the home of Forseti, a god of whom we know nothing beyond what Snorri tells us: "Forseti is the son of Baldr and Nanna, daughter of Nep. All those who come to him with hard cases to settle go away satisfied; he is the best judge among gods and men."

16. *Noatun* ("Ships'-Haven"): the home of Njorth, who calms the waves; cf. stanza 11 and *Voluspo*, 21.

17. *Vithi*: this land is not mentioned elsewhere. *Vithar* avenged his father, Othin, by slaying the wolf Fenrir.]

[18. Stanzas 18-20 appear also in Snorri's Edda. Very possibly they are an interpolation here. *Eldhrimnir* ("Sooty with Fire"): the great kettle in Valhall, wherein the gods' cook, *Andhrimnir* ("The Sooty-Faced") daily cooks the flesh of the boar *Sæhrimnir* ("The Blackened"). His flesh suffices for all the heroes there gathered, and each evening he becomes whole again, to be cooked the next morning.

19. *Freki* ("The Greedy") and *Geri* ("The Ravenous"): the two wolves who sit by Othin's side at the feast, and to whom he gives all the food set before him, since wine is food and drink alike for him. *Heerfather*: Othin.

20, *Mithgarth* ("The Middle Home"): the earth. *Hugin* ("Thought") and *Munin* ("Memory"): the two ravens who sit on Othin's shoulders, and fly forth daily to bring him news of the world.]

[21. *Thund* ("The Swollen" or "The Roaring"): the river surrounding Valhall. *Thjothvitnir's fish*: presumably the sun, which was caught by the wolf Skoll (cf. *Voluspo*, 40), Thjothvitnir meaning "the mighty wolf." Such a phrase, characteristic of all Skaldic poetry, is rather rare in the Edda. The last two lines refer to the attack on Valhall by the people of Hel; cf. Voluspo, 51.

22. *Valgrind* ("The Death-Gate"): the outer gate of Valhall; cf. *Sigurtharkvitha en skamma*, 68 and note.

23. This and the following stanza stand in reversed order in *Regius*. Snorri quotes stanza 23 as a proof of the vast size of Valhall. The last two lines refer to the final battle with Fenrir and the other enemies.

24. This stanza is almost certainly an interpolation, brought in through a confusion of the first two lines with those of stanza 23. Its description of Thor's house, Bilskirnir (cf. stanza 4 and [fp. 94] note) has nothing to do with that of Valhall. Snorri quotes the stanza in his account of Thor.]

[25. The first line in the original is, as indicated in the translation, too long, and various attempts to amend it have been made. *Heithrun*: the she-goat who lives on the twigs of the tree *Lærath* (presumably the ash Yggdrasil), and daily gives mead which, like the boar's flesh, suffices for all the heroes in Valhall. In Snorri's *Edda* Gangleri foolishly asks whether the heroes drink water, whereto Har replies, "Do you imagine that Othin invites kings and earls and other noble men, and then gives them water to drink?"

26. Eikthyrnir ("The Oak-Thorned," i.e., with antlers, "thorns," like an oak): this animal presumably represents the clouds. The first line, like that of stanza 25, is too long in the original. *Lærath*: cf. stanza 25, note. *Hvergelmir*: according to Snorri, this spring, "the Cauldron-Roaring," was in the midst of Niflheim, the world of darkness and the dead, beneath the third root of the ash Yggdrasil. Snorri gives a list of the rivers flowing thence nearly identical with the one in the poem.]

[27. The entire passage from stanza 27 through stanza 35 is confused. The whole thing may well be an interpolation. Bugge calls stanzas 27-30 an interpolation, and editors who have accepted the passage as a whole have rejected various lines. The spelling of the names of the rivers varies greatly in the manuscripts and editions. It is needless here to point out the many attempted emendations of this list. For a passage presenting similar problems, cf. *Voluspo*, 10-16. Snorri virtually quotes stanzas 27-29 in his prose, though not consecutively. The name *Rin*, in line 3, is identical with that for the River Rhine which appears frequently in the hero poems, but the similarity is doubt less purely accidental.

28. *Slith* may possibly be the same river as that mentioned in Voluspo, 36, as flowing through the giants' land. *Leipt*: in *Helgakvitha Hundingsbana II*, 29, this

river is mentioned as one by which a solemn oath is sworn, and Gering points the parallel to the significance of the Styx among the Greeks. The other rivers here named are not mentioned elsewhere in the poems.]

[29. This stanza looks as though it originally had had nothing to do with the two preceding it. Snorri quotes it in his description of the three roots of Yggdrasil, and the three springs be neath them. "The third root of the ash stands in heaven and beneath this root is a spring which is very holy, and is called Urth's well." (Cf. *Voluspo*, 19) "There the gods have their judgment-seat, and thither they ride each day over Bifrost, which is also called the Gods' Bridge." Thor has to go on foot in the last days of the destruction, when the bridge is burning. Another interpretation, however, is that when Thor leaves the heavens (i.e., when a thunder-storm is over) the rainbow-bridge becomes hot in the sun. Nothing more is known of the rivers named in this stanza. Lines 3-4 are almost certainly interpolated from stanza 30.

30. This stanza, again possibly an interpolation, is closely paraphrased by Snorri following the passage quoted in the previous note. *Glath*("Joyous"): identified in the *Skaldskaparmal* with Skinfaxi, the horse of day; cf. *Vafthruthnismol*, 12. *Gyllir*: "Golden." *Gler*: "Shining."*Skeithbrimir*: "Swift-Going." *Silfrintopp*: "Silver-Topped." Sinir: "Sinewy." *Gisl*: the meaning is doubtful; Gering suggests "Gleaming."*Falhofnir*: [fp. 97]"Hollow-Hoofed." *Golltopp* ("Gold-Topped"): this horse be longed to Heimdall (cf. Voluspo, i and 46). It is noteworthy that gold was one of the attributes of Heimdall's belongings, and, because his teeth were of gold, he was also called Gullintanni ("Gold-Toothed").*Lettfeti*: "Light-Feet." Othin's eight footed horse, *Sleipnir*, is not mentioned in this list.]

[31. The first of these roots is the one referred to in stanza 26; the second in stanza 29 (cf. notes). Of the third root there is nothing noteworthy recorded. After this stanza it is more than possible that one has been lost, paraphrased in the prose of Snorri's Edda thus: "An eagle sits in the branches of the ash tree, and he is very wise; and between his eyes sits the hawk who is called Vethrfolnir."

32. *Ratatosk* ("The Swift-Tusked"): concerning this squirrel, the Prose Edda has to add only that he runs up and down the tree conveying the abusive language of the eagle (see note on stanza 31) and the dragon *Nithhogg* (cf. *Voluspo*, 39 and note) to each other. The hypothesis that Ratatosk "represents the undying hatred between the sustaining and the destroying elements-the gods and the giants," seems a trifle far-fetched.

33. Stanzas 33-34 may well be interpolated, and are certainly in bad shape in the Mss. Bugge points out that they are probably of later origin than those

90

surrounding them. Snorri [fp. 98] closely paraphrases stanza 33, but without
elaboration, and nothing further is known of the *four harts*. It may be guessed,
however, that they are a late multiplication of the single hart mentioned in stanza
26, just as the list of dragons in stanza 34 seems to have been expanded out of
Nithhogg, the only authentic dragon under the root of the ash. *Highest twigs*: a
guess; the Mss. words are baffling. Something has apparently been lost from lines
3-4, but there is no clue as to its nature.]

[34. Cf. note on previous stanza. Nothing further is known of any of the serpents
here listed, and the meanings of many of the names are conjectural. Snorri quotes
this stanza. Editors have altered it in various ways in an attempt to regularize the
meter. *Goin* and *Moin*: meaning obscure. *Grafvitnir*: "The Gnawing
Wolf." *Grabak*: "Gray-Back." *Grafvolluth*: "The Field
Gnawer." *Ofnir* and *Svafnir* ("The Bewilderer" and "The Sleep-Bringer"): it is
noteworthy that in stanza 54 Othin gives himself these two names.

35. Snorri quotes this stanza, which concludes the passage, beginning with stanza
25, describing Yggdrasil. If we assume that stanzas 27-34 are later interpolations--
possibly excepting 32--this section of the poem reads clearly enough.]

[36. Snorri quotes this list of the Valkyries, concerning whom cf. Voluspo, 31 and
note, where a different list of names is given. *Hrist*: "Shaker."*Mist*:
"Mist." *Skeggjold*: "Ax-Time." *Skogul*: "Raging" (?). *Hild*: "Warrior." *Thruth*:
"Might." *Hlok*: "Shrieking." *Herfjotur*: "Host-Fetter." *Gol*:
"Screaming." *Geironul*: "Spear-Bearer." *Randgrith*: "Shield-Bearer." *Rathgrith*:
Gering guesses "Plan-Destroyer." *Reginleif*: "Gods'-Kin." Manuscripts and
editions vary greatly in the spelling of these names, and hence in their
significance.

37. Müllenhoff suspects stanzas 37-41 to have been interpolated, and Edzardi
thinks they may have come from the *Vafthruthnismol*. Snorri closely paraphrases
stanzas 37-39, and quotes 40-41. *Arvak* ("Early Waker") and *Alsvith* ("All Swift"):
the horses of the sun, named also in*Sigrdrifumol*, 15. According to Snorri: "There
was a man called Mundilfari, who had two children; they were so fair and lovely
that he called his son Mani and his daughter Sol. The gods were angry at this
presumption, and took the children and set them up in heaven; and they bade Sol
drive the horses that drew the car of the sun [fp. 100] which the gods had made to
light the world from the sparks which flew out of Muspellsheim. The horses were
called Alsvith and Arvak, and under their yokes the gods set two bellows to cool
them, and in some songs these are called 'the cold iron.'"]

[38. *Svalin* ("The Cooling"): the only other reference to this shield is in *Sigrdrifumol*, 15.

39. *Skoll* and *Hati*: the wolves that devour respectively the sun and moon. The latter is the son of Hrothvitnir ("The Mighty Wolf," i. e. Fenrir); cf. *Voluspo*, 40, and *Vafthruthnismol*, 46-47, in which Fenrir appears as the thief. *Ironwood*: a conjectural emendation of an obscure phrase; cf. *Voluspo*, 40.

40. This and the following stanza are quoted by Snorri. They seem to have come from a different source from the others of this poem; Edzardi suggests an older version of the *Vafthruthnismol*. This stanza is closely parallel to *Vafthruthnismol*, 21, which see, as also *Voluspo*, 3. Snorri, following this account, has a few details to add. The stones were made out of Ymir's teeth and such of his bones as were broken. Mithgarth was a mountain-wall made out of Ymir's eyebrows, and set around the earth because of the enmity of the giants.]

[42. With this stanza Othin gets back to his immediate situation, bound as he is between two fires. He calls down a blessing on the man who will reach into the fire and pull aside the great kettle which, in Icelandic houses, hung directly under the smoke vent in the roof, and thus kept any one above from looking down into the interior. On *Ull*, the archer-god, cf. stanza 5 and note. He is specified here apparently for no better reason than that his name fits the initial-rhyme.

43. This and the following stanza are certainly interpolated, for they have nothing to do with the context, and stanza 45 continues the dramatic conclusion of the poem begun in stanza 42. This stanza is quoted by Snorri. *Ivaldi* ("The Mighty"): he is known only as the father of the craftsmen-dwarfs who made not only the ship Skithblathnir, but also Othin's spear Gungnir, and the golden hair for Thor's wife, Sif, after Loki had maliciously cut her own hair off. *Skithblathnir*: this ship ("Wooden-Bladed") always had a fair wind, whenever the sail was set; it could be folded up at will and put in the pocket. *Freyr*: concerning him and his father, see Voluspo, 21, note, and *Skirnismol*, introductory prose and note.]

[44. Snorri quotes this stanza. Like stanza 43 an almost certain interpolation, it was probably drawn in by the reference to Skithblathnir in the stanza interpolated earlier. It is presumably in faulty condition. One Ms. has after the fifth line half of a sixth,--"Brimir of swords," *Yggdrasil*: cf. stanzas 25-35. *Skithblathnir*: cf. stanza 43, note. *Sleipnir*: Othin's eight-legged horse, one of Loki's numerous progeny, borne by him to the stallion Svathilfari. This stallion belonged to the giant who built a fortress for the gods, and came so near to finishing it, with Svathilfari's aid, as to make the gods fear he would win his promised reward--Freyja and the sun and moon. To delay the work, Loki turned himself into a mare, whereupon the stallion ran away, and the giant failed to complete his task within the stipulated time. *Bilrost*: probably another form of Bifrost (which Snorri has in his version of the stanza), on which cf. stanza 29. *Bragi*: the god of poetry. He is one of the later figures among the gods, and is mentioned only three times in the poems of the *Edda*. In Snorri's *Edda*, however, he is of great importance. His wife is Ithun, goddess of youth. Perhaps the Norwegian skald Bragi Boddason, the oldest recorded skaldic poet, had been traditionally apotheosized as early as the tenth century. *Hobrok*: nothing further is known of him. *Garm*: cf. Voluspo, 44.

45. With this stanza the narrative current of the poem is resumed. Ægir: the sea-god; cf. *Lokasenna*, introductory prose.]

[46. Concerning the condition of stanzas 46-50, quoted by Snorri, nothing definite can be said. Lines and entire stanzas of this "catalogue" sort undoubtedly came and went with great freedom all through the period of oral transmission. Many of the names are not mentioned elsewhere, and often their significance is sheer guesswork. As in nearly every episode Othin appeared in disguise, the number of his names was necessarily almost limitless. *Grim*: "The Hooded." *Gangleri*: "The Wanderer." *Herjan*: "The Ruler." *Hjalmberi*: "The Helmet-Bearer." *Thekk*: "The Much-Loved." *Thrithi*: "The Third" (in Snorri's Edda the stories are all told in the form of answers to questions, the speakers being Har, Jafnhar and Thrithi. Just what this tripartite form of Othin signifies has been the source of endless debate. Probably this line is late enough to betray the somewhat muddled influence of early Christianity.) *Thuth* and *Uth*: both names defy guesswork. *Helblindi*: "Hel-Blinder" (two manuscripts have *Herblindi*--"Host-Blinder"). *Hor*: "The High One."

47. *Sath*: "The Truthful." *Svipal*: "The Changing." *Sanngetal*: "The Truth-Teller." *Herteit*: "Glad of the Host." *Hnikar*: "The Overthrower."*Bileyg*: "The Shifty-Eyed." *Baleyg*: "The Flaming-Eyed." *Bolverk*: "Doer of Ill" (cf. Hovamol, 104 and note). *Fjolnir*: "The Many-Shaped."*Grimnir*: "The Hooded." *Glapswith*: "Swift in Deceit." *Fjolsvith*: "Wide of Wisdom."

48. *Sithhott*: "With Broad Hat." *Sithskegg*: "Long-Bearded." [fp. 104] *Sigfather*: 'Father of Victory." *Hnikuth*: "Overthrower." *Valfather*: 'Father of the Slain." *Atrith*: "The Rider." *Farmatyr*: "Helper of Cargoes" (i. e., god of sailors).]

[49. Nothing is known of Asmund, of Othin's appearance as Jalk, or of the occasion when he "went in a sledge" as Kjalar ("Ruler of Keels"?).*Thror* and *Vithur* are also of uncertain meaning. *Oski*: "God of Wishes." *Biflindi*: the manuscripts vary widely in the form of this name.*Jafnhor*:

93

"Equally High" (cf. note on stanza 46). *Omi*: "The Shouter." *Gondlir*: "Wand Bearer." *Harbarth*: "Graybeard" (cf. *Harbarthsljoth*, introduction).

50. Nothing further is known of the episode here mentioned Sokkmimir is presumably Mithvitnir's son. Snorri quotes the names Svithur and Svithrir, but omits all the remainder of the stanza.]

[51. Again the poem returns to the direct action, Othin addressing the terrified Geirröth. The manuscripts show no lacuna. Some editors supply a second line from paper manuscripts: "Greatly by me art beguiled."

53. *Ygg*: Othin ("The Terrible"). *The maids*: the three Norns.

54. Possibly out of place, and probably more or less corrupt. *Thund*: "The Thunderer." *Vak*: "The Wakeful." *Skilfing*: "The Shaker." *Vofuth*: "The Wanderer." *Hroptatyr*: "Crier of the Gods." *Gaut*: "Father." *Ofnir and Svafnir*: cf. stanza 34.]

SKIRNISMOL

The Ballad of Skirnir

INTRODUCTORY NOTE

The *Skirnismol* is found complete in the *Codex Regius*, and through stanza 27 in the *Arnamagnæan Codex*. Snorri quotes the concluding stanza. In *Regius* the poem is entitled "For Scirnis" ("Skirnir's journey").

The *Skirnismol* differs sharply from the poems preceding it, in that it has a distinctly ballad quality. As a matter of fact, however, its verse is altogether dialogue, the narrative being supplied in the prose "links," concerning which cf. introductory note to the *Grimnismol*. The dramatic effectiveness and vivid characterization of the poem seem to connect it with the *Thrymskvitha*, and the two may possibly have been put into their present form by the same man. Bugge's guess that the Skirnismol was the work of the author of the *Lokasenna* is also possible, though it has less to support it.

Critics have generally agreed in dating the poem as we now have it as early as the first half of the tenth century; Finnur Jonsson puts it as early as goo, and claims it, as usual, for Nor way. Doubtless it was current in Norway, in one form or another, before the first Icelandic settlements, but his argument that the thistle (stanza 31) is not an Icelandic plant has little weight, for such curse-formulas must have traveled freely from place to place. In view of the evidence pointing to a western origin for many or all of the Eddic poems, Jonsson's reiterated "Digtet er sikkert norsk og ikke islandsk" is somewhat exasperating. Wherever the *Skirnismol* was composed, it has been preserved in exceptionally good condition, and seems to be practically devoid of interpolations or lacunæ.

Freyr, the son of Njorth, had sat one day in Hlithskjolf, and looked over all the worlds. He looked into Jotunheim, and saw there a fair maiden, as she went from her father's house to her bower. Forthwith he felt a mighty love-sickness. Skirnir was the name of Freyr's servant; Njorth bade him ask speech of Freyr. He said:

1. "Go now, Skirnir! | and seek to gain
Speech from my son;
And answer to win, | for whom the wise one
Is mightily moved."

Skirnir spake:
2. "Ill words do I now | await from thy son,
If I seek to get speech with him,
And answer to win, | for whom the wise one
Is mightily moved."

Skirnir spake:
3. "Speak prithee, Freyr, | foremost of the gods,
For now I fain would know;
Why sittest thou here | in the wide halls,
Days long, my prince, alone?"

Freyr spake.
4. "How shall I tell thee, | thou hero young,
Of all my grief so great?
Though every day | the elfbeam dawns,
It lights my longing never."

Skirnir spake:
5. "Thy longings, methinks, | are not so large
That thou mayst not tell them to me;

Since in days of yore | we were young together,
We two might each other trust."

Freyr spake:
6. "From Gymir's house | I beheld go forth
A maiden dear to me;
Her arms glittered, | and from their gleam
Shone all the sea and sky.

7. "To me more dear | than in days of old
Was ever maiden to man;
But no one of gods | or elves will grant
That we both together should be."

Skirnir spake:
8. "Then give me the horse | that goes through the dark
And magic flickering flames;
And the sword as well | that fights of itself
Against the giants grim."

Freyr spake:
9. "The horse will I give thee | that goes through the dark
And magic flickering flames,
And the sword as well | that will fight of itself
If a worthy hero wields it."

Skirnir spake to the horse:
10. "Dark is it without, | and I deem it time
To fare through the wild fells,
(To fare through the giants' fastness;)
We shall both come back, | or us both together
The terrible giant will take."

Skirnir rode into Jotunheim to Gymir's house. There were fierce
dogs bound before the gate of the fence which was around Gerth's
hall. He rode to where a herdsman sat on a hill, and said:

97

11. "Tell me, herdsman, | sitting on the hill,
And watching all the ways,
How may I win | a word with the maid
Past the hounds of Gymir here?"

The herdsman spake:
12. "Art thou doomed to die | or already dead,
Thou horseman that ridest hither?
Barred from speech | shalt thou ever be
With Gymir's daughter good."

Skirnir spake:
13. "Boldness is better | than plaints can be
For him whose feet must fare;
To a destined day has mine age been doomed,
And my life's span thereto laid."

Gerth spake:
14. "What noise is that which now so loud
I hear within our house?
The ground shakes, and the home of Gymir
Around me trembles too."

The Serving-Maid spake:
15. "One stands without who has leapt from his steed,
And lets his horse loose to graze;"

. . . .
. . . .

Gerth spake:
16. "Bid the man come in, and drink good mead
Here within our hall;
Though this I fear, that there without
My brother's slayer stands.

17. "Art thou of the elves | or the offspring of gods,
Or of the wise Wanes?
How camst thou alone | through the leaping flame
Thus to behold our home?"

Skirnir spake:
18. "I am not of the elves, | nor the offspring of gods,
Nor of the wise Wanes;
Though I came alone | through the leaping flame
Thus to behold thy home.

19. "Eleven apples, | all of gold,
Here will I give thee, Gerth,
To buy thy troth | that Freyr shall be
Deemed to be dearest to you."

Gerth spake:
20. "I will not take | at any man's wish
These eleven apples ever;
Nor shall Freyr and I | one dwelling find
So long as we two live."

Skirnir spake:
21. "Then do I bring thee | the ring that was burned
Of old with Othin's son;
From it do eight | of like weight fall
On every ninth night."

Gerth spake:
22. "The ring I wish not, | though burned it was
Of old with Othin's son;
In Gymir's home | is no lack of gold
In the wealth my father wields."

Skirnir spake:
23. "Seest thou, maiden, | this keen, bright sword

That I hold here in my hand?
Thy head from thy neck | shall I straightway hew,
If thou wilt not do my will."

Gerth spake:
24. "For no man's sake | will I ever suffer
To be thus moved by might;
But gladly, methinks, | will Gymir seek
To fight if he finds thee here."

Skirnir spake:
25. "Seest thou, maiden, | this keen, bright sword
That I hold here in my hand?
Before its blade the | old giant bends,--
Thy father is doomed to die.

26. "I strike thee, maid, | with my magic staff,
To tame thee to work my will;
There shalt thou go | where never again
The sons of men shall see thee.

27. "On the eagle's hill | shalt thou ever sit,
And gaze on the gates of Hel;
More loathsome to thee | than the light-hued snake
To men, shall thy meat become.

28. "Fearful to see, | if thou comest forth,
Hrimnir will stand and stare,
(Men will marvel at thee;)
More famed shalt thou grow | than the watchman of the gods!
Peer forth, then, from thy prison,

29. "Rage and longing, | fetters and wrath,
Tears and torment are thine;
Where thou sittest down | my doom is on thee
Of heavy heart And double dole.

30. "In the giants' home | shall vile things harm thee
Each day with evil deeds;
Grief shalt thou get | instead of gladness,
And sorrow to suffer with tears.

31. "With three-headed giants | thou shalt dwell ever,
Or never know a husband;
(Let longing grip thee, | let wasting waste thee,--)
Be like to the thistle | that in the loft
Was cast and there was crushed.

32. "I go to the wood, | and to the wet forest,
To win a magic wand;

. . . .

I won a magic wand.

33. "Othin grows angry, | angered is the best of the gods,
Freyr shall be thy foe,
Most evil maid, | who the magic wrath
Of gods hast got for thyself.

34. "Give heed, frost-rulers, | hear it, giants.
Sons of Suttung,
And gods, ye too,
How I forbid | and how I ban
The meeting of men with the maid,
(The joy of men with the maid.)

35. "Hrimgrimnir is he, | the giant who shall have thee
In the depth by the doors of Hel;
To the frost-giants' halls | each day shalt thou fare,
Crawling and craving in vain,
(Crawling and having no hope.)

36. "Base wretches there | by the root of the tree
Will hold for thee horns of filth;

A fairer drink | shalt thou never find,
Maid, to meet thy wish,
(Maid, to meet my wish.)

37. "I write thee a charm | and three runes therewith,
Longing and madness and lust;
But what I have writ | I may yet unwrite
If I find a need therefor."

Gerth spake:
38. "Find welcome rather, | and with it take
The frost-cup filled with mead;
Though I did not believe | that I should so love
Ever one of the Wanes."

Skirnir spake:
39. "My tidings all | must I truly learn
Ere homeward hence I ride:
How soon thou wilt | with the mighty son
Of Njorth a meeting make."

Gerth spake:
40. Barri there is, | which we both know well,
A forest fair and still;
And nine nights hence | to the son of Njorth
Will Gerth there grant delight."

Then Skirnir rode home. Freyr stood without, and spoke to him, and
asked for tidings:

41. "Tell me, Skimir, | ere thou take off the saddle,
Or farest forward a step:
What hast thou done | in the giants' dwelling
To make glad thee or me?"

Skirnir spoke:
42. "Barri there is, | which we both know well,
A forest fair and still;
And nine nights hence | to the son of Njorth
Will Gerth there grant delight."

Freyr spake:
43. "Long is one night, | longer are two;
How then shall I bear three?
Often to me | has a month seemed less
Than now half a night of desire."

[*Prose. Freyr:* concerning his father, Njorth, and the race of the Wanes in general, cf. *Voluspo*, 21 and note. Snorri thus describes Njorth's family: "Njorth begat two children in Noatun; the son was named Freyr, and the daughter Freyja; they were fair of aspect and mighty. Freyr is the noblest of the gods; he rules over rain and sunshine, and therewith the fruitfulness of the earth; it is well to call upon him for plenty and welfare, for he rules over wealth for mankind. Freyja is the noblest of the goddesses. When she rides to the fight, she has one-half of the slain, and Othin has half. When she goes on a journey, she drives her two cats, and sits in a cart. Love-songs please her well, and it is good to call on her in love-matters." *Hlithskjolf:* Othin's watch-tower; cf. *Grimnismol*, introductory prose. *He said*: both manuscripts have "Then Skathi said:" (Skathi was Njorth's wife), but Bugge's emendation, based on Snorri's version, is doubtless correct.]

1. *My son*: both manuscripts, and many editors, have "our son," which, of course, goes with the introduction of Skathi in the prose. As the stanza is clearly addressed to Skirnir, the change of pronouns seems justified. The same confusion occurs in stanza 2, where Skirnir in the manuscripts is made to speak of Freyr as [fp. 108]"your son" (plural). The plural pronoun in the original involves a metrical error, which is corrected by the emendation.]

[4. Elfbeam: the sun, so called because its rays were fatal to elves and dwarfs; cf. *Alvissmol*, 35.

6. *Gymir*: a mountain-giant, husband of Aurbotha, and father of Gerth, fairest among women. This is all Snorri tells of him in his paraphrase of the story.

7. Snorri's paraphrase of the poem is sufficiently close so that his addition of another sentence to Freyr's speech makes it probable [fp. 110] that a stanza has

dropped out between 7 and 8. This has been tentatively reconstructed, thus: "Hither to me shalt thou bring the maid, / And home shalt thou lead her here, / If her father wills it or wills it not, / And good reward shalt thou get." Finn Magnusen detected the probable omission of a stanza here as early as 1821.]

[8. *The sword*: Freyr's gift of his sword to Skirnir eventually proves fatal, for at the last battle, when Freyr is attacked by Beli, whom he kills bare-handed, and later when the fire-demon, Surt, slays him in turn, he is weaponless; cf. *Voluspo*, 53 and note. *Against the giants grim*: the condition of this line makes it seem like an error in copying, and it is possible that it should be identical with the fourth line of the next stanza.]

[10. Some editors reject line 3 as spurious.

12. Line 2 is in neither manuscript, and no gap is indicated. I have followed Grundtvig's conjectural emendation.

13. This stanza is almost exactly like many in the first part of [fp. 112] the *Hovamol*, and may well have been a separate proverb. After this stanza the scene shifts to the interior of the house.]

[15. No gap indicated in either manuscript. Bugge and Niedner have attempted emendations, while Hildebrand suggests that the last two lines of stanza 14 are spurious, 14, 12, and 15 thus forming a single stanza, which seems doubtful.

16. *Brother's slayer*: perhaps the brother is Beli, slain by Freyr; the only other references are in *Voluspo*, 53, and in Snorri's paraphrase of the *Skirnismol*, which merely says that Freyr's gift of his sword to Skirnir "was the reason why he was weaponless when he met Beli, and he killed him bare-handed." Skirnir himself seems never to have killed anybody.]

[17. *Wise Wanes*: Cf. *Voluspo*, 21 and note.

18. The *Arnamagnæan Codex* omits this stanza.

19. *Apples*: the apple was the symbol of fruitfulness, and also of eternal youth. According to Snorri, the goddess Ithun had charge of the apples which the gods ate whenever they felt themselves growing old.]

[21. *Ring*: the ring Draupnir ("Dropper") was made by the dwarfs for Othin, who laid it on Baldr's pyre when the latter's corpse was burned (Cf. *Voluspo*, 32 and note, and *Baldrs Draumar*). Baldr, however, sent the ring back to Othin from hell. How Freyr obtained it is nowhere stated. Andvari's ring (Andvaranaut) had a similar power of creating gold; cf. *Reginsmol*, prose [fp. 115] after stanza 4 and note. Lines 3 and 4 of this stanza, and the first two of stanza 22, are missing in the *Arnamagnæan Codex*.]

[25. The first two lines are abbreviated in both manuscripts.]

26. With this stanza, bribes and threats having failed, Skirnir begins a curse which, by the power of his magic staff, is to fall on Gerth if she refuses Freyr.

27. *Eagle's hill*: the hill at the end of heaven, and consequently overlooking hell, where the giant Hræsvelg sits "in an eagle's guise," and makes the winds with his wings; cf. *Vafthruthnismol*, 37, also Voluspo, 50. The second line is faulty in both manuscripts; Hildebrand's emendation corrects the error, but omits an effective touch; the manuscript line may be rendered "And look and hanker for hell." The Arnamagnæan Codex breaks off with the fourth line of this stanza.

28. *Hrimnir*: a frost-giant, mentioned elsewhere only in *Hyndluljoth*, 33. Line 3 is probably spurious. *Watchman of the gods*: Heimdall; cf.*Voluspo*, 46.]

[29. Three nouns of doubtful meaning, which I have rendered *rage, longing,* and *heart* respectively, make the precise force of this stanza obscure. Niedner and Sijmons mark the entire stanza as interpolated, and Jonsson rejects line 5.

30. In *Regius* and in nearly all the editions the first two lines of this stanza are followed by lines 3-5 of stanza 35. I have followed Niedner, Sijmons, and Gering. The two words here translated *vile things* are obscure; Gering renders the phrase simply "Kobolde."

31. The confusion noted as to the preceding stanza, and a metrical error in the third line, have led to various rearrangements and emendations; line 3 certainly looks like an interpolation. *Three-headed giants*: concerning giants with numerous heads, cf. *Vafthruthnismol*, 33, and*Hymiskvitha*, 8.]

[32. No gap indicated in the manuscript; Niedner makes the line here given as 4 the first half of line 3, and fills out the stanza thus: "with which I will tame you, / Maid, to work my will." The whole stanza seems to be either interpolated or out of place; it would fit better after stanza 25.

33. Jonsson marks this stanza as interpolated. The word translated *most evil* is another case of guesswork.

34. Most editors reject line 3 as spurious, and some also reject line 6. Lines 2 and 3 may have been expanded out of a single line running approximately "Ye gods and Suttung's sons." *Suttung*: concerning this giant cf. Hovamol, 104 and note.]

[35. Most editors combine lines 1-2 with stanza 36 (either with the first two lines thereof or the whole stanza), as lines 3-5 stand in the manuscript after line 2 of stanza 30. *Hrimgrimnir* ("The Frost-Shrouded"): a giant not elsewhere mentioned. Line 5, as a repetition of line 4, is probably a later addition.

36. For the combination of this stanza with the preceding one, cf. note on stanza 35. The scribe clearly did not consider that the stanza began with line I, as the first word thereof in the manuscript does not begin with a capital letter and has no period before it. The first word of line 3, however, is so marked. Line 5 may well be spurious.

37. Again the scribe seems to have been uncertain as to the stanza divisions. This time the first line is preceded by a period, but begins with a small letter. Many editors have made line 2 [fp. 119] into two half-lines. *A charm*: literally, the rune Thurs (b); the runic letters all had magic attributes; cf. *Sigrdrifumol*, 6-7 and notes.]

[40. Barri: "The Leafy."]

[42. Abbreviated to initial letters in the manuscript.

43. The superscription is lacking in *Regius*. Snorri quotes this one stanza in his prose paraphrase, *Gylfaginning*, chapter 37 The two versions are substantially the same, except that Snorri makes the first line read, "Long is one night, long is the second."]

HARBARTHSLJOTH

The Poem of Harbarth

INTRODUCTORY NOTE

The Harbarthsljoth is found complete in the *Codex Regius*, where it follows the *Skirnismol*, and from the fourth line of stana 19 to the end of the poem in the *Arnamagnæan Codex*, of which it occupies the first page and a half.

The poem differs sharply from those which precede it in the *Codex Regius*, both in metrical form and in spirit. It is, indeed, the most nearly formless of all the Eddic poems. The normal metre is the Malahattr (cf. Introduction, where an example is given). The name of this verse-form means "in the manner of conversation," and the Harbarthsljoth's verse fully justifies the term. The Atli poems exemplify the conventional use of Malahattr, but in the Harbarthsljoth the form is used with extraordinary freedom, and other metrical forms are frequently employed. A few of the speeches of which the poem is composed cannot be twisted into any known Old Norse metre, and appear to be simply prose.

How far this confusion is due to interpolations and faulty transmission of the original poem is uncertain. Finnur Jonsson has attempted a wholesale purification of the poem, but his arbitrary condemnation of words, lines, and entire stanzas as spurious is quite unjustified by any positive evidence. I have accepted Mogk's theory that the author was "a first-rate psychologist, but a poor poet," and have translated the poem as it stands in the manuscripts. I have preserved the metrical confusion of the original by keeping throughout so far as possible to the metres found in the poem; if the rhythm of the translation is often hard to catch, the difficulty is no less with the original Norse.

The poem is simply a contest of abuse, such as the early Norwegian and Icelander delighted in, the opposing figures being Thor and Othin, the latter appearing in the disguise of the ferryman Harbarth. Such billingsgate lent itself readily to changes, interpolations and omissions, and it is little wonder that the poem is chaotic. It consists mainly of boasting and of references, often luckily obscure, to disreputable events in the life of one or the other of the disputants. Some editors have sought to read a complex symbolism into it, particularly by representing it as a contest between the noble or warrior class (Othin) and the peasant (Thor). But it seems a pity to take such a vigorous piece of broad farce too seriously.

Verse-form, substance, and certain linguistic peculiarities, notably the suffixed articles, point to a relatively late date (eleventh century) for the poem in its present form. Probably it had its origin in the early days, but its colloquial nature and its vulgarity made it readily susceptible to changes.

Owing to the chaotic state of the text, and the fact that none of the editors or commentators have succeeded in improving it much, I have not in this case attempted to give all the important emendations and suggestions. The stanza-divisions are largely arbitrary.

———————————

Thor was on his way back from a journey in the East, and came to a sound; on the other side of the sound was a ferryman with a boat. Thor called out:

1. "Who is the fellow yonder, | on the farther shore of the sound?"

The ferryman spake:
2. "What kind of a peasant is yon, | that calls o'er the bay?"

Thor spake:
3. "Ferry me over the sound; | I will feed thee therefor in the

morning;
A basket I have on my back, | and food therein, none better;
At leisure I ate, | ere the house I left,
Of herrings and porridge, | so plenty I had."

The ferryman spake:
4. "Of thy morning feats art thou proud, | but the future thou
knowest not wholly;
Doleful thine home-coming is: | thy mother, me thinks, is dead."

Thor spake:
5. "Now hast thou said | what to each must seem
The mightiest grief, | that my mother is dead."

The ferryman spake:
6. "Three good dwellings, | methinks, thou hast not;
Barefoot thou standest, | and wearest a beggar's dress;
Not even hose dost thou have."

Thor spake:
7. "Steer thou hither the boat; | the landing here shall I show thee;
But whose the craft | that thou keepest on the shore?"

The ferryman spake:
8. "Hildolf is he | who bade me have it,
A hero wise; | his home is at Rathsey's sound.
He bade me no robbers to steer, | nor stealers of steeds,
But worthy men, | and those whom well do I know.
Say now thy name, | if over the sound thou wilt fare."

Thor spake:
9. "My name indeed shall I tell, | though in danger I am,

And all my race; | I am Othin's son,
Meili's brother, | and Magni's father,

The strong one of the gods; | with Thor now speech canst thou get.
And now would I know | what name thou hast."

The ferryman spake:
10. "Harbarth am I, | and seldom I hide my name."

Thor spake:
11. "Why shouldst thou hide thy name, | if quarrel thou hast not?"

Harbarth spake:
12. "And though I had a quarrel, | from such as thou art
Yet none the less | my life would I guard,
Unless I be doomed to die."

Thor spake:
13. "Great trouble, methinks, | would it be to come to thee,
To wade the waters across, | and wet my middle;
Weakling, well shall I pay | thy mocking words,
if across the sound I come."

Harbarth spake:
14. "Here shall I stand | and await thee here;
Thou hast found since Hrungnir died | no fiercer man."

Thor spake:
15. "Fain art thou to tell | how with Hrungnir I fought,
The haughty giant, | whose head of stone was made;
And yet I felled him, | and stretched him before me.
What, Harbarth, didst thou the while?"

Harbarth spake:
16. "Five full winters | with Fjolvar was I,
And dwelt in the isle | that is Algrön called;
There could we fight, | and fell the slain,
Much could we seek, | and maids could master."

Thor spake:
17. "How won ye success with your women?"

Harbarth spake:
18. "Lively women we had, | if they wise for us were;
Wise were the women we had, | if they kind for us were;
For ropes of sand | they would seek to wind,
And the bottom to dig | from the deepest dale.
Wiser than all | in counsel I was,
And there I slept | by the sisters seven,
And joy full great | did I get from each.
What, Thor, didst thou the while?"

Thor spake:
19. "Thjazi I felled, | the giant fierce,
And I hurled the eyes | of Alvaldi's son
To the heavens hot above;
Of my deeds the mightiest | marks are these,
That all men since can see.
What, Harbarth, didst thou the while?"

Harbarth spoke:
20. "Much love-craft I wrought | with them who ride by night,
When I stole them by stealth from their husbands;
A giant hard | was Hlebarth, methinks:
His wand he gave me as gift,
And I stole his wits away."

Thor spake:
21. "Thou didst repay good gifts with evil mind."

Harbarth spake:
22. "The oak must have | what it shaves from another;
In such things each for himself.
What, Thor, didst thou the while?"

Thor spake:

23. "Eastward I fared, | of the giants I felled
Their ill-working women | who went to the mountain;
And large were the giants' throng | if all were alive;
No men would there be | in Mithgarth more.
What, Harbarth, didst thou the while?"

Harbarth spake:

24. "In Valland I was, | and wars I raised,
Princes I angered, | and peace brought never;
The noble who fall | in the fight hath Othin,
And Thor hath the race of the thralls."

Thor spake:

25. "Unequal gifts | of men wouldst thou give to the gods,
If might too much thou shouldst have."

Harbarth spake:

26. "Thor has might enough, | but never a heart;
For cowardly fear | in a glove wast thou fain to crawl,
And there forgot thou wast Thor;
Afraid there thou wast, | thy fear was such,
To fart or sneeze | lest Fjalar should hear."

Thor spake:

27. "Thou womanish Harbarth, | to hell would I smite thee straight,
Could mine arm reach over the sound."

Harbarth spake:

28. "Wherefore reach over the sound, | since strife we have none?
What, Thor, didst thou do then?"

Thor spake:

29. "Eastward I was, | and the river I guarded well,
Where the sons of Svarang | sought me there;
Stones did they hurl; | small joy did they have of winning;

Before me there | to ask for peace did they fare.
What, Harbarth, didst thou the while?"

Harbarth spake:
30. "Eastward I was, | and spake with a certain one,
I played with the linen-white maid, | and met her by stealth;
I gladdened the gold-decked one, | and she granted me joy."

Thor spake:
31. "Full fair was thy woman-finding."

Harbarth spake:
32. "Thy help did I need then, Thor, | to hold the white maid fast."

Thor spake:
33. "Gladly, had I been there, | my help to thee had been given."

Harbarth spake:
34. "I might have trusted thee then, | didst thou not betray thy troth."

Thor spake:
35. "No heel-biter am I, in truth, | like an old leather shoe in spring."

Harbarth spoke:
36. "What, Thor, didst thou the while?"

Thor spake:
37. "In Hlesey the brides | of the Berserkers slew I;
Most evil they were, | and all they betrayed."

Harbarth spake:
38, "Shame didst thou win, | that women thou slewest, Thor."

Thor spake:
39. "She-wolves they were like, | and women but little;
My ship, which well | I had trimmed, did they shake;

With clubs of iron they threatened, | and Thjalfi they drove off.
What, Harbarth, didst thou the while?"

Harbarth spake:
40. "In the host I was | that hither fared,
The banners to raise, | and the spear to redden."

Thor spake:
41. "Wilt thou now say | that hatred thou soughtest to bring us?"

Harbarth spake:
42. "A ring for thy hand | shall make all right for thee,
As the judge decides | who sets us two at peace."

Thor spake:
43. "Where foundest thou | so foul and scornful a speech?
More foul a speech | I never before have heard."

Harbarth spake:
44. "I learned it from men, | the men so old,
Who dwell in the hills of home."

Thor spake:
45. "A name full good | to heaps of stones thou givest
When thou callest them hills of home."

Harbarth spake:
46. "Of such things speak I so."

Thor spake:
47. "Ill for thee comes | thy keenness of tongue,
If the water I choose to wade;
Louder, I ween, | than a wolf thou cryest,
If a blow of my hammer thou hast."

Harbarth spake:
48. "Sif has a lover at home, | and him shouldst thou meet;
More fitting it were | on him to put forth thy strength."

Thor spake:
49. "Thy tongue still makes thee say | what seems most ill to me,
Thou witless man! Thou liest, I ween."

Harbarth spake:
50. "Truth do I speak, | but slow on thy way thou art;
Far hadst thou gone | if now in the boat thou hadst fared."

Thor spake:
51. "Thou womanish Harbarth! | here hast thou held me too long."

Harbarth spake:
52. "I thought not ever | that Asathor would be hindered
By a ferryman thus from faring."

Thor spake:
53. "One counsel I bring thee now: | row hither thy boat;
No more of scoffing; | set Magni's father across."

Harbarth spake:
54. "From the sound go hence; | the passage thou hast not."

Thor spake:
55. "The way now show me, since thou takest me not o'er the water."

Harbarth spake:
56. "To refuse it is little, to fare it is long;
A while to the stock, and a while to the stone;
Then the road to thy left, till Verland thou reachest;
And there shall Fjorgyn her son Thor find,
And the road of her children she shows him to Othin's realm."

Thor spake:
57. "May I come so far in a day?"

Harbarth spake:
58. "With toil and trouble perchance,
While the sun still shines, or so I think."

Thor spake:
59. "Short now shall be our speech, for thou speakest in mockery only;

The passage thou gavest me not I shall pay thee if ever we meet."

Harbarth spake:
60. "Get hence where every evil thing shall have thee!"

[*Prose. Harbarth* ("Gray-Beard"): Othin. On the nature of the prose notes found in the manuscripts, cf. *Grimnismol*, introduction. *Thor*: the journeys of the thunder-god were almost as numerous as those of Othin;
cf. *Thrymskvitha* and *Hymiskvitha*. Like the Robin Hood of the British ballads, Thor was often temporarily worsted, but always managed to come out ahead in the end. His "Journey in the East" is presumably the famous episode, related in full by Snorri, in the course of which he en countered the giant Skrymir, and in the house of Utgartha-Loki lifted the cat which turned out to be Mithgarthsorm.
The *Hymiskvitha* relates a further incident of this journey.]

[2. The superscriptions to the speeches are badly confused in the manuscripts, but editors have agreed fairly well as to where they belong. 3. From the fact that in *Regius* line 3 begins with a capital letter, it is possible that lines 3-4 constitute the ferryman's reply, with something lost before stanza 4.

4. *Thy mother*: Jorth (Earth).

5. Some editors assume a lacuna after this stanza.

6. *Three good dwellings*: this has been generally assumed to mean three separate establishments, but it may refer simply to [fp. 124] the three parts of a single farm, the dwelling proper, the cattle barn and the storehouse; i.e., Thor is not even a respectable peasant.]

[9. *Hildolf* ("slaughtering wolf"): not elsewhere mentioned in the *Edda*. *Rathsey* ("Isle of Counsel"): likewise not mentioned elsewhere.

9. *In danger*: Thor is "sekr," i.e., without the protection of any law, so long as he is in the territory of his enemies, the [fp. 125] giants. *Meili*: a practically unknown son of Othin, mentioned here only in the *Edda*. *Magni*: son of Thor and the giantess Jarnsaxa; after Thor's fight with Hrungnir (cf. stanza 14, note) Magni, though but three days old, was the only one of the gods strong enough to lift the dead giant's foot from Thor's neck. After rescuing his father, Magni said to him: "There would have been little trouble, father, had I but come sooner; I think I should have sent this giant to hell with my fist if I had met him first." Magni and his brother, Mothi, inherit Thor's hammer.]

[12. This stanza is hopelessly confused as to form, but none of the editorial rearrangements have materially altered the meaning. *Doomed to die*: the word "feigr" occurs constantly in the Old Norse poems and sagas; the idea of an inevitable but unknown fate seems to have been practically universal through out the pre-Christian period. On the concealment of names from enemies, cf. *Fafnismol*, prose after stanza 1.]

[13. This stanza, like the preceding one, is peculiarly chaotic in the manuscript, and has been variously emended.

14. *Hrungnir*: this giant rashly wagered his head that his horse, Gullfaxi, was swifter than Othin's Sleipnir. In the race, which Hrungnir lost, he managed to dash uninvited into the home of the gods, where he became very drunk. Thor ejected him, and accepted his challenge to a duel. Hrungnir, terrified, had a helper made for him in the form of a dummy giant nine miles high and three miles broad. Hrungnir himself had a three-horned heart of stone and a head of stone; his shield was of stone and his weapon was a grindstone. But Thjalfi, Thor's servant, told him the god would attack him out of the ground, wherefore Hrungnir laid down his shield and stood on it. The hammer Mjollnir shattered both the grindstone and Hrungnir's [fp. 127] head, but part of the grindstone knocked Thor down, and the giant fell with his foot on Thor's neck (cf. note on stanza 9). Meanwhile Thjalfi dispatched the dummy giant without trouble.]

[16. *Fjolvar*: not elsewhere mentioned in the poems; perhaps the father of the "seven sisters" referred to in stanza 18. *Algrön*: "The All-Green": not mentioned elsewhere in the *Edda*.

17. Thor is always eager for stories of this sort; cf. stanzas 31 and 33.

117

19. Lines 1-2 are obscure, but apparently Harbarth means that the women were wise to give in to him cheerfully, resistance to his power being as impossible as (lines 3-4) making ropes of sand or digging the bottoms out of the valleys. Nothing further is known of these unlucky "seven sisters."]

[19. *Thjazi*: this giant, by a trick, secured possession of the goddess Ithun and her apples (cf. *Skirnismol*, 19, note), and carried her off into Jotunheim. Loki, through whose fault she had been betrayed, was sent after her by the gods. He went in Freyja's "hawk's-dress" (cf.*Thrymskvitha*, 3), turned Ithun into a nut, and flew back with her. Thjazi, in the shape of an eagle, gave chase. But the gods kindled a fire which burnt the eagle's wings, and then they killed him. Snorri's prose version does not attribute this feat particularly to Thor. Thjazi's daughter was Skathi, whom the gods permitted to marry Njorth as a recompense for her father's death. *Alvaldi*: of him we know only that he was the father of Thjazi, Ithi and Gang, who divided his wealth, each taking a mouthful of gold. The name is variously spelled. It is not known which stars were called "Thjazi's Eyes." In the middle of line 4 begins the fragmentary version of the poem found in the Arnamagnæan Codex.

20. *Riders by night*: witches, who were supposed to ride on wolves in the dark. Nothing further is known of this adventure.]

[22. *The oak, etc.*: this proverb is found elsewhere (*e.g.*, *Grettissaga*) in approximately the same words. its force is much like our "to the victor belong the spoils."

23. Thor killed no women of the giants' race on the "journey to the East" so fully described by Snorri, his great giant-killing adventure being the one narrated in the Thrymskvitha.

24. *Valland*: this mythical place ("Land of Slaughter") is elsewhere mentioned, but not further characterised; cf. prose introduction to *Volundarkvitha*, and *Helreith Brynhildar*, 2. On the bringing of slain heroes to Othin, cf. *Voluspo*, 31 and note, [fp. 130] and, for a somewhat different version, *Grimnismol*, 14. Nowhere else is it indicated that Thor has an asylum for dead peasants.]

[26. The reference here is to one of the most familiar episodes in Thor's eastward journey. He and his companions came to a house in the forest, and went in to spend the night. Being disturbed by an earthquake and a terrific noise, they all crawled into a smaller room opening from the main one. In the morning, however, they discovered that the earthquake had been occasioned by the giant Skrymir's lying down near them, and the noise by his snoring. The house in which they had

118

taken refuge was his glove, the smaller room being the thumb. Skrymir was in fact Utgartha-Loki himself. That he is in this stanza called Fjalar (the name occurs also in *Hovamol*, 14) is probably due to a confusion of the names by which Utgartha-Loki went. Loki taunts Thor with this adventure in *Lokasenna*, 60 and 62, line 3 of this stanza being perhaps interpolated from *Lokasenna*, 60, 4.]

[29. *The river*: probably Ifing, which flows between the land of the gods and that of the giants; cf. *Vafthruthnismol*, 16. *Sons of Svarang*: presumably the giants; Svarang is not else where mentioned in the poems, nor is there any other account of Thor's defense of the passage.

30. Othin's adventures of this sort were too numerous to make it possible to identify this particular person. By *stealth*: so the *Arnamagnæan Codex*; *Regius*, followed by several editors, has "long meeting with her."]

[35. Heel-biter: this effective parallel to our "back-biter" is not found elsewhere in Old Norse.

37. Hlesey: "the Island of the Sea-God" (Hler = Ægir), identified with the Danish island Läsö, in the Kattegat. It appears again, much out of place, in *Oddrunargratr*, 28. *Berserkers*: originally men who could turn themselves into bears, hence the name, "bear-shirts"; cf. the werewolf or loupgarou. Later the name was applied to men who at times became seized with a madness for bloodshed; cf. *Hyndluljoth*, 23 and note. The women here mentioned are obviously of the earlier type.]

[39. *Thjalfi*: Thor's servant; cf. note on stanza 14.

40. To what expedition this refers is unknown, but apparently Othin speaks of himself as allied to the foes of the gods.

41. *Hatred*: so *Regius*; the other manuscript has, apparently, "sickness."

42. Just what Othin means, or why his words should so have enraged Thor, is not evident, though he may imply that Thor is open to bribery. Perhaps a passage has dropped out before stanza 43.]

[44. Othin refers to the dead, from whom he seeks information through his magic power.

48. Sit: Thor's wife, the lover being presumably Loki; cf. Lokasenna, 54.]

[52. *Asathor*: Thor goes by various names in the poems: *e.g.*, Vingthor, Vingnir, Hlorrithi. Asathor means "Thor of the Gods."

53. *Magni*: Thor's son; cf. stanza 9 and note.]

[56. *Line 2*: the phrases mean simply "a long way"; cf. "over stock and stone." *Verland*: the "Land of Men" to which Thor must come from the land of the giants. The *Arnamagnæan Codex* has "Valland" (cf. stanza 24 and note), but this is obviously an error. *Fjorgyn*: a feminine form of the same name, which belongs to Othin (cf. Voluspo, 56 and note); here it evidently means Jorth (Earth), Thor's mother. *The road*: the rainbow bridge, Bifrost; cf. *Grimnismol*, 29 and note.

58. Line 2: so *Regius*; the other manuscript has "ere sunrise."]

[60. The *Arnamagnæan Codex* clearly indicates Harbarth as the speaker of this line, but *Regius* has no superscription, and begins the line with a small letter not preceded by a period, thereby assigning it to Thor.]

HYMISKVITHA

The Lay of Hymir

INTRODUCTORY NOTE

The *Hymiskvitha* is found complete in both manuscripts; in *Regius* it follows the *Harbarthsljoth*, while in the *Arnamagnæan Codex* it comes after the *Grimnismol*. Snorri does not quote it, although he tells the main story involved.

The poem is a distinctly inferior piece of work, obviously based on various narrative fragments, awkwardly pieced together. Some critics, Jessen and Edzardi for instance, have maintained that the compiler had before him three distinct poems, which he simply put together; others, like Finnur Jonsson and Mogk, think that the author made a new poem of his own on the basis of earlier poems, now lost. It seems probable that he took a lot of odds and ends of material concerning Thor, whether in prose or in verse, and worked them together in a perfunctory way, without much caring how well they fitted. His chief aim was probably to impress the credulous imaginations of hearers greedy for wonders.

The poem is almost certainly one of the latest of those dealing with the gods, though Finnur Jonsson, in order to support his theory of a Norwegian origin, has to date it relatively early. If, as seems probable, it was produced in Iceland, the chances are that it was composed in the first half of the eleventh century. Jessen, rather recklessly, goes so far as to put it two hundred years later. In any case, it belongs to a period of literary decadence,--the great days of Eddic poetry would never have permitted the nine hundred headed person found in Hymir's home-- and to one in which the usual forms of diction in mythological poetry had yielded somewhat to the verbal subtleties of skaldic verse.

121

While the skaldic poetry properly falls outside the limits of this book, it is necessary here to say a word about it. There is preserved, in the sagas and elsewhere, a very considerable body of lyric poetry, the authorship of each poem being nearly always definitely stated, whether correctly or otherwise. This type of poetry is marked by an extraordinary complexity of diction, with a peculiarly difficult vocabulary of its own. It was to explain some of the "kennings" which composed this special vocabulary that Snorri wrote one of the sections of the *Prose Edda*. As an illustration, in a single stanza of one poem in the *Egilssaga*, a sword is called "the halo of the helm," "the wound-hoe," "the blood-snake" (possibly; no one is sure what the compound word means) and "the ice of the girdle," while men appear in the same stanza as "Othin's ash-trees," and battle is spoken of as "the iron game." One of the eight lines has defied translation completely.

Skaldic diction made relatively few inroads into the earlier Eddic poems, but in the *Hymiskvitha* these circumlocutions are fairly numerous. This sets the poem somewhat apart from the rest of the mythological collection. Only the vigor of the two main stories-- Thor's expedition after Hymir's kettle and the fishing trip in which he caught Mithgarthsorm--saves it from complete mediocrity.

1. Of old the gods | made feast together,
And drink they sought | ere sated they were;
Twigs they shook, | and blood they tried:
Rich fare in Ægir's | hall they found.

2. The mountain-dweller | sat merry as boyhood,
But soon like a blinded | man he seemed;
The son of Ygg | gazed in his eyes:
"For the gods a feast | shalt thou forthwith get."

3. The word-wielder toil | for the giant worked,
And so revenge | on the gods he sought;

He bade Sif's mate | the kettle bring:
"Therein for ye all | much ale shall I brew."

4. The far-famed ones | could find it not,
And the holy gods | could get it nowhere;
Till in truthful wise | did Tyr speak forth,
And helpful counsel | to Hlorrithi gave.

5. "There dwells to the east | of Elivagar
Hymir the wise | at the end of heaven;
A kettle my father | fierce doth own,
A mighty vessel | a mile in depth."

Thor spake:
6. "May we win, dost thou think, | this whirler of water?"
Tyr spake:
"Aye, friend, we can, | if cunning we are."

7. Forward that day | with speed they fared,
From Asgarth came they | to Egil's home;
The goats with horns | bedecked he guarded;
Then they sped to the hall | where Hymir dwelt.

8. The youth found his grandam, | that greatly he loathed,
And full nine hundred | heads she had;
But the other fair | with gold came forth,
And the bright-browed one | brought beer to her son.

9. "Kinsman of giants, | beneath the kettle
Will I set ye both, | ye heroes bold;
For many a time | my dear-loved mate
To guests is wrathful | and grim of mind."

10. Late to his home | the misshapen Hymir,
The giant harsh, | from his hunting came;

The icicles rattled | as in he came,
For the fellow's chin-forest | frozen was.

11. "Hail to thee, Hymir! | good thoughts mayst thou have;
Here has thy son | to thine hall now come;
(For him have we waited, | his way was long;)
And with him fares | the foeman of Hroth,
The friend of mankind, | and Veur they call him.

12. "See where under | the gable they sit!
Behind the beam | do they hide themselves."
The beam at the glance | of the giant broke,
And the mighty pillar | in pieces fell.

13. Eight fell from the ledge, | and one alone,
The hard-hammered kettle, | of all was whole;
Forth came they then, | and his foes he sought,
The giant old, | and held with his eyes.

14. Much sorrow his heart | foretold when he saw
The giantess' foeman | come forth on the floor;
Then of the steers | did they bring in three;
Their flesh to boil | did the giant bid.

15. By a head was each | the shorter hewed,
And the beasts to the fire | straight they bore;
The husband of Sif, | ere to sleep he went,
Alone two oxen | of Hymir's ate.

16. To the comrade hoary | of Hrungnir then
Did Hlorrithi's meal | full mighty seem;
"Next time at eve | we three must eat
The food we have | s the hunting's spoil."

17. .   .   .   .
Fain to row on the sea | was Veur, he said,
If the giant bold | would give him bait.

Hymir spake:
18. "Go to the herd, | if thou hast it in mind,
Thou slayer of giants, | thy bait to seek;
For there thou soon | mayst find, methinks,
Bait from the oxen | easy to get."

19. Swift to the wood | the hero went,
Till before him an ox | all black he found;
From the beast the slayer | of giants broke
The fortress high | of his double horns.

Hymir spake:
20. "Thy works, methinks, | are worse by far,
Thou steerer of ships, | than when still thou sittest."
.   .   .   .
.   .   .   .

21. The lord of the goats | bade the ape-begotten
Farther to steer | the steed of the rollers;
But the giant said | that his will, forsooth,
Longer to row | was little enough.

22. Two whales on his hook | did the mighty Hymir
Soon pull up | on a single cast;
In the stern the kinsman | of Othin sat,
And Veur with cunning | his cast prepared.

23. The warder of men, | the worm's destroyer,
Fixed on his hook | the head of the ox;
There gaped at the bait | the foe of the gods,
The girdler of all | the earth beneath.

24. The venomous serpent | swiftly up
To the boat did Thor, | the bold one, pull;
With his hammer the loathly | hill of the hair
Of the brother of Fenrir | he smote from above.

25. The monsters roared, | and the rocks resounded,
And all the earth | so old was shaken;
.   .   .   .
Then sank the fish | in the sea forthwith.

26. .   .   .   .
Joyless as back | they rowed was the giant;
Speechless did Hymir | sit at the oars,
With the rudder he sought | a second wind.

Hymir spake:
27. "The half of our toil | wilt thou have with me,
And now make fast | our goat of the flood;
Or home wilt thou bear | the whales to the house,
Across the gorge | of the wooded glen?"

28. Hlorrithi stood | and the stem he gripped,
And the sea-horse with water | awash he lifted;
Oars and bailer | and all he bore
With the surf-swine home | to the giant's house.

29. His might the giant | again would match,
For stubborn he was, | with the strength of Thor;
None truly strong, | though stoutly he rowed,
Would he call save one | who could break the cup.

30. Hlorrithi then, | when the cup he held,
Struck with the glass | the pillars of stone;
As he sat the posts | in pieces he shattered,
Yet the glass to Hymir whole they brought.

31. But the loved one fair | of the giant found
A counsel true, | and told her thought:
"Smite the skull of Hymir, | heavy with food,
For harder it is | than ever was glass."

32. The goats' mighty ruler | then rose on his knee,
And with all the strength | of a god he struck;
Whole was the fellow's | helmet-stem,
But shattered the wine-cup | rounded was.

Hymir spake:
33. "Fair is the treasure | that from me is gone,
Since now the cup | on my knees lies shattered;"
So spake the giant: | "No more can I say
In days to be, | 'Thou art brewed, mine ale.'

34. "Enough shall it be | if out ye can bring
Forth from our house | the kettle here."
Tyr then twice | to move it tried,
But before him the kettle | twice stood fast.

35. The father of Mothi | the rim seized firm,
And before it stood | on the floor below;
Up on his head | Sif's husband raised it,
And about his heels | the handles clattered.

36. Not long had they fared, | ere backwards looked
The son of Othin, | once more to see;
From their caves in the east | beheld he coming
With Hymir the throng | of the many-headed.

37. He stood and cast | from his back the kettle,
And Mjollnir, the lover | of murder, he wielded;
. . . .
So all the whales | of the waste he slew.

38. Not long had they fared | ere one there lay
Of Hlorrithi's goats | half-dead on the ground;
In his leg the pole-horse | there was lame;
The deed the evil | Loki had done.

39. But ye all have heard,-- | for of them who have
The tales of the gods, | who better can tell?
What prize he won | from the wilderness-dweller,
Who both his children | gave him to boot.

40. The mighty one came | to the council of gods,
And the kettle he had | that Hymir's was;
So gladly their ale | the gods could drink
In Ægir's hall | at the autumn-time.

[1. *Twigs*: Vigfusson comments at some length on "the rite practised in the
heathen age of inquiring into the future by dipping bunches of chips or twigs into
the blood (of sacrifices) and shaking them." But the two operations may have been
separate, the twigs being simply "divining-rods" marked with runes. In either case,
the gods were seeking information by magic as to where they could find plenty to
drink.*Ægir*: a giant who is also the god of the sea; little is known of him outside of
what is told here and in the introductory prose to the *Lokasenna*, though Snorri
has a brief account of him, giving his home as Hlesey (Läsö, cf. *Harbarthsljoth*,
37). *Grimnismol*, 45, has a reference to this same feast.]

[2. *Mountain-dweller*: the giant (Ægir). *Line 2*: the principal word in the original
has defied interpretation, and any translation of the line must be largely
guesswork. *Ygg*: Othin; his son is Thor. Some editors assume a gap after this
stanza.

3. *Word-wielder*: Thor. *The giant*: Ægir. *Sif*: Thor's wife; cf. Harbarthsljoth,
48. *The kettle*: Ægir's kettle is possibly the sea itself.

4. *Tyr*: the god of battle; his two great achievements were thrusting his hand into
the mouth of the wolf Fenrir so that the gods might bind him, whereby he lost his
hand (cf. *Voluspo*, 39, note), and his fight with the hound Garm in the last battle,
in which they kill each other. *Hlorrithi*: Thor.

5. *Elivagar* ("Stormy Waves"): possibly the Milky Way; [fp. 141] cf. *Vafthruthnismol*, 31, note. *Hymir*: this giant figures only in this episode. It is not clear why Tyr, who is elsewhere spoken of as a son of Othin, should here call Hymir his father. Finnur Jonsson, in an attempt to get round this difficulty, deliberately changed the word "father" to "grandfather," but this does not help greatly.]

[6. Neither manuscript has any superscriptions, but most editors have supplied them as above. From this point through stanza it the editors have varied considerably in grouping the lines into stanzas. The manuscripts indicate the third lines of stanzas 7, 8, 9, and to as beginning stanzas, but this makes more complications than the present arrangement. It is possible that, as Sijmons suggests, two lines have been lost after stanza 6.

7. *Egil*: possibly, though by no means certainly, the father of Thor's servant, Thjalfi, for, according to Snorri, Thor's first stop on this journey was at the house of a peasant whose children, Thjalfi and Roskva, he took into his service; cf. stanza 38, note. The *Arnamagnæan Codex* has "Ægir" instead of "Egil," but, aside from the fact that Thor had just left Ægir's house, the sea-god can hardly have been spoken of as a goat-herd.

8. *The youth*: Tyr, whose extraordinary grandmother is Hymir's mother. We know nothing further of her, or of the other, [fp. 141] who is Hymir's wife and Tyr's mother. It may be guessed, however, that she belonged rather to the race of the gods than to that of the giants.]

[11. Two or three editors give this stanza a superscription ("The concubine spake", "The daughter spake"). Line 3 is commonly regarded as spurious. *The foeman of Hroth*: of course this means Thor, but nothing is known of any enemy of his by this name. Several editors have sought to make a single word meaning "the famous enemy" out of the phrase. Concerning Thor as the friend of man, particularly of the peasant class, cf. introduction to Harbarthsljoth. *Veur*: another name, of uncertain meaning, for Thor.]

[13. *Eight*: the giant's glance, besides breaking the beam, knocks down all the kettles with such violence that all but the one under which Thor and Tyr are hiding are broken.

14. Hymir's wrath does not permit him to ignore the duties of a host to his guests, always strongly insisted on.

15. Thor's appetite figures elsewhere; cf. *Thrymskvitha*, 24.

16. *The comrade of Hrungnir*: Hymir, presumably simply because both are giants; cf. *Harbarthsljoth*, 14 and note.]

[17. The manuscripts indicate no lacuna, and many editors unite stanza 17 with lines 1 and 2 of 18. Sijmons and Gering assume a gap after these two lines, but it seems more probable that the missing passage, if any, belonged before them, supplying the connection with the previous stanza.

18. The manuscripts have no superscription. Many editors combine lines 3 and 4 with lines 1 and 2 of stanza 19. In Snorri's extended paraphrase of the story, Hymir declines to go fishing with Thor on the ground that the latter is too small a person to be worth bothering about. "You would freeze," he says, "if you stayed out in mid-ocean as long as I generally do." *Bait* (line 4): the word literally means "chaff," hence any small bits; Hymir means that Thor should collect dung for bait.

19. Many editors combine lines 3 and 4 with stanza 20. *Fortress*, etc.: the ox's head; cf. introductory note concerning the diction of this poem. Several editors assume a lacuna after stanza 19, but this seems unnecessary.]

[20. The manuscripts have no superscription. *Steerer of ships*: probably merely a reference to Thor's intention to go fishing. The lacuna after stanza 20 is assumed by most editors.

21. *Lord of the goats*: Thor, because of his goat-drawn chariot. *Ape-begotten*: Hymir; the word "api," rare until relatively late times in its literal sense, is fairly common with the meaning of "fool." Giants were generally assumed to be stupid. *Steed of the rollers*: a ship, because boats were pulled up on shore by means of rollers.

23. *Warder of men*: Thor; cf. stanza 11. *Worm's destroyer*: likewise Thor, who in the last battle slays, and is slain by, Mithgarthsorm; cf. *Voluspo*, 56. *The foe of the gods*: Mithgarthsorm, who lies in the sea, and surrounds the whole earth.]

[24. *Hill of the hair*: head,--a thoroughly characteristic skaldic phrase. *Brother of Fenrir*: Mithgarthsorm was, like the wolf Fenrir and the goddess Hel, born to Loki and the giantess Angrbotha (cf. *Voluspo*, 39 and note), and I have translated this line accordingly; but the word used in the text has been guessed as meaning almost anything from "comrade" to "enemy."

25. No gap is indicated in the manuscripts, but that a line or more has been lost is highly probable. In Snorri's version, Thor pulls so hard on the line that he drives both his feet through the flooring of the boat, and stands on bottom. When he pulls

the serpent up, Hymir cuts the line with his bait-knife, which explains the serpent's escape. Thor, in a rage, knocks Hymir overboard with his hammer, and then wades ashore. The lines of stanzas 25 and 26 have been variously grouped.

26. No gap is indicated in the manuscripts, but line 2 begins with a small letter. *A second wind*: another direction, i. e., he put about for the shore.]

[27. No superscription in the manuscripts. In its place Bugge supplies a line-- "These words spake Hymir, | the giant wise." The manuscripts reverse the order of lines 2 and 3, and in both of them line 4 stands after stanza 28. *Goat of the flood*: boat.

28. *Sea-horse*: boat. *Surf-swine*: the whales.

29. Snorri says nothing of this episode of Hymir's cup. The glass which cannot be broken appears in the folklore of various races.

31. *The loved one*: Hymir's wife and Tyr's mother; cf. stanza 8 and note. The idea that a giant's skull is harder than stone or anything else is characteristic of the later Norse folk-stories, and [fp. 148] in one of the so-called "mythical sagas" we find a giant actually named Hard-Skull.]

[32. *Helmet-stem*: head.

33. The manuscripts have no superscription. Line 4 in the manuscripts is somewhat obscure, and Bugge, followed by some editors, suggests a reading which may be rendered (beginning with the second half of line 3): "No more can I speak / Ever again | as I spoke of old."

35, *The father of Mothi and Sif's husband*: Thor.]

[36. *The many-headed*: The giants, although rarely designated as a race in this way, sometimes had two or more heads; cf. stanza 8, *Skirnismol*, V and *Vafthruthnismol*, 33. Hymir's mother is, however, the only many-headed giant actually to appear in the action of the poems, and it is safe to assume that the tradition as a whole belongs to the period of Norse folk-tales of the *märchen* order.

37. No gap is indicated in the manuscripts. Some editors put the missing line as 2, some as 3, and some, leaving the present three lines together, add a fourth, and

metrically incorrect, one from late paper manuscripts: "Who with Hymir followed after." *Whales of the waste*: giants.

38. According to Snorri, when Thor set out with Loki (not Tyr) for the giants' land, he stopped first at a peasant's house (cf. stanza 7 and note). There he proceeded to cook his own goats for supper. The peasant's son, Thjalfi, eager to get at the marrow, split one of the leg-bones with his knife. The next morning, when Thor was ready to proceed with his journey, he called the goats to life again, but one of them proved irretrievably lame. His wrath led the peasant to give him both his children as [fp. 150] servants (cf. stanza 39). Snorri does not indicate that Loki was in any way to blame.]

[39. This deliberate introduction of the story-teller is exceedingly rare in the older poetry.

40. The translation of the last two lines is mostly guess work, as the word rendered "gods" is uncertain, and the one rendered "at the autumn-time" is quite obscure.]

LOKASENNA

Loki's Wrangling

INTRODUCTORY NOTES

The *Lokasenna* is found only in *Regius*, where it follows the *Hymiskvitha*; Snorri quotes four lines of it, grouped together as a single stanza.

The poem is one of the most vigorous of the entire collection, and seems to have been preserved in exceptionally good condition. The exchange or contest of insults was dear to the Norse heart, and the *Lokasenna* consists chiefly of Loki's taunt; to the assembled gods and goddesses, and their largely ineffectual attempts to talk back to him. The author was evidently well versed in mythological fore, and the poem is full of references to incidents not elsewhere recorded. As to its date and origin there is the usual dispute, but the latter part of the tenth century and Iceland seem the best guesses.

The prose notes are long and of unusual interest. The introductory one links the poem closely to the *Hymiskvitha*, much as the *Reginsmol*, *Fafnismol* and *Sigrdrifumol* are linked together; the others fill in the narrative gaps in the dialogue--very like stage directions,--and provide a conclusion by relating Loki's punishment, which, presumably, is here connected with the wrong incident. It is likely that often when the poem was recited during the two centuries or so before it was committed to writing, the speaker inserted some such explanatory comments, and the compiler of the collection followed this example by adding such explanations as he thought necessary. The *Lokasenna* is certainly much older than the *Hymiskvitha*, the connection between them being purely one of subject-matter; and the twelfth-century compiler evidently knew a good deal less about mythology than the author whose work he was annotating.

Ægir, who was also called Gymir, had prepared ale for the gods, after he had got the mighty kettle, as now has been told. To this feast came Othin and Frigg, his wife. Thor came not, as he was on a journey in the East. Sif, Thor's wife, was there, and Brag, with Ithun, his wife. Tyr, who had but one hand, was there; the wolf Fenrir had bitten off his other hand when they had bound him. There were Njorth and Skathi his wife, Freyr and Freyja, and Vithar, the son of Othin. Loki was there, and Freyr's servants Byggvir and Beyla. Many were there of the gods and elves.

Ægir had two serving-men, Fimafeng and Eldir. Glittering gold they had in place of firelight; the ale came in of itself; and great was the peace. The guests praised much the ability of Ægir's serving-men. Loki might not endure that, and he slew Fimafeng. Then the gods shook their shields and howled at Loki and drove him away to the forest, and thereafter set to drinking again. Loki turned back, and outside he met Eldir. Loki spoke to him:

1. "Speak now, Eldir, | for not one step
Farther shalt thou fare;
What ale-talk here | do they have within,
The sons of the glorious gods?"

Eldir spake:
2. "Of their weapons they talk, | and their might in war,
The sons of the glorious gods;
From the gods and elves | who are gathered here
No friend in words shalt thou find."

Loki spake:
3. "In shall I go | into Ægir's hall,
For the feast I fain would see;
Bale and hatred | I bring to the gods,
And their mead with venom I mix."

Eldir spake:
4. "If in thou goest | to Ægir's hall,
And fain the feast wouldst see,
And with slander and spite | wouldst sprinkle the gods,
Think well lest they wipe it on thee."

Loki spake:
5. "Bethink thee, Eldir, | if thou and I
Shall strive with spiteful speech;
Richer I grow | in ready words
If thou speakest too much to me."

Then Loki went into the hall, but when they who were there saw
who had entered, they were all silent.

Loki spake:
6. "Thirsty I come | into this thine hall,
I, Lopt, from a journey long,
To ask of the gods | that one should give
Fair mead for a drink to me.

7. "Why sit ye silent, | swollen with pride,
Ye gods, and no answer give?
At your feast a place | and a seat prepare me,
Or bid me forth to fare."

Bragi spake:
8. "A place and a seat | will the gods prepare
No more in their midst for thee;
For the gods know well | what men they wish
To find at their mighty feasts."

Loki spake:
9. "Remember, Othin, | in olden days
That we both our blood have mixed;

Then didst thou promise | no ale to pour,
Unless it were brought for us both."

Othin spake:
10. "Stand forth then, Vithar, | and let the wolf's father
Find a seat at our feast;
Lest evil should Loki | speak aloud
Here within Ægir's hall."

Then Vithar arose and poured drink for Loki; but before he drank he spoke to the gods:

11. "Hail to you, gods! | ye goddesses, hail!
Hail to the holy throng!
Save for the god | who yonder sits,
Bragi there on the bench."

Bragi spake:
12. "A horse and a sword | from my hoard will I give,
And a ring gives Bragi to boot,
That hatred thou makst not | among the gods;
So rouse not the great ones to wrath."

Loki spake:
13. "In horses and rings | thou shalt never be rich,
Bragi, but both shalt thou lack;
Of the gods and elves | here together met
Least brave in battle art thou,
(And shyest thou art of the shot.)"

Bragi spake:
14. "Now were I without | as I am within,
And here in Ægir's hall,
Thine head would I bear | in mine hands away,
And pay thee the price of thy lies."

Loki spake:
15. "In thy seat art thou bold, | not so are thy deeds,
Bragi, adorner of benches!
Go out and fight | if angered thou feelest,
No hero such forethought has."

Ithun spake:
16. "Well, prithee, Bragi, | his kinship weigh,
Since chosen as wish-son he was;
And speak not to Loki | such words of spite
Here within Ægir's hall."

Loki spake:
17. "Be silent, Ithun! | thou art, I say,
Of women most lustful in love,
Since thou thy washed-bright | arms didst wind
About thy brother's slayer."

Ithun spake:
18. "To Loki I speak not | with spiteful words
Here within Ægir's hall;
And Bragi I calm, | who is hot with beer,
For I wish not that fierce they should fight."

Gefjun spake:
19. "Why, ye gods twain, | with bitter tongues
Raise hate among us here?
Loki is famed | for his mockery foul,
And the dwellers in heaven he hates."

Loki spake:
20. "Be silent, Gefjun! | for now shall I say
Who led thee to evil life;
The boy so fair | gave a necklace bright,
And about him thy leg was laid."

Othin spake:
21. "Mad art thou, Loki, | and little of wit,
The wrath of Gefjun to rouse;
For the fate that is set | for all she sees,
Even as I, methinks."

Loki spake:
22. "Be silent, Othin! | not justly thou settest
The fate of the fight among men;
Oft gavst thou to him | who deserved not the gift,
To the baser, the battle's prize."

Othin spake:
23. "Though I gave to him | who deserved not the gift,
To the baser, the battle's prize;
Winters eight | wast thou under the earth,
Milking the cows as a maid,
(Ay, and babes didst thou bear;
Unmanly thy soul must seem.)"

Loki spake:
24. "They say that with spells | in Samsey once
Like witches with charms didst thou work;
And in witch's guise | among men didst thou go;
Unmanly thy soul must seem."

Frigg spake:
25. "Of the deeds ye two | of old have done
Ye should make no speech among men;
Whate'er ye have done | in days gone by,
Old tales should ne'er be told."

Loki spake:
26. "Be silent, Frigg! | thou art Fjorgyn's wife,
But ever lustful in love;

For Vili and Ve, | thou wife of Vithrir,
Both in thy bosom have lain."

Frigg spake:
27. "If a son like Baldr | were by me now,
Here within Ægir's hall,
From the sons of the gods | thou shouldst go not forth
Till thy fierceness in fight were tried."

Loki spake:
28. "Thou wilt then, Frigg, | that further I tell
Of the ill that now I know;
Mine is the blame | that Baldr no more
Thou seest ride home to the hall."

Freyja spake:
29. "Mad art thou, Loki, | that known thou makest
The wrong and shame thou hast wrought;
The fate of all | does Frigg know well,
Though herself she says it not."

Loki spake:
30. "Be silent, Freyja! | for fully I know thee,
Sinless thou art not thyself;
Of the gods and elves | who are gathered here,
Each one as thy lover has lain."

Freyja spake:
31. "False is thy tongue, | and soon shalt thou find
That it sings thee an evil song;
The gods are wroth, | and the goddesses all,
And in grief shalt thou homeward go."

Loki spake:
32. "Be silent, Freyja! | thou foulest witch,
And steeped full sore in sin;

In the arms of thy brother | the bright gods caught thee
When Freyja her wind set free."

Njorth spake:
33. "Small ill does it work | though a woman may have
A lord or a lover or both;
But a wonder it is | that this womanish god
Comes hither, though babes he has borne."

Loki spake:
34. "Be silent, Njorth; | thou wast eastward sent,
To the gods as a hostage given;
And the daughters of Hymir | their privy had
When use did they make of thy mouth."

Njorth spake:
35. "Great was my gain, | though long was I gone,
To the gods as a hostage given;
The son did I have | whom no man hates,
And foremost of gods is found."

Loki spake:
36. "Give heed now, Njorth, | nor boast too high,
No longer I hold it hid;
With thy sister hadst thou | so fair a son,
Thus hadst thou no worse a hope."

Tyr spake:
37. "Of the heroes brave | is Freyr the best
Here in the home of the gods;
He harms not maids | nor the wives of men,
And the bound from their fetters he frees."

Loki spake:
38. "Be silent, Tyr! | for between two men
Friendship thou ne'er couldst fashion;

Fain would I tell | how Fenrir once
Thy right hand rent from thee."

Tyr spake:
39. "My hand do I lack, | but Hrothvitnir thou,
And the loss brings longing to both;
Ill fares the wolf | who shall ever await
In fetters the fall of the gods."

Loki spake:
40. "Be silent, Tyr! | for a son with me
Thy wife once chanced to win;
Not a penny, methinks, | wast thou paid for the wrong,
Nor wast righted an inch, poor wretch."

Freyr spake:
41. "By the mouth of the river | the wolf remains
Till the gods to destruction go;
Thou too shalt soon, | if thy tongue is not stilled,
Be fettered, thou forger of ill."

Loki spake:
42. "The daughter of Gymir | with gold didst thou buy,
And sold thy sword to boot;
But when Muspell's sons | through Myrkwood ride,
Thou shalt weaponless wait, poor wretch."

Byggvir spake:
43. "Had I birth so famous | as Ingunar-Freyr,
And sat in so lofty a seat,
I would crush to marrow | this croaker of ill,
And beat all his body to bits."

Loki spake:
44. "What little creature | goes crawling there,
Snuffling and snapping about?

At Freyr's ears ever | wilt thou be found,
Or muttering hard at the mill."

Byggvir spake:
45. "Byggvir my name, | and nimble am I,
As gods and men do grant;
And here am I proud | that the children of Hropt
Together all drink ale."

Loki spake:
46. "Be silent, Byggvir! | thou never couldst set
Their shares of the meat for men;
Hid in straw on the floor, | they found thee not
When heroes were fain to fight."

Heimdall spake:
47. "Drunk art thou, Loki, | and mad are thy deeds,
Why, Loki, leavst thou this not?
For drink beyond measure | will lead all men
No thought of their tongues to take."

Loki spake:
48. "Be silent, Heimdall! | in days long since
Was an evil fate for thee fixed;
With back held stiff | must thou ever stand,
As warder of heaven to watch."

Skathi spake:
49. "Light art thou, Loki, | but longer thou mayst not
In freedom flourish thy tail;
On the rocks the gods bind thee | with bowels torn
Forth from thy frost-cold son."

Loki spake:
50. "Though on rocks the gods bind me | with bowels torn
Forth from my frost-cold son,

I was first and last | at the deadly fight
There where Thjazi we caught."

Skathi spake:
51. "Wert thou first and last | at the deadly fight
There where Thjazi was caught,
From my dwellings and fields | shall ever come forth
A counsel cold for thee."

Loki spake:
52. "More lightly thou spakest | with Laufey's son,
When thou badst me come to thy bed;
Such things must be known | if now we two
Shall seek our sins to tell."

Then Sif came forward and poured mead for Loki in a crystal cup,
and said:

53. "Hail too thee, Loki, | and take thou here
The crystal cup of old mead;
For me at least, | alone of the gods,
Blameless thou knowest to be."

He took the horn, and drank therefrom:

54. "Alone thou wert | if truly thou wouldst
All men so shyly shun;
But one do I know | full well, methinks,
Who had thee from Hlorrithi's arms,--
(Loki the crafty in lies.)"

Beyla spake:
55. "The mountains shake, | and surely I think
From his home comes Hlorrithi now;
He will silence the man | who is slandering here
Together both gods and men."

Loki spake:
56. "Be silent, Beyla! | thou art Byggvir's wife,
And deep art thou steeped in sin;
A greater shame | to the gods came ne'er,
Befouled thou art with thy filth."

Then came Thor forth, and spake:

57. "Unmanly one, cease, | or the mighty hammer,
Mjollnir, shall close thy mouth;
Thy shoulder-cliff | shall I cleave from thy neck,
And so shall thy life be lost."

Loki spake:
58. "Lo, in has come | the son of Earth:
Why threaten so loudly, Thor?
Less fierce thou shalt go | to fight with the wolf
When he swallows Sigfather up."

Thor spake:
59. "Unmanly one, cease, | or the mighty hammer,
Mjollnir, shall close thy mouth;
I shall hurl thee up | and out in the East,
Where men shall see thee no more."

Loki spake:
60. "That thou hast fared | on the East-road forth
To men shouldst thou say no more;
In the thumb of a glove | didst thou hide, thou great one,
And there forgot thou wast Thor."

Thor spake:
61. "Unmanly one, cease, | or the mighty hammer,
Mjollnir, shall close thy mouth;
My right hand shall smite thee | with Hrungnir's slayer,
Till all thy bones are broken."

Loki spake:
62. "Along time still | do I think to live,
Though thou threatenest thus with thy hammer;
Rough seemed the straps | of Skrymir's wallet,
When thy meat thou mightest not get,
(And faint from hunger didst feel.)"

Thor spake:
63. "Unmanly one, cease, | or the mighty hammer,
Mjollnir, shall close thy mouth;
The slayer of Hrungnir | shall send thee to hell,
And down to the gate of death."

Loki spake:
64. "'1 have said to the gods | and the sons of the god,
The things that whetted my thoughts;
But before thee alone | do I now go forth,
For thou fightest well, I ween.

65. "Ale hast thou brewed, | but, Ægir, now
Such feasts shalt thou make no more;
O'er all that thou hast | which is here within
Shall play the flickering flames,
(And thy back shall be burnt with fire.)"

And after that Loki hid himself in Franang's waterfall in the guise of a salmon, and there the gods took him. He was bound with the bowels of his son Vali, but his son Narfi was changed to a wolf. Skathi took a poison-snake and fastened it up over Loki's face, and the poison dropped thereon. Sigyn, Loki's wife, sat there and held a shell under the poison, but when the shell was full she bore away the poison, and meanwhile the poison dropped on Loki. Then he struggled so hard that the whole earth shook therewith; and now that is called an earthquake.

[*Prose. Ægir*: the sea-god; Snorri gives Hler as another of his names, but he is not elsewhere called Gymir, which is the name of the giant, Gerth's father, in the Skirnismol. On Ægir cf. *Grimnismol*, 45, and *Hymiskvitha*, 1. *Frigg*: though Othin's wife is often mentioned, she plays only a minor part in the Eddic poems; cf. *Voluspo*, 34, *Vafthruthnismol*, I, and *Grimnismol*, introductory prose. *Thor*: the compiler is apparently a trifle confused as to Thor's movements; the "Journey in the East" here mentioned cannot be the one described in the *Hymiskvitha*, nor yet the one narrated by Snorri, as Loki was with Thor through out that expedition. He probably means no more than that Thor was off killing giants.*Sif*: concerning Thor's wife the chief incident is that Loki cut off her hair, and, at the command of the wrathful Thor, was compelled to have the dwarfs fashion her a new supply of hair out of gold; cf. *Harbarthsljoth*, 48. *Bragi*: the god of poetry; cf. *Grimnismol*, 44 and note. *Ithun*: the goddess of youth; cf. note on *Skirnismol*, 19. Ithun is not mentioned by name in any other of the Eddic poems, but Snorri tells in detail how the giant Thjazi stole her and her apples, explaining the reference in *Harbarthsljoth*, 19 (q. v.). *Tyr*: the god of battle; cf. *Hymiskvitha*, 4, and (concerning his dealings with the wolf Fenrir) *Voluspo*, 39, note. *Njorth*: the chief of the Wanes, and father of Freyr and Freyja; cf. (concerning the whole family) *Skirnismol*, introductory prose and note, also *Voluspo*, 21 and note. *Skathi*: Njorth's wife was the daughter of the giant Thjazi; cf. *Harbarthsljoth*, 19, note, and *Grimnismol*, 17. *Vithar*: the silent god, the son of Othin who avenged his father by slaying the wolf Fenrir; cf. *Voluspo*, 54, *Vafthruthnismol*, 51, and *Grimnismol*, 17. *Loki*: the mischief-making fire-god; in addition to the many references to his career in the Lokasenna, cf. particularly *Voluspo*, 32 and 35, and notes. *Byggvir and Beyla*: not mentioned elsewhere in the poems; Freyr's conspicuous servant is Skirnir, hero of the Skirnismol. *Fimafeng* ("The Swift Handler") [fp. 153] and *Eldir* ("The Man of the Fire"): mentioned only in connection with this incident. *Glittering gold*: Ægir's use of gold to light his hall, which was often thought of as under the sea, was responsible for the phrase "flame of the flood," and sundry kindred phrases, meaning "gold."]

[9. *Bragi*: cf. note on introductory prose. Why Loki taunts him with cowardice (stanzas 11 13 15) is not clear, for poetry, of which Bragi was the patron, was generally associated in the Norse mind with peculiar valor, and most of the skaldic poets were likewise noted fighters.

9. There exists no account of any incident in which Othin and Loki thus swore blood-brotherhood, but they were so often allied in enterprises that the idea is wholly reasonable. The common process of "mingling blood" was carried out quite literally, and the promise of -which Loki speaks is characteristic of those which, in the sagas, often accompanied the ceremony; cf. Brot af Sigurtharkvithu, 18 and note.

10. In stanzas 10-31 the manuscript has nothing to indicate the identity of the several speakers, but these are uniformly clear [fp. 156] enough through the context. *Vithar*: cf. note on introductory prose. *The wolf's father*: Loki; cf. *Voluspo*, 39 and note.]

[13. Sijmons makes one line of lines 4-5 by cutting out a part of each; Finnur Jonsson rejects 5 as spurious.

14. The text of line 4 is somewhat obscure, and has been [fp. 157] variously emended, one often adopted suggestion making the line read, "Little is that for thy lies."]

[15. *Adorner of benches*: this epithet presumably implies that Bragi is not only slothful, but also effeminate, for a very similar word, "pride of the benches," means a bride.

16. *Ithun*: Bragi's wife; cf. note on introductory prose. The goddesses who, finding that their husbands are getting the worst of it, take up the cudgels with Loki, all find themselves confronted with undeniable facts in their own careers; cf. stanzas 26 (Frigg), 52 (Skathi) and 54 (Sif). Gefjun and Freyja are silenced in similar fashion. *Wish-son*: adopted son; Loki was the son of the giant Farbauti and the giantess Laufey, and hence was not of the race of the gods, but had been virtually adopted by Othin, who subsequently had good reason to regret it.]

[17. We do not even know who Ithun's brother was, much less who slew him.

19. *Gefjun*: a goddess, not elsewhere mentioned in the poems, who, according to Snorri, was served by the women who died maidens. Beyond this nothing is known of her. Lines 3-4 in the manuscript are puzzling, and have been freely emended.

20. Nothing is known of the incident here mentioned. There is a good deal of confusion as to various of the gods and goddesses, and it has been suggested that Gefjun is really Frigg under an other name, with a little of Freyja--whose attributes were frequently confused with Frigg's--thrown in. Certainly Othin's [fp. 159] answer (stanza 21, lines 3-4) fits Frigg perfectly, for she shared his knowledge of the future, whereas it has no relation to any thing known of Gefjun. As for the necklace (line 3), it may be the Brisings' necklace, which appears in the *Thrymskvitha* as Freyja's, but which, in some mythological writings, is assigned to Frigg.]

[21. Snorri quotes line 1; cf. note on stanza 29.

23. There is no other reference to Loki's having spent eight years underground, or to his cow-milking. On one occasion, however, he did bear offspring. A giant had undertaken to build the gods a fortress, his reward being Freyja and the sun and moon, provided the work was done by a given time. His sole helper was his horse, Svathilfari. The work being nearly done, and the gods fearing to lose Freyja and the sun and moon, Loki [fp. 160] turned himself into a mare, and so effectually distracted Svathilfari from his task that shortly afterwards Loki gave birth to Othin's eight-legged horse, Sleipnir. In such contests of abuse a man was not infrequently taunted with having borne children; cf. *Helgakvitha Hundingsbana* I, 39-45. One or two of the last three lines may be spurious.]

[24. *Samsey*: perhaps the Danish island of Samsö. Othin was the god of magic, but there is no other reference to his ever having disguised himself as a witch.

25. *Frigg*: Othin's wife; cf. note to introductory prose.

26. *Fjorgyn*: Othin; cf. *Voluspo*, 56 and note. *Vili and Ve*: Othin's brothers, who appear merely as, with Othin, the sons of Bur and Bestla; cf.*Voluspo*, 4.
The *Ynglingasaga* says that, during one of Othin's protracted absences, his two brothers took Frigg as their mistress. *Vithrir*: another name for Othin.]

[27. On the death of Baldr, slain through Loki's cunning by the blind Hoth, cf. *Voluspo*, 32 and note.

29. *Freyja*: daughter of Njorth and sister of Freyr; cf. note on introductory prose. Snorri, in speaking of Frigg's knowledge of the future, makes a stanza out of *Lokasenna*, 21, 1; 47, 2; 29, 3-4, thus: "Mad art thou, Loki, | and little of wit, / Why, Loki, leavst thou this not? / The fate of all | does Frigg know well, / Though herself she says it not."

30. According to Snorri, Freyja was a model of fidelity to her husband, Oth.]

[32. Before each of stanzas 32-42 the manuscript indicates the speaker, through the initial letter of the name written in the margin. *Thy brother*: Freyr; there is no other indication that such a relation existed between these two, but they themselves were the product of such a union; cf. stanza 36 and note.

33. *Njorth*: father of Freyr and Freyja, and given by the Wanes as a hostage, in exchange for Hönir, at the close of the first war; Cf. *Voluspo*, 21 and note, also *Skirnismol*, introductory prose and note. *Babes*: cf. stanza 23 and note. Bugge suggests that this clause may have been a late insertion.]

[34. *Daughters of Hymir*: we have no clue to who these were, though Hymir is doubtless the frost-giant of the *Hymiskvitha* (q.v.). Loki's point is that Njorth is not a god, but the product of an inferior race (the Wanes).

35. *The son*: Freyr.

36. *Thy sister*: the *Ynglingasaga* supports this story of Njorth's having had two children by his sister before he came among the gods. Snorri, on the other hand, specifically says that Freyr and Freyja were born after Njorth came to the gods.

37. *Tyr*: the god of battle; cf. notes on *Hymiskvitha*, 4, and *Voluspo*, 39. *Freyr*; concerning his noble qualities cf. *Skirnismol*, introductory prose and note.]

[38. Snorri mentions Tyr's incompetence as a peacemaker. *Fenrir*: the wolf, Loki's son; cf. *Voluspo*, 39.

39. *Hrothvitnir* ("The Mighty Wolf"): Fenrir, who awaits in chains the final battle and death at the hands of Vithar. The manuscript has a metrical error in line 3, which has led to various emendations, all with much the same meaning.

40. *Thy wife*: there is no other reference to Tyr's wife, nor do we know who was the son in question.]

[41. *The mouth of the river*: according to Snorri, the chained Fenrir "roars horribly, and the slaver runs from his mouth, and makes the river called Vam; he lies there till the doom of the gods." Freyr's threat is actually carried out; cf. concluding prose.

42. *The daughter of Gymir*: Gerth, heroine of the *Skirnismol*, which gives the details of Freyr's loss of his sword. *Muspell's sons*: the name Muspell is not used elsewhere in the poems; Snorri uses it frequently, but only in this same phrase, "Muspell's sons." They are the dwellers in the fire-world, Muspellsheim, led by Surt against the gods in the last battle; cf. Voluspo, 47 and 52 and notes. *Myrkwood*: here the dark forest bounding the fire-world; in the *Atlakvitha* (stanza 3) the name is used of another boundary forest.

43. *Byggvir*: one of Freyr's two servants; cf. introductory prose. *Ingunar-Freyr*: the name is not used elsewhere in the poems, or by Snorri; it may be the genitive of a woman's name, Ingun, the unknown sister of Njorth who was Freyr's mother (cf. stanza 36), or a corruption of the name Ingw, used for Freyr (Fro) in old German mythology.]

[44. Beginning with this stanza, the names of the speakers are lacking in the manuscript. *The mill*: i.e., at slaves' tasks.

45. Nothing further is known of either Byggvir's swiftness or his cowardice. *Hropt*: Othin.

47. *Heimdall*: besides being the watchman of the gods (cf. *Voluspo*, 27), he appears also as the god of light (cf. *Thrymskvitha*, 14), and possibly also as a complex cultural deity in the [fp. 167] *Rigsthula*. He was a son of Othin, born of nine sisters; cf. *Hyndluljoth*, 37-40. In the last battle he and Loki slay one an other. Line 2 is quoted by Snorri; cf. stanza 29, note.]

[49. Skathi: the wife of Njorth, and daughter of the giant Thjazi, concerning whose death cf. *Harbarthsljoth*, 19, note. Bowels, etc.: according to the prose note at the end of the *Lokasenna*, the gods bound Loki with the bowels of his son Vali, and changed his other son, Narfi, into a wolf. Snorri turns the story about Vali being the wolf, who tears his brother to pieces, the gods then using Narfi's intestines to bind Loki. Narfi--and presumably Vali--were the sons of Loki and his wife, Sigyn. They appear only in this episode, though Narfi (or Nari) is named by Snorri in his list of Loki's children. Cf. concluding prose, and note.]

[52. *Laufey's son*: Loki; not much is known of his parents beyond their names. His father was the giant Farbauti, his mother Laufey, sometimes called Nal. There is an elaborate but far fetched hypothesis explaining these three on the basis of a nature-myth. There is no other reference to such a relation between Skathi and Loki as he here suggests.

53. *Sif*: Thor's wife; cf. *Harbarthsljoth*, 48, where her infidelity is again mentioned. The manuscript omits the proper name [fp. 169] from the preceding prose, and a few editors have, obviously in error, attributed the speech to Beyla.]

[54. *Hlorrithi*: Thor. Line 3 is probably spurious.

55. *Beyla*: Freyr's servant, wife of Byggvir; cf. introductory prose and note.

57. *Mjollnir*: concerning Thor's famous hammer see particularly *Thrymskvitha*, 1 and note. *Shoulder-cliff*: head; concerning [fp. 170] the use of such diction in the *Edda*, cf. introductory note to *Hymiskvitha*. The manuscript indicates line 3 as the beginning of a stanza, but this is apparently a scribal error.]

[58. *Son of Earth*: Thor, son of Othin and Jorth (Earth). The manuscript omits the word "son," but all editors have agreed in supplying it. *The wolf*: Fenrir, Loki's son, who slays Othin (Sigfather: "Father of Victory") in the final battle. Thor, according to Snorri and to the Voluspo, 56, fights with Mithgarthsorm and not with Fenrir, who is killed by Vithar.

59. Lines 1-2 are abbreviated in the manuscript, as also in stanzas 61 and 63.

60. Loki's taunt that Thor hid in the thumb of Skrymir's glove is similar to that of Othin, *Harbarthsljoth*, 26, in the note to which the story is outlined. Line 4 is identical with line 5 of *Harbarthsljoth*, 26.]

[61. *Hrungnir's slayer*: the hammer; the story of how Thor slew this stone-headed giant is indicated in *Harbarthsljoth*, 14-15, and outlined in the note to stanza 14 of that poem.

62. On the day following the adventure of the glove, Thor, Loki and Thor's servants proceed on their way in company with Skrymir, who puts all their food in his wallet. At evening Skrymir goes to sleep, and Thor tries to get at the food, but cannot loosen the straps of the wallet. In a rage he smites Skrymir three times on the head with his hammer, but the giant--who, it subsequently appears, deftly dodges the blows--is totally undisturbed. Line 5 may well be spurious.]

[65. *The flames*: the fire that consumes the world on the last day; cf. *Voluspo*, 57. Line 5 may be spurious.

Prose: Snorri tells the same story, with minor differences, but makes it the consequence of Loki's part in the slaying of Baldr, which undoubtedly represents the correct tradition. The compiler of the poems either was confused or thought the incident was [fp. 173] useful as indicating what finally happened to Loki. Possibly he did not mean to imply that Loki's fate was brought upon him by his abuse of the gods, but simply tried to round out the story. *Franang*: "Gleaming Water." *Vali and Narfi*: cf. stanza 49 and note. *Sigyn*: cf. *Voluspo*, 35, the only other place where she is mentioned in the poems. Snorri omits the naive note about earth quakes, his narrative ending with the words, "And there he lies till the destruction of the gods."]

THRYMSKVITHA

The Lay of Thrym

INTRODUCTORY NOTE

The *Thrymskvitha* is found only in the *Codex Regius*, where it follows the *Lokasenna*. Snorri does not quote from it, nor, rather oddly, does the story occur in the *Prose Edda*.

Artistically the *Thrymskvitha* is one of the best, as it is, next to the *Voluspo*, the most famous, of the entire collection. It has, indeed, been called "the finest ballad in the world," and not without some reason. Its swift, vigorous action, the sharpness of its characterization and the humor of the central situation combine to make it one of the most vivid short narrative poems ever composed. Of course we know nothing specific of its author, but there can be no question that he was a poet of extraordinary ability. The poem assumed its present form, most critics agree, somewhere about 900, and thus it is one of the oldest in the collection. It has been suggested, on the basis of stylistic similarity, that its author may also have composed the *Skirnismol*, and possibly *Baldrs Draumar*. There is also some resemblance between the *Thrymskvitha* and the *Lokasenna* (note, in this connection, Bugge's suggestion that the *Skirnismol* and the *Lokasenna* may have been by the same man), and it is not impossible that all four poems have a single authorship.

The *Thrymskvitha* has been preserved in excellent condition, without any serious gaps or interpolations. In striking contrast to many of the poems, it contains no prose narrative links, the story being told in narrative verse--a rare phenomenon in the poems of the *Edda*.

1. Wild was Vingthor | when he awoke,
And when his mighty | hammer he missed;

He shook his beard, | his hair was bristling,
As the son of Jorth | about him sought.

2. Hear now the speech | that first he spake:
"Harken, Loki, | and heed my words,
Nowhere on earth | is it known to man,
Nor in heaven above: | our hammer is stolen."

3. To the dwelling fair | of Freyja went they,
Hear now the speech | that first he spake:
"Wilt thou, Freyja, | thy feather-dress lend me,
That so my hammer | I may seek?"

Freyja spake:
4. "Thine should it be | though of silver bright,
And I would give it | though 'twere of gold."
Then Loki flew, | and the feather-dress whirred,
Till he left behind him | the home of the gods,
And reached at last | the realm of the giants.

5. Thrym sat on a mound, | the giants' master,
Leashes of gold | he laid for his dogs,
And stroked and smoothed | the manes of his steeds.

Thrym spake:
6. "How fare the gods, | how fare the elves?
Why comst thou alone | to the giants' land?"

Loki spake:
"Ill fare the gods, | ill fare the elves!
Hast thou hidden | Hlorrithi's hammer?"

Thrym spake:
7. "I have hidden | Hlorrithi's hammer,
Eight miles down | deep in the earth;

And back again | shall no man bring it
If Freyja I win not | to be my wife."

8. Then Loki flew, | and the feather-dress whirred,
Till he left behind him | the home of the giants,
And reached at last | the realm of the gods.
There in the courtyard | Thor he met:
Hear now the speech | that first he spake:

9. "Hast thou found tidings | as well as trouble?
Thy news in the air | shalt thou utter now;
Oft doth the sitter | his story forget,
And lies he speaks | who lays himself down."

Loki spake:
10. "Trouble I have, | and tidings as well:
Thrym, king of the giants, | keeps thy hammer,
And back again | shall no man bring it
If Freyja he wins not | to be his wife."

11. Freyja the fair | then went they to find
Hear now the speech | that first he spake:
"Bind on, Freyja, | the bridal veil,
For we two must haste | to the giants' home."

12. Wrathful was Freyja, | and fiercely she snorted,
And the dwelling great | of the gods was shaken,
And burst was the mighty | Brisings' necklace:
"Most lustful indeed | should I look to all
If I journeyed with thee | to the giants' home."

13. Then were the gods | together met,
And the goddesses came | and council held,
And the far-famed ones | a plan would find,
How they might Hlorrithi's | hammer win.

14. Then Heimdall spake, | whitest of the gods,
Like the Wanes he knew | the future well:
"Bind we on Thor | the bridal veil,
Let him bear the mighty | Brisings' necklace;

15. "Keys around him | let there rattle,
And down to his knees | hang woman's dress;
With gems full broad | upon his breast,
And a pretty cap | to crown his head."

16. Then Thor the mighty | his answer made:
"Me would the gods | unmanly call
If I let bind | the bridal veil."

17. Then Loki spake, | the son of Laufey:
"Be silent, Thor, | and speak not thus;
Else will the giants | in Asgarth dwell
If thy hammer is brought not | home to thee."

8. Then bound they on Thor | the bridal veil,
And next the mighty | Brisings' necklace.

19. Keys around him | let they rattle,
And down to his knees | hung woman's dress;
With gems full broad | upon his breast,
And a pretty cap | to crown his head.

20. Then Loki spake, | the son of Laufey:
"As thy maid-servant thither | I go with thee;
We two shall haste | to the giants' home."

21. Then home the goats | to the hall were driven,
They wrenched at the halters, | swift were they to run;
The mountains burst, | earth burned with fire,
And Othin's son | sought Jotunheim.

22. Then loud spake Thrym, | the giants' leader:
"Bestir ye, giants, | put straw on the benches;
Now Freyja they bring | to be my bride,
The daughter of Njorth | out of Noatun.

23. "Gold-horned cattle | go to my stables,
Jet-black oxen, | the giant's joy;
Many my gems, | and many my jewels,
Freyja alone | did I lack, methinks."

24. Early it was | to evening come,
And forth was borne | the beer for the giants;
Thor alone ate an ox, | and eight salmon,
All the dainties as well | that were set for the women;
And drank Sif's mate | three tuns of mead.

25. Then loud spake Thrym, | the giants' leader:
"Who ever saw bride | more keenly bite?
I ne'er saw bride | with a broader bite,
Nor a maiden who drank | more mead than this!"

26. Hard by there sat | the serving-maid wise,
So well she answered | the giant's words:
"From food has Freyja | eight nights fasted,
So hot was her longing | for Jotunheim."

27. Thrym looked 'neath the veil, | for he longed to kiss,
But back he leaped | the length of the hall:
"Why are so fearful | the eyes of Freyja?
Fire, methinks, | from her eyes burns forth."

28. Hard by there sat | the serving-maid wise,
So well she answered | the giant's words:
"No sleep has Freyja | for eight nights found,
So hot was her longing | for Jotunheim."

29. Soon came the giant's | luckless sister,
Who feared not to ask | the bridal fee:
"From thy hands the rings | of red gold take,
If thou wouldst win | my willing love,
(My willing love | and welcome glad.)"

30: Then loud spake Thrym, | the giants' leader:
"Bring in the hammer | to hallow the bride;
On the maiden's knees | let Mjollnir lie,
That us both the band | of Vor may bless."

31. The heart in the breast | of Hlorrithi laughed
When the hard-souled one | his hammer beheld;
First Thrym, the king | of the giants, he killed,
Then all the folk | of the giants he felled.

32. The giant's sister | old he slew,
She who had begged | the bridal fee;
A stroke she got | in the shilling's stead,
And for many rings | the might of the hammer.

33. And so his hammer | got Othin's son.

[1. *Vingthor* ("Thor the Hurler"): another name for Thor, equivalent to Vingnir
(*Vafthruthnismol*, 51). Concerning Thor and his hammer, Mjollnir,
cf. *Hymiskvitha, Lokasenna*, and *Harbarthsljoth, passim. Jorth*: Earth, Thor's
mother, Othin being his father.]

[2. *Loki*: cf. *Lokasenna, passim.*

3. *Freyja*: Njorth's daughter, and sister of Freyr; cf. *Lokasenna*, introductory prose
and note, also *Skirnismol*, introductory prose. Freyja's house was Sessrymnir
("Rich in Seats") built in Folkvang ("Field of the Folk"); cf. *Grimnismol*,
14. *Feather-dress*: this flying equipment of Freyja's is also used in the story of
Thjazi, wherein Loki again borrows the "hawk's dress" of Freyja, this time to
rescue Ithun; cf.*Harbarthsljoth*, 19 and note.

157

4. The manuscript and most editions have lines 1-2 in inverse order. Several editors assume a lacuna before line I, making a stanza out of the two conjectural lines (Bugge actually supplies them) and lines 1-2 of stanza 4. Thus they either make a separate stanza out of lines 3-5 or unite them in a six-line stanza with 5. The manuscript punctuation and capitalization--not [fp. 176] wholly trustworthy guides--indicate the stanza divisions as in this translation.]

[5. *Thrym*: a frost-giant. Gering declares that this story of the theft of Thor's hammer symbolizes the fact that thunderstorms rarely occur in winter.

6. Line 1: cf. *Voluspo*, 48, 1. The manuscript does not indicate Loki as the speaker of lines 3-4. *Hlorrithi*: Thor.

7. No superscription in the manuscript. Vigfusson made up [fp. 177] and inserted lines like "Then spake Loki the son of Laufey" whenever he thought they would be useful.]

[9. The manuscript marks line 2, instead of line I, as the beginning of a stanza, which has caused editors some confusion in grouping the lines of stanzas 8 and 9.

10. No superscription in the manuscript.

12. Many editors have rejected either line 2 or line s. Vigfusson inserts one of his own lines before line 4. *Brisings' necklace*: a marvelous necklace fashioned by the dwarfs, here called Brisings (i.e., "Twiners"); cf. *Lokasenna*, 20 and note.]

[13. Lines 1-3 are identical with *Baldrs Draumar*, I, 1-3.

14. *Heimdall*: the phrase "whitest of the gods" suggests that Heimdall was the god of light as well as being the watchman. His wisdom was probably connected with his sleepless watching over all the worlds; cf. *Lokasenna*, 17 and note. On the Wanes Cf. *Voluspo*, 21 and note. They are not elsewhere spoken of as peculiarly gifted with knowledge of future events.

16. Possibly a line has been lost from this stanza.

17. *Laufey*: Loki's mother, cf. *Lokasenna*, 52 and note.]

[18-19. The manuscript abbreviates all six lines, giving only the initial letters of the words. The stanza division is thus arbitrary; some editors have made one stanza of the six lines, others have combined the last two lines of stanza 19 with stanza 20. It is possible that a couple of lines have been lost.

21. *Goats*: Thor's wagon was always drawn by goats; cf. *Hymiskvitha*, 38 and note. *Jotunheim*: the world of the giants.

22. *Njorth*: cf. *Voluspo*, 21, and *Grimnismol*, 11 and 16. *Noatun* [fp. 180] ("Ships'-Haven"): Njorth's home, where his wife, Skathi, found it impossible to stay; cf. *Grimnismol*, 11 and note.]

[24. Grundtvig thinks this is all that is left of two stanzas describing Thor's supper. Some editors reject line 4. in line 3 the manuscript has "he," the reference being, of course, to Thor, on whose appetite cf. *Hymiskvitha*, 15. *Sif*: Thor's wife; cf. *Lokasenna*, note to introductory prose and stanza 53.]

[27. For clearness I have inserted Thrym's name in place of the pronoun of the original. *Fire*: the noun is lacking in the manuscript; most editors have inserted it, however, following a late paper manuscript.

28. In the manuscript the whole stanza is abbreviated to initial letters, except for "sleep," "Freyja," and "found."

29. *Luckless*: so the manuscript, but many editors have altered the word "arma" to "aldna," meaning "old," to correspond with line 1 of stanza 32. Line 5 may well be spurious.

30. *Hallow*: just what this means is not clear, but there are {footnote po.

181 references to other kinds of consecration, though not of a bride, with the "sign of the hammer." According to Vigfusson, "the hammer was the holy sign with the heathens, answering to the cross of the Christians." In Snorri's story of Thor's resuscitation of his cooked goat (cf. *Hymiskvitha*, 38, note) the god "hallows" the goat with his hammer. One of the oldest runic signs, sup posed to have magic power, was named Thor's-hammer. *Vor*: the goddess of vows, particularly between men and women; Snorri lists a number of little-known goddesses similar to Vor, all of them apparently little more than names for Frigg.]}

[33. Some editors reject this line, which, from a dramatic stand point, is certainly a pity. In the manuscript it begins with a capital letter, like: the opening of a new stanza.]

ALVISSMOL

The Ballad of Alvis

INTRODUCTORY NOTE

No better summary of the Alvissmol can be given than Gering's statement that "it is a versified chapter from the skaldic Poetics." The narrative skeleton, contained solely in stanzas 1-8 and in 35, is of the slightest; the dwarf Alvis, desirous of marrying Thor's daughter, is compelled by the god to answer a number of questions to test his knowledge. That all his answers are quite satisfactory makes no difference whatever to the outcome. The questions and answers differ radically from those of the *Vafthruthnismol*. Instead of being essentially mythological, they all concern synonyms. Thor asks what the earth, the sky, the moon, and so on, are called " in each of all the worlds," but there is no apparent significance in the f act that the gods call the earth one thing and the giants call it another; the answers are simply strings of poetic circumlocutions, or "kennings." Concerning the use of these "kennings" in skaldic poetry, cf. introductory note to the *Hymiskvitha*.

Mogk is presumably right in dating the poem as late as the twelfth century, assigning it to the period of "the Icelandic renaissance of skaldic poetry." It appears to have been the work of a man skilled in poetic construction,--Thor's questions, for instance, are neatly balanced in pairs,--and fully familiar with the intricacies of skaldic diction, but distinctly weak in his mythology. In other words, it is learned rather than spontaneous poetry. Finnur Jonsson's attempt to make it a tenth century Norwegian poem baffles logic. Vigfusson is pretty sure the poem shows marked traces of Celtic influence, which is by no means incompatible with Mogk's theory (cf. introductory note to the *Rigsthula*).

The poem is found only in *Regius*, where it follows the Thrymskvitha. Snorri quotes stanzas 2c, and 30, the manuscripts of the*Prose Edda* giving the name of the poem as *Alvissmol, Alsvinnsmol* or *Olvismol*. It is apparently in excellent condition, without serious errors of transmission, although interpolations or omissions in such a poem might have been made so easily as to defy detection.

The translation of the many synonyms presents, of course, unusual difficulties, particularly as many of the Norse words can be properly rendered in English only by more or less extended phrases. I have kept to the original meanings as closely as I could without utterly destroying the metrical structure.

Alvis spake:
1. "Now shall the bride | my benches adorn,
And homeward haste forthwith;
Eager for wedlock | to all shall I seem,
Nor at home shall they rob me of rest."

Thor spake:
2. "What, pray, art thou? | Why so pale round the nose?
By the dead hast thou lain of late?
To a giant like | dost thou look, methinks;
Thou wast not born for the bride."

Alvis spake:
3. "Alvis am I, | and under the earth
My home 'neath the rocks I have;
With the wagon-guider | a word do I seek,
Let the gods their bond not break."

Thor spake:
4. "Break it shall I, | for over the bride
Her father has foremost right;

At home was I not | when the promise thou hadst,
And I give her alone of the gods."

Alvis spake:
5. "What hero claims | such right to hold
O'er the bride that shines so bright?
Not many will know thee, | thou wandering man!
Who was bought with rings to bear thee?"

Thor spake:
6. "Vingthor, the wanderer | wide, am I,
And I am Sithgrani's son;
Against my will | shalt thou get the maid,
And win the marriage word."

Alvis spake:
7. "Thy good-will now | shall I quickly get,
And win the marriage word;
I long to have, | and I would not lack,
This snow-white maid for mine."

Thor spake:
8. "The love of the maid | I may not keep thee
From winning, thou guest so wise,
If of every world | thou canst tell me all
That now I wish to know.

9. "Answer me, Alvis! | thou knowest all,
Dwarf, of the doom of men:
What call they the earth, | that lies before all,
In each and every world?"

Alvis spake:
10. " 'Earth' to men, 'Field' | to the gods it is,
'The Ways' is it called by the Wanes;

'Ever Green' by the giants, | 'The Grower' by elves,
'The Moist' by the holy ones high."

Thor spake:
11. "Answer me, Alvis! | thou knowest all,
Dwarf, of the doom of men:
What call they the heaven, | beheld of the high one,
In each and every world?"

Alvis spake:
12. " 'Heaven' men call it, | 'The Height' the gods,
The Wanes 'The Weaver of Winds';
Giants 'The Up-World,' | elves 'The Fair-Roof,'
The dwarfs 'The Dripping Hall.'"

Thor spake:
13. "Answer me, Alvis! | thou knowest all,
Dwarf, of the doom of men.:
What call they the moon, | that men behold,
In each and every world?"

Alvis spake:
14. "'Moon' with men, 'Flame' | the gods among,
'The Wheel' in the house of hell;
'The Goer' the giants, | 'The Gleamer' the dwarfs,
The elves 'The Teller of Time."

Thor spake:
15. "Answer me, Alvis! | thou knowest all,
Dwarf, of the doom of men:
What call they the sun, | that all men see,
In each and every world?"

Alvis spake:
16. "Men call it 'Sun,' | gods 'Orb of the Sun,'
'The Deceiver of Dvalin' the dwarfs;

The giants 'The Ever-Bright,' | elves 'Fair Wheel,'
'All-Glowing' the sons of the gods."

Thor spake:
17. "Answer me, Alvis! | thou knowest all,
Dwarf, of the doom of men:
What call they the clouds, | that keep the rains,
In each and every world?"

Alvis spake:
18. "'Clouds' men name them, | 'Rain-Hope' gods call them,
The Wanes call them 'Kites of the Wind';
'Water-Hope' giants, | 'Weather-Might' elves,
'The Helmet of Secrets' in hell."

Thor spake:
19. "Answer me, Alvis! | thou knowest all,
Dwarf, of the doom of men:
What call they the wind, | that widest fares,
In each and every world?"

Alvis spake:
20. "'Wind' do men call it, | the gods 'The Waverer,'
'The Neigher' the holy ones high;
'The Wailer' the giants, | 'Roaring Wender' the elves,
In hell 'The Blustering Blast.'

Thor spake:
21. "Answer me, Alvis! | thou knowest all
Dwarf, of the doom of men:
What call they the calm, | that quiet lies,
In each and every world?"

Alvis spake:
22. " 'Calm' men call it, | 'The Quiet' the gods,
The Wanes 'The Hush of the Winds';

'The Sultry' the giants, | elves 'Day's Stillness,'
The dwarfs 'The Shelter of Day.'

Thor spake:
23. "Answer me, Alvis! | thou knowest all,
Dwarf, of the doom of men:
What call they the sea, | whereon men sail,
In each and every world?"

Alvis spake:
24. " 'Sea' men call it, | gods 'The Smooth-Lying,'
'The Wave' is it called by the Wanes;
'Eel-Home' the giants, | 'Drink-Stuff' the elves,
For the dwarfs its name is 'The Deep.'

Thor spake:
25. "Answer me, Alvis! | thou knowest all,
Dwarf, of the doom of men:
What call they the fire, | that flames for men,
In each of all the worlds?"

Alvis spake:
26. " 'Fire' men call it, | and 'Flame' the gods,
By the Wanes is it 'Wildfire' called;
'The Biter' by giants, | 'The Burner' by dwarfs,
'The Swift' in the house of hell."

Thor spake:
27. "Answer me, Alvis! | thou knowest all,
Dwarf, of the doom of men:
What call they the wood, | that grows for mankind,
In each and every world?"

Alvis spake:
28. "Men call it 'The Wood, | gods 'The Mane of the Field,'
'Seaweed of Hills' in hell;

'Flame-Food' the giants, | 'Fair-Limbed' the elves,
'The Wand' is it called by the Wanes."

Thor spake:
29. "Answer me, Alvis! | thou knowest all,
Dwarf, of the doom of men:
What call they the night, | the daughter of Nor,
In each and every world?"

Alvis spake:
30. "'Night' men call it, | 'Darkness' gods name it,
'The Hood' the holy ones high;
The giants 'The Lightless,' | the elves 'Sleep's joy"
The dwarfs 'The Weaver of Dreams.'"

Thor spake:
31. "Answer me, Alvis! | thou knowest all,
Dwarf, of the doom of men:
What call they the seed, | that is sown by men,
In each and every world?"

Alvis spake:
32. "Men call it 'Grain,' | and 'Corn' the gods,
'Growth' in the world of the Wanes;
'The Eaten' by giants, | 'Drink-Stuff' by elves,
In hell 'The Slender Stem.'

Thor spake:
33. "Answer me, Alvis! | thou knowest all,
Dwarf, of the doom of men:
What call they the ale, | that is quaffed of men,
In each and every world?"

Alvis spake:
34. "'Ale' among men, | 'Beer' the gods among,
In the world of the Wanes 'The Foaming';

'Bright Draught' with giants, | 'Mead' with dwellers in hell,
'The Feast-Draught' with Suttung's sons."

Thor spake:
.3.5. "In a single breast | I never have seen
More wealth of wisdom old;
But with treacherous wiles | must I now betray thee:
The day has caught thee, dwarf!
(Now the sun shines here in the hall.)"

[1. *Alvis* ("All-Knowing"): a dwarf, not elsewhere mentioned. The manuscript
nowhere indicates the speakers' name. The bride in question is Thor's daughter;
Thruth ("Might") is the only daughter of his whose name is recorded, and she does
not appear elsewhere in the poems. Her mother was Sif, Thor's wife, whereas the
god's sons were born of a giantess. *Benches*: cf. *Lokasenna*, 15 and note.

2. The dwarfs, living beyond the reach of the sun, which was fatal to them (cf.
stanzas 16 and 35), were necessarily pale. Line 3 is, of course, ironical.

3. *Wagon-guider*: Thor, who travels habitually on his goat drawn wagon. Bugge
changes "Vagna vets" to "Vapna verþs," [fp. 185] rendering the line "I am come to
seek the cost of the weapons." In either case, Alvis does not as yet recognize
Thor.]

[4. Apparently the gods promised Thor's daughter in marriage to Alvis during her
father's absence, perhaps as a reward for some craftsmanship of his (cf. Bugge's
suggestion as to stanza 3). The text of line 4 is most uncertain.

5. *Hero*: ironically spoken; Alvis takes Thor for a tramp, the god's uncouth
appearance often leading to such mistakes; cf. *Harbarthsljoth*, 6. Line 4 is a trifle
uncertain; some editors alter the wording to read "What worthless woman bore
thee?"

6. *Vingthor* ("Thor the Hurler"): cf. *Thrymskvitha*, 1. *Sithgrani* ("Long-Beard"):
Othin.]

[8. *Every world*: concerning the nine worlds, cf. Voluspo, 2 and note. Many
editors follow this stanza with one spoken by Alvis, found in late paper

manuscripts, as follows: "Ask then, Vingthor, since eager thou art / The lore of the dwarf to learn; / Oft have I fared in the nine worlds all, / And wide is my wisdom of each."

10. *Men*, etc.: nothing could more clearly indicate the author's mythological inaccuracy than his confusion of the inhabitants of the nine worlds. Men (dwellers in Mithgarth) appear in each of Alvis's thirteen answers; so do the gods (Asgarth) and the giants (Jotunheim). The elves (Alfheim) appear in eleven [fp. 187] answers, the Wanes (Vanaheim) in nine, and the dwarfs (who occupied no special world, unless one identifies them with the dark elves of Svartalfaheim) in seven. The dwellers "in hell" appear in six stanzas; the phrase probably refers to the world of the dead, though Mogk thinks it may mean the dwarfs. In stanzas where the gods are already listed appear names else where applied only to them,--"holy ones," "sons of the gods" and "high ones,"--as if these names meant beings of a separate race. "Men" appears twice in the same stanza, and so do the giants, if one assumes that they are "the sons of Suttung." Altogether it is useless to pay much attention to the mythology of Alvis's replies.]

[11. Lines I, 2, and 4 of Thor's questions are regularly abbreviated in the manuscript. *Beheld*, etc.: the word in the manuscript is almost certainly an error, and all kinds of guesses have been made to rectify it. All that can be said is that it means "beheld of" or "known to" somebody.]

[14. *Flame*: a doubtful word; Vigfusson suggests that it properly means a "mock sun." *Wheel*: the manuscript adds the adjective "whirling," to the destruction of the metre; cf. *Hovamol*, 84, 3.

16. *Deceiver of Dvalin*: Dvalin was one of the foremost dwarfs; cf. *Voluspo*, 14, *Fafnismol*, 13, and *Hovamol*, 144. The [fp. 189] sun "deceives" him because, like the other dwarfs living under ground, he cannot live in its light, and always fears lest sunrise may catch him unaware. The sun's rays have power to turn the dwarfs into stone, and the giantess Hrimgerth meets a similar fate (cf. *Helgakvitha Hjorvarthssonar*, 30). Alvis suffers in the same way; cf. stanza 35.]

[20. Snorri quotes this stanza in the *Skaldskaparmal*. *Waverer*: the word is uncertain, the Prose Edda manuscripts giving it in various forms.*Blustering Blast*: two *Prose Edda* manuscripts give a totally different word, meaning "The Pounder."]

[22. *Hush*, etc.: the manuscript, by inserting an additional letter, makes the word practically identical with that translated "Kite" in stanza 18. Most editors have agreed as to the emendation.

169

24. *Drink-Stuff*: Gering translates the word thus; I doubt it, but can suggest nothing better.]

[26. *Wildfire*: the word may mean any one of various things, including "Wave," which is not unlikely.

28. *In hell*: the word simply means "men," and it is only a guess, though a generally accepted one, that here it refers to the dead.]

[29. *Nor*: presumably the giant whom Snorri calls Norvi or Narfi, father of Not (Night) and grandfather of Dag (Day). Cf. *Vafthruthnismol*, 25.

30. Snorri quotes this stanza in the *Skaldskaparmal*. The various *Prose Edda* manuscripts differ considerably in naming the gods, the giants, etc. *Lightless*: some manuscripts have "The Unsorrowing."

32. *Grain*: the two words translated "grain" and "corn" apparently both meant primarily barley, and thence grain in [fp. 193] general, the first being the commoner term of the two. *Drink-Stuff*: the word is identical with the one used, and commented on, in stanza 24, and again I have followed Gering's interpretation for want of a better one. If his guess is correct, the reference here is evidently to grain as the material from which beer and other drinks are brewed.]

[34. *Suttung's sons*: these ought to be the giants, but the giants are specifically mentioned in line 3. The phrase "Suttung's sons" occurs in Skirnismol, 34, clearly meaning the giants. Concerning Suttung as the possessor of the mead of poetry, cf. Hovamol, 104.]

[35. Concerning the inability of the dwarfs to endure sunlight, which turns them into stone, cf. stanza 16 and note. Line 5 may be spurious.]

BALDRS DRAUMAR

Baldr's Dreams

INTRODUCTORY NOTE

Baldrs Draumar is found only in the *Arnamagnæan Codex*, where it follows the *Harbarthsljoth* fragment. It is preserved in various late paper manuscripts, with the title *Vegtamskvitha* (The Lay of Vegtam), which has been used by some editors.

The poem, which contains but fourteen stanzas, has apparently been preserved in excellent condition. Its subject-matter and style link it closely with the Voluspo. Four of the five lines of stanza 11 appear, almost without change, in the *Voluspo*, 32-33, and the entire poem is simply an elaboration of the episode outlined in those and the preceding stanzas. It has been suggested that *Baldrs Draumar* and the *Voluspo* may have been by the same author. There is also enough similarity in style between*Baldrs Draumar* and the *Thrymskvitha* (note especially the opening stanza) to give color to Vigfusson's guess that these two poems had a common authorship. In any case, *Baldrs Draumar* presumably assumed its present form not later than the first half of the tenth century.

Whether the Volva (wise-woman) of the poem is identical with the speaker in the *Voluspo* is purely a matter for conjecture. Nothing definitely opposes such a supposition. As in the longer poem she foretells the fall of the gods, so in this case she prophesies the first incident of that fall, the death of Baldr. Here she is called up from the dead by Othin, anxious to know the meaning of Baldr's evil dreams; in the *Voluspo* it is likewise intimated that the Volva has risen from the grave.

The poem, like most of the others in the collection, is essentially dramatic rather than narrative, summarizing a story which was doubtless familiar to every one who heard the poem recited.

---

1. Once were the gods | together met,
And the goddesses came | and council held,
And the far-famed ones | the truth would find,
Why baleful dreams | to Baldr had come.

2. Then Othin rose, | the enchanter old,
And the saddle he laid | on Sleipnir's back;
Thence rode he down | to Niflhel deep,
And the hound he met | that came from hell.

3. Bloody he was | on his breast before,
At the father of magic | he howled from afar;
Forward rode Othin, | the earth resounded
Till the house so high | of Hel he reached.

4. Then Othin rode | to the eastern door,
There, he knew well, | was the wise-woman's grave;
Magic he spoke | and mighty charms,
Till spell-bound she rose, | and in death she spoke:

5. "What is the man, | to me unknown,
That has made me travel | the troublous road?
I was snowed on with snow, | and smitten with rain,
And drenched with dew; | long was I dead."

Othin spake:
6. "Vegtam my name, | I am Valtam's son;
Speak thou of hell, | for of heaven I know:
For whom are the benches | bright with rings,
And the platforms gay | bedecked with gold?"

172

The Wise-Woman spake:
7. "Here for Baldr | the mead is brewed,
The shining drink, | and a shield lies o'er it;
But their hope is gone | from the mighty gods.
Unwilling I spake, | and now would be still."

Othin spake:
8. "Wise-woman, cease not! | I seek from thee
All to know | that I fain would ask:
Who shall the bane | of Baldr become,
And steal the life | from Othin's son?"

The Wise-Woman spake:
9. "Hoth thither bears | the far-famed branch,
He shall the bane | of Baldr become,
And steal the life | from Othin's son.
Unwilling I spake, | and now would be still."

Othin spake:
10. "Wise-woman, cease not! | I seek from thee
All to know | that I fain would ask:
Who shall vengeance win | for the evil work,
Or bring to the flames | the slayer of Baldr?"

The Wise-Woman spake:
11. "Rind bears Vali | in Vestrsalir,
And one night old | fights Othin's son;
His hands he shall wash not, | his hair he shall comb not,
Till the slayer of Baldr | he brings to the flames.
Unwilling I spake, | and now would be still."

Othin spake:
12. "Wise-woman, cease not! | I seek from thee
All to know | that I fain would ask:
What maidens are they | who then shall weep,
And toss to the sky | the yards of the sails?"

The Wise-Woman spake:
13. "Vegtam thou art not, | as erstwhile I thought;
Othin thou art, | the enchanter old."

Othin spake:
"No wise-woman art thou, | nor wisdom hast;
Of giants three | the mother art thou."

The Wise-Woman spake:
14. "Home ride, Othin, | be ever proud;
For no one of men | shall seek me more
Till Loki wanders | loose from his bonds,
And to the last strife | the destroyers come."

[1. Lines 1-3 are identical with *Thrymskvitha*, 13, 1-3. *Baldr*: concerning this best and noblest of the gods, the son of Othin and [fp. 196] Frigg, who comes again among the survivors after the final battle, cf. *Voluspo*, 32 and 62, and notes. He is almost never mentioned anywhere except in connection with the story of his death, though Snorri has one short passage praising his virtue and beauty. After stanza 1 two old editions, and one later one, insert four stanzas from late paper manuscripts.]

[2. *Sleipnir*: Othin's eight-legged horse, the son of Loki and the stallion Svathilfari; cf. Lokasenna, 23, and *Grimnismol*, 44, and notes. *Niflhel*: the murky ("nifl") dwelling of Hel, goddess of the dead. *The hound*: Garm; cf. *Voluspo*, 44.

3. *Father of magic*: Othin appears constantly as the god of magic. *Hel*: offspring of Loki and the giantess Angrbotha, as were the wolf Fenrir and Mithgarthsorm. She ruled the world of the unhappy dead, either those who had led evil lives or, according to another tradition, those who had not died in battle. The [fp. 197] manuscript marks line 3 as the beginning of a stanza, and thus the editions vary in their grouping of the lines of this and the succeeding stanzas.]

[6. The manuscript has no superscriptions indicating the speakers. *Vegtam* ("The Wanderer"): Othin, as usual, conceals his identity, calling himself the son of Valtam ("The Fighter"). In this instance he has unusual need to do so, for as the wise-woman belongs apparently to the race of the giants, she would be unwilling to answer a god's questions. *Heaven*: the word used includes all the upper worlds, in contrast to hell.*Benches*, etc.: the adornment of the benches and raised platforms, or elevated parts of the house, was a regular part of the preparation for a feast of welcome. The text of the two last lines is somewhat uncertain.

7. Grundtvig, followed by, Edzardi, thinks a line has been lost between lines 3 and 4.]

[9. Concerning the blind Hoth, who, at Loki's instigation, cast the fatal mistletoe at Baldr, cf. *Voluspo*, 32-33 and notes. In the manuscript the last line is abbreviated, as also in stanza 11.

10. In the manuscript lines 1-2 are abbreviated, as also in stanza 12.

11. *Rind*: mentioned by Snorri as one of the goddesses. Concerning her son Vali, begotten by Othin for the express purpose of avenging Baldr's death, and his slaying of Hoth the day after his birth, cf. *Voluspo*, 33-34, where the lines of this stanza appear practically verbatim.*Vestrsalir* ("The Western Hall"): not else where mentioned in the poems.]

[12. The manuscript marks the third line as the beginning of a stanza; something may have been lost. Lines 3.4 are thoroughly obscure. According to Bugge the maidens who are to weep for Baldr are the daughters of the sea-god Ægir, the waves, whose grief will be so tempestuous that they will toss the ships up to the very sky. "Yards of the sails" is a doubtfully accurate rendering; the two words, at any rate in later Norse nautical speech, meant respectively the "tack" and the "sheet" of the square sail.

13. Possibly two separate stanzas. *Enchanter*: the meaning of the original word is most uncertain.]

[14. Concerning Loki's escape and his relation to the destruction of the gods, cf. *Voluspo*, 35 and 51, and notes. While the wise-woman probably means only that she will never speak again till the end of the world, it has been suggested, and is certainly possible, that she intends to give Loki her counsel, thus revenging herself on Othin.]

RIGSTHULA

The Song of Rig

INTRODUCTORY NOTE

The *Rigsthula* is found in neither of the principal codices. The only manuscript containing it is the so-called *Codex Wormanius*, a manuscript of Snorri's *Prose Edda*. The poem appears on the last sheet of this manuscript, which unluckily is incomplete, and thus the end of the poem is lacking. In the *Codex Wormanius* itself the poem has no title, but a fragmentary parchment included with it calls the poem the *Rigsthula*. Some late paper manuscripts give it the title of *Rigsmol*.

The *Rigsthula* is essentially unlike anything else which editors have agreed to include in the so-called *Edda*. It is a definitely cultural poem, explaining, on a mythological basis, the origin of the different castes of early society: the thralls, the peasants, and the warriors. From the warriors, finally, springs one who is destined to become a king, and thus the whole poem is a song in praise of the royal estate. This fact in itself would suffice to indicate that the *Rigsthula* was not composed in Iceland, where for centuries kings were regarded with profound disapproval.

Not only does the *Rigsthula* praise royalty, but it has many of the earmarks of a poem composed in praise of a particular king. The manuscript breaks off at a most exasperating point, just as the connection between the mythical "Young Kon" (Konr ungr, konungr, "king"; but cf. stanza 44, note) and the monarch in question is about to be established. Owing to the character of the Norse settlements in Iceland, Ireland, and the western islands generally, search for a specific king leads back to either Norway or Denmark; despite the arguments advanced by Edzardi, Vigfusson, Powell, and others, it seems most improbable that such a poem

177

should have been produced elsewhere than on the Continent, the region where Scandinavian royalty most flourished. Finnur Jonsson's claim for Norway, with Harald the Fair-Haired as the probable king in question, is much less impressive than Mogk's ingenious demonstration that the poem was in all probability composed in Denmark, in honor of either Gorm the Old or Harald Blue-Tooth. His proof is based chiefly on the evidence provided by stanza 49, and is summarized in the note to that stanza.

The poet, however, was certainly not a Dane, but probably a wandering Norse singer, who may have had a dozen homes, and who clearly had spent much time in some part of the western island world chiefly inhabited by Celts. The extent of Celtic influence on the Eddic poems in general is a matter of sharp dispute. Powell, for example, claims almost all the poems for the "Western Isles," and attributes nearly all their good qualities to Celtic influence. Without here attempting to enter into the details of the argument, it may be said that the weight of authoritative opinion, while clearly recognizing the marks of Celtic influence in the poems, is against this view; contact between the roving Norsemen of Norway and Iceland and the Celts of Ireland and the "Western Isles," and particularly the Orkneys, was so extensive as to make the presumption of an actual Celtic home for the poems seem quite unnecessary.

In the case of the *Rigsthula* the poet unquestionably had not only picked up bits of the Celtic speech (the name Rig itself is almost certainly of Celtic origin, and there are various other Celtic words employed), but also had caught something of the Celtic literary spirit. This explains the cultural nature of the poem, quite foreign to Norse poetry in general. On the other hand, the style as a whole is vigorously Norse, and thus the explanation that the poem was composed by an itinerant Norse poet who had lived for some time in the Celtic islands, and who was on a visit to the court of a Danish king, fits the ascertainable facts exceedingly well. As Christianity was introduced into Denmark around 960, the *Rigsthula* is not likely to have been composed much after that date, and probably belongs to the first half of the tenth century. Gorm the Old died about the year 935, and was succeeded by Harald Blue-Tooth, who died about 985.

The fourteenth (or late thirteenth) century annotator identifies Rig with Heimdall, but there is nothing in the poem itself, and very little anywhere else, to warrant this, and it seems likely that the poet had Othin, and not Heimdall, in mind, his purpose being to trace the origin of the royal estate to the chief of the gods. The evidence bearing on this identification is briefly summed up in the note on the introductory prose passage, but the question involves complex and baffling problems in mythology, and from very early times the status of Heimdall was unquestionably confusing to the Norse mind.

They tell in old stories that one of the gods, whose name was Heimdall, went on his way along a certain seashore, and came to a dwelling, where he called himself Rig. According to these stories is the following poem:

1. Men say there went | by ways so green
Of old the god, | the aged and wise,
Mighty and strong | did Rig go striding.
. . . .

2. Forward he went | on the midmost way,
He came to a dwelling, | a door on its posts;
In did he fare, | on the floor was a fire,
Two hoary ones | by the hearth there sat,
Ai and Edda, | in olden dress.

3. Rig knew well | wise words to speak,
Soon in the midst | of the room he sat,
And on either side | the others were.

4. A loaf of bread | did Edda bring,
Heavy and thick | and swollen with husks;
Forth on the table | she set the fare,
And broth for the meal | in a bowl there was.
(Calf's flesh boiled | was the best of the dainties.)

5. Rig knew well | wise words to speak,
Thence did he rise, | made ready to sleep;
Soon in the bed | himself did he lay,

6. Thus was he there | for three nights long,
Then forward he went | on the midmost way,
And so nine months | were soon passed by.

7. A son bore Edda, | with water they sprinkled him,
With a cloth his hair | so black they covered;
Thræll they named him, | .   .   .   .   .

8. The skin was wrinkled | and rough on his hands,
Knotted his knuckles, | .   .   .   .   .
Thick his fingers, | and ugly his face,
Twisted his back, | and big his heels.

9. He began to grow, | and to gain in strength,
Soon of his might | good use he made;
With bast he bound, | and burdens carried,
Home bore faggots | the whole day long.

10. One came to their home, | crooked her legs,
Stained were her feet, | and sunburned her arms,
Flat was her nose; | her name was Thir.

11. Soon in the midst | of the room she sat,
By her side there sat | the son of the house;
They whispered both, | and the bed made ready,
Thræll and Thir, | till the day was through.

180

12. Children they had, | they lived and were happy,
Fjosnir and Klur | they were called, methinks,
Hreim and Kleggi, | Kefsir, Fulnir,
Drumb, Digraldi, | Drott and Leggjaldi,
Lut and Hosvir; | the house they cared for,
Ground they dunged, | and swine they guarded,
Goats they tended, | and turf they dug.

13. Daughters had they, | Drumba and Kumba,
Ökkvinkalfa, | Arinnefla,
Ysja and Ambott, | Eikintjasna,
Totrughypja | and Tronubeina;
And thence has risen | the race of thralls.

14. Forward went Rig, | his road was straight,
To a hall he came, | and a door there hung;
In did he fare, | on the floor was a fire:
Afi and Amma | owned the house.

15. There sat the twain, | and worked at their tasks:
The man hewed wood | for the weaver's beam;
His beard was trimmed, | o'er his brow a curl,
His clothes fitted close; | in the corner a chest.

16. The woman sat | and the distaff wielded,
At the weaving with arms | outstretched she worked;
On her head was a band, | on her breast a smock;
On her shoulders a kerchief | with clasps there was.

17. Rig knew well | wise words to speak,
Soon in the midst | of the room he sat,
And on either side | the others were.

18. Then took Amma | .   .   .   .   .
The vessels full | with the fare she set,
Calf's flesh boiled | was the best of the dainties.

19. Rig knew well | wise words to speak,
He rose from the board, | made ready to sleep;
Soon in the bed | himself did he lay,
And on either side | the others were.

20. Thus was he there | for three nights long,
Then forward he went | on the midmost way,
And so nine months | were soon passed by.

21. A son bore Amma, | with water they sprinkled him,
Karl they named him; | in a cloth she wrapped him,
He was ruddy of face, | and flashing his eyes.

22. He began to grow, | and to gain in strength,
Oxen he ruled, | and plows made ready,
Houses he built, | and barns he fashioned,
Carts he made, | and the plow he managed.

23. Home did they bring | the bride for Karl,
In goatskins clad, | and keys she bore;
Snör was her name, | 'neath the veil she sat;
A home they made ready, | and rings exchanged,
The bed they decked, | and a dwelling made.

24. Sons they had, | they lived and were happy:
Hal and Dreng, | Holth, Thegn and Smith,
Breith and Bondi, | Bundinskeggi,
Bui and Boddi, | Brattskegg and Segg.

25. Daughters they had, | and their names are here:
Snot, Bruth, Svanni, | Svarri, Sprakki,
Fljoth, Sprund and Vif, | Feima, Ristil:
And thence has risen | the yeomen's race.

26. Thence went Rig, | his road was straight,
A hall he saw, | the doors faced south;

The portal stood wide, | on the posts was a ring,
Then in he fared; | the floor was strewn.

27. Within two gazed | in each other's eyes,
Fathir and Mothir, | and played with their fingers;
There sat the house-lord, | wound strings for the bow,
Shafts he fashioned, | and bows he shaped.

28. The lady sat, | at her arms she looked,
She smoothed the cloth, | and fitted the sleeves;
Gay was her cap, | on her breast were clasps,
Broad was her train, | of blue was her gown,
Her brows were bright, | her breast was shining,
Whiter her neck | than new-fallen snow.

29. Rig knew | well wise words to speak,
Soon in the midst | of the room he sat,
And on either side | the others were.

30. Then Mothir brought | a broidered cloth,
Of linen bright, | and the board she covered;
And then she took | the loaves so thin,
And laid them, white | from the wheat, on the cloth.

31. Then forth she brought | the vessels full,
With silver covered, | and set before them,
Meat all browned, | and well-cooked birds;
In the pitcher was wine, | of plate were the cups,
So drank they and talked | till the day was gone.

32. Rig knew well | wise words to speak,
Soon did he rise, | made ready to sleep;
So in the bed | himself did he lay,
And on either side | the others were.

33. Thus was he there | for three nights long,
Then forward he went | on the midmost way,
And so nine months | were soon passed by.

34. A son had Mothir, | in silk they wrapped him,
With water they sprinkled him, | Jarl he was;
Blond was his hair, | and bright his cheeks,
Grim as a snake's | were his glowing eyes.

35. To grow in the house | did Jarl begin,
Shields he brandished, | and bow-strings wound,
Bows he shot, | and shafts he fashioned,
Arrows he loosened, | and lances wielded,
Horses he rode, | and hounds unleashed,
Swords he handled, | and sounds he swam.

36. Straight from the grove | came striding Rig,
Rig came striding, | and runes he taught him;
By his name he called him, | as son he claimed him,
And bade him hold | his heritage wide,
His heritage wide, | the ancient homes.

37. .   .   .   .
Forward he rode | through the forest dark,
O'er the frosty crags, | till a hall he found.

38. His spear he shook, | his shield he brandished,
His horse he spurred, | with his sword he hewed;
Wars he raised, | and reddened the field,
Warriors slew he, | and land he won.

39. Eighteen halls | ere long did he hold,
Wealth did he get, | and gave to all,
Stones and jewels | and slim-flanked steeds,
Rings he offered, | and arm-rings shared.

40. His messengers went | by the ways so wet,
And came to the hall | where Hersir dwelt;
His daughter was fair | and slender-fingered,
Erna the wise | the maiden was.

41. Her hand they sought, | and home they brought her,
Wedded to Jarl | the veil she wore;
Together they dwelt, | their joy was great,
Children they had, | and happy they lived.

42. Bur was the eldest, | and Barn the next,
Joth and Athal, | Arfi, Mog,
Nith and Svein, | soon they began-
Sun and Nithjung-- | to play and swim;
Kund was one, | and the youngest Kon.

43. Soon grew up | the sons of Jarl,
Beasts they tamed, | and bucklers rounded,
Shafts they fashioned, | and spears they shook.

44. But Kon the Young | learned runes to use,
Runes everlasting, | the runes of life;
Soon could he well | the warriors shield,
Dull the swordblade, | and still the seas.

45. Bird-chatter learned he, | flames could he lessen.,
Minds could quiet, | and sorrows calm;

. . . .

The might and strength | of twice four men.

46. With Rig-Jarl soon | the runes he shared,
More crafty he was, | and greater his wisdom;
The right he sought, | and soon he won it,
Rig to be called, | and runes to know.

47. Young Kon rode forth | through forest and grove,
Shafts let loose, | and birds he lured;
There spake a crow | on a bough that sat:
"Why lurest thou, Kon, | the birds to come?

48. " 'Twere better forth | on thy steed to fare,
.   .   .   .   . | and the host to slay.

49. "The halls of Dan | and Danp are noble,
Greater their wealth | than thou bast gained;
Good are they | at guiding the keel,
Trying of weapons, | and giving of wounds.

[*Prose.* It would be interesting to know how much the annotator meant by the phrase *old stories*. Was he familiar with the tradition in forms other than that of the poem? If so, his introductory note was scanty, for, outside of identifying *Rig* as *Heimdall*, he provides no information not found in the poem. Probably he meant simply to refer to the poem itself as a relic of antiquity, and the identification of Rig as Heimdall may well have been an attempt at constructive criticism of his own. The note was presumably written somewhere about 1300, or even later, and there is no reason for crediting the annotator with any considerable knowledge of mythology. There is little to favor the identification of Rig with Heimdall, the watchman of the gods, beyond a few rather vague passages in the other poems. Thus in *Voluspo*, I, the Volva asks hearing "from Heimdall's sons both high and low"; in *Grimnismol*, 13, there is a very doubtful line which may mean that Heimdall "o'er men holds sway, it is said," and in "the Short Voluspo" (*Hyndluljoth*, 40) he is called "the kinsman of men." On the other hand, everything in the *Rigsthula*, including the phrase "the aged and wise" in stanza I, and the references to runes in stanzas 36, 44, and 46, fits Othin exceedingly well. It seems probable that the annotator was wrong, and that Rig is Othin, and not Heimdall. *Rig*: almost certainly based on the Old Irish word for "king," "ri" or "rig."

1. No gap is indicated, but editors have generally assumed one. Some editors, however, add line 1 of stanza 2 to stanza 1.]

[2. Most editions make line 5 a part of the stanza, as here, but some indicate it as the sole remnant of one or more stanzas descriptive of Ai and Edda, just as Afi

186

and Amma, Fathir and Mothir, are later described. *Ai and Edda*: Great-Grandfather and Great-Grandmother; the latter name was responsible for Jakob Grimm's famous guess at the meaning of the word "Edda" as applied to the whole collection (cf. Introduction).

3. A line may have been lost from this stanza.

4. Line 5 has generally been rejected as spurious.

5. The manuscript has lines 1-2 in inverse order, but marks the word "Rig" as the beginning of a stanza.]

[6. The manuscript does not indicate that these lines form a separate stanza, and as only one line and a fragment of another are left of stanza 7, the editions have grouped the lines in all sorts of ways, with, of course, various conjectures as to where lines may have been lost.

7. After line 1 the manuscript has only four words: "cloth," "black," "named," and "Thræll." No gap is anywhere indicated. Editors have pieced out the passage in various ways. *Water*, etc.: concerning the custom of sprinkling water on children, which long antedated the introduction of Christianity, cf. *Hovamol*, 159 and note. *Black*: dark hair, among the blond Scandinavians, was the mark of a foreigner, hence of a slave. *Thræll*: Thrall or Slave.

8. In the manuscript line 1 of stanza 9 stands before stanza 8, neither line being capitalized as the beginning of a stanza. I have followed Bugge's rearrangement. The manuscript indicates no gap in line 2, but nearly all editors have assumed one, Grundtvig supplying "and rough his nails."

9. The manuscript marks line 2 as the beginning of a stanza.]

[10. A line may well have dropped out, but the manuscript is too uncertain as to the stanza-divisions to make any guess safe. *Crooked*: the word in the original is obscure. *Stained*: literally, "water was on her soles." *Thir*: "Serving-Woman."

12. There is some confusion as to the arrangement of th lines and division into stanzas of 12 and 13. The names mean: *Fjosnir*, "Cattle-Man"; *Klur*, "The Coarse"; *Hreim*, "The Shouter"; *Kleggi*, "The Horse-Fly"; *Kefsir*, "Concubine-Keeper"; *Fulnir*, "The Stinking"; *Drumb*, "The Log"; *Digraldi*, "The Fat"; *Drott*, "The Sluggard"; *Leggjaldi*, "The Big-Legged"; *Lut*, "The Bent"; *Hosvir*, "The Grey."]

[13. The names mean: *Drumba*, "The Log"; *Kumba*, "The Stumpy"; *Ökkvinkalfa*, "Fat-Legged"; *Arinnefla*, "Homely Nosed"; *Ysja*, "The Noisy"; *Ambott*, "The Servant"; *Eikintjasna*, "The Oaken Peg" (?); *Totrughypja*, "Clothed in Rags"; *Tronubeina*, "Crane-Legged."

14. In the manuscript line 4 stands after line 4 of stanza 16, but several editors have rearranged the lines, as here. *Afi and Amma*: Grandfather and Grandmother.

15. There is considerable confusion among the editors as to where this stanza begins and ends.

16. The manuscript marks line 3 as the beginning of a stanza.]

[17. The manuscript jumps from stanza 17, line I, to stanza 19, line 2. Bugge points out that the copyist's eye was presumably led astray by the fact that 17, I, and 19, I, were identical. Lines 2-3 of 17 are supplied from stanzas 3 and 29.

18. I have followed Bugge's conjectural construction of the missing stanza, taking lines 2 and 3 from stanzas 31 and 4.

19. The manuscript marks line 2 as the beginning of a stanza.

20. The manuscript omits line 2, supplied by analogy with stanza 6.]

[21. Most editors assume a lacuna, after either line 2 or line 3. Sijmons assumes, on the analogy of stanza 8, that a complete stanza describing *Karl* ("Yeoman") has been lost between stanzas 21 and 22.

22. No line indicated in the manuscript as beginning a stanza. *Cart*: the word in the original, "kartr," is one of the clear signs of the Celtic influence noted in the introduction.

23. *Bring*: the word literally means "drove in a wagon"--a mark of the bride's social status. *Snör*: "Daughter-in-Law." Bugge, followed by several editors, maintains that line 4 was wrongly interpolated here from a missing stanza describing the marriage of Kon.

24. No line indicated in the manuscript as beginning a stanza. The names mean: *Hal*, "Man"; *Dreng*, "The Strong"; *Holth*, "The Holder of Land"; *Thegn*, "Freeman"; *Smith*, "Craftsman"; *Breith*, "The Broad-Shouldered"; *Bondi*, "Yeoman"; *Bundinskeggi*, "With Beard Bound" (i.e., not allowed to hang unkempt); *Bui*, "Dwelling-Owner"; *Boddi*, "Farm-Holder"; *Brattskegg*, "With Beard Carried High"; *Segg*, "Man."]

[25. No line indicated in the manuscript as beginning a stanza. The names mean: *Snot*, "Worthy Woman"; *Bruth*, "Bride"; *Svanni*, "The Slender"; *Svarri*, "The Proud"; *Sprakki*, "The Fair"; *Fljoth*, "Woman" (?); *Sprund*, "The Proud"; *Vif*, "Wife"; *Feima*, "The Bashful"; *Ristil*, "The Graceful."

26. Many editors make a stanza out of line 4 and lines 1-2 of the following stanza. *Strewn*: with fresh straw in preparation for a feast; cf.*Thrymskvitha*, 22.

27. *Fathir and Mothir*: Father and Mother. Perhaps lines 3-4 should form a stanza with 28, 1-3.

28. Bugge thinks lines 5-6, like 23, 4, got in here from the lost stanzas describing Kon's bride and his marriage.]

[31. The manuscript of lines 1-3 is obviously defective, as there are too many words for two lines, and not enough for the full three. The meaning, however, is clearly very much as indicated in the translation. Gering's emendation, which I have followed, consists simply in shifting "set before them" from the first line to the second--where the manuscript has no verb,--and supplying the verb "brought" in line 1. The various editions contain all sorts of suggestions.

32. The manuscript begins both line 1 and line 2 with a capital [fp. 212] preceded by a period, which has led to all sorts of strange stanza-combinations and guesses at lost lines in the various editions. The confusion includes stanza 33, wherein no line is marked in the manuscript as beginning a stanza.]

[34. *Jarl*: "Nobly-Born."

35. Various lines have been regarded as interpolations, 3 and 6 being most often thus rejected.

36. Lines I, 2, and 5 all begin with capitals preceded by periods, a fact which, taken in conjunction with the obviously defective state of the following stanza, has led to all sorts of conjectural emendations. The exact significance of Rig's

giving his own name to Jarl (cf. stanza 46), and thus recognizing him, potentially at least, as a king, depends on the conditions under [fp. 213] which the poem was composed (cf. Introductory Note). The whole stanza, particularly the reference to the teaching of magic (runes), fits Othin far better than Heimdall.]

[37. Something--one or two lines, or a longer passage--has clearly been lost, describing the beginning of Jarl's journey. Yet many editors, relying on the manuscript punctuation, make 37 and 38 into a single stanza.

39. The manuscript marks both lines 1 and 2 as beginning stanzas.

40. *Hersir*: "Lord"; the hersir was, in the early days before the establishment of a kingdom in Norway, the local chief, and [fp. 214] hence the highest recognized authority. During and after the time of Harald the Fair-Haired the name lost something of its distinction, the hersir coming to take rank below the jarl. *Erna*: "The Capable."]

[42. The names mean: *Bur*, "Son"; *Barn*, "Child"; *Joth*, "Child"; *Athal*, "Offspring"; *Arfi*, "Heir"; *Mog*, "Son"; *Nith*, "Descendant"; *Svein*, "Boy"; *Sun*, "Son"; *Nithjung*, "Descend ant"; *Kund*, "Kinsman"; *Kon*, "Son" (of noble birth). Concerning the use made of this last name, see note on stanza 44. It is curious that there is no list of the daughters of Jarl and Erna, and accordingly Vigfusson inserts here the names listed in stanza 25. Grundtvig rearranges the lines of stanzas 42 and 43.

44. The manuscript indicates no line as beginning a stanza. Kon the Young: a remarkable bit of fanciful etymology; the [fp. 215] phrase is "Konr ungr," which could readily be contracted into "Konungr," the regular word meaning "king." The "kon" part is actually not far out, but the second syllable of "konungr" has nothing to do with "ungr" meaning "young." *Runes*: a long list of just such magic charms, dulling swordblades, quenching flames, and so on, is given in *Hovamol*, 147-163]

[45. The manuscript indicates no line as beginning a stanza. *Minds*: possibly "seas,'" the word being doubtful. Most editors assume the gap as indicated.

4.6. The manuscript indicates no line as beginning a stanza *Rig-Jarl*: Kon's father; cf stanza 36.

47. This stanza has often been combined with 48, either as a whole or in part. *Crow*: birds frequently play the part of mentor in Norse literature; cf., for example, *Helgakvitha Hundingsbana* I, 5, and *Fafnismol*, 32.]

[48. This fragment is not indicated as a separate stanza in the manuscript. Perhaps half a line has disappeared, or, as seems more likely, the gap includes two lines and a half. Sijmons actually constructs these lines, largely on the basis of stanzas 35 and 38, Bugge fills in the half-line lacuna as indicated above with "The sword to wield."

49. *Dan and Danp*: These names are largely responsible for the theory that the *Rigsthula* was composed in Denmark. According to the Latin epitome of the *Skjöldungasaga* by Arngrimur Jonsson, "Rig (Rigus) was a man not the least among the great ones of his time. He married the daughter of a certain Danp, lord of Danpsted, whose name was Dana; and later, having won the royal title for his province, left as his heir his son by Dana, called Dan or Danum, all of whose subjects were called Danes." This may or may not be conclusive, and it is a great pity that the manuscript breaks off abruptly at this stanza.]

HYNDLULJOTH

The Poem of Hyndla

INTRODUCTORY NOTE

The Hyndluljoth is found in neither of the great manuscripts of the Poetic Edda, but is included in the so-called *Flateyjarbok* (Book of the Flat Island), an enormous compilation made some where about 1400. The lateness of this manuscript would of itself be enough to cast a doubt upon the condition in which the poem has been preserved, and there can be no question that what we have of it is in very poor shape. It is, in fact, two separate poems, or parts of them, clumsily put together. The longer one, the *Poem of Hyndla* proper, is chiefly a collection of names, not strictly mythological but belonging to the semi-historical hero-sagas of Norse tradition. The wise-woman, Hyndla, being asked by Freyja to trace the ancestry of her favorite, Ottar, for the purpose of deciding a wager, gives a complex genealogy including many of the heroes who appear in the popular sagas handed down from days long before the Icelandic settlements. The poet was learned, but without enthusiasm; it is not likely that he composed the *Hyndluljoth* much before the twelfth century, though the material of which it is compounded must have been very much older. Although the genealogies are essentially continental, the poem seems rather like a product of the archæological period of Iceland.

Inserted bodily in the *Hyndluljoth* proper is a fragment of fifty-one lines, taken from a poem of which, by a curious chance, we know the name. Snorri quotes one stanza of it, calling it "the short *Voluspo*." The fragment preserved gives, of course, no indication of the length of the original poem, but it shows that it was a late and very inferior imitation of the great *Voluspo*. Like the Hyndluljoth proper, it apparently comes from the twelfth century; but there is nothing whatever to indicate that the two poems were

192

the work of the same man, or were ever connected in any way until some blundering copyist mixed them up. Certainly the connection did not exist in the middle of the thirteenth century, when Snorri quoted "the short *Voluspo*."

Neither poem is of any great value, either as mythology or as poetry. The author of "the short *Voluspo*" seems, indeed, to have been more or less confused as to his facts; and both poets were too late to feel anything of the enthusiasm of the earlier school. The names of Hyndla's heroes, of course, suggest an unlimited number of stories, but as most of these have no direct relation to the poems of the *Edda*, I have limited the notes to a mere record of who the persons mentioned were, and the saga-groups in which they appeared.

Freyja spake:
1. "Maiden, awake! | wake thee, my friend,
My sister Hyndla, | in thy hollow cave!
Already comes darkness, | and ride must we
To Valhall to seek | the sacred hall.

2. "The favor of Heerfather | seek we to find,
To his followers gold | he gladly gives;
To Hermoth gave he | helm and mail-coat,
And to Sigmund he gave | a sword as gift.

3. "Triumph to some, | and treasure to others,
To many wisdom | and skill in words,
Fair winds to the sailor, | to the singer his art,
And a manly heart | to many a hero.

4. "Thor shall I honor, | and this shall I ask,
That his favor true | mayst thou ever find;
. . . .
Though little the brides | of the giants he loves.

5. "From the stall now | one of thy wolves lead forth,
And along with my boar | shalt thou let him run;
For slow my boar goes | on the road of the gods,
And I would not weary | my worthy steed."

Hyndla spake:
6. "Falsely thou askest me, | Freyja, to go,
For so in the glance | of thine eyes I see;
On the way of the slain | thy lover goes with thee.
Ottar the young, | the son of Instein."

Freyja spake:
7. "Wild dreams, methinks, | are thine when thou sayest
My lover is with me | on the way of the slain;
There shines the boar | with bristles of gold,
Hildisvini, | he who was made
By Dain and Nabbi, | the cunning dwarfs.

8. "Now let us down | from our saddles leap,
And talk of the race | of the heroes twain;
The men who were born | of the gods above,
. . . .

9. "A wager have made | in the foreign metal
Ottar the young | and Angantyr;
We must guard, for the hero | young to have,
His father's wealth, | the fruits of his race.

10. "For me a shrine | of stones he made,--
And now to glass | the rock has grown;--
Oft with the blood | of beasts was it red;
In the goddesses ever | did Ottar trust.

11. "Tell to me now | the ancient names,
And the races of all | that were born of old:
Who are of the Skjoldungs, | who of the Skilfings,

194

Who of the Othlings, | who of the Ylfings,
Who are the free-born, | who are the high-born,
The noblest of men | that in Mithgarth dwell?"

Hyndla spake:
12. "Thou art, Ottar, | the son of Instein,
And Instein the son | of Alf the Old,
Alf of Ulf, | Ulf of Sæfari,
And Sæfari's father | was Svan the Red.

13. "Thy mother, bright | with bracelets fair,
Hight, methinks, | the priestess Hledis;
Frothi her father, | and Friaut her mother;--
Her race of the mightiest | men must seem.

14. "Of old the noblest | of all was Ali,
Before him Halfdan, | foremost of Skjoldungs;
Famed were the battles | the hero fought,
To the corners of heaven | his deeds were carried.

15. "Strengthened by Eymund, | the strongest of men,
Sigtrygg he slew | with the ice-cold sword;
His bride was Almveig, | the best of women,
And eighteen boys | did Almveig bear him.

16. "Hence come the Skjoldungs, | hence the Skilfings,
Hence the Othlings, | hence the Ynglings,
Hence come the free-born, | hence the high-born,
The noblest of men | that in Mithgarth dwell:
And all are thy kinsmen, | Ottar, thou fool!

17. "Hildigun then | her mother hight,
The daughter of Svava | and Sækonung;
And all are thy kinsmen, | Ottar, thou fool!
It is much to know,-- | wilt thou hear yet more?

18. "The mate of Dag | was a mother of heroes,
Thora, who bore him | the bravest of fighters,
Frathmar and Gyrth | and the Frekis twain,
Am and Jofurmar, | Alf the Old;
It is much to know,-- | wilt thou hear yet more?

19. "Her husband was Ketil, | the heir of Klypp,
He was of thy mother | the mother's-father;
Before the days | of Kari was Frothi,
And horn of Hild | was Hoalf then.

20. "Next was Nanna, | daughter of Nokkvi,
Thy father's kinsman | her son became;
Old is the line, | and longer still,
And all are thy kinsmen, | Ottar, thou fool!

21. "Isolf and Osolf, | the sons of Olmoth,
Whose wife was Skurhild, | the daughter of Skekkil,
Count them among | the heroes mighty,
And all are thy kinsmen, | Ottar, thou fool!

22. "Gunnar the Bulwark, | Grim the Hardy,
Thorir the Iron-shield, | Ulf the Gaper,
Brodd and Hörvir | both did I know;
In the household they were | of Hrolf the Old.

23. "Hervarth, Hjorvarth, | Hrani, Angantyr,
Bui and Brami, | Barri and Reifnir,
Tind and Tyrfing, | the Haddings twain,--
And all are thy kinsmen, | Ottar, thou fool!

24. "Eastward in Bolm | were born of old
The sons of Arngrim | and Eyfura;
With berserk-tumult | and baleful deed
Like fire o'er land | and sea they fared,
And all are thy kinsmen, | Ottar, thou fool!

25. "The sons of Jormunrek | all of yore
To the gods in death | were as offerings given;
He was kinsman of Sigurth,-- | hear well what I say,--
The foe of hosts, | and Fafnir's slayer.

26., "From Volsung's seed | was the hero sprung,
And Hjordis was born | of Hrauthung's race,
And Eylimi | from the Othlings came,--
And all are thy kinsmen, | Ottar, thou fool!

27. "Gunnar and Hogni, | the heirs of Gjuki,
And Guthrun as well, | who their sister was;
But Gotthorm was not | of Gjuki's race,
Although the brother | of both he was:
And all are thy kinsmen, | Ottar, thou fool!

28. "Of Hvethna's sons | was Haki the best,
And Hjorvarth the father | of Hvethna was;

. . . .

29. "Harald Battle-tooth | of Auth was born,
Hrörek the Ring-giver | her husband was;
Auth the Deep-minded | was Ivar's daughter,
But Rathbarth the father | of Randver was:
And all are thy kinsmen, | Ottar, thou fool!"

*   *   *

Fragment of "The Short Voluspo"

30. Eleven in number | the gods were known,
When Baldr o'er the hill | of death was bowed;
And this to avenge | was Vali swift,
When his brother's slayer | soon he slew.

31. The father of Baldr | was the heir of Bur,

. . . .

32. Freyr's wife was Gerth, | the daughter of Gymir,
Of the giants' brood, | and Aurbotha bore her;
To these as well | was Thjazi kin,
The dark-loving giant; | his daughter was Skathi.

33. Much have I told thee, | and further will tell;
There is much that I know;-- | wilt thou hear yet more?

34. Heith and Hrossthjof, | the children of Hrimnir.

. . . .

35. The sybils arose | from Vitholf's race,
From Vilmeith all | the seers are,
And the workers of charms | are Svarthofthi's children,
And from Ymir sprang | the giants all.

36. Much have I told thee, | and further will tell;
There is much that I know;-- | wilt thou hear yet more?

37. One there was born | in the bygone days,
Of the race of the gods, | and great was his might;
Nine giant women, | at the world's edge,
Once bore the man | so mighty in arms.

38. Gjolp there bore him, | Greip there bore him,
Eistla bore him, | and Eyrgjafa,
Ulfrun bore him, | and Angeyja,
Imth and Atla, | and Jarnsaxa.

39. Strong was he made | with the strength of earth,
With the ice-cold sea, | and the blood of swine.

40. One there was born, | the best of all,
And strong was he made | with the strength of earth;
The proudest is called | the kinsman of men
Of the rulers all | throughout the world.

41. Much have I told thee, | and further will tell;
There is much that I know;-- | wilt thou hear yet more?

42. The wolf did Loki | with Angrbotha win,
And Sleipnir bore he | to Svathilfari;
The worst of marvels | seemed the one
That sprang from the brother | of Byleist then.

43. A heart ate Loki,-- | in the embers it lay,
And half-cooked found he | the woman's heart;--
With child from the woman | Lopt soon was,
And thence among men | came the monsters all.

44. The sea, storm-driven, | seeks heaven itself,
O'er the earth it flows, | the air grows sterile;
Then follow the snows | and the furious winds,
For the gods are doomed, | and the end is death.

45. Then comes another, | a greater than all,
Though never I dare | his name to speak;
Few are they now | that farther can see
Than the moment when Othin | shall meet the wolf.

*   *   *

Freyja spake:
46. "To my boar now bring | the memory-beer,
So that all thy words, | that well thou hast spoken,
The third morn hence | he may hold in mind,
When their races Ottar | and Angantyr tell."

Hyndla spake:
47. "Hence shalt thou fare, | for fain would I sleep,
From me thou gettest | few favors good;
My noble one, out | in the night thou leapest
As. Heithrun goes | the goats among.

48. "To Oth didst thou run, | who loved thee ever,
And many under | thy apron have crawled;
My noble one, out | in the night thou leapest,
As Heithrun goes | the goats among."

Freyja spake:
49. "Around the giantess | flames shall I raise,
So that forth unburned | thou mayst not fare."

Hyndla spake:
50. "Flames I see burning, | the earth is on fire,
And each for his life | the price must lose;
Bring then to Ottar | the draught of beer,
Of venom full | for an evil fate."

Freyja spake:
51. "Thine evil words | shall work no ill,
Though, giantess, bitter | thy baleful threats;
A drink full fair | shall Ottar find,
If of all the gods | the favor I get."

[1. Freyja: The names of the speakers do not appear in the manuscripts. On Freyja cf. *Voluspo*, 21 and note; *Skirnismol*, introductory prose and note; *Lokasenna*, introductory prose and note. As stanzas 9-10 show, Ottar has made a wager of his entire inheritance with Angantyr regarding the relative loftiness of their ancestry, and by rich offerings (Hyndla hints at less commendable methods) has induced Freyja to assist him in establishing his genealogy. Freyja, having turned Ottar for purposes of disguise into a boar, calls on the giantess Hyndla ("She-Dog") to aid her. Hyndla does not appear elsewhere in the poems.

2. *Heerfather*: Othin; cf. *Voluspo*, 30. Hermoth: mentioned in the *Prose Edda* as a son of Othin who is sent to Hel to ask for the return of the slain Baldr. *Sigmund*: according to the *Volsungasaga* Sigmund was the son of Volsung, and hence Othin's great-great-grandson (note that Wagner eliminates all the intervening generations by the simple expedient of using [fp. 219] Volsung's name as one of Othin's many appellations). Sigmund alone was able to draw from the tree the sword which a mysterious stranger (Othin, of course) had thrust into it (compare the first act of Wagner's *Die Walküre).*]

[3. Sijmons suggests that this stanza may be an interpolation.

4. No lacuna after line 2 is indicated in the manuscript. Editors have attempted various experiments in rearranging this and the following stanza.

5. Some editors, following Simrock, assign this whole stanza to Hyndla; others assign to her lines 3-4. Giving the entire stanza to Freyja makes better sense than any other arrangement, but is dependent on changing the manuscript's "thy" in line 3 to "my", as suggested by Bugge. The boar on which Freyja rides ("my worthy steed") is, of course, Ottar.

6. Hyndla detects Ottar, and accuses Freyja of having her [fp. 220] lover with her. Unless Ottar is identical with Oth (cf. Voluspo, 25 and note), which seems most unlikely, there is no other reference to this love affair. *The way of the slain*: the road to Valhall.]

[7. Various experiments have been made in condensing the stanza into four lines, or in combining it with stanza 8. *Hildisvini* ("Battle-Swine"): perhaps Freyja refers to the boar with golden bristles given, according to Snorri, to her brother Freyr by the dwarfs. *Dain*: a dwarf; cf. *Voluspo*, 11. *Nabbi*: a dwarf nowhere else mentioned.

8. The first line is obviously corrupt in the manuscript, and has been variously emended. The general assumption is that in the interval between stanzas 7 and 8 Freyja and Hyndla have arrived at Valhall. No lacuna is indicated in the manuscript.

9. *Foreign metal*: gold. The word *valr*, meaning "foreign," [fp. 221] and akin to "Welsh," is interesting in this connection, and some editors interpret it frankly as "Celtic," i.e., Irish.]

[10. *To glass*: i.e., the constant fires on the altar have fused the stone into glass. Glass beads, etc., were of very early use, though the use of glass for windows probably did not begin in Iceland much before 1200.

11. Possibly two stanzas, or perhaps one with interpolations. The manuscript omits the first half of line 4, here filled out from stanza 16, line 2.*Skjoldungs*: the descendants of Skjold, a mythical king who was Othin's son and the ancestor of the Danish kings; cf. Snorri's *Edda,Skaldskaparmal*, 43. *Skilfings*: mentioned by Snorri as descendants of King Skelfir, a mythical ruler in "the East." In *Grimnismol*, 54, the name Skilfing appears as one of Othin's many appellations. *Othlings*: Snorri derives this race from Authi, the son of Halfdan the Old (cf. stanza 14).*Ylfings*: some editors have changed this to "Ynglings," as in stanza 16, referring to the descendants of Yng or Yngvi, another son of Halfdan, but the reference may be to the same mythical family to which Helgi Hundingsbane belonged (cf. *Helgakvitha Hundingsbana* I, 5).]

[12. *Instein*: mentioned in the *Halfssaga* as one of the warriors of King Half of Horthaland (the so-called Halfsrekkar). The others mentioned in this stanza appear in one of the later mythical accounts of the settlement of Norway.

14. Stanzas 14-16 are clearly interpolated, as Friaut (stanza 13, line S) is the daughter of Hildigun (stanza 17, line 1). *Halfdan* the Old, a mythical king of Denmark, called by Snorri "the most famous of all kings," of whom it was foretold that "for three hundred years there should be no woman and no man in his line who was not of great repute." After the. slaying of Sigtrygg he married Almveig (or Alvig), daughter of King Eymund of Holmgarth (i.e., Russia), who bore him eighteen [fp. 223] sons, nine at one birth. These nine were all slain, but the other nine were traditionally the ancestors of the most famous families in Northern hero lore.]

[16. Compare stanza 11. All or part of this stanza may be interpolated.

17. *Hildigun* (or Hildiguth): with this the poem returns to Ottar's direct ancestry, Hildigun being Friaut's mother. *Line 4*: cf. the refrain-line in the *Voluspo* (stanzas 27, 29, etc.).

18. Another interpolation, as Ketil (stanza 19, line 1) is the husband of Hildigun (stanza 17). *Dag*: one of Halfdan's sons, and ancestor of the Döglings. Line 5 may be a late addition.

19. *Ketil*: the semi-mythical Ketil Hortha-Kari, from whom various Icelandic families traced their descent. *Hoalf*: probably King Half of Horthaland, hero of the Halfssaga, and son of Hjorleif and Hild (cf. stanza 12, note).]

[20. *Nanna*: the manuscript has "Manna." Of Nanna and her father, Nokkvi, we know nothing, but apparently Nanna's son married a sister of Instein, Ottar's father.

21. *Olmoth*: one of the sons of Ketil Hortha-Kari. *Line 4*: here, and generally hereafter when it appears in the poem, this refrain-line is abbreviated in the manuscript to the word "all."

22. An isolated stanza, which some editors place after stanza 24, others combining lines 1-2 with the fragmentary stanza 23 In the manuscript lines 3-4 stand after stanza 24, where they fail to connect clearly with anything. *Hrolf the Old*: probably King Hrolf Gautreksson of Gautland, in the saga relating to whom (*Fornaldar sögur* III, 57 ff.) appear the names of Thorir the iron-shield and Grim Thorkelsson.]

[23. Stanzas 23 and 24 name the twelve Berserkers, the sons of Arngrim and Eyfura, the story of whom is told in the *Hervararsaga* and the *Orvar-Oddssaga*. Saxo Grammaticus tells of the battle between them and Hjalmar and Orvar-Odd. Line 1 does not appear in the manuscript, but is added from the list of names given in the sagas. The Berserkers were wild warriors, distinguished above all by the fits of frenzy to which they were subject in battle; during these fits they howled like wild beasts, foamed at the mouth, and gnawed the iron rims of their shields. At such times they were proof against steel or fire, but when the fever abated they were weak. The etymology of the word berserk is disputed; probably, however, it means "bear-shirt."

24. The manuscript omits the first half of line I, here supplied from the *Orvar-Oddssaga*. *Bolm*: probably the island of Bolmsö, in the Swedish province of Smaland. In the manuscript and in most editions stanza 24 is followed by lines 3-4 of stanza 22. Some editors reject line 5 as spurious.

25. In the manuscript line 1 stands after line 4 of stanza 29. Probably a stanza enumerating Jormunrek's sons has been lost. Many editors combine lines 3-4 of stanza 22 and lines 2-4 of [fp. 226] stanza 25 into one stanza. *Jormunrek*: the historical Ermanarich, king of the Goths, who died about 376. According to Norse tradition, in which Jormunrek played a large part, he slew his own sons (cf. *Guthrunarhvot* and *Hamthesmol*). In the saga Jormunrek married Sigurth's daughter, Svanhild. Stanzas 25-27 connect Ottar's descent with the whole

Volsung-Sigurth-Jormunrek-Gjuki genealogy. The story of Sigurth is the basis for most of the heroic poems of the Edda, of the famous *Volsungasaga*, and, in Germany, of the *Nibelungenlied*. On his battle with the dragon *Fafnir* cf. *Fafnismol*.]

[26. *Volsung*: Sigurth's grandfather and Othin's great-grand son. *Hjordis*: daughter of King Eylimi, wife of Sigmund and mother of Sigurth. *Othlings*: cf. stanza 11.

27. *Gunnar*, *Hogni*, and *Guthrun*: the three children of the Burgundian king *Gjuki* and his wife Grimhild (Kriemhild); Guthrun was Sigurth's wife. *Gotthorm*, the third brother, who killed Sigurth at Brynhild's behest, was Grimhild's son, and thus a step-son of Gjuki. These four play an important part in the heroic cycle of Eddic poems. Cf. *Gripisspo*, introductory note.]

[28. In the manuscript and in many editions these two lines stand between stanzas 33 and 34. The change here made follows Bugge. The manuscript indicates no gap between stanzas 27 and 29. *Hvethna*: wife of King Halfdan of Denmark.

29. The manuscript and many editions include line 1 of stanza 25 after line 4 of stanza 29. The story of *Harald Battle-tooth* is told in detail by Saxo Grammaticus. Harald's father was *Hrörek*, king of Denmark; his mother was *Auth*, daughter of *Ivar*, king of Sweden. After Ivar had treachreously detroyed {*sic* Hrörek, Auth fled with Harald to Russia, where she married King *Rathbarth*. Harald's warlike career in Norway, and his death on the Bravalla-field at the hands of his nephew, Sigurth Ring, son of Randver and grandson of Rathbarth and Auth, were favorite saga themes.

30. At this point begins the fragmentary and interpolated "short *Voluspo*" identified by Snorri. The manuscript gives no indication of the break in the poem's continuity. *Eleven*: there [fp. 228] are various references to the "twelve" gods (including Baldr) Snorri (*Gylfaginning*, 20-33) lists the following twelve in addition to Othin: Thor, Baldr, Njorth, Freyr, Tyr, Bragi, Heimdall, Hoth, Vithar, Vali, Ull and Forseti; he adds Loki as of doubtful divinity. Baldr and Vali: cf. *Voluspo*, 32-33.]}

[31. The fragmentary stanzas 31-34 have been regrouped in various ways, and with many conjectures as to omissions, none of which are indicated in the manuscript. The order here is as in the manuscript, except that lines 1-2 of stanza 28 have been transposed from after line 2 of stanza 33. *Bur's heir*: Othin; cf. *Voluspo*, 4.

32. *Freyr, Gerth, Gymir*: cf. *Skirnismol. Aurbotha*: a giantess, mother of Gerth. *Thjazi and Skathi*: cf. *Lokasenna*, 49, and Harbarthsljoth, 19. 33. Cf. Voluspo, 44 and 27.

34. *Heith* ("Witch") and *Hrossthjof* ("Horse-thief"): the only other reference to the giant *Hrimnir* (*Skirnismol*, 28) makes no mention of his children.]

[35. This stanza is quoted by Snorri (*Gylfaginning*, 5). Of *Vitholf* ("Forest Wolf'), *Vilmeith* ("Wish-Tree") and *Svarthofthi* ("Black Head") nothing further is known. Ymir: cf. *Voluspo*, 3.

37. According to Snorri (*Gylfaginning*, 27) Heimdall was the son of Othin and of nine sisters. As Heimdall was the watch man of the gods, this has given rise to much "solar myth" discussion. The names of his nine giantess mothers are frequently said to denote attributes of the sea.

38. The names of Heimdall's mothers may be rendered "Yelper," "Griper," "Foamer," "Sand-Strewer," "She-Wolf," "Sorrow-Whelmer," "Dusk," "Fury," and "Iron-Sword."]

[39. It has been suggested that these lines were interpolated from *Guthrunarkvitha* II, 22. Some editors add the refrain of stanza 36. *Swine's blood*: to Heimdall's strength drawn from earth and sea was added that derived from sacrifice.

40. In the manuscript this stanza stands after stanza 44. Regarding Heimdall's kinship to the three great classes of men, cf. *Rigsthula*, introductory note, wherein the apparent confusion of his attributes with those of Othin is discussed.

42. Probably a lacuna before this stanza. Regarding the wolf Fenrir, born of Loki and the giantess *Angrbotha*, cf. *Voluspo*, 39 and note.*Sleipnir*: Othin's eight-legged horse, born of the stallion *Svathilfari* and of Loki in the guise of a mare (cf. *Grimnismol*, 44). *The worst*: doubtless referring to Mithgarthsorm, another child of Loki. *The brother of Byleist*: Loki; cf. *Voluspo*, 51.]

[43. Nothing further is known of the myth here referred to, wherein Loki (Lopt) eats the cooked heart of a woman and thus himself gives birth to a monster. The reference is not likely to be to the serpent, as, according to Snorri (*Gylfaginning*, 34), the wolf, the serpent, and Hel were all the children of Loki and Angrbotha.

44. Probably an omission, perhaps of considerable length, before this stanza. For the description of the destruction of the world, cf. *Voluspo*, 57.

45. Cf. *Voluspo*, 65, where the possible reference to Christianity is noted. With this stanza the fragmentary "short *Voluspo*" ends, and the dialogue between Freyja and Hyndla continues.

46. Freyja now admits the identity of her boar as Ottar, who [fp. 232] with the help of the "memory-beer" is to recall the entire genealogy he has just heard, and thus win his wager with Angantyr.]

[47. *Heithrun*: the she-goat that stands by Valhall (cf. *Grimnismol*, 25), the name being here used simply of she-goats in general, in caustic comment on Freyja's morals. Of these Loki entertained a similar view; cf. *Lokasenna*, 30.

48. *Oth*: cf. stanza 6 and note, and *Voluspo*, 25 and note. Lines 3-4, abbreviated in the manuscript, are very likely repeated here by mistake.

49. The manuscript repeats once again lines 3-4 of stanza 47 as the last two lines of this stanza. It seems probable that two lines have been lost, to the effect that Freyja will burn the giantess alive "If swiftly now | thou dost not seek, / And hither bring | the memory-beer."]

SVIPDAGSMOL

The Ballad of Svipdag

INTRODUCTORY NOTE

The two poems, *Grougaldr* (*Groa's Spell*) and *Fjolsvinnsmol* (the *Ballad of Fjolsvith*), which many editors have, very wisely, united under the single title of Svipdagsmol, are found only in paper manuscripts, none of them antedating the seventeenth century. Everything points to a relatively late origin for the poems: their extensive use of "kennings" or poetical circumlocutions, their romantic spirit, quite foreign to the character of the unquestionably older poems, the absence of any reference to them in the earlier documents, the frequent errors in mythology, and, finally, the fact that the poems appear to have been preserved in unusually good condition. Whether or not a connecting link of narrative verse joining the two parts has been lost is an open question; on the whole it seems likely that the story was sufficiently well known so that the reciter of the poem (or poems) merely filled in the gap with a brief prose summary in pretty much his own words. The general relationship between dialogue and narrative in the Eddic poems is discussed in the introductory note to the *Grimnismol*, in connection with the use of prose links.

The love story of Svipdag and Mengloth is not referred to elsewhere in the *Poetic Edda*, nor does Snorri mention it; however, Groa, who here appears as Svipdag's mother, is spoken of by Snorri as a wise woman, the wife of Orvandil, who helps Thor with her magic charms. On the other hand, the essence of the story, the hero's winning of a bride ringed about by flames, is strongly suggestive of parts of the Sigurth-Brynhild traditions. Whether or not it is to be regarded as a nature or solar myth depends entirely on one's view of the whole "solar myth" school of criticism, not so highly esteemed today as formerly; such an interpretation is certainly not necessary to explain what is, under any circumstances, a very charming romance told, in the main, with dramatic effectiveness.

In later years the story of Svipdag and Mengloth became popular throughout the North, and was made the subject of many Danish and Swedish as well as Norwegian ballads. These have greatly assisted in the reconstruction of the outlines of the narrative surrounding the dialogue poems here given.

I. GROUGALDR

GROA'S SPELL

Svipdag spake:
1. "Wake thee, Groa! | wake, mother good!
At the doors of the dead I call thee;
Thy son, bethink thee, | thou badst to seek
Thy help at the hill of death."

Groa spake:
2. "What evil vexes | mine only son,
What baleful fate hast thou found,
That thou callest thy mother, | who lies in the mould,
And the world of the living has left?"

Svipdag spake:
3. "The woman false | whom my father embraced
Has brought me a baleful game;
For she bade me go forth | where none may fare,
And Mengloth the maid to seek."

Groa spake:
4. "Long is the way, | long must thou wander,

But long is love as well;
Thou mayst find, perchance, | what thou fain wouldst have,
If the fates their favor will give."

Svipdag spake:
5. "Charms full good | then chant to me, mother,
And seek thy son to guard;
For death do I fear | on the way I shall fare,
And in years am I young, methinks."

Groa spake:
6. "Then first I will chant thee | the charm oft-tried,
That Rani taught to Rind;
From the shoulder whate'er | mislikes thee shake,
For helper thyself shalt thou have.

7. "Then next I will chant thee, | if needs thou must travel,
And wander a purposeless way:
The bolts of Urth | shall on every side
Be thy guards on the road thou goest.

8. "Then third I will chant thee, | if threatening streams
The danger of death shall bring:
Yet to Hel shall turn | both Horn and Ruth,
And before thee the waters shall fail.

9. "Then fourth I will chant thee, | if come thy foes
On the gallows-way against thee:
Into thine hands | shall their hearts be given,
And peace shall the warriors wish.

10. "Then fifth I will chant thee, | if fetters perchance
Shall bind thy bending limbs:
O'er thy thighs do I chant | a loosening-charm,
And the lock is burst from the limbs,
And the fetters fall from the feet.

11. "Then sixth I will chant thee, | if storms on the sea
Have might unknown to man:
Yet never shall wind | or wave do harm,
And calm is the course of thy boat.

12. "Then seventh I chant thee, | if frost shall seek
To kill thee on lofty crags:
The fatal cold | shall not grip thy flesh,
And whole thy body shall be.

13. "Then eighth will I chant thee, | if ever by night
Thou shalt wander on murky ways:
Yet never the curse | of a Christian woman
From the dead shall do thee harm.

14. "Then ninth will I chant thee, | if needs thou must strive
With a warlike giant in words:
Thy heart good store | of wit shall have,
And thy mouth of words full wise.

15. "Now fare on the way | where danger waits,
Let evils not lessen thy love!
I have stood at the door | of the earth-fixed stones,
The while I chanted thee charms.

16. "Bear hence, my son, | what thy mother hath said,
And let it live in thy breast;
Thine ever shall be the | best of fortune,
So long as my words shall last."

II. FJOLMINNSMOL

THE LAY OF FJOLSVITH

17. Before the house | he beheld one coming
To the home of the giants high.

Svipdag spake:
"What giant is here, | in front of the house,
And around him fires are flaming?"

Fjolsvith spake:
3. "What seekest thou here? | for what is thy search?
What, friendless one, fain wouldst thou know?
By the ways so wet | must thou wander hence,
For, weakling, no home hast thou here."

Svipdag spake:
19. "What giant is here, | in front of the house,
To the wayfarer welcome denying?"

Fjolsvith spake:
"Greeting full fair | thou never shalt find,
So hence shalt thou get thee home.

20. "Fjolsvith am I, | and wise am I found,
But miserly am I with meat;
Thou never shalt enter | within the house,--
Go forth like a wolf on thy way!"

Svipdag spake:
21. "Few from the joy | of their eyes will go forth,
When the sight of their loves they seek;
Full bright are the gates | of the golden hall,
And a home shall I here enjoy."

Fjolsvith spake:
22. "Tell me now, fellow, | what father thou hast,
And the kindred of whom thou camst."

Svipdag spake:
"Vindkald am I, | and Varkald's son,
And Fjolkald his father was.

23. "Now answer me, Fjolsvith, | the question I ask,
For now the truth would I know:
Who is it that holds | and has for his own
The rule of the hall so rich?"

Fjolsvith spake:
224. "Mengloth is she, | her mother bore her
To the son of Svafrthorin;
She is it that holds | and has for her own
The rule of the hall so rich."

Svipdag spake:
25. "Now answer me, Fjolsvith, | the question I ask,
For now the truth would I know:
What call they the gate? | for among the gods
Ne'er saw man so grim a sight."

Fjolsvith spake:
26. "Thrymgjol they call it; | 'twas made by the three,
The sons of Solblindi;
And fast as a fetter | the farer it holds,
Whoever shall lift the latch."

Svipdag spake:
27. "Now answer me, Fjolsvith, | the question I ask,
For now the truth would I know:
What call they the house? | for no man beheld
'Mongst the gods so grim a sight."

Fjolsvith spake:
28. "Gastropnir is it, | of old I made it
From the limbs of Leirbrimir;

I braced it so strongly | that fast it shall stand
So long as the world shall last."

Svipdag spake:
29. "Now answer me, Fjolsvith, | the question I ask,
For now the truth would I know:
What call they the tree | that casts abroad
Its limbs o'er every land?"

Fjolsvith spake:
30. "Mimameith its name, | and no man knows
What root beneath it runs;
And few can guess | what shall fell the tree,
For fire nor iron shall fell it."

Svipdag spake:
31. "Now answer me, Fjolsvith, | the question I ask,
For now the truth would I know:
What grows from the seed | of the tree so great,
That fire nor iron shall fell?"

Fjolsvith spake:
32. "Women, sick | with child, shall seek
Its fruit to the flames to bear;
Then out shall come | what within was hid,
And so is it mighty with men."

Svipdag spake:
33. "Now answer me, Fjolsvith, | the question I ask,
For now the truth would I know:
What cock is he | on the highest bough,
That glitters all with gold?"

Fjolsvith spake:
34. "Vithofnir his name, | and now he shines
Like lightning on Mimameith's limbs;

And great is the trouble | with which he grieves
Both Surt and Sinmora."

Svipdag spake:
35. "Now answer me, Fjolsvith, | the question I ask,
For now the truth would I know:
What call they the hounds, | that before the house
So fierce and angry are?"

Fjolsvith spake:
36. "Gif call they one, | and Geri the other,
If now the truth thou wouldst know;
Great they are, | and their might will grow,
Till the gods to death are doomed."

Svipdag spake:
37. "Now answer me, Fjolsvith, | the question I ask,
For now the truth would I know:
May no man hope | the house to enter,
While the hungry hounds are sleeping?"

Fjolsvith spake:
38. "Together they sleep not, | for so was it fixed
When the guard to them was given;
One sleeps by night, | the next by day,
So no man may enter ever."

Svipdag spake:
39, "Now answer me, Fjolsvith, | the question I ask,
For now the truth would I know:
Is there no meat | that men may give them,
And leap within while they eat?"

Fjolsvith spake:
40. "Two wing-joints there be | in Vithofnir's body,
If now the truth thou wouldst know;

That alone is the meat | that men may give them,
And leap within while they eat."

Svipdag spake:
41. "Now answer me, Fjolsvith, | the question I ask,
For now the truth would I know:
What weapon can send | Vithofnir to seek
The house of Hel below?"

Fjolsvith spake:
42. "Lævatein is there, | that Lopt with runes
Once made by the doors of death;
In Lægjarn's chest | by Sinmora lies it,
And nine locks fasten it firm."

Svipdag spake:
43. "Now answer me, Fjolsvith, | the question I ask,
For now the truth would I know:
May a man come thence, | who thither goes,
And tries the sword to take?"

Fjolsvith spake:
44. "Thence may he come | who thither goes,
And tries the sword to take,
If with him he carries | what few can win,
To give to the goddess of gold."

Svipdag spake:
45. "Now answer me, Fjolsvith, | the question I ask,
For now the truth would I know:
What treasure is there | that men may take
To rejoice the giantess pale?"

Fjolsvith spake:
46. "The sickle bright | in thy wallet bear,
Mid Vithofnir's feathers found;

To Sinmora give it, | and then shall she grant
That the weapon by thee be won."

Svipdag spake:
47. "Now answer me, Fjolsvith, | the question I ask,
For now the truth would I know:
What call they the hall, | encompassed here
With flickering magic flames?"

Fjolsvith spake:
48. "Lyr is it called, | and long it shall
On the tip of a spear-point tremble;
Of the noble house | mankind has heard,
But more has it never known."

Svipdag spake:
49. "Now answer me, Fjolsvith, | the question I ask,
For now the truth would I know:
What one of the gods | has made so great
The hall I behold within?"

Fjolsvith spake:
50. "Uni and Iri, | Bari and Jari,
Var and Vegdrasil,
Dori and Ori, | Delling, and there
Was Loki, the fear of the folk."

Svipdag spake:
51. "Now answer me, Fjolsvith, | the question I ask,
For now the truth would I know:
What call they the mountain | on which the maid
Is lying so lovely to see?"

Fjolsvith spake:
52. "Lyfjaberg is it, | and long shall it be
A joy to the sick and the sore;

For well shall grow | each woman who climbs it,
Though sick full long she has lain."

Svipdag spake:
53. "Now answer me, Fjolsvith, | the question I ask,
For now the truth would I know:
What maidens are they | that at Mengloth's knees
Are sitting so gladly together?"

Fjolsvith spake:
54. "Hlif is one named, | Hlifthrasa another,
Thjothvara call they the third;
Bjort and Bleik, | Blith and Frith,
Eir and Aurbotha."

Svipdag spake:
55. "Now answer me, Fjolsvith, | the question I ask,
For now the truth would I know:
Aid bring they to all | who offerings give,
If need be found therefor?"

Fjolsvith spake:
56. "Soon aid they all | who offerings give
On the holy altars high;
And if danger they see | for the sons of men,
Then each from ill do they guard."

Svipdag spake:
57. "Now answer me, Fjolsvith, | the question I ask,
For now the truth would I know:
Lives there the man | who in Mengloth's arms
So fair may seek to sleep?"

Fjolsvith spake:
58. "No man there is | who in Mengloth's arms
So fair may seek to sleep,

Save Svipdag alone, | for the sun-bright maid
Is destined his bride to be."

Svipdag spake:
59. "Fling back the gates! | make the gateway wide!
Here mayst thou Svipdag see!
Hence get thee to find | if gladness soon
Mengloth to me will give."

Fjolsvith spake:
60. "Hearken, Mengloth, | a man is come;
Go thou the guest to see!
The hounds are fawning, | the house bursts open,--
Svipdag, methinks, is there."

Mengloth spake:
61. "On the gallows high | shall hungry ravens
Soon thine eyes pluck out,
If thou liest in saying | that here at last
The hero is come to my hall.

62. "Whence camest thou hither? | how camest thou here?
What name do thy kinsmen call thee?
Thy race and thy name | as a sign must I know,
That thy bride I am destined to be."

Svipdag spake:
63. "Svipdag am I, | and Solbjart's son;
Thence came I by wind-cold ways;

With the words of Urth | shall no man war,
Though unearned her gifts be given."

Mengloth spake:
64. "Welcome thou art, | for long have I waited;
The welcoming kiss shalt thou win!

For two who love | is the longed-for meeting
The greatest gladness of all.

65. "Long have I sat | on Lyfjaberg here,
Awaiting thee day by day;
And now I have | what I ever hoped,
For here thou art come to my hall.

66. "Alike we yearned; | I longed for thee,
And thou for my love hast longed;
But now henceforth | together we know
Our lives to the end we shall live."

[1. *Svipdag* ("Swift Day"): the names of the speakers are lacking in the manuscripts.

3. *The woman*: Svipdag's stepmother, who is responsible for [fp. 236] his search for *Mengloth* ("Necklace-Glad"). This name has suggested that Mengloth is really Frigg, possessor of the famous Brisings' necklace, or else Freyja (cf. *Lokasenna*, 20: note).]

[6. For this catalogue of charms (stanzas 6-14) cf. the *Ljothatal* (*Hovamol*, 147-165). *Rani and Rind*: the manuscripts, have these words in inverse relation; I have followed Neckel's emendation. Rind was the giantess who became the mother of Vali, Othin's son, the one-night-old avenger of Baldr (cf. *Voluspo*, 33-34, and *Baldrs Draumar*, 11 and note). Rani is presumably Othin, who, according to a skaldic poem, won Rind by magic.

7. Urth: one of the three Norns, or Fates; Cf. *Voluspo*, 20.]

[8. *Horn and Ruth*: these two rivers, here used merely to symbolize all dangerous streams, are not included in the catalogue of rivers given in*Grimnismol*, 27-29, for which reason some editors have changed the names to Hron and Hrith.

10. This stanza is a close parallel to *Hovamol*, 150, and the fifth line may well be an interpolation from line 4 of that stanza.]

[13. *A dead Christian woman*: this passage has distressed many editors, who have sought to emend the text so as to make it mean simply "a dead witch." The fact seems to be, however, that this particular charm was composed at a time when Christians were regarded by all conservative pagans as emissaries of darkness. A dead woman's curse would naturally be more potent, whether she was Christian or otherwise, than a living one's. Presumably this charm is much older than the poem in which it here stands.

16. At this point Groa's song ends, and Svipdag, thus fortified, goes to seek Mengloth. All the link that is needed between the poems is approximately this: "Then Svipdag searched long for [fp. 239] Mengloth, and at last he came to a great house set all about with flames. And before the house there was a giant."]

[17. Most editors have here begun a new series of stanza numbers, but if the *Grougaldr* and the *Fjolsvinnsmol* are to be considered, as a single poem, it seems more reasonable to continue the stanza numbers consecutively. Bugge thinks a stanza has been lost before 17, including Fjolsvith's name, so that the "he" in line 1 might have something to refer to. However, just such a prose link as I have suggested in the note on stanza 16 would serve the purpose. Editors have suggested various rearrange merits in the lines of stanzas 17-19. The substance, however, is clear enough. The giant *Fjolsvith* ("Much-Wise"), the warder of the house in which Mengloth dwells, sees Svipdag coming and stops him with the customary threats. The assignment of the [fp. 240] speeches in stanzas 17-20, in the absence of any indications in the manuscripts, is more or less guesswork.]

[22. *Vindkald* ("Wind-Cold"), *Varkald* ("Cold of Early Spring') and *Fjolkald* ("Much Cold"): Svipdag apparently seeks to persuade Fjolsvith that he belongs to the frost giants.]

[24. Svafrthorin: who he was, or what his name means, or who his son was, are all unknown.

26. *Thrymgjol* ("Loud-Clanging"): this gate, like the gate of the dead, shuts so fast as to trap those who attempt to use it (cf. *Sigurtharkvitha en skamma*, 68 and note). it was made by the dwarfs, sons of *Solblindi* ("Sun-Blinded"), the traditional crafts men, who could not endure the light of day.]

[28. *Gastropnir*: "quest-Crusher." *Leirbrimir's* ("Clay-Giant's") limbs: a poetic circumlocution for "clay"; cf. the description of the making of earth from the body of the giant Ymir, *Vafthruthnismol*, 21.

30. *Mimameith* ("Mimir's Tree"): the ash Yggdrasil, that overshadows the whole world. The well of Mimir was situated at its base; Cf. *Voluspo*, 27-29.]

[32. Gering suggests that two stanzas have been lost between stanzas 15 and 16, but the giant's answer fits the question quite well enough. The fruit of Yggdrasil, when cooked, is here assumed to have the power of assuring safe childbirth.

34. *Vithofnir* ("Tree-Snake"): apparently identical with either the cock Gollinkambi (cf. *Voluspo*, 43) or Fjalar (cf. *Voluspo*, 42), the former of which wakes the gods to battle, and the latter the giants. *Surt*: the giant mentioned in *Voluspo*, 52, as ruler of the fire-world; here used to represent the giants in general, who are constantly in terror of the cock's eternal watchfulness. *Sinmora*: presumably Surt's wife, the giantess who possesses the weapon by which alone the cock Vithofnir may be slain.]

[35. The last two lines have been variously emended.

36. *Gif* and *Geri*: both names signify "Greedy." The first part of line 3 is conjectural; the manuscripts indicate the word "eleven," which clearly fails to make sense.]

[42. *Lævetein* ("Wounding Wand"): the manuscripts differ as to the form of this name. The suggestion that the reference is to the mistletoe with which Baldr was killed seems hardly reason able. *Lopt*: Loki. *Lægjarn* ("Lover of Ill"): Loki; cf. *Voluspo*, 35, [fp. 246] where the term appears as an adjective applied to Loki. This is Falk's emendation for the manuscripts' "Sægjarn," meaning "Sea Lover." *Sinmora*: cf. stanza 34.]

[44. *Goddess of gold*: poetic circumlocution for "woman," here meaning Sinmora.]

46. *Sickle*: i.e., tail feather. With this the circle of impossibilities is completed. To get past the dogs, they must be fed with the wing-joints of the cock Vithofnir; the cock can be killed only [fp. 247] with the sword in Sinmora's possession, and Sinmora will give up the sword only in return for the tail feather of the cock.]

[48. *Lyr* ("Heat-Holding"): just what the spear-point reference means is not altogether clear. Presumably it refers to the way in which the glowing brightness of the lofty hall makes it seem to quiver and turn in the air, but the tradition, never baffled by physical laws, may have actually balanced the whole building on a single point to add to the difficulties of entrance.

50. *Loki*, the one god named, was the builder of the hall, with the aid of the nine dwarfs. Jari, Dori, and Ori appear in the Voluspo catalogue of the dwarfs (stanzas 13 and 15); *Delling* appears in *Hovamol*, 161, and *Vafthruthnismol*, 25, in the latter case, however, the name quite possibly referring to some one else. The other dwarfs' names do not appear elsewhere. The manuscripts differ as to the forms of many of these names.]

[52. *Lyfjaberg* ("Hill of Healing"): the manuscripts vary as to this name; I have followed Bugge's suggestion. This stanza implies that Mengloth is a goddess of healing, and hence, per haps, an hypostasis of Frigg, as already intimated by her name (cf. stanza 3, note). In stanza 54 Eir appears as one of Mengloth's handmaidens, and Eir, according to Snorri (*Gylfaginning*, 35) is herself the Norse Hygeia. Compare this stanza with stanza 32.

54. The manuscripts and editions show many variations in these names. They may be approximately rendered thus: Helper, Help-Breather, Folk-Guardian, Shining, White, Blithe, Peaceful, Kindly (?), and Gold-Giver.]

[55. One of the manuscripts omits stanzas 55 and 56.

56. The first line is based on a conjectural emendation.]

[63. Solbjart ("Sun-B right"): not elsewhere mentioned. *The words of Urth*: i.e., the decrees of fate; cf. stanza 7.]

[65. Lyfjaberg cf. stanza 52 and note.]

THE POETIC EDDA

VOLUME II

LAYS OF THE HEROES

VÖLUNDARKVITHA

The Lay of Völund

INTRODUCTORY NOTE

Between the *Thrymskvitha* and the *Alvissmol* in the *Codex Regius* stands the *Völundarkvitha*. It was also included in the *Arnamagnæan Codex*, but unluckily it begins at the very end of the fragment which has been preserved, and thus only a few lines of the opening prose remain. This is doubly regrettable because the text in *Regius* is unquestionably in very bad shape, and the other manuscript would doubtless have been of great assistance in the reconstruction of the poem.

There has been a vast amount written regarding the Weland tradition as a whole, discussing particularly the relations between the *Völundarkvitha* and the Weland passage in *Deor's Lament*. There can be little question that the story came to the North from Saxon regions, along with many of the other early hero tales. In stanza 16 the Rhine is specifically mentioned as the home of treasure; and the presence of the story in Anglo-Saxon poetry probably as early as the first part of the eighth century proves beyond a doubt that the legend cannot have been a native product of Scandinavia. In one form or another, however, the legend of the smith persisted for centuries throughout all the Teutonic lands, and the name of Wayland Smith is familiar to all readers of Walter Scott, and even of Rudyard Kipling's tales of England.

In what form this story reached the North is uncertain. Sundry striking parallels between the diction of the *Völundarkvitha*and that of the Weland passage in *Deor's Lament* make it distinctly probable that a Saxon song on this subject had found its way to Scandinavia or Iceland. But the prose introduction to the poem mentions the "old sagas" in which Völund was celebrated, and in the *Thithrekssaga* we have definite evidence of the existence of such prose narrative in the form of the*Velentssaga* (Velent, Völund, Weland, and Wayland all being, of course, identical), which gives a long story for which the*Völundarkvitha* can have supplied relatively little, if any, of the material. It is probable, then, that Weland stories were current in both prose and verse in Scandinavia as early as the latter part of the ninth century.

Once let a figure become popular in oral tradition, and the number and variety of the incidents connected with his name will increase very rapidly. Doubtless there were scores of Weland stories current in the eighth, ninth, and tenth centuries, many of them with very little if any traditional authority. The main one, however, the story of the laming of the smith by King Nithuth (or by some other enemy) and of Weland's terrible revenge, forms the basis of the *Völundarkvitha*. To this, by way of introduction, has been added the story of Völund and the wan-maiden, who, to make things even more complex, is likewise aid to be a Valkyrie. Some critics maintain that these two sections were originally two distinct poems, merely strung together by the compiler with the help of narrative prose links; but the poem as a whole has a kind of dramatic unity which suggests rather that an early poet--for linguistically the poem belongs among the oldest of the Eddic collection--used two distinct legends, whether in prose or verse, as the basis for the composition of a new and homogeneous poem.

The swan-maiden story appears, of course, in many places quite distinct from the Weland tradition, and, in another form, became one of the most popular of German folk tales. Like the story of Weland, however, it is of German rather than Scandinavian origin, and the identification of the swan-maidens as Valkyries, which may have taken place before the legend reached the North, may, on the other hand, have been simply an attempt to connect southern tradition with figures well known in northern mythology.

The *Völundarkvitha* is full of prose narrative links, including an introduction. The nature of such prose links has already been discussed in the introductory note to the *Grimnismol*; the *Völundarkvitha* is a striking illustration of the way in which the function of the earlier Eddic verse was limited chiefly to dialogue or description, the narrative outline being provided, if at all, in prose. This prose was put in by each reciter according to his fancy and knowledge, and his estimate of his hearers' need for such explanations; some of it, as in this instance, eventually found its way into the written record.

The manuscript of the *Völundarkvitha* is in such bad shape, and the conjectural emendations have been so numerous, that in the notes I have attempted to record only the most important of them.

There was a king in Sweden named Nithuth. He had two sons and one daughter; her name was Bothvild. There were three brothers, sons of a king of the Finns: one was called Slagfith, another Egil, the third Völund. They went on snowshoes and hunted wild beasts. They came into Ulfdalir and there they built themselves a house; there was a lake there which is called Ulfsjar. Early one morning they found on the shore of the lake three women, who were spinning flax. Near them were their swan garments, for they were Valkyries. Two of them were daughters of King Hlothver, Hlathguth the Swan-White and Hervor the All-Wise, and the third was Olrun, daughter of Kjar from Valland. These did they bring home to their hall with them. Egil took Olrun, and Slagfith Swan-White, and Völund All-Wise. There they dwelt seven winters; but then they flew away to find battles, and came back no more. Then Egil set forth on his snowshoes to follow Olrun, and Slagfith followed Swan White, but Völund stayed in Ulfdalir. He was a most skillful man, as men know from old tales. King Nithuth had him taken by force, as the poem here tells.

1. Maids from the south | through Myrkwood flew,
Fair and young, | their fate to follow;
On the shore of the sea | to rest them they sat,
The maids of the south, | and flax they spun.

2. . .   .   .
Hlathguth and Hervor, | Hlothver's children,
And Olrun the Wise | Kjar's daughter was.

3. . .   .   .
One in her arms | took Egil then
To her bosom white, | the woman fair.

4. Swan-White second,-- | swan-feathers she wore,
.   .   .   .
And her arms the third | of the sisters threw
Next round Völund's | neck so white.

5. There did they sit | for seven winters,
In the eighth at last | came their longing again,
(And in the ninth | did need divide them).
The maidens yearned | for the murky wood,
The fair young maids, | their fate to follow.

6. Völund home | from his hunting came,
From a weary way, | the weather-wise bowman,
Slagfith and Egil | the hall found empty,
Out and in went they, | everywhere seeking.

7. East fared Egil | after Olrun,
And Slagfith south | to seek for Swan-White;
Völund alone | in Ulfdalir lay,

.   .   .   .

8. Red gold he fashioned | with fairest gems,
And rings he strung | on ropes of bast;
So for his wife | he waited long,
If the fair one home | might come to him.

9. This Nithuth learned, | the lord of the Njars,
That Völund alone | in Ulfdalir lay;

By night went his men, | their mail-coats were studded,
Their shields in the waning | moonlight shone.

10. From their saddles the gable | wall they sought,
And in they went | at the end of the hall;
Rings they saw there | on ropes of bast,
Seven hundred | the hero had.

11. Off they took them, | but all they left
Save one alone | which they bore away.
 .   .   .   .
 .   .   .   .

12. Völund home | from his hunting came,
From a weary way, | the weather-wise bowman;
A brown bear's flesh | would he roast with fire;
Soon the wood so dry | was burning well,

13. On the bearskin he rested, | and counted the rings,
The master of elves, | but one he missed;
That Hlothver's daughter | had it he thought,
And the all-wise maid | had come once more.

14. So long he sat | that he fell asleep,
His waking empty | of gladness was;
Heavy chains | he saw on his hands,
And fetters bound | his feet together.

Völund spake:
15. "What men are they | who thus have laid
Ropes of bast | to bind me now?"

Then Nithuth called, | the lord of the Njars:
"How gottest thou, Völund, | greatest of elves,
These treasures of ours | in Ulfdalir?"

Völund spake:
16. "The gold was not | on Grani's way,
(The wind-dried wood | that Völund's was).
Far, methinks, is our realm | from the hills of the Rhine;
I mind me that treasures | more we had
When happy together | at home we were."

17. Without stood the wife | of Nithuth wise,
And in she came | from the end of the hall;
On the floor she stood, | and softly spoke:
"Not kind does he look | who comes from the wood."

King Nithuth gave to his daughter Bothvild the gold ring that he had taken from the bast rope in Völund's house, and he himself wore the sword that Völund had had. The queen spake:

18. "The glow of his eyes | is like gleaming snakes,
His teeth he gnashes | if now is shown
The sword, or Bothvild's | ring he sees;
Let them straightway cut | his sinews of strength,
And set him then | in Sævarstath."

So was it done: the sinews in his knee-joints were cut, and he was set in an island which was near the mainland, and was called Sævarstath. There he smithied for the king all kinds of precious things. No man dared to go to him, save only the king himself. Völund spake:

228

19. "At Nithuth's girdle | gleams the sword
That I sharpened keen | with cunningest craft,
(And hardened the steel | with highest skill;)
The bright blade far | forever is borne,
(Nor back shall I see it | borne to my smithy;)
Now Bothvild gets | the golden ring
(That was once my bride's,-- | ne'er well shall it be.)"

20. He sat, nor slept, | and smote with his hammer,
Fast for Nithuth | wonders he fashioned;
Two boys did go | in his door to gaze,
Nithuth's sons, | into Sævarstath.

21. They came to the chest, | and they craved the keys,
The evil was open | when in they looked;
To the boys it seemed | that gems they saw,
Gold in plenty | and precious stones.

Völund spake:
22. "Come ye alone, | the next day come,
Gold to you both | shall then be given;
Tell not the maids | or the men of the hall,
To no one say | that me you have sought."

23. .   .   .   .
Early did brother | to brother call:
"Swift let us go | the rings to see."

24. They came to the chest, | and they craved the keys,
The evil was open | when in they looked;
He smote off their heads, | and their feet he hid
Under the sooty | straps of the bellows.

25. Their skulls, once hid | by their hair, he took,
Set them in silver | and sent them to Nithuth;

Gems full fair | from their eyes he fashioned,
To Nithuth's wife | so wise he gave them.

26. And from the teeth | of the twain he wrought
A brooch for the breast, | to Bothvild he sent it;

.　.　.　.　.　.　.　.　.　.

27. Bothvild then | of her ring did boast,

.　.　.　.　.　.　.　.　.　.

.　.　.　.　.　| "The ring I have broken,
I dare not say it | save to thee."

Völund spake:
28. 'I shall weld the break | in the gold so well
That fairer than ever | thy father shall find it,
And better much | thy mother shall think it,
And thou no worse | than ever it was."

29. Beer he brought, | he was better in cunning,
Until in her seat | full soon she slept.

Völund spake:
"Now vengeance I have | for all my hurts,
Save one alone, | on the evil woman."

30.　.　.　.　.　.　.　.　.　.　.
.　.　.　.　.　.　.　.　.　.
Quoth Völund: "Would | that well were the sinews
Maimed in my feet | by Nithuth's men."

31. Laughing Völund | rose aloft,
Weeping Bothvild | went from the isle,
For her lover's flight | and her father's wrath.

32. Without stood the wife | of Nithuth wise,
And in she came | from the end of the hall;

But he by the wall | in weariness sat:
"Wakest thou, Nithuth, | lord of the Njars?"

Nithuth spake:
33. "Always I wake, | and ever joyless,
Little I sleep | since my sons were slain;
Cold is my head, | cold was thy counsel,
One thing, with Völund | to speak, I wish.

34. .   .   .   .
"Answer me, Völund, | greatest of elves,
What happed with my boys | that hale once were?"

Völund spake:
35. "First shalt thou all | the oaths now swear,
By the rail of ship, | and the rim of shield,
By the shoulder of steed, | and the edge of sword,
That to Völund's wife | thou wilt work no ill,
Nor yet my bride | to her death wilt bring,
Though a wife I should have | that well thou knowest,
And a child I should have | within thy hall.

36. "Seek the smithy | that thou didst set,
Thou shalt find the bellows | sprinkled with blood;
I smote off the heads | of both thy sons,
And their feet 'neath the sooty | straps I hid.

37. "Their skulls, once hid | by their hair, I took,
Set them in silver | and sent them to Nithuth;
Gems full fair | from their eyes I fashioned,
To Nithuth's wife | so wise I gave them.

38. "And from the teeth | of the twain I wrought
A brooch for the breast, | to Bothvild I gave it;
Now big with child | does Bothvild go,
The only daughter | ye two had ever."

Nithuth spake:

39. "Never spakest thou word | that worse could hurt me,
Nor that made me, Völund, | more bitter for vengeance;
There is no man so high | from thy horse to take thee,
Or so doughty an archer | as down to shoot thee,
While high in the clouds | thy course thou takest."

40. Laughing Völund | rose aloft,
But left in sadness | Nithuth sat.

. . . .

41. Then spake Nithuth, | lord of the Njars:
"Rise up, Thakkrath, | best of my thralls,
Bid Bothvild come, | the bright-browed maid,
Bedecked so fair, | with her father to speak."

42. . . . .
"Is it true, Bothvild, | that which was told me;
Once in the isle | with Völund wert thou?"

Bothvild spake:

43. "True is it, Nithuth, | that which was told thee,
Once in the isle | with Völund was I,
An hour of lust, | alas it should be!
Nought was my might | with such a man,
Nor from his strength | could I save myself."

[*Prose. Nithuth* ("Bitter Hater"): here identified as a king of Sweden, is in the poem (stanzas 9, 15 and 32) called lord of the Njars, which may refer to the people of the Swedish district of Nerike. In any case, the scene of the story has moved from Saxon lands into the Northeast. The first and last sentences of the introduction refer to the second part of the poem; the rest of it concerns the swan-maidens episode. *Bothvild*("Warlike Maid"): Völund's victim in the latter part of the poem. *King of the Finns*: this notion, clearly later than the poem, which calls Völund an elf, may perhaps be ascribed to the annotator who composed the prose introduction. The Finns, meaning the dwellers in Lapland, were generally credited with magic powers. *Egil* appears in the *Thithrekssaga* as Völund's brother, but *Slagfith* is not elsewhere mentioned. *Ulfdalir*("Wolf-Dale"), *Ulfsjar* ("Wolf-Sea"), *Valland* ("Slaughter-Land"): mythical, places without historical identification. *Valkyries*: cf. *Voluspo*, 31 and note; there is nothing in the poem to identify the three swan maidens as Valkyries except one obscure word in line 2 of stanza 1 and again in line 5 of stanza 5, which may mean, as Gering translates it, "helmed," or else "fair and wise." I suspect that the annotator, anxious to give the Saxon legend as much northern local color as possible, was mistaken in his mythology, and that [fp. 255] the poet never conceived of his swan-maidens as Valkyries at all. However, this identification of swan-maidens with Valkyries was not uncommon; cf. *Helreith Brynhildar*, 7. The three maidens' names, *Hlathguth*, *Hervor*, and *Olrun*, do not appear in the lists of Valkyries. *King Hlothver*: this name suggests the southern origin of the story, as it is the northern form of Ludwig; the name appears again in *Guthrunarkvitha* II, 26, and that of *Kjar* is found in *Atlakvitha*, 7, both of these poems being based on German stories. It is worth noting that the composer of this introductory note seems to have had little or no information beyond what was actually contained in the poem as it has come down to us; he refers to the "old stories" about Völund, but either he was unfamiliar with them in detail or else he thought it needless to make use of them. His note simply puts in clear and connected form what the verse tells somewhat obscurely; his only additions are making Nithuth a king of Sweden and Völund's father a king of the Finns, supplying the name Ulfsjar for the lake, identifying the swan-maidens as Valkyries, and giving Kjar a home in Valland.]

[1. The manuscript indicates line 3 as the beginning of a stanza; two lines may have been lost before or after lines 1-2, [fp. 256] and two more, or even six, with the additional stanza describing the theft of the swan-garments, after line 4. *Myrkwood*: a stock name for a magic, dark forest; cf. *Lokasenna*, 42.]

[2. In the manuscript these two lines stand after stanza 16; editors have tried to fit them into various places, but the prose indicates that they belong here, with a gap assumed.

3. In the manuscript these two lines follow stanza 1, with no gap indicated, and the first line marked as the beginning of a stanza. Many editors have combined them with stanza 4.

4. No lacuna indicated in the manuscript; one editor fills the stanza out with a second line running: "Then to her breast Slagfith embraced."

5. Line 3 looks like an interpolation, but line 5, identical with line 2 of stanza 1, may be the superfluous one.]

[6. The phrase "Völund home from a weary way" is an emendation of Bugge's, accepted by many editors. Some of those who do not include it reject line 4, and combine the remainder of the stanza with all or part of stanza 7.

7. The manuscript marks the second, and not the first, line as the beginning of a stanza. Some editors combine lines 2-3 with all or part of stanza 8. No gap is indicated in the manuscript, but many editors have assumed one, some of them accepting Bugge's suggested "Till back the maiden bright should come."

8. No line in this stanza is indicated in the manuscript as be ginning a new stanza; editors have tried all sorts of experiments in regrouping the lines into stanzas with those of stanzas 7 and 9. In line 3 the word long is sheer guesswork, as the line in the manuscript contains a metrical error.

9. Some editors combine the first two lines with parts of stanza 8, and the last two with the first half of stanza 10. *Njars*: [fp. 258] there has been much, and inconclusive, discussion as to what this name means; probably it applies to a semi-mythical people somewhere vaguely in "the East."]

[10. Some editors combine lines 3-4 with the fragmentary stanza 11.

11. No gap indicated in the manuscript; some editors combine these lines with lines 3-4 of stanza to, while others combine them with the first two lines of stanza 12. The one ring which Nithuth's men steal is given to Bothvild, and proves the cause of her undoing.

12. The manuscript indicates line 3, and not line 1, as the beginning of a stanza, which has given rise to a large amount of conjectural rearrangement. Line 2 of the original is identical with the phrase added by Bugge in stanza 6. Line 5 may be [fp. 259] spurious, or lines 4-5 may have been expanded out of a single line running "The wind-dried wood for | Völund burned well."]

[13. *Elves*: the poem here identifies Völund as belonging to the race of the elves. *Hlothver's daughter*: Hervor; many editors treat the adjective "all-wise" here as a proper name.

15. In this poem the manuscript indicates the speakers. Some editors make lines 1-2 into a separate stanza, linking lines 3-5 (or 4-5) with stanza 16. Line 3 is very possibly spurious, a mere expansion of "Nithuth spake." Nithuth, of course, has come with his men to capture Völund, and now charges him with having stolen his treasure.

16. The manuscript definitely assigns this stanza to Völund, but many editors give the first two lines to Nithuth. In the manuscript [fp. 260] stanza 16 is followed by the two lines of stanza 2, and many editions make of lines 3-4 of stanza 16 and stanza 2 a single speech by Völund. *Grani's way*: Grani was Sigurth's horse, on which he rode to slay Fafnir and win Andvari's hoard; this and the reference to the *Rhine* as the home of wealth betray the southern source of the story. If lines 1-2 belong to Völund, they mean that Nithuth got his wealth in the Rhine country, and that Völund's hoard has nothing to do with it; if the speaker is Nithuth, they mean that Völund presumably has not killed a dragon, and that he is far from the wealth of the Rhine, so that he must have stolen his treasure from Nithuth himself.]

[17. Line 1 is lacking in the manuscript, lines 2-4 following immediately after the two lines here given as stanza 2. Line 1, borrowed from line I of stanza 32, is placed here by many editors, following Bugge's suggestion. Certainly it is Nithuth's wife who utters line 4. *Who comes from the wood*: Völund, noted as a hunter. Gering assumes that with the entrance of Nithuth's wife the scene has changed from Völund's house to Nithuth's, but I cannot see that this is necessary.

Prose. The annotator inserted this note rather clumsily in the midst of the speech of Nithuth's wife.]

[18. In the manuscript lines 2-3 stand before line 1; many editors have made the transposition here indicated. Some editors reject line 3 as spurious. *Sævarstath*: "Sea-Stead."

19. This stanza is obviously in bad shape. Vigfusson makes two stanzas of it by adding a first line: "Then did Völund speak, | sagest of elves." Editors have rejected various lines, and some have regrouped the last lines with the first two of [fp. 262] stanza 20. The elimination of the passages in parenthesis produces a four-line stanza which is metrically correct, but it has little more than guesswork to support it.]

[20. The editions vary radically in combining the lines of this stanza with those of stanzas 19 and 21, particularly as the manuscript indicates the third line as the beginning of a stanza. The meaning, however, remains unchanged.

211. Several editions make one stanza out of lines 1-4 of stanza 20 and lines 1-2 of stanza 21, and another out of the next four lines. *The evil was open*: i.e., the gold in the chest was destined to be their undoing.

22. The manuscript indicates line 3 as the beginning of a stanza, and several editors have adopted this grouping. In the *Thithrekssaga* Völund sends the boys away with instructions not to come back until just after a fall of snow, and then to approach his dwelling walking backward. The boys do this, and when, after he has killed them, Völund is questioned regarding them, he points to the tracks in the snow as evidence that they had left his house.]

[23. No gap indicated in the manuscript. Some editors assume it, as here; some group the lines with lines 3-4 of stanza 22, and some with lines 1-2 of stanza 24.

24. Some editions begin a new stanza with line 3.

25. The manuscript indicates line 3 as the beginning of a stanza, and many editors have adopted this grouping.

26. These two lines have been grouped in various ways, either with lines 3-4 of stanza 25 or with the fragmentary stanza 27 No gap is indicated in the manuscript, but the loss of something is so obvious that practically all editors have noted it, although they have differed as to the number of lines lost.

27. No gap indicated in the manuscript; the line and a half [fp. 263] might be filled out (partly with the aid of late paper manuscripts) thus: "But soon it broke, | and swiftly to Völund / She bore it and said--"]

[29. The manuscript does not name Völund as the speaker before line 3; Vigfusson again inserts his convenient line, "Then Völund spake, sagest of elves." A few editions combine lines 3-4 with the two lines of stanza 30.

30. No gap indicated in the manuscript; some editors combine the two lines with lines 3-4 of stanza 29, and many with the three lines of stanza 31.]

[31. Something has probably been lost before this stanza, explaining how Völund made himself wings, as otherwise, owing to his lameness, he could not leave the island. The *Thithrekssaga* tells the story of how Völund's brother, Egil, shot birds and gave him the feathers, out of which he made a feather-garment. This break in the narrative illustrates the lack of knowledge apparently possessed by the compiler who was responsible for the prose notes; had he known the story told in the *Thithrekssaga*, it is hardly conceivable that he would have failed to indicate the necessary connecting link at this point. Some editors reject line 3 as spurious. The manuscript does not indicate any lacuna.

32. The manuscript indicates line 4 as the beginning of a stanza, and many editors have followed this arrangement.

33. The manuscript does not name the speaker. It indicates line 3 as the beginning of a new stanza. Vigfusson adds before line 1, "Then spake Nithuth, lord of the Njars."

34. No gap indicated in the manuscript, but it seems clear [fp. 266] that something has been lost. Some editors combine these two lines with lines 3-4 of stanza 33. Völund is now flying over Nithuth's hall.]

[35. The manuscript does not name the speaker; Vigfusson again makes two full stanzas with the line, "Then did Völund speak, sagest of elves." Some editors begin a new stanza with line 4, while others reject as interpolations lines 2-3 or 5-7. *Völund's wife*: the reference is to Bothvild, as Völund wishes to have his vengeance fall more heavily on her father than on her.

36. Lines 3-4 are nearly identical with lines 3-4 of stanza 24.

37. Identical, except for the pronouns, with stanza 25.]

[38. Lines 1-2: Cf. stanza 26.

39. The manuscript does not name the speaker. Either line 4 or line 5 may be an interpolation; two editions reject lines 3-5, combining lines 1-2 with stanza 40. In the *Thithrekssaga* Nithuth actually compels Egil, Völund's brother, to shoot at Völund. The latter has concealed a bladder full of blood under his left arm, and when his brother's arrow pierces this, Nithuth assumes that his enemy has been killed. This episode likewise appears among the scenes from Völund's career rudely carved on an ancient casket of ivory, bearing an Anglo-Saxon inscription in runic letters, which has been preserved.

40. Line 1: cf. stanza 3 1. The manuscript indicates no lacuna.]

[41. The first line is a conjectural addition. *Thakkrath* is probably the northern form of the Middle High German name Dancrat.

42. The manuscript indicates no gap, but indicates line 3 as the beginning of a stanza; Vigfusson's added "Then Nithuth spake, lord of the Njars" seems plausible enough.

43. The manuscript does not name the speaker. Different editors have rejected one or another of the last three lines, and as the manuscript indicates line 4 as the beginning of a new stanza, the loss of two or three lines has likewise been suggested. According to the *Thithrekssaga*, the son of Völund and Bothvild was Vithga, or Witege, one of the heroes of Dietrich of Bern.]

HELGAKVITHA HJORVARTHSSONAR

The Lay of Helgi the Son of Hjorvarth

INTRODUCTORY NOTE

The three Helgi lays, all found in the *Codex Regius*, have been the subjects of a vast amount of discussion, in spite of which many of the facts regarding them are still very far from settled. It is, indeed, scarcely possible to make any unqualified statement regarding these three poems for which a flat contradiction cannot be found in the writings of some scholar of distinction. The origin of the Helgi tradition, its connection with that of Sigurth, the authorship, date and home of the poems, the degree to which they have been altered from their original forms, the status of the composer of the copious prose notes: these and many other allied questions have been and probably always will be matters of dispute among students of the *Edda's* history.

Without attempting to enter into the discussion in detail, certain theories should be noted. Helgi appears originally to have been a Danish popular hero, the son of King Halfdan. Saxo Grammaticus has a good deal to say about him in that capacity, and it has been pointed out that many of the place names in the Helgi lays can be pretty clearly identified with parts of Denmark and neighboring stretches of the Baltic. The Danish Helgi, according to Saxo, was famed as the conqueror of Hunding and Hothbrodd, the latter as the result of a naval expedition at the head of a considerable fleet.

From Denmark the story appears to have spread northward into Norway and westward into the Norse settlements among the islands. Not many of its original features remained, and new ones were added here and there, particularly with regard to Helgi's love affair

239

with Sigrun. The victories over Hunding and Hothbrodd, however, were generally retained, and out of material relating to these two fights, and to the Helgi-Sigrun story, were fashioned the two lays of Helgi Hundingsbane.

How the Helgi legend became involved with that of the Volsungs is an open question. Both stories travelled from the South, and presumably about the same time, so it is not unnatural that some confusion should have arisen. At no time, however, was the connection particularly close so far as the actual episodes of the two stories were concerned. In the two lays of Helgi Hundingsbane the relationship is established only by the statement that Helgi was the son of Sigmund and Borghild; Sigurth is not mentioned, and in the lay of Helgi the son of Hjorvarth there is no connection at all. On the other hand, Helgi does not appear in any of the Eddic poems dealing directly with the Volsung stories, although in one passage of doubtful authenticity (cf. *Reginsmol*, introductory note) his traditional enemy, Hunding, does, represented by his sons. In the *Volsungasaga* the story of Helgi, including the fights with Hunding and Hothbrodd and the love affair with Sigrun, is told in chapters 8 and 9 without otherwise affecting the course of the narrative. Here, as in the Helgi lays, Helgi is the son of Sigmund Volsungsson and Borghild; Sigurth, on the other hand, is the son of Sigmund and Hjordis, the latter being the daughter of King Eylimi. Still another son, who complicates both stories somewhat, is Sinfjotli, son of Sigmund and his own sister, Signy. Sinfjotli appears in both of the Helgi Hundingsbane lays and in the *Volsungasaga*, but not in any of the Eddic poems belonging to the Volsung cycle (cf. *Fra Dautha Sinfjotla* and note).

There is a certain amount of resemblance between the story of Helgi and Sigrun and that of Sigurth and Brynhild, particularly as the annotator responsible for the prose notes insists that Sigrun was a Valkyrie. Whether this resemblance was the cause of bringing the two stories together, or whether the identification of Helgi as Sigmund's son resulted in alterations of the love story in the Helgi poems, cannot be determined. The first of the three Helgi poems, the lay of Helgi the son of Hjorvarth, is a somewhat distant cousin of the other two. The Helgi in question is apparently the same traditional figure, and he leads a naval expedition, but he is not the son of Sigmund, there is no connection with the Volsung cycle, and his wife is Svava, not Sigrun. At the same time, the points of general resemblance with the two Helgi Hundingsbane lays are such as to indicate a common origin, provided one goes far enough back. The annotator brings the stories together by the naive expedient of having Helgi "born again," and not once only, but twice. The first Helgi lay, is manifestly in bad shape, and includes at least two distinct poems, differentiated not only by subject matter but by metrical form. Although the question is debatable, the longer of these poems (stanzas 1-11 and 31-43) seems in turn to have been compounded out of fragments of two or more Helgi poems. The first five stanzas are a dialogue between a bird and Atli, one of Hjorvarth's followers, concerning the winning of Sigrlin, who is destined to be Hjorvarth's wife and Helgi's mother. Stanzas 6-11 are a dialogue between Helgi and a Valkyrie (the accompanying prose so calls her, and identifies her as Svava, but there is nothing in the verse to prove this). Stanzas 12-30 form a fairly consecutive unit, in which Atli, on guard over Helgi's ship, has a vigorous argument with a giantess, Hrimgerth, whence this section has sometimes been called the *Hrimgertharmol*(*Lay of Hrimgerth*). The last section, stanzas 31-43, is, again fairly consecutive, and tells of the death of Helgi following the rash oath of his brother, Hethin, to win Svava for himself.

Parts I, II, and IV may all have come from the same poem or they may not; it is quite impossible to tell surely. All of them are generally dated by commentators not later than the first half of the tenth century, whereas the *Hrimgertharmol* (section III) is placed considerably later. When and by whom these fragments were pieced together is another vexed question, and this involves a consideration of the prose notes and links, of which the *Helgakvitha Hjorvarthssonar* has a larger amount than any other poem in

241

the *Edda*. These prose links contain practically all the narrative, the verse being almost exclusively dialogue. Whoever composed them seems to have been consciously trying to bring his chaotic verse material into some semblance of unity, but he did his work pretty clumsily, with manifest blunders and contradictions. Bugge has advanced the theory that these prose passages are to be regarded as an original and necessary part of the work, but this hardly squares with the evidence.

It seems probable, rather, that as the Helgi tradition spread from its native Denmark through the Norse regions of the North and West, and became gradually interwoven, although not in essentials, with the other great hero cycle from the South, that of the Volsungs, a considerable number of poems dealing with Helgi were composed, at different times and in different places, reflecting varied forms of the story. Many generations after wards, when Iceland's literary period had arrived, some zealous scribe committed to writing such poems or fragments of poems as he knew, piecing them together and annotating them on the basis of information which had reached him through other channels. The prose notes to *Helgakvitha Hundingsbana II* frankly admit this patchwork process: a section of four stanzas (13-16) is introduced with the phrase, "as is said in the Old Volsung Lay"; the final prose note cites an incident "told in the *Karuljoth* (*Lay of Kara*)," and a two-line speech is quoted "as it was written before in the *Helgakvitha*."

The whole problem of the origin, character and home of the Helgi poems has been discussed in great detail by Bugge in his*Helge-Digtene i den Ældre Edda, Deres Hjem og Forbindelser*, which, as translated by W. H. Schofield under the title *The Home of the Eddic Poems*, is available for readers of English. This study is exceedingly valuable, if not in all respects convincing. The whole matter is so complex and so important in the history of Old Norse literature, and any intelligent reading of the Helgi poems is so dependent on an understanding of the conditions under which they have come down to us, that I have here discussed the question more extensively than

242

the scope of a mere introductory note to a single poem would warrant.

(I)

OF HJORVARTH AND SIGRLIN

Hjorvarth was the name of a king, who had four wives: one was called Alfhild, and their son was named Hethin; the second was called Særeith, and their son was named Humlung; the third was called Sinrjoth, and their son was named Hymling. King Hjorvarth had made a great vow to have as wife whatsoever woman he knew was fairest. He learned that King Svafnir had a daughter fairer than all others, whose name was Sigrlin. Ithmund was the name of one of his jarls; he had a son called Atli, who went to woo Sigrlin on behalf of the king. He dwelt the winter long with King Svafnir. There was a jarl called Franmar, Sigrlin's foster-father; his daughter was named Alof. The jarl told him that the maiden's hand was denied, and Atli went home. Atli, the jarl's son, stood one day in a certain wood; a bird sat in the branches up over him, and it had heard that his men called Hjorvarth's wives the fairest of women. The bird twittered, and Atli hearkened to what it spoke. It said:

1. "Sawest thou Sigrlin, | Svafnir's daughter,
The fairest maid | in her home-land found?
Though Hjorvath's wives | by men are held
Goodly to see | in Glasir's wood."

Atli spake:
2. "Now with Atli, | Ithmund's son,
Wilt thou say more, | thou bird so wise?"

The bird spake:
"I may if the prince | an offering makes,
And I have what I will | from the house of the king."

Atli spake:
3. "Choose not Hjorvarth, | nor sons of his,
Nor the wives so fair | of the famous chief;
Ask not the brides | that the prince's are;
Fair let us deal | in friendly wise."

The bird spake:
4. "A fane will I ask, | and altars many,
Gold-horned cattle | the prince shall give me,
If Sigrlin yet | shall sleep in his arms,
Or free of will | the hero shall follow."

This was before Atli went on his journey; but when he came home, and the king asked his tidings, he said:

5. "Trouble we had, | but tidings none,
Our horses failed | in the mountains high,
The waters of Sæmorn | we needs must wade;
Svafnir's daughter, | with rings bedecked,
She whom we sought, | was still denied us."

The king bade that they should go another time, and he went with them himself, But when they came up on the mountain, they saw Svavaland burning and mighty dust-clouds from many steeds. The king rode from the mountain forward into the land, and made a night's stay hard by a stream. Atli kept watch and went over the stream; he found there a house. A great bird sat on the housetop to guard it, but he was asleep. Atli hurled his spear at the bird and slew it, and in the house he found Sigrlin the king's daughter and Alof the jarl's daughter, and he brought them both thence with him. Jarl Franmar had changed himself into the likeness of an eagle, and guarded them from the enemy host by magic. Hrothmar was the name of a king, a wooer of Sigrlin; he slew the king of Svavaland and had plundered and burned his land. King Hjorvarth took Sigrlin, and Atli took Alof.

(II)

Hjorvarth and Sigrlin had a son, mighty and of noble stature; he was a silent man, and no name stuck fast to him. He sat on a hill, and saw nine Valkyries riding; one of them was the fairest of all. She spake:

6. "Late wilt thou, Helgi, | have hoard of rings,
Thou battle-tree fierce, | or of shining fields,--
The eagle screams soon,-- | if never thou speakest,
Though, hero, hard | thy heart may cry."

Helgi spake:
7. "What gift shall I have | with Helgi's name,
Glorious maid, | for the giving is thine?
All thy words | shall I think on well,
But I want them not | if I win not thee."

The Valkyrie spake:
8. "Swords I know lying | in Sigarsholm,
Fifty there are | save only four;
One there is | that is best of all,
The shield-destroyer, | with gold it shines.

9. "In the hilt is fame, | in the haft is courage,
In the point is fear, | for its owner's foes;
On the blade there lies | a blood-flecked snake,
And a serpent's tail | round the flat is twisted."

Eylimi was the name of a king, whose daughter was Svava; she was a Valkyrie, and rode air and sea. She gave Helgi this name, and shielded him oft thereafter in battle. Helgi spake:

10. "Hjorvarth, king, | unwholesome thy counsels,
Though famed thou art | in leading the folk,

Letting fire the homes of heroes eat,
Who evil deed had never done thee.

11. "Yet Hrothmar still the hoard doth hold,
The wealth that once our kinsmen wielded;
Full seldom care the king disturbs,
Heir to dead men he deems himself."

Hjorvarth answered that he would give Helgi a following if he fain
would avenge his mother's father. Then Helgi got the sword that
Svava had told him of. So he went, and Atli with him, and they slew
Hrothmar, and they did many great deeds.

(III)

He slew the giant Hati, whom he found sitting on a certain
mountain. Helgi and Atli lay with their ships in Hatafjord. Atli kept
watch during the first part of the night. Hrimgerth, Hati's daughter,
spake:

12. "Who are the heroes | in Hatafjord?
The ships are covered with shields;
Bravely ye look, | and little ye fear,
The name of the king would I know."

Atli spake:
13. "Helgi his name, | and never thou mayst
Harm to the hero bring;
With iron is fitted | the prince's fleet,
Nor can witches work us ill."

Hrimgerth spake:
14. "Who now, thou mighty | man, art thou?
By what name art thou known to men?
He trusts thee well, | the prince who wills
That thou stand at the stem of his ship."

246

Atli spake:

15. "Atli am I, | and ill shalt thou find me,
Great hate for witches I have;
Oft have I been | in the dripping bows,
And to dusk-riders death have brought.

16. "Corpse-hungry giantess, | how art thou called?
Say, witch, who thy father was!
Nine miles deeper | down mayst thou sink,
And a tree grow tall on thy bosom."

Hrimgerth spake:

17. "Hrimgerth am I, | my father was Hati,
Of giants the most in might;
Many a woman | he won from her home,
Ere Helgi hewed him down."

Atli spake:

18. "Witch, in front | of the ship thou wast,
And lay before the fjord;
To Ron wouldst have given | the ruler's men,
If a spear had not stuck in thy flesh."

Hrimgerth spake:

19. "Dull art thou, Atli, | thou dreamest, methinks,
The lids lie over thine eyes;
By the leader's ships | my mother lay,
Hlothvarth's sons on the sea I slew.

20. "Thou wouldst neigh, Atli, | but gelded thou art,
See, Hrimgerth hoists her tail;
In thy hinder end | is thy heart, methinks,
Though thy speech is a stallion's cry."

Atli spake:

21. "A stallion I seem | if thou seekest to try me,

And I leap to land from the sea;
I shall smite thee to bits, | if so I will,
And heavy sinks Hrimgerth's tail."

Hrimgerth spake:
22. "Go ashore then, Atli, | if sure of thy might,
Let us come to Varin's cove;
Straight shall thy rounded | ribs be made
If thou comest within my claws."

Atli spake:
23. "I will not go | till the warriors wake,
Again their chief to guard;
I should wonder not, | foul witch, if up
From beneath our keel thou shouldst come."

Hrimgerth spake:
24. "Awake now, Helgi, | and Hrimgerth requite,
That Hati to death thou didst hew;
If a single night | she can sleep by the prince,
Then requited are all her ills."

Helgi spake:
25. " 'Tis Lothin shall have thee,-- | thou'rt loathsome to men,--
His home in Tholley he has;
Of the wild-dwellers worst | is the giant wise,
He is meet as a mate for thee."

Hrimgerth spake:
26. "More thou lovest her | who scanned the harbor,
Last night among the men;
(The gold-decked maid | bore magic, methinks,
When the land from the sea she sought,
And fast she kept your fleet;)
She alone is to blame | that I may not bring
Death to the monarch's men."

Helgi spake:
27. "Hrimgerth, mark, | if thy hurts I requite,
Tell now the truth to the king;
Was there one who the ships | of the warrior warded,
Or did many together go?"

Hrimgerth spake:
28. "Thrice nine there were, | but one rode first,
A helmed maid white of hue;
Their horses quivered, | there came from their manes
Dew in the dales so deep,
(Hail on the woods so high,
Thence men their harvest have,
But ill was the sight I saw.)"

Atli spake:
29. "Look eastward, Hrimgerth, | for Helgi has struck thee
Down with the runes of death;
Safe in harbor floats | the prince's fleet,
And safe are the monarch's men."

Helgi spake:
30. "It is day, Hrimgerth, | for Atli held thee
Till now thy life thou must lose;
As a harbor mark | men shall mock at thee,
Where in stone thou shalt ever stand."

(IV)

King Helgi was a mighty warrior. He came to King Eylimi and sought the hand of his daughter, Svava. Then Helgi and Svava exchanged vows, and greatly they loved each other. Svava was at home with her father, while Helgi was in the field; Svava was still a Valkyrie as before.

Hethin was at home with his father, King Hjorvarth, in Norway. Hethin was coming home alone from the forest one Yule-eve, and found a troll-woman; she rode on a wolf, and had snakes in place of a bridle. She asked Hethin for his company. "Nay," said he. She said, "Thou shalt pay for this at the king's toast." That evening the great vows were taken; the sacred boar was brought in, the men laid their hands thereon, and took their vows at the king's toast. Hethin vowed that he would have Svava, Eylimi's daughter, the beloved of his brother Helgi; then such great grief seized him that he went forth on wild paths southward over the land, and found Helgi, his brother. Helgi said:

3 1. "Welcome, Hethin! | what hast thou to tell
Of tidings new | that from Norway come?
Wherefore didst leave | thy land, O prince,
And fared alone | to find us here?"

Hethin spake:
32. "A deed more evil | I have done
Than, brother mine, | thou e'er canst mend;
For I have chosen | the child of the king,
Thy bride, for mine | at the monarch's toast."

Helgi spake:
33. "Grieve not, Hethin, | for true shall hold
The words we both | by the beer have sworn;
To the isle a warrior | wills that I go,
(There shall I come | the third night hence;)
And doubtful must be | my coming back,
(So may all be well, | if fate so wills.)"

Hethin spake:
34. "Thou saidst once, Helgi, | that Hethin was
A friend full good, | and gifts didst give him;
More seemly it were | thy sword to redden,
Than friendship thus | to thy foe to-give."

Helgi spoke thus because he foresaw his death, for his following-spirits had met Hethin when he saw the woman riding on the wolf. Alf was the name of a king, the son of Hrothmar, who had marked out a battle-place with Helgi at Sigarsvoll after a stay of three nights. Then Helgi spake:

35. "On a wolf there rode, | when dusk it was,
A woman who fain | would have him follow;
Well she knew | that now would fall
Sigrlin's son | at Sigarsvoll."

There was a great battle, and there Helgi got a mortal wound.

36. Sigar riding | did Helgi send
To seek out Eylimi's | only daughter:
"Bid her swiftly | ready to be,
If her lover | alive she would find."

Sigar spake:
37. "Hither now | has Helgi sent me,
With thee, Svava, | thyself to speak;
The hero said | he fain would see thee
Ere life the nobly | born should leave."

Svava spake:
A "What chanced with Helgi, | Hjorvarth's son?
Hard to me | is harm now come;
If the sea smote him, | or sword bit him,
Ill shall I bring | to all his foes."

Sigar spake:
39. "In the morn he fell | at Frekastein,
The king who was noblest | beneath the sun;
Alf has the joy | of victory all,
Though need therefor | is never his."

Helgi spake:

40. "Hail to thee, Svava! | thy sorrow rule,
Our meeting last | in life is this;
Hard the wounds | of the hero bleed,
And close to my heart | the sword has come.

41. "I bid thee, Svava,-- | weep not, bride,--
If thou wilt hearken | to these my words,
The bed for Hethin | have thou ready,
And yield thy love | to the hero young."

Svava spake:

42. "A vow I had | in my dear-loved home,
When Helgi sought | with rings to have me,
That not of my will, | if the warrior died,
Would I fold in my arms | a man unfamed."

Hethin spake:

43. "Kiss me, Svava, | I come not back,
Rogheim to see, | or Rothulsfjoll,
Till vengeance I have | for the son of Hjorvarth,
The king who was noblest | beneath the sun."

Of Helgi and Svava it is said that they were born again.

[*Prose*: In the manuscript the sub-title, "Of Hjorvarth and Sigrlin," stands as the title for the whole poem, though it clearly applies only to the first five stanzas. Most editions employ the title here given. *Hjorvarth*: the name is a not uncommon one; [fp. 273] there are two men of that name mentioned in the mythical heroic genealogies of the *Hyndluljoth* (stanzas 23 and 28), and Hjorvarth appears in *Helgakvitha Hundingsbana* I (stanza 14) and II (prose after stanza 12) as a son of Hunding. This particular Hjorvarth is called by the annotator, but not directly so in the verse, a king of Norway. The name means "Sword-Guardian." *Four wives*: polygamy, while very infrequent, appears occasionally in the Norse sagas. *Alfhild*: "Elf-Warrior." *Hethin*: "Fur-Clothed" (?). *Særeith*: "Sea-Rider." *Sinrjoth*: "Ever-Red." The fourth wife, not here named, may be Sigrlin. It has been suggested that Særeith and Sinrjoth may be northern and southern forms of the same name, as also*Humlung* and *Hymling*, their sons. *Svafnir*: the annotator calls him king of Svavaland, apparently a place on the mainland which could be reached from Norway either by land or by sea. *Sigrlin*: "The Conquering Serpent." *Atli*: Norse form of the Gothic Attila (Etzel). *Alof*: perhaps a feminine form of Olaf. *A bird*: compare the counsel given by the birds to Sigurth after the slaying of Fafnir (Fafnismol, stanzas 32-38). This is one of the many curious resemblances between the Helgi and the Sigurth stories.]

[1. *Glasir's wood*: Snorri in the *Skaldskaparmal* quotes a half stanza to the effect that "Glasir stands with golden leaves before Othin's hall," and calls it "the fairest wood among gods and men." The phrase as used here seems to mean little.

4. The bird's demands would indicate that it is in reality one of the gods. *Gold-horned cattle*: cf. *Thrymskvitha*, 23. There [fp. 275] are other references to gilding the horns of cattle, particularly for sacrificial purposes.]

[*Prose*. The annotator contradicts himself here, as he had already stated that Atli was on his way home.

5. Possibly the remains of two stanzas, or perhaps a line has been added. *Sæmorn*: this river is nowhere else mentioned.

Prose. Sigrlin and Alof, protected by the latter's father, Franmar, have fled before the ravaging army of Sigrlin's rejected [fp. 276] suitor, Hrothmar. The beginning of a new section (II) is indicated in the manuscript only by the unusually large capital letter with which "Hjorvarth" begins. *No name*, etc.: this probably means that Helgi had always been so silent that he would answer to no name, with the result that he had none. *Valkyries*: cf. *Voluspo*, 31 and note. The annotator insists here and in the prose after stanza 9 that Svava was a Valkyrie, but there is nothing in the verse to prove it, or, indeed, to identify the Svava of the last section of the poem with the person who gave Helgi his name. In the *Volsungasaga* Sigmund himself names his son Helgi, and gives him a sword, following Helgakvitha *Hundingsbana* I.]

[6. *Battle-free*: poetic phrase for "warrior." *Shining fields*: the words in the manuscript may form a proper name, Rothulsvoll, having this meaning.

7. *Gift*: not only was it customary to give gifts with the naming [fp. 276] of a child, but the practice frequently obtained when a permanent epithet was added to the name of an adult.]

253

[8. *Sigarsholm* ("Isle of Sigar"): a place not identified, but probably related to the Sigarsvoll where Helgi was slain (stanza 35).

9. The sword is carved with magic runes and with snakes. *Fame*: the original word is uncertain.

Prose. Eylimi: this name is another link with the Sigurth story, as it is likewise the name of the father of Sigurth's mother, Hjordis.

10. With this stanza begins a new episode, that of Helgi's [fp. 277] victory over King Hrothmar, who had killed his mother's father (cf. prose after stanza 5). It has been suggested, in consequence, that stanzas 10-11 may be a separate fragment. The verse tells nothing of the battle, merely giving Helgi's reproaches to his father for having left Svafnir's death and the burning of Svavaland unavenged.]

[*Prose*. The manuscript does not indicate any break, but the episode which forms the basis of the *Hrimgertharmol* (stanzas 12-30) clearly begins with the slaying of the giant Hati ("The Hateful"). *Hatafjord*: "Hati's Fjord." *Hrimgerth*: "Frost Shrouded"]

[13. *Iron*: the keels of Norse ships were sometimes fitted with iron "shoes" at bow and stern, but it is not certain that this practice much antedated the year 1000, and thus this line has raised some question as to the antiquity of this stanza, if not of the entire *Hrimgertharmol*, which may have been composed as late as the eleventh century.

15. The manuscript does not indicate the speaker. The pun on "Atli" and "atall" (meaning "ill") is untranslatable.]

[17. The manuscript does not indicate the speaker.

18. From this point to the end the manuscript does not indicate the speakers. *Ron*: wife of the sea-god Ægir, who draws drowning men into the sea with her net. There is no other reference to the wounding of Hrimgerth.

19. Apparently both Hrimgerth and her mother, Hati's wife, had sought to destroy Helgi's ships, and had actually killed some of his companions, the sons of *Hlothvarth*, concerning whom nothing more is known. Many editors assume that a stanza containing a speech by Atli has been lost after stanza 19.]

[20. Apparently Hrimgerth has assumed the form of a mare.

22. *Varin's cove*: the name of Varin appears twice in place names in *Helgakvitha Hundingsbana I* (stanzas 27 and 39). The sagas mention a mythical King Varin who lived at Skorustrond in Rogaland (Norway).]

[25. Of the giant *Lothin* ("The Shaggy") and his home in *Tholley* ("Pine Island") nothing is known. Cf. *Skirnismol*, 35.

26. Something is clearly wrong with this stanza, and the manuscript indicates line 6 as the beginning of a new one. Perhaps a line (between lines 4 and 5) has been lost, or perhaps the lines in parenthesis are interpolations. Hrimgerth here refers to Svava, or to the protectress with whom the annotator has identified her, as having saved Helgi and his, ships from the vengeance of the giantesses. In the original line 1 includes Helgi's name, which makes it metrically incorrect.]

[28. Again something is clearly wrong, and the last three lines look like interpolations, though some editors have tried to reconstruct two full stanzas. The passage suggests the identification of the Valkyries with the clouds.

29. Some editions give this speech to Helgi. *Eastward*: Atli and Helgi have held Hrimgerth in talk till sunrise, and the sun's rays turn her into stone. But dwarfs rather than giants were the victims of sunlight; cf. *Alvissmol*, stanzas 16 and 35.]

[30. Most editions give this stanza to Atli. With this the *Hrimgertharmol* ends, and after the next prose passage the meter reverts to that of the earlier sections.

Prose. The manuscript does not indicate a new section of the poem. *Eylimi*: cf. note on prose after stanza 9. *Valkyrie*: here, as before, the annotator has apparently nothing but his own imagination on which to base his statement. Svava in the ensuing stanzas certainly does not behave like a Valkyrie. *Norway*: the annotator doubtless based this statement on the reference to Norway in line 2 of stanza 31. *Yule-eve*: the Yule feast, marking the new year, was a great event in the heathen North. It was a time of feasting and merrymaking, vows ("New Year's resolutions"), ghosts and witches; the spirits had their greatest power on Yule-eve. *The king's toast*: vows made at the passing of the king's cup at the Yule feast were particularly sacred. *Sacred boar*: a boar consecrated to Freyr, an integral part of the Yule rites. Hethin's vow, which is, of course, the vengeance of the troll-woman, is too sacred to be broken, but he immediately realizes the horror of his oath.]

[31. *From Norway*: Bugge uses this phrase as evidence that the poem was composed in one of the Icelandic settlements of the western islands, but as the annotator himself seems to have thought that Hethin came to Helgi by land ("on wild paths southward"), this argument does not appear to have much weight.

32. The second line is conjectural; a line has; clearly been lost from this stanza, and various emendations have been suggested.]

[33. Perhaps this is the remnant of two stanzas, or perhaps two lines (probably the ones in parenthesis) have been interpolated. *The isle*: duels were commonly fought on islands, probably to guard against treacherous interference, whence the usual name for a duel was "isle-going." A duel was generally fought three days after the challenge. Reckoning the lapse of time by nights instead of days was a common practice throughout the German and Scandinavian peoples.

Prose. Some editors place all or part of this prose passage after stanza 35. *Following-spirits*: the "fylgja" was a female guardian spirit whose appearance generally betokened death. The belief was common throughout the North, and has come down to recent times in Scottish and Irish folk-lore. Individuals and sometimes whole families had these following-spirits, but it was most unusual for a person to have more than one of them. *Alf*: son of the Hrothmar who killed Helgi's grandfather, and [fp. 287] who was in turn later killed by Helgi. *Sigarsvoll* ("Sigar's Field"): cf. stanza 8 and note; the Sigar in question may be the man who appears as Helgi's messenger in stanzas 36-39.]

[36. Sigar ("The Victorious"): cf. the foregoing note.]

[39. *Frekastein* ("Wolf-Crag"): the name appears several times in the Helgi lays applied to battlefields; cf. *Helgakvitha Hundingsbana* I, 46 and 55, and II, 18 and 24. *Need*: i. e., Alf deserves no credit for the victory, which was due to the troll woman's magic.]

[41. One or two editors ascribe this stanza to Hethin.

43. A few editions make the extraordinary blunder of ascribing this speech to the dying Helgi. The point, of course, is that Hethin will satisfy Svava's vow by becoming famous as the slayer of Alf. *Rogheim* ("Rome of Battle") and *Rothulsfjoll* ("Sun-Mountain"): nowhere else mentioned; Hethin means simply that he will not come back to Svava till he has won fame.

Prose. Regarding this extraordinary bit see the prose note at the end of Helgakvitha *Hundingsbana II*. Gering thinks the reborn Helgi Hjorvarthsson was Helgi Hundingsbane, while Svava, according to the annotator himself, became Sigrun. The point seems to be simply that there were so many Helgi stories current, and the hero died in so many irreconcilable ways, that tradition had to have him born over again, not once only but several times, to accommodate his many deaths, and to avoid splitting him up into several Helgis. Needless to say, the poems themselves know nothing of this rebirth, and we owe the suggestion entirely to the annotator, who probably got it from current tradition.]

HELGAKVITHA HUNDINGSBANA I

The First Lay of Helgi Hundingsbane

INTRODUCTORY NOTE

The general subject of the Helgi lays is considered in the introduction to *Helgakvitha Hjorvarthssonar*, and it is needless here to repeat the statements there made. The first lay of Helgi Hundingsbane is unquestionably one of the latest of the Eddic poems, and was composed probably not earlier than the second quarter of the eleventh century. It presents several unusual characteristics. For one thing, it is among the few essentially narrative poems in the whole collection, telling a consecutive story in verse, and, except for the abusive dialogue between Sinfjotli and Gothmund, which clearly was based on another and older poem, it does so with relatively little use of dialogue. It is, in fact, a ballad, and in the main an exceedingly vigorous one. The annotator, who added his prose narrative notes so freely in the other Helgi poems, here found nothing to do. The available evidence indicates that narrative verse was a relatively late development in Old Norse poetry, and it is significant that most of the poems which consist chiefly, not of dialogue, but of narrative stanzas, such as the first Helgi Hundingsbane lay and the two Atli lays, can safely be dated, on the basis of other evidence, after the year 1000.

The first Helgi Hundingsbane lay is again differentiated from most of the Eddic poems by the character of its language. It is full of those verbal intricacies which were the delight of the Norse skalds, and which made Snorri's dictionary of poetic phrases an absolute necessity. Many of these I have paraphrased in the translation; some I have simplified or wholly avoided. A single line will serve to indicate the character of this form of complex diction (stanza 56,

258

line 4): "And the horse of the giantess raven's-food had." This means simply that wolves (giantesses habitually rode on wolves) ate the bodies of the dead.

Except for its intricacies of diction, and the possible loss of a stanza here and there, the poem is comparatively simple. The story belongs in all its essentials to the Helgi tradition, with the Volsung cycle brought in only to the extent of making Helgi the son of Sigmund, and in the introduction of Sinfjotli, son of Sigmund and his sister Signy, in a passage which has little or nothing to do with the course of the narrative, and which looks like an expansion of a passage from some older poem, perhaps from the "old Volsung lay" to which the annotator of the second Helgi Hundingsbane lay refers (prose after stanza 12). There are many proper names, some of which betray the confusion caused by the blending of the two sets of traditions; for example, Helgi appears indiscriminately as an Ylfing (which presumably he was before the Volsung story became involved) and as a Volsung. Granmar and his sons are called Hniflungs (Nibelungen) in stanza 50, though they seem to have had no connection with this race. The place names have aroused much debate as to the localization of the action, but while some of them probably reflect actual places, there is so much geographical confusion, and such a profusion of names which are almost certainly mythical, that it is hard to believe that the poet had any definite locations in mind.

1. In olden days, | when eagles screamed,
And holy streams | from heaven's crags fell,
Was Helgi then, | the hero-hearted,
Borghild's son, | in Bralund born.

2. 'Twas night in the dwelling, | and Norns there came,
Who shaped the life | of the lofty one;
They bade him most famed | of fighters all
And best of princes | ever to be.

259

3. Mightily wove they | the web of fate,
While Bralund's towns | were trembling all;
And there the golden | threads they wove,
And in the moon's hall | fast they made them.

4. East and west | the ends they hid,
In the middle the hero | should have his land;
And Neri's kinswoman | northward cast
A chain, and bade it | firm ever to be.

5. Once sorrow had | the Ylfings' son,
And grief the bride | who the loved one had borne.

* * * * * *

Quoth raven to raven, | on treetop resting,
Seeking for food, | "There is something I know.

6. "In mail-coat stands | the son of Sigmund,
A half-day old; | now day is here;
His eyes flash sharp | as the heroes' are,
He is friend of the wolves; | full glad are we."

7. The warrior throng | a ruler thought him,
Good times, they said, | mankind should see;
The king himself | from battle-press came,
To give the prince | a leek full proud.

8. Helgi he named him, | and Hringstathir gave him,
Solfjoll, Snæfjoll, | and Sigarsvoll,
Hringstoth, Hotun, | and Himinvangar,
And a blood-snake bedecked | to Sinfjotli's brother.

9. Mighty he grew | in the midst of his friends,
The fair-born elm, | in fortune's glow;

To his comrades gold | he gladly gave,
The hero spared not | the blood-flecked hoard.

10. Short time for war | the chieftain waited,
When fifteen winters | old he was;
Hunding he slew, | the hardy wight
Who long had ruled | o'er lands and men.

11. Of Sigmund's son | then next they sought
Hoard and rings, | the sons of Hunding;
They bade the prince | requital pay
For booty stolen | and father slain.

12. The prince let not | their prayers avail,
Nor gold for their dead | did the kinsmen get;
Waiting, he said, | was a mighty storm
Of lances gray | and Othin's grimness.

13. The warriors forth | to the battle went,
The field they chose | at Logafjoll;
Frothi's peace | midst foes they broke,
Through the isle went hungrily | Vithrir's hounds.

14. The king then sat, | when he had slain
Eyjolf and Alf, | 'neath the eagle-stone;
Hjorvarth and Hovarth, | Hunding's sons,
The kin of the spear-wielder, | all had he killed.

15. Then glittered light | from Logafjoll,
And from the light | the flashes leaped;

. . . .

16. . . . .
High under helms | on heaven's field;
Their byrnies all | with blood were red,
And from their spears | the sparks flew forth.

17. Early then | in wolf-wood asked
The mighty king | of the southern maid,
If with the hero | home would she
Come that night; | the weapons clashed.

18. Down from her horse | sprang Hogni's daughter,--
The shields were still,-- | and spake to the hero:
"Other tasks | are ours, methinks,
Than drinking beer | with the breaker of rings.

19. "My father has pledged | his daughter fair
As bride to Granmar's | son so grim;
But, Helgi, I | once Hothbrodd called
As fine a king | as the son of a cat.

20. "Yet the hero will come | a few nights hence,
· · · ·   · · · ·
Unless thou dost bid him | the battle-ground seek,
Or takest the maid | from the warrior mighty."

Helgi spake:
21. "Fear him not, | though Isung he felled,
First must our courage | keen be tried,
Before unwilling | thou fare with the knave;
Weapons will clash, | if to death I come not."

22. Messengers sent | the mighty one then,
By land and by sea, | a host to seek,
Store of wealth | of the water's gleam,
And men to summon, | and sons of men.

23. "Bid them straightway | seek the ships,
And off Brandey | ready to be!"
There the chief waited | till thither were come
Men by hundreds | from Hethinsey.

24. Soon off Stafnsnes | stood the ships,
Fair they glided | and gay with gold;
Then Helgi spake | to Hjorleif asking:
"Hast thou counted | the gallant host?"

25. The young king answered | the other then:
"Long were it to tell | from Tronueyr
The long-stemmed ships | with warriors laden
That come from without | into Orvasund.

26. .   .   .   .
"There are hundreds twelve | of trusty men,
But in Hotun lies | the host of the king,
Greater by half; | I have hope of battle."

27. The ship's-tents soon | the chieftain struck,
And waked the throng | of warriors all;
(The heroes the red | of dawn beheld;)
And on the masts | the gallant men
Made fast the sails | in Varinsfjord.

28. There was beat of oars | and clash of iron,
Shield smote shield | as the ships'-folk rowed;
Swiftly went | the warrior-laden
Fleet of the ruler | forth from the land.

29. So did it sound, | when together the sisters
Of Kolga struck | with the keels full long,
As if cliffs were broken | with beating surf,

.   .   .   .

30. Helgi bade higher | hoist the sails,
Nor did the ships'-folk | shun the waves,
Though dreadfully | did Ægir's daughters
Seek the steeds | of the sea to sink.

31. But from above | did Sigrun brave
Aid the men and | all their faring;
Mightily came | from the claws of Ron
The leader's sea-beast | off Gnipalund.

32. At evening there | in Unavagar
Floated the fleet | bedecked full fair;
But they who saw | from Svarin's hill,
Bitter at heart | the host beheld.

33. Then Gothmund asked, | goodly of birth,
. . . .
"Who is the monarch | who guides the host,
And to the land | the warriors leads?"

34. Sinfjotli answered, | and up on an oar
Raised a shield all red | with golden rim;
A sea-sentry was he, | skilled to speak,
And in words with princes | well to strive.

35. "Say tonight | when you feed the swine,
And send your bitches | to seek their swill,
That out of the East | have the Ylfings come,
Greedy for battle, | to Gnipalund.

36. "There will Hothbrodd | Helgi find,
In the midst of the fleet, | and flight he scorns;
Often has he | the eagles gorged,
Whilst thou at the quern | wert slave-girls kissing."

Gothmund spake:
37. "Hero, the ancient | sayings heed,
And bring not lies | to the nobly born.
. . . .
. . . .

38. "Thou hast eaten | the entrails of wolves,
And of thy brothers | the slayer been;
Oft wounds to suck | thy cold mouth sought,
And loathed in rocky | dens didst lurk."

Sinfjotli spake:
39. "A witch in Varin's | isle thou wast,
A woman false, | and lies didst fashion;
Of the mail-clad heroes | thou wouldst have
No other, thou saidst, | save Sinfjotli only.

40. "A Valkyrie wast thou, | loathly Witch,
Evil and base, | in Allfather's home;
The warriors all | must ever fight,
Woman subtle, | for sake of thee.

41. ".   .   .   .   .

.   .   .   .
Nine did we | in Sogunes
Of wolf-cubs have; | I their father was."

Gothmund spake:
42. "Thou didst not father | Fenrir's-wolves,
Though older thou art | than all I know;
For they gelded thee | in Gnipalund,
The giant-women | at Thorsnes once.

43. "Under houses the stepson | of Siggeir lay,
Fain of the wolf's cry | out in the woods;
Evil came then all | to thy hands,
When thy brothers' | breasts thou didst redden,
Fame didst thou win | for foulest deeds.

44. "In Bravoll wast thou | Grani's bride,
Golden-bitted | and ready to gallop;

265

I rode thee many | a mile, and down
Didst sink, thou giantess, | under the saddle."

Sinfjotli spake:
45. "A brainless fellow | didst seem to be,
When once for Gollnir | goats didst milk,
And another time | when as Imth's daughter
In rags thou wentest; | wilt longer wrangle?"

Gothmund spake:
46. "Sooner would I | at Frekastein
Feed the ravens | with flesh of thine
Than send your bitches | to seek their swill,
Or feed the swine; | may the fiends take you!"

Helgi spake:
47. "Better, Sinfjotli, | thee 'twould beseem
Battle to give | and eagles to gladden,
Than vain and empty | words to utter,
Though ring-breakers oft | in speech do wrangle.

48. "Good I find not | the sons of Granmar,
But for heroes 'tis seemly | the truth to speak;
At Moinsheimar | proved the men
That hearts for the wielding | of swords they had."

49. Mightily then | they made to run
Sviputh and Sveggjuth | to Solheimar;
(By dewy dales | and chasms dark,
Mist's horse shook | where the men went by;)
The king they found | at his courtyard gate,
And told him the foeman | fierce was come.

50. Forth stood Hothbrodd, | helmed for battle,
Watched the riding | of his warriors;

. . . .
"Why are the Hniflungs | white with fear?"

Gothmund spake:
51. "Swift keels lie | hard by the land,
(Mast-ring harts | and mighty yards,
Wealth of shields | and well-planed oars;)
The king's fair host, | the Ylfings haughty;
Fifteen bands | to land have fared,
But out in Sogn | are seven thousand.

52. "At anchor lying | off Gnipalund
Are fire-beasts black, | all fitted with gold;
There wait most | of the foeman's men,
Nor will Helgi long | the battle delay."

Hothbrodd spake:
53. "Bid the horses run | to the Reginthing,
Melnir and Mylnir | to Myrkwood now,
(And Sporvitnir | to Sparinsheith;)
Let no man seek | henceforth to sit
Who the flame of wounds | knows well to wield.

54. "Summon Hogni, | the sons of Hring,
Atli and Yngvi | and Alf the Old;
Glad they are | of battle ever;
Against the Volsungs | let us go."

55. Swift as a storm | there smote together
The flashing blades | at Frekastein;
Ever was Helgi, | Hunding's slayer,
First in the throng | where warriors fought;
(Fierce in battle, | slow to fly,
Hard the heart | of the hero was.)

56. From heaven there came | the maidens helmed,-- ˙
The weapon-clang grew,-- | who watched o'er the king;
Spake Sigrun fair,-- | the wound-givers flew,
And the horse of the giantess | raven's-food had:--

57. "Hail to thee, hero! | full happy with men,
Offspring of Yngvi, | shalt ever live,
For thou the fearless | foe hast slain
Who to many the dread | of death had brought.

58. "Warrior, well | for thyself hast won
Red rings bright | and the noble bride;
Both now, warrior, | thine shall be,
Hogni's daughter | and Hringstathir,
Wealth and triumph; | the battle wanes."

[1. The manuscript contains the superscription: "Here begins the lay of Helgi
Hundingbane and h. (Hothbrodd?) The lay of the Volsungs."*Eagles*, etc.: the
screaming of eagles and water pouring from heaven were portents of the birth of a
hero. *Borghild*: Sigmund's first wife;*Bralund* was her home, not Sigmund's.

2. *Norns*: cf. *Voluspo*, 20 and note. Here it is the Norns who [fp. 292] preside over
Helgi's early destiny, and not a Valkyrie, as in *Helgakvitha Hjorvarthssonar*.]

[3. Line 2 is largely guesswork, the manuscript being obscure. *Moon's hall*: the
sky.

4. *East*, etc.: the Norris give Helgi fame in the East, West, and North; in the North
his renown is particularly to endure. This suggests that the poet was aware of the
spread of the Helgi story over many lands. *Neri's kinswoman*: evidently one of the
Norns, but nothing further is known of Neri, and the word may not be a proper
name at all.

5. The manuscript indicates no gap, but it looks as though something had been lost
after line 2. *Ylfings' son*: Sigmund is evidently meant, though calling him an
Ylfing (cf. *Hyndluljoth*, 11 and note) is a manifest error. Helgi, in the tradition as
it came from Denmark, was undoubtedly an Ylfing, and the poet, in order to

combine the two legends, has to treat the Ylfings and Volsungs as if they were the same family.]

[6. *Sigmund*: the chief link between the Helgi and Sigurth stories. He was the son of Volsung, great-grandson of Othin. His children by his first wife, Borghild, were Helgi and Hamund (belonging to the Helgi cycle); his son by his second wife, Hjordis, was Sigurth. An incestuous connection with his sister, Signy (cf. Wagner's Siegmund and Sieglinde) resulted in the birth of Sinfjotli (cf. *Fra Dautha Sinfjotla* and note).

7. *The king*: Sigmund, who gives his son a symbol of the lands which he bestows on him. Regarding the leek, cf. *Voluspo*, 4; *Guthrunarkvitha*I, 17, and *Sigrdrifumol*, 7.

8. *Hringstathir* ("Ring-Stead"): quite possibly the historical Ringsted, long a possession of the Danish kings, and thus a relic of the old Helgi tradition. *Hringstoth* may be another form of the same name. *Solfjoll* ("Sun-Mountain") and *Snæfjoll* ("Snow-Mountain") are fictitious names. Regarding *Sigarsvoll* cf. *Helgakvitha Hjorvarthssonar*, stanzas 8 and 35. Saxo mentions a Danish king named Sigar, and the frequency with which the name appears in the Helgi poems may be taken as a reminiscence of Denmark. *Hotun* ("High Place"): possibly the village of Tune in Seeland. *Himinvangar* ("Heaven's Field"): an imaginary place. Blood-snake: a sword. *Sinfjotli*: cf. note on stanza 6.]

[9. *Elm*: a not uncommon word for "man." *Blood-flecked*: i.e., won in battle.

10. *Fifteen*: until early in the eleventh century a Norwegian or Icelandic boy became "of age" at twelve, and Maurer cites this passage as added proof of the poem's lateness. Hunding: the annotator (introductory prose to *Helgakvitha Hundingsbana* II) calls him king of Hundland, which shows no great originality. Saxo mentions a Hunding who was a Saxon king ruling in Jutland, probably the origin of Helgi's traditional foe.

12. *Storm*, etc.: war.

13. *Logafjoll* ("Flame-Mountain"): a mythical name. *Frothi*: [fp. 295] a traditional king of Denmark, whose peaceful reign was so famous that "Frothi's peace" became a by-word for peace of any kind. *Vithrir's hounds*: wolves; Vithrir is Othin, and his hounds are the wolves Freki and Geri.]

[14. In this poem Helgi kills all the sons of Hunding, but in the poems of the Sigurth cycle, and the prose notes attached thereto, Sigmund and his father-in-law, Eylimi, are killed by Hunding's sons, on whom Sigurth subsequently takes vengeance (cf. *Fra Dautha Sinfjotla* and *Reginsmol*).

15. No gap indicated in the manuscript, but almost certainly something has been lost mentioning more specifically the coming of the Valkyries. The lightning which accompanies them suggests again their identification with the clouds (cf. *Helgakvitha Hjorvarthssonar*, 28).

16. Some editions fill out the first line: "He saw there mighty maidens riding." The manuscript indicates line 4 as the beginning of a new stanza.]

[17. *Wolf-wood*: dark forest; the original word is not altogether clear. *Southern*: this variety of Valkyrie, like the swan maidens of the *Völundarkvitha*, was clearly regarded as of southern (i.e., German) origin. Here again there is a confusion of traditions; the Valkyries of the *Voluspo* were as essentially Norse as any part of the older mythology. I doubt if a poet much earlier than the author of the first Helgi Hundingsbane lay would have made his Sigrun, daughter of Hogni, a Valkyrie. It is to be noted that the same complication appears in the Sigurth story, where the undoubted Valkyrie, Brynhild-Sigrdrifa (the latter name is really only an epithet) is hopelessly mixed up with the quite human Brynhild, daughter of Buthli.

18. *Breaker of rings*: generous prince, because the breaking of rings was the customary form of distributing gold.

19. *Granmar*: the annotator gives an account of him and his family in the prose following stanza 12 of *Helgakvitha Hundingsbana II*.

20. No gap indicated in the manuscript; some editors combine the stanza with the fragmentary stanza 21, and others fill in with "And home will carry | Hogni's daughter."]

[21. The manuscript has only lines 1 and 4 with the word "first" of line 2, and does not indicate Helgi as the speaker. The *Volsungasaga*, which follows this poem pretty closely, expands Helgi's speech, and lines 2-3 are conjectural versifications of the saga's prose. *Isung*: nothing is known of him beyond the fact, here indicated, that Hothbrodd killed him.

22. *Water's gleam*: gold.

23. *Brandey* ("Brand-Isle"): not mentioned elsewhere. *Hethinsey* ("Hethin's Isle"): possibly the island of Hiddensee, east of Rügen.]

[24. *Stafnsnes* ("Steersman's Cape"): an unidentifiable promontory. *Fair*: a guess, as the adjective in the manuscript is obscure. *Hjorleif* does not appear elsewhere, and seems to be simply one of Helgi's lieutenants.

25. *Tronueyr*: "Crane-Strand." *Long-stemmed*: literally "long-headed," as the high, curving stem of a Norse ship was often carved to represent a head and neck. *Orvasund*: almost certainly the Danish Öresund, off Seeland. Such bits of geography as this followed Helgi persistently.

26. No gap indicated in the manuscript. *Hotun*: cf. stanza 8 and note.

27. Line 3 seems to have been interpolated from line 4 of *Helgakvitha Hundingsbana* II, 42. *Ship's-tents*: the awnings spread over the deck to shelter the crews from sun and rain when the ships were at anchor. *Varinsfjord*: cf. *Helgakvitha Hjorvarthssonar*, 22 and note.]

[28. The manuscript indicates line 3 as the beginning of a new stanza, and some editions follow this arrangement, making lines 1-2 a separate stanza.

29. The manuscript indicates no gap, and some editions combine the stanza with lines 3-4 of stanza 28. *Sisters of Kolga*: the waves, Kolga ("The Gold") being one of the daughters of the sea-god, Ægir. As the *Volsungasaga* says, "Now there was a great storm."

30. Helgi demonstrates his courage, whatever one may think of his seamanship. *Ægir's daughters*: the waves; cf. stanza 29 and note.]

[31. Sigrun here appears again as a Valkyrie. *Ron*: Ægir's wife; cf. *Helgakvitha Hjorvarthssonar*, 18 and note. *Sea-beast*: ship. *Gnipalund*: "Crag-Wood."

32. *Unavagar*: "Friendly Waves." *Svarin's hill*: the hill where Granmar had his dwelling.

33. Here begins the long dialogue between Gothmund, one of Gramnar's sons, and Sinfjotli, Helgi's half-brother. Two lines (stanza 33, lines 3-4) are quoted by the annotator in the prose note following stanza 16 of the second Helgi Hundingsbane lay, and the dialogue, in much abbreviated form, together with Helgi's admonition to Sinfjotli to cease talking, is closely paralleled in stanzas 22-27 of that poem. It

has been suggested that this whole passage (stanzas 33-48) is an interpolation, perhaps from "the Old Volsung lay." This may be, but it seems more probable that the poet used an older poem simply as the basis for this passage, borrowing a little but making up a great deal more. The manuscript indicates no gap in stanza 33.

34. *Sinfjotli*: cf. note on stanza 6. *Red*: raising a red shield was the signal for war.]

[35. *Ylfings*: cf. stanza 5 and note.

36. *Quern*: turning the hand mill was, throughout antiquity, the task of slaves.

37. The manuscript does not name the speakers in this dialogue. No gap indicated in the manuscript, and editors have attempted various combinations of stanzas 37 and 38.

38. *Wolves*: the Volsungasaga tells that Sigmund and Sinfjotli lived in the woods for a time as werewolves. *Brothers*: [fp. 302] Sinfjotli killed the two sons of his mother, Signy, and her husband, Siggeir, as part of the vengeance wreaked on Siggeir for the treacherous murder of Sigmund's father, Volsung, and nine of his brothers (cf. *Fra Dautha Sinfjotla* and note). The manuscript marks line 3 as the beginning of a new stanza.]

[39. *Varin's isle*: cf. stanza 27 and note, and *Helgakvitha Hjorvarthssonar*, 22. Reproaching a man with having been a woman and borne children was not uncommon.

40. This stanza may be an interpolation in the dialogue passage. *Allfather*: Othin. We have no information regarding Gothmund's career, but it looks as though Sinfjotli were drawing solely on his imagination for his taunts, whereas Gothmund's insults have a basis in Sinfjotli's previous life.

41. No gap indicated in the manuscript; some editors combine the two lines with stanza 40, some regard them as the first instead of the last lines of a separate stanza, and some assume the lacuna here indicated. *Sogunes* ("Saga's Cape"): of the goddess Saga little is known; cf.*Grimnismol*, 7.]

[42. *Fenrir's-wolves*: wolves in general. *Thorsnes*: "Thor's Cape."

43. The phrase "under houses," which follows the manuscript, may be an error for "in wolf-caves." Line 3 (or 4) may be an interpolation. The manuscript indicates line 5 as the beginning of a new stanza. *Siggeir*: cf. stanza 38, note.

44. Several editions assign this stanza to Sinfjotli instead of to Gothmund. *Bravoll* ("Field of the Brow"): not elsewhere mentioned in the poems. *Grani*: Sigurth's horse (cf. *Völundarkvitha*, 16 and note); Gothmund means that Sinfjotli had turned into a mare, after the fashion of Loki (cf. *Grimnismol*, 44, note). The meaning of line 4 in the original is uncertain.

45. A few editions give this stanza to Gothmund. *Gollnir*: [fp. 304] possibly a giant. *Imth*: nothing is known of him or his daughter.]

[46. A few editions give this stanza to Sinfjotli. *Frekastein*: cf. *Helgakvitha Hjorvarthssonar*, 39 and note. A stanza may have been lost after stanza 46, parallel to stanza 25 of the second Helgi Hundingsbane lay.

47. *Ring-breakers*: cf. stanza 318 and note.

48. *Moinsheimar*: a battlefield of which nothing is known, where, however, the sons of Granmar appear to have fought bravely.

49. Here the scene shifts to the shore among Hothbrodd's followers. [fp. 305] *Sviputh* and *Sveggjuth* ("Swift" and "Lithe"): horses' names. *Mist's horse*: the Valkyrie's name is the same as the English word "mist," and the "horse" on which the mist rides is the earth. The two lines in parenthesis may be interpolated, or line 5 may begin a new stanza, as the manuscript indicates.]

[50. No gap indicated in the manuscript. *Hniflungs*: cf. introductory note.

51. Lines 2-3 may be interpolated, or a new stanza may begin, as the manuscript indicates, with line 5. Many editors combine lines 5-6 with all or part of stanza 52. Possibly Gothmund is not the speaker. *Mast-ring harts*: ships, so called from the ring attaching the yard to the mast. *Ylfings*: cf. stanza 5 and note. *Sogn*: this name, which actually belongs in western Norway, seems to have been used here with no particular significance.

52. The manuscript indicates line 3 as beginning a new stanza; some editors combine lines 3-4 with all or part of stanza [fp. 306]53, while others assume the loss of two lines following line 4. *Fire-beasts*: dragons,, i.e., ships. The Norse ships of war, as distinguished from merchant vessels, were often called dragons because of their shape and the carving of their stems.]

[53. The manuscript does not indicate the speaker, and a few editors assume the loss of one or two lines embodying the phrase "Hothbrodd spake." In the manuscript line 3, which many editors have suspected of being spurious, stands before line 2. Possibly lines 4-5 are the remains of a separate stanza. *Reginthing* ("The Great Council"): apparently the council-place for the whole country, as distinct from the local council, or "herathsthing." *Melnir* ("Bit-Bearer"), *Mylnir* ("The Biter") and *Spornvitnir* ("Spur-Wolf"): horses' names. *Myrkwood*: a not uncommon name for a dark forest; cf. *Lokasenna*, 42, and *Atlakvitha*, 3. *Sparinsheith* ("Sparin's Heath"): nothing more is known of Sparin or his heath. *Flame of wounds*: sword.

54. *Hogni*: the father of Sigrun; cf. *Helgakvitha Hundingsbana* [fp. 307] II, 18. Of Hring and his sons nothing further is known. Volsungs: here for the first time the poet gives Helgi and Sinfjotli the family name to which, as sons of Sigmund Volsungsson, they are entitled.]

[55. The manuscript indicates line 5 as the beginning of a new stanza, but many editors have rejected lines 5-6 as spurious, while others regard them as the first half of a stanza the last two lines of which have been lost.

56. *Wound-givers*: probably this means "Valkyries," but there is considerable doubt as to the original word. *Horse*, etc.: i.e., the wolf (because giantesses customarily had wolves for their steeds) ate corpses (the food of birds of prey).

57. *Yngvi*: one of the sons of Halfdan the Old, and traditional ancestor of the Ynglings, with whom the Ylfings seem to have been confused (cf. *Hynduljoth*, 11 and note). The confusion between the Ylfings (or Ynglings) and Volsungs was carried far [fp. 308] enough so that Sigurth himself is once called a descendant of Yngvi (*Reginsmol*, 14). Gering identifies the name of Yngvi with the god Freyr, but the Volsungs certainly claimed descent from Othin, not Freyr, and there is nothing to indicate that Helgi in the Danish tradition was supposed to be descended from Freyr, whereas his descent from Yngvi Halfdansson fits well with the rest of his story. However, cf. *Sigurtharkvitha en skamma*, 24 and note.]

[58. This entire stanza may be an interpolation; nearly every edition has a different way of dealing with it. *Hringstathir*: as this place had been given to Helgi by his father (cf. stanza 8 and note), the poet has apparently made a mistake in naming it here as a conquest from Granmar's sons, unless, indeed, they had previously captured it from Helgi, which seems unlikely.]

HELGAKVITHA HUNDINGSBANA II

The Second Lay of Helgi Hundingsbane

INTRODUCTORY NOTE

As the general nature of the Helgi tradition has been considered in the introductory note to *Helgakvitha Hjorvarthssonar*, it is necessary here to discuss only the characteristics of this particular poem. The second Helgi Hundingsbane lay is in most respects the exact opposite of the first one: it is in no sense consecutive; it is not a narrative poem, and all or most of it gives evidence of relatively early composition, its origin probably going well back into the tenth century.

It is frankly nothing but a piece of, in the main, very clumsy patchwork, made up of eight distinct fragments, pieced together awkwardly by the annotator with copious prose notes. One of these fragments (stanzas 13-16) is specifically identified as coming from "the old Volsung lay." What was that poem, and how much more of the extant Helgi-lay compilation was taken from it, and did the annotator know more of it than he included in his patchwork? Conclusive answers to these questions have baffled scholarship, and probably always will do so. My own guess is that the annotator knew little or nothing more than he wrote down; having got the first Helgi Hundingsbane lay, which was obviously in fairly good shape, out of the way, he proceeded to assemble all the odds and ends of verse about Helgi which he could get hold of, putting them together on the basis of the narrative told in the first Helgi lay and of such stories as his knowledge of prose sagas may have yielded.

Section I (stanzas 1-4) deals with an early adventure of Helgi's, -in which he narrowly escapes capture when he ventures into Hunding's

275

home in disguise. Section II (stanzas 5-12) is a dialogue between Helgi and Sigrun at their first meeting. Section III (stanzas 13-16, the "old Volsung lay" group) is another dialogue between Helgi and Sigrun when she invokes his aid to save her from Hothbrodd. Section IV (stanzas 17-20, which may well be from the same poem as Section III, is made up of speeches by Helgi and Sigrun after the battle in which Hothbrodd is killed; stanza 21, however, is certainly an interpolation from another poem, as it is in a different meter. Section V (stanzas 22-27) is the dispute between Sinfjotli and Gothmund, evidently in an older form than the one included in the first Helgi Hundingsbane lay. Section VI (stanzas 28-37) gives Dag's speech to his sister, Sigrun, telling of Helgi's death, her curse on her brother and her lament for her slain husband. Section VII (stanza 38) is the remnant of a dispute between Helgi and Hunding, here inserted absurdly out of place. Section VIII (stanzas 39-50) deals with the return of the dead Helgi and Sigrun's visit to him in the burial hill.

Sijmons maintains that sections I and II are fragments of the Kara lay mentioned by the annotator in his concluding prose note, and that sections IV, VI, and VIII are from a lost Helgi-Sigrun poem, while Section III comes, of course, from the "old Volsung lay." This seems as good a guess as any other, conclusive proof being quite out of the question.

Were it not for sections, VI and VIII the poem would be little more than a battle-ground for scholars, but those two sections are in many ways as fine as anything in Old Norse poetry. Sigrun's curse of her brother for the slaying of Helgi and her lament for her dead husband, and the extraordinary vividness of the final scene in the burial hill, have a quality which fully offsets the baffling confusion of the rest of the poem.

King Sigmund, the son of Volsung, had as wife Borghild, from Bralund. They named their son Helgi, after Helgi Hjorvarthsson; Hagal was Helgi's foster-father. Hunding was the name of a powerful king, and Hundland is named from him. He was a mighty warrior, and had many sons with him on his campaigns. There was enmity and strife between these two, King Hunding and King Sigmund, and each slew the other's kinsmen. King Sigmund and his family were called Volsungs and Ylfings. Helgi went as a spy to the home of King Hunding in disguise. Hæming, a son of King Hunding's, was at home. When Helgi went forth, then he met a young herdsman, and said:

1. "Say to Hæming | that Helgi knows
Whom the heroes | in armor hid;
A gray wolf had they | within their hall,
Whom King Hunding | Hamal thought."

Hamal was the name of Hagal's son. King Hunding sent men to Hagal to seek Helgi, and Helgi could not save himself in any other way, so he put on the clothes of a bond-woman and set to work at the mill. They sought Helgi but found him not.

2. Then Blind spake out, | the evil-minded:
" Of Hagal's bond-woman | bright are the eyes;
Yon comes not of churls | who stands at the quern;
The millstones break, | the boards are shattered.

3. "The hero has | a doom full hard,
That barley now | he needs must grind;
Better befits | his hand to feel
The hilt of the sword | than the millstone's handle."

Hagal answered and said:

4. "Small is the wonder | if boards are splintered
By a monarch's daughter | the mill is turned;

277

Once through clouds | she was wont to ride,
And battles fought | like fighting men,
(Till Helgi a captive | held her fast;
Sister she is | of Sigar and Hogni,
Thus bright are the eyes | of the Ylfings' maid.)"

Helgi escaped and went to a fighting ship. He slew King Hunding, and thenceforth was called Helgi Hundingsbane.

(II)

He lay with his host in Brunavagar, and they had there a strand-slaughtering, and ate the flesh raw. Hogni was the name of a king. His daughter was Sigrun; she was a Valkyrie and rode air and water; she was Svava reborn. Sigrun rode to Helgi's ship and said:

5. "Who rules the ship | by the shore so steep?
Where is the home | ye warriors have?
Why do ye bide | in Brunavagar,
Or what the way | that ye wish to try?"

Helgi spake:
6 "Hamal's the ship | by the shore so steep,
Our home in Hlesey | do we have;
For fair wind bide we | in Brunavagar,
Eastward the way | that we wish to try."

Sigrun spake:
7. "Where hast thou, warrior, | battle wakened,
Or gorged the birds | of the sisters of Guth?
Why is thy byrnie | spattered with blood,
Why helmed dost feast | on food uncooked?"

Helgi spake:
8. "Latest of all, | the Ylfings' son
On the western sea, | if know thou wilt,

278

Captured bears | in Bragalund,
And fed the eagles | with edge of sword.
Now is it shown | why our shirts are bloody,
And little our food | with fire is cooked."

Sigrun spake:
9. "Of battle thou tellest, | and there was bent
Hunding the king | before Helgi down;
There was carnage when thou | didst avenge thy kin,
And blood flowed fast | on the blade of the sword."

Helgi spake:
10. "How didst thou know | that now our kin,
Maiden wise, | we have well avenged?
Many there are | of the sons of the mighty
Who share alike | our lofty race."

Sigrun spake:
11. "Not far was I | from the lord of the folk,
Yester morn, | when the monarch was slain;
Though crafty the son | of Sigmund, methinks,
When he speaks of the fight | in slaughter-runes.

12. "On the long-ship once | I saw thee well,
When in the blood-stained | bow thou wast,
 (And round thee icy | waves were raging;)
Now would the hero | hide from me,
But to Hogni's daughter | is Helgi known."

(III)

Granmar was the name of a mighty king, who dwelt at Svarin's hill.
He had many sons; one was named Hothbrodd, another Gothmund,
a third Starkath. Hothbrodd was in a kings' meeting, and he won the
promise of having Sigrun, Hogni's daughter, for his wife. But when
she heard this, she rode with the Valkyries over air and sea to seek

Helgi. Helgi was then at Logafjoll, and had fought with Hunding's sons; there he killed Alf and Eyolf, Hjorvarth and Hervarth. He was all weary with battle, and sat under the eagle-stone. There Sigrun found him, and ran to throw her arms about his neck, and kissed him, and told him her tidings, as is set forth in the old Volsung lay:

13. Sigrun the joyful | chieftain sought,
Forthwith Helgi's | hand she took;
She greeted the hero | helmed and kissed him,
The warrior's heart | to the woman turned.

14. From her heart the daughter | of Hogni spake,
Dear was Helgi, | she said, to her;
"Long with all | my heart I loved
Sigmund's son | ere ever I saw him.

15. "At the meeting to Hothbrodd | mated I was,
But another hero | I fain would have;
Though, king, the wrath | of my kin I fear,
Since I broke my father's | fairest wish."

Helgi spake:
16. "Fear not ever | Hogni's anger,
Nor yet thy kinsmen's | cruel wrath;
Maiden, thou | with me shalt live,
Thy kindred, fair one, | I shall not fear."

(IV)

Helgi then assembled a great sea-host and went to Frekastein. On the sea he met a perilous storm; lightning flashed overhead and the bolts struck the ship. They saw in the air that nine Valkyries were riding, and recognized Sigrun among them. Then the storm abated, and they came safe and sound to land. Granmar's sons sat on a certain mountain as the ships sailed toward the land. Gothmund leaped on a horse and rode for news to a promontory near the harbor; the Volsungs were even then lowering their sails. Then Gothmund said, as is written before in the Helgi lay:

"Who is the king | who captains the fleet,
And to the land | the warriors leads?"

Sinfjotli, Sigmund's son, answered him, and that too is written. Gothmund rode home with his tidings of the host; then Granmar's sons summoned an army. Many kings came there; there were Hogni, Sigrun's father, and his sons Bragi and Dag. There was a great battle, and all Granmar's sons were slain and all their allies; only Dag, Hogni's son, was spared, and he swore loyalty to the Volsungs. Sigrun went among the dead and found Hothbrodd at the coming of death. She said:

17. "Never shall Sigrun | from Sevafjoll,
Hothbrodd king, | be held in thine arms;
Granmar's sons | full cold have grown,
And the giant-steeds gray | on corpses gorge."

Then she sought out Helgi, and was full of joy He said:

18. "Maid, not fair | is all thy fortune,
The Norris I blame | that this should be;
This morn there fell | at Frekastein
Bragi and Hogni | beneath my hand.

19. "At Hlebjorg fell | the sons of Hrollaug,
Starkath the king | at Styrkleifar;
Fighters more noble | saw I never,
The body fought | when the head had fallen.

20. "On the ground full low | the slain are lying,
Most are there | of the men of thy race;
Nought hast thou won, | for thy fate it was
Brave men to bring | to the battle-field."

Then Sigrun wept. | Helgi said:

21. "Grieve not, Sigrun, | the battle is gained,
The fighter can shun not his fate."
Sigrun spake:
"To life would I call | them who slaughtered lie,
If safe on thy breast I might be."

(V)

This Gothmund the son of Granmar spoke:

22. "What hero great | is guiding the ships?
A golden flag | on the stem he flies;
I find not peace in | the van of your faring,
And round the fighters | is battle-light red."

Sinfjotli spake:
23. "Here may Hothbrodd | Helgi find,
The hater of flight, | in the midst of the fleet;
The home of all | thy race he has,
And over the realm | of the fishes he rules."

Gothmund spake:
24. "First shall swords | at Frekastein
Prove our worth | in place of words;
Time is it, Hothbrodd, | vengeance to have,
If in battle worsted | once we were."

Sinfjotli spake:
25. "Better, Gothmund, | to tend the goats,
And climb the rocks | of the mountain cliffs;
A hazel switch | to hold in thy hand
More seemly were | than the hilt of a sword."

26. "Better, Sinfjotli, | thee 'twould beseem
Battles to give, | and eagles to gladden,
Than vain and empty | speech to utter,
Though warriors oft | with words do strive.

27. "Good I find not | the sons of Granmar,
But for heroes 'tis seemly | the truth to speak;
At Moinsheimar | proved the men
That hearts for the wielding | of swords they had,
(And ever brave | the warriors are.)"

(VI)

Helgi took Sigrun to wife, and they had sons. Helgi did not reach old age. Dag, the son of Hogni, offered sacrifice to Othin to be avenged for his father's death; Othin gave Dag his spear. Dag found Helgi, his brother-in-law, at a place which is called Fjoturlund. He thrust the spear through Helgi's body. Then Helgi fell, and Dag rode to Sevafjoll and told Sigrun the tidings:

28. "Sad am I, sister, | sorrow to tell thee,
Woe to my kin | unwilling I worked;
In the morn there fell | at Fjoturlund
The noblest prince | the world has known,
(And his heel he set | on the heroes' necks.)"

Sigrun spake:
29. "Now may every | oath thee bite
That with Helgi | sworn thou hast,
By the water | bright of Leipt,
And the ice-cold | stone of Uth.

30. "The ship shall sail not | in which thou sailest,
Though a favoring wind | shall follow after;

The horse shall run not | whereon thou ridest,
Though fain thou art | thy foe to flee.

31.. . . . .

. . . .

"The sword shall bite not | which thou bearest,
Till thy head itself | it sings about.

32. "Vengeance were mine | for Helgi's murder,
Wert thou a wolf | in the woods without,
Possessing nought | and knowing no joy,
Having no food | save corpses to feed on."

Dag spake:
33. "Mad art thou, sister, | and wild of mind,
Such a curse | on thy brother to cast;
Othin is ruler | of every ill,
Who sunders kin | with runes of spite.

34. "Thy brother rings | so red will give thee,
All Vandilsve | and Vigdalir;
Take half my land | to pay the harm,
Ring-decked maid, | and as meed for thy sons."

Sigrun spake:
35. "I shall sit not happy | at Sevafjoll,
Early or late, | my life to love,
If the light cannot show, | in the leader's band,
Vigblær bearing him | back to his home,
(The golden-bitted; | I shall greet him never.)

36. "Such the fear | that Helgi's foes
Ever felt, | and all their kin,
As makes the goats | with terror mad
Run from the wolf | among the rocks.

37. "Helgi rose | above heroes all
Like the lofty ash | above lowly thorns,
Or the noble stag, | with dew besprinkled,
Bearing his head | above all beasts,
(And his horns gleam bright | to heaven itself.)

A hill was made in Helgi's memory. And when he came to Valhall,
then Othin bade him rule over every thing with himself.

(VII)

Helgi said:
A "Thou shalt, Hunding, | of every hero
Wash the feet, | and kindle the fire,
Tie up dogs, | and tend the horses,
And feed the swine | ere to sleep thou goest."

(VIII)

One of Sigrun's maidens went one evening to Helgi's hill, and saw
that Helgi rode to the hill with many men, The maiden said:

39. "Is this a dream | that methinks I see,
Or the doom of the gods, | that dead men ride,
And hither spurring | urge your steeds,
Or is home-coming now | to the heroes granted?"

Helgi spake:
40. "No dream is this | that thou thinkest to see,
Nor the end of the world, | though us thou beholdest,
And hither spurring | we urge our steeds,
Nor is home-coming now | to the heroes granted."

The maiden went home and said to Sigrun:

41. "Go forth, Sigrun, | from Sevafjoll,
If fain the lord | of the folk wouldst find;
(The hill is open, | Helgi is come;)
The sword-tracks bleed; | the monarch bade
That thou his wounds | shouldst now make well."

Sigrun went in the hill to Helgi, and said:

42. "Now am I glad | of our meeting together,
As Othin's hawks, | so eager for prey,
When slaughter and flesh | all warm they scent,
Or dew-wet see | the red of day.

43. "First will I kiss | the lifeless king,
Ere off the bloody | byrnie thou cast;
With frost thy hair | is heavy, Helgi,
And damp thou art | with the dew of death;
(Ice-cold hands | has Hogni's kinsman,
What, prince, can I | to bring thee ease?)"

Helgi spake:
44. "Thou alone, Sigrun | of Sevafjoll,
Art cause that Helgi | with dew is heavy;
Gold-decked maid, | thy tears are grievous,
(Sun-bright south-maid, | ere thou sleepest;)
Each falls like blood | on the hero's breast,
(Burned-out, cold, | and crushed with care.)

45. "Well shall we drink | a noble draught,
Though love and lands | are lost to me;
No man a song | of sorrow shall sing,
Though bleeding wounds | are on my breast;
Now in the hill | our brides we hold,
The heroes' loves, | by their husbands dead."

Sigrun made ready a bed in the hill.

46. "Here a bed | I have made for thee, Helgi,
To rest thee from care, | thou kin of the Ylfings;
I will make thee sink | to sleep in my arms,
As once I lay | with the living king."

Helgi spake:
47. "Now do I say | that in Sevafjoll
Aught may happen, | early or late,
Since thou sleepest clasped | in a corpse's arms,
So fair in the hill, | the daughter of Hogni!
(Living thou comest, | a daughter of kings.)

48. "Now must I ride | the reddened ways,
And my bay steed set | to tread the sky;

Westward I go | to wind-helm's bridges,
Ere Salgofnir wakes | the warrior throng."

Then Helgi and his followers rode on their way, and the women went home to the dwelling. Another evening Sigrun bade the maiden keep watch at the hill. And at sunset when Sigrun came to the hill she said:

49. "Now were he come, | if come he might,
Sigmund's son, | from Othin's seat;
Hope grows dim | of the hero's return
When eagles sit | on the ash-tree boughs,
And men are seeking | the meeting of dreams."

The Maiden said:
50. "Mad thou wouldst seem | alone to seek,
Daughter of heroes, | the house of the dead;
For mightier now | at night are all
The ghosts of the dead | than when day is bright."

Sigrun was early dead of sorrow and grief. It was believed in olden times that people were born again, but that is now called old wives' folly. Of Helgi and Sigrun it is said that they were born again; he became Helgi Haddingjaskati, and she Kara the daughter of Halfdan, as is told in the Lay of Kara, and she was a Valkyrie.

[*Prose.* In the manuscript the poem is headed "Of the Volsungs," but most editions give it the title used here. Sigmund: cf. *Helgakvitha Hundingsbana I*, 6 and note, which also mentions Volsung. *Borghild* and *Bralund*: cf. *Helgakvitha Hundingsbana I*, 1 and note. *Helgi*: the annotator's explanation that the child [fp. 311] was named after Helgi Hjorvarthsson is a naive way of getting around the difficulties created by the two sets of Helgi stories. He might equally well have said that the new Helgi was the old one born again, as he accounts for Sigrun in this way ("she was Svava reborn"). *Hagal*: not elsewhere mentioned; it was a common custom to have boys brought up by foster-parents.*Hunding* and *Hundland*: cf. *Helgakvitha Hundingsbana I*, 10 and note. *Volsungs* and *Ylfings*: regarding this confusion of family names cf.*Helgakvitha Hundingsbana I*, 5 and note. *Hæming*: his name does not appear in the list of Hunding's sons. It is quite possible that these opening stanzas (1-4) do not refer to Hunding at all.]

[1. Helgi appears to have stayed with Hunding under the name of Hamal, but now, thinking himself safe, he sends word of who he really is.*Hunding*: it has been suggested that the compiler may have inserted this name to fit what he thought the story ought to be, in place of Hæming, or even Hadding. If stanzas 1-4 are a fragment of the *Karuljoth* (*Lay of Kara*), this latter suggestion is quite reasonable, for in that poem, which we do not possess, but which supplied material for the compilers of the *Hromundar saga Greipssonar*, Helgi appears as Helgi Haddingjaskati (cf. final prose note). Nothing beyond this one name connects stanzas 1-4 with Hunding.]

[*Prose. Hagal*: Helgi's foster-father, who naturally protects him.

2. The manuscript indicates line 2 as the beginning of the stanza, the copyist evidently regarding line 1 as prose. This has caused various rearrangements in the different editions. *Blind*: leader of the band sent to capture Helgi.

3. The manuscript marks line 3 as the beginning of a stanza. *Barley*: the word literally means "foreign grain," and would afford an interesting study to students of early commerce.

4. Possibly two stanzas with one line lost, or perhaps the lines in parenthesis are spurious; each editor has his own guess, Sigar and Hogni: it seems unlikely that Hagal refers to the Hogni who was Sigrun's father, for this part of the story has nothing whatever to do with Sigrun. As Hagal is, of course, deliberately [fp. 313] lying, it is useless to test any part of his speech for accuracy.]

[*Prose*. No division indicated in the manuscript. *Brunavagar* ("Bruni's Sea"): mentioned only in this section. *Strand-slaughtering*: a killing on the shore of cattle stolen in a raid. *Hogni* and *Sigrun*: cf. *Helgakvitha Hundingsbana I*, 17 and note; the annotator's notion of Sigrun as the reincarnated Svava (cf. *Helgakvitha Hjorvarthssonar*, concluding prose note) represents a naive form of scholarship. There is nothing in stanzas 5-12 which clearly identifies Sigrun as a Valkyrie, or which, except for the last line of stanza 12, identifies the speaker as Sigrun. Some editors, therefore, call her simply "the Valkyrie," while [fp. 314] Vigfusson, who thinks this section is also a remnant of the *Karuljoth*, calls her Kara.]

[6. The manuscript does not indicate the speakers. *Hamal*: Helgi's assumption of this name seems to link this section (stanzas 5-12) with stanza 1. *Hlesey* ("Island of Hler"--i.e., Ægir, the sea-god): generally identified as the Danish island of Läsö; cf. *Harbarthsljoth*, 37 and note.

7. *Guth*: a Valkyrie (cf. *Voluspo*, 31) the birds of her sisters are the kites and ravens.

8. The manuscript indicates line 5 as the beginning of a new stanza; some editors reject lines 1-2, while others make lines 5-6 into a fragmentary stanza. *Ylfings*: cf. introductory prose and note. *Bragalund* ("Bragi's Wood"): a mythical place. *Bears*: presumably Berserkers, regarding whom cf. *Hyndluljoth*, 23.]

[10. Helgi's meaning in lines 3-4 is that, although he has al ready declared himself an Ylfing (stanza 8, line 1), there are many heroes of that race, and he does not understand how Sigrun knows him to be Helgi.

11. *Slaughter-runes*: equivocal or deceptive speech regarding the battle. The word "rune" had the meaning of "magic" or "mystery" long before it was applied to the signs or characters with which it was later identified.

12. Some editors reject line 3, others line 5. The manuscript omits Helgi's name in line 5, thereby destroying both the sense and the meter. Vigfusson, following his *Karuljoth* theory (cf. [fp. 316] note on prose following stanza 4), changes Hogni to Halfdan, father of Kara.]

[*Prose*. The manuscript indicates no division. Most of this prose passage is evidently based on *Helgakvitha Hundingsbana I*; the only new features are the introduction of Starkath as a third son of Granmar, which is clearly an error based on a misunderstanding of stanza 19, and the reference to the *kings' meeting*, based on stanza 15. Kings' meetings, or councils, were by no means unusual; the North in early days was prolific in kings. For the remaining names, cf. *Helgakvitha Hundingsbana I*: [fp. 317] *Granmar*, stanza 19; *Hothbrodd*, stanza 33; *Gothmund*, stanza 33; *Svarin's hill*, stanza 32; *Logafjoll*, stanza 13; .41f, *Eyjolf, Hjorvarth* and *Hervarth*, stanza 14. The *old Volsung lay*: cf. Introductory Note.]

[13. Some editions combine lines 3-4, Or line 4, with part of stanza 14.

14. The lines of stanzas 14 and 15 are here rearranged in accordance with Bugge's emendation; in the manuscript they stand as follows: lines 3-4 of stanza 14; stanza 15; lines 1-2 of stanza 14. This confusion has given rise to various editorial conjectures.

Prose. The manuscript indicates no division. Here again, the annotator has drawn practically all his information from *Helgakvitha* [fp. 317]*Hundingsbana I*, which he specifically mentions and even quotes. The only new features are the names of Hogni's sons, *Bragi* and *Dag*. Bragi is mentioned in stanza 19, though it is not there stated that he is Hogni's son. Dag, who figures largely in stanzas 28-34, is a puzzle, for the verse never names him, and it is an open question where the annotator got his name. *Frekastein*: cf. *Helgakvitha Hjorvarthssonar*, 39 and note. As is written: the two lines are quoted, with a change of two words, from *Holgakvitha Hundingsbana I*, 33. *Sinfjotli*: cf. *Helgakvitha Hundingsbana I*, 6 and note, and stanzas 33-48, in which the whole dialogue is given. *Loyalty*: apparently the annotator got this bit of information out of stanza 29, in which Sigrun refers to the oaths which her brother had sworn to Helgi.]

[17. *Sevafjoll* ("Wet Mountain"). mentioned only in this poem. *Giant-steeds*: wolves, the usual steeds of giantesses; cf. *Helgakvitha Hundingsbana I*, 56.

18. *Maid*: the word thus rendered is the same doubtful one which appears in *Völundarkvitha*, 1 and 5, and which may mean specifically a Valkyrie (Gering translates it "helmed" or "heroic") or simply "wise." Cf. *Völundarkvitha*, note on

introductory prose. *Norns*: cf. *Voluspo*, 20 and note. In stanza 33 Dag similarly lays the blame for the murder he has committed on Othin. *Bragi*: probably Sigrun's brother.

19. This stanza looks like an interpolation, and there is little [fp. 320] or nothing to connect it with the slaying of Gramnar's sons. In the manuscript line 2, indicated as the beginning of a stanza, precedes line 1. *Hlebjorg* ("Sea-Mountain") and *Styrkleifar* ("Battle-Cliffs"): place names not elsewhere mentioned. Of *Hrollaug's sons* nothing further is known. *Starkath*: this name gives a hint of the origin of this stanza, for Saxo Grammaticus tells of the slaying of the Swedish hero Starkath ("The Strong") the son of Storverk, and describes how his severed head bit the ground in anger (cf. line 4). In all probability this stanza is from an entirely different poem, dealing with the Starkath story, and the annotator's attempt to identify the Swedish hero as a third son of Granmar is quite without foundation.]

[21. The difference of meter would of itself be enough to indicate that this stanza comes from an entirely different poem. A few editions assign the whole stanza to Helgi, but lines 3-4. are almost certainly Sigrun's, and the manuscript begins line 3 with a large capital letter following a period.]

[22. With this stanza begins the dispute between Gothmund and Sinfjotli which, together with Helgi's rebuke to his half brother, appears at much greater length in *Helgakvitha Hundingsbana* I, 33-48. It is introduced here manifestly in the wrong place. The version here given is almost certainly the older of the two, but the resemblance is so striking, and in some cases (notably in Helgi's rebuke) the stanzas are so nearly identical, that it seems probable that the composer of the first Helgi Hundingsbane lay borrowed directly from the poem of which the present dialogue is a fragment. Flag: the banner ("gunnfani," cf. "gonfalon") here serves as the signal for war instead of the red shield mentioned in*Helgakvitha Hundingsbana* I, 34. *Battle-light*: perhaps the "northern lights."

23. Lines 3-4 are obscure, and in the manuscript show signs of error. Helgi had not at this time, so far as we know, conquered any of Hothbrodd's land. *The realm of the fishes*, in line 4, presumably means the sea, but the word here translated "fishes" is obscure, and many editors treat it as a proper name, "the realm of the Fjorsungs," but without further suggestion as to who or what the Fjorsungs are.]

[24. The word here translated *swords* is a conjectural emendation; the manuscript implies merely an invitation to continue the quarrel at Frekastein. *Hothbrodd*: apparently he is here considered as present during the dispute; some editors, in defiance of the meter, have emended the line to mean "Time is it for Hothbrodd | vengeance to have."

26-27. Cf. *Helgakvitha Hundingsbana* I, 47-48, which are nearly identical. Stanza 27 in the manuscript is abbreviated to the first letters of the words, except for line 5, which does not appear in the other poem, and which looks like an interpolation.]

[*Prose.* Here begins a new section of the poem, dealing with Helgi's death at the hands of *Dag*, Sigrun's brother. The note is based wholly on stanzas 28-34, except for the introduction of Dag's name (cf. note on prose following stanza 16), and the reference to *Othin's spear*, the weapon which made victory certain, and which the annotator brought in doubtless on the strength of Dag's statement that Othin was responsible for Helgi's death (stanza 33). *Fjoturlund* ("Fetter-Wood"): mentioned only here and in stanza 28.

28. Line 5 looks like an interpolation.

29. *Leipt*: this river is mentioned in *Grimnismol*, 29. *Uth*: a [fp. 324] daughter of the sea-god Ægir; regarding her sacred stone we know nothing. According to the annotator, Dag's life had been spared because he swore loyalty to Helgi.]

[31. No gap indicated in the manuscript, but most editors have assumed that either the first or the last two lines have been lost. Bugge adds a line: "The shield shall not help thee which thou holdest."

34. *Vandilsve* ("Vandil's Shrine): who Vandil was we do not [fp. 325] know; this and Vigdalir ("Battle-Dale") are purely mythical places.]

[35. Line 5 may be spurious. *Vigblær* ("Battle-Breather") Helgi's horse.

37. Line 5 (or possibly line 4) may be spurious. Cf. *Guthrunarkvitha I*, 17, and *Guthrunarkvitha II*, 2.

Prose. Valhall, etc.: there is no indication as to where the annotator got this notion of Helgi's sharing Othin's rule. It is [fp. 326] most unlikely that such an idea ever found place in any of the Helgi poems, or at least in the earlier ones; probably it was a late development of the tradition in a period when Othin was no longer taken seriously.]

[38. This stanza apparently comes from an otherwise lost passage containing a contest of words between Helgi and Hunding; indeed the name of Hunding may have been substituted for another one beginning with "H," and the stanza originally have had no connection with Helgi at all. The annotator inserts it here through an obvious misunderstanding, taking it to be Helgi's application of the power conferred on him by Othin.

39. Here begins the final section (stanzas 39-50), wherein Sigrun visits the dead Helgi in his burial hill. *Doom of the gods*: the phrase "ragna rök" has been rather unfortunately Anglicized into the work "ragnarok" (the Norse term is not a proper name), [fp. 326] and *rök*, "doom," has been confused with *rökkr*, "darkness," and so translated "dusk of the Gods," or "Götterdämmerung."]

[40. In the manuscript most of this stanza is abbreviated to the first letters of the words.

41. Line 5 (or possibly line 2) may be spurious. Sword-tracks: wounds. One edition places stanza 48 after stanza 42, and an other does the same with stanza 50.]

[43. Possibly lines 5-6 are spurious, or part of a stanza the rest of which has been lost. It has also been suggested that two lines may have been lost after line 2, making a new stanza of lines 3-6. *Kinsman*: literally "son-in-law."

44.. Lines 4 and 6 have been marked by various editors as probably spurious. Others regard lines 1-2 as the beginning of a stanza the rest of which has been lost, or combine lines 5-6 with lines 5-6 of stanza 45 to make a new stanza. *South-maid*: cf. *Helgakvitha Hundingsbana I*, 17 and note.

45. Both lines 3-4 and lines 5-6 have been suspected by editors of being interpolated, and the loss of two lines has also been suggested.*Brides*: the plural here is perplexing. Gering insists that only Sigrun is meant, and translates the word as singular, but both "brides" and "loves" are uncompromisingly plural in [fp. 329] the text. Were the men of Helgi's ghostly following likewise visited by their wives? The annotator may have thought so, for in the prose he mentions the "women" returning to the house, al though, of course, this may refer simply to Sigrun and the maid.]

[47. Line 5 (or possibly line 4) may be interpolated.

48. *Wind-helm*: the sky; the bridge is Bifrost, the rainbow (cf. *Grimnismol*, 29). *Salgofnir* ("Hall-Crower"): the cock Gollinkambi who awakes the gods and warriors for the last battle.]

[49. Many editors assign this speech to the maid. Line 5 (or 4) may be spurious. *Meeting of dreams* ("Dream-Thing'"): sleep.

Prose. The attitude of the annotator is clearly revealed by his contempt for those who put any faith in such "old wives' folly" as the idea that men and women could be reborn. As in the case of Helgi Hjorvarthsson, the theory of the hero's rebirth seems to have developed in order to unite around a single Helgi

[fp. 331]

the various stories in which the hero is slain. *The Lay of Kara* (*Karuljoth*) is lost, although, as has been pointed out, parts of the *Helgakvitha Hundingsbana II* may be remnants of it, but we find the main outlines of the story in the *Hromundar saga Greipssonar*, whose compilers appear to have known the *Karuljoth*. In the saga Helgi Haddingjaskati (Helgi the Haddings' Hero) is protected by the Valkyrie Kara, who flies over him in the form of a swan (note once more the Valkyrie swan-maiden confusion); but in his fight with Hromund he swings his sword so high that he accidentally gives Kara a mortal wound, where upon Hromund cuts off his head. As this makes the third recorded death of Helgi (once at the hands of Alf, once at those of Dag, and finally in the fight with Hromund), the phenomenon of his rebirth is not surprising. The points of resemblance in all the Helgi stories, including the one told in the lost *Karuljoth*, are sufficiently striking so that it is impossible not to see in them a common origin, and not to believe that Helgi the son of Hjorvarth, Helgi the son of Sigmund and Helgi the Haddings'-Hero (not to mention various other Helgis who probably figured in songs and stories now lost) were all originally the same Helgi who appears in the early traditions of Denmark.]

FRA DAUTHA SINFJOTLA

Of Sinfjotli's Death

INTRODUCTORY NOTE

It has been pointed out that the Helgi tradition, coming originally from Denmark, was early associated with that of the Volsungs, which was of German, or rather of Frankish, origin (cf. Introductory Note to *Helgakvitha Hjorvarthssonar*). The connecting links between these two sets of stories were few in number, the main point being the identification of Helgi as a son of Sigmund Volsungsson. Another son of Sigmund, however, appears in the Helgi poems, though not in any of the poems dealing with the Volsung cycle proper. This is Sinfjotli, whose sole function in the extant Helgi lays is to have a wordy dispute with Gothmund Granmarsson.

Sinfjotli's history is told in detail in the early chapters of the *Volsungasaga*. The twin sister of Sigmund Volsungsson, Signy, had married Siggeir, who hated his brother-in-law by reason of his desire to possess a sword which had belonged to Othin and been won by Sigmund. Having treacherously invited Volsung and his ten sons to visit him, Siggeir slew Volsung and captured his sons, who were set in the stocks. Each night a wolf ("some men say that she was Siggeir's mother") came out of the woods and ate up one of the brothers, till on the tenth night Sigmund alone was left. Then, however, Signy aided him to escape, and incidentally to kill the wolf. He vowed vengeance on Siggeir, and Signy, who hated her husband, was determined to help him. Convinced that Sigmund must have a helper of his own race, Signy changed forms with a witch, and in this guise sought out Sigmund, who, not knowing who she was, spent three nights with her. Thereafter she gave birth to a boy, whom she named Sinfjotli ("The Yellow-Spotted"?), whom she sent to Sigmund. For a time they lived in the woods, occasionally turning

295

into wolves (whence perhaps Sinfjotli's name). When Sinfjotli was full grown, he and his father came to Siggeir's house, but were seen and betrayed by the two young sons of Signy and Siggeir, whereupon Sinfjotli slew them. Siggeir promptly had Sigmund and Sinfjotli buried alive, but Signy managed to smuggle Sigmund's famous sword into the grave, and with this the father and son dug themselves out. The next night they burned Siggeir's house, their enemy dying in the flames, and Signy, who had at the last refused to leave her husband, from a sense of somewhat belated loyalty, perishing with him.

Was this story, which the Volsungasaga relates in considerable detail, the basis of an old poem which has been lost? Almost certainly it was, although, as I have pointed out, many if not most of the old stories appear to have been handed down rather in prose than in verse, for the Volsungasaga quotes two lines of verse regarding the escape from the grave. At any rate, Sinfjotli early became a part of the Volsung tradition, which, in turn, formed the basis for no less than fifteen poems generally included in the Eddic collection. Of this tradition we may recognize three distinct parts: the Volsung-Sigmund-Sinfjotli story; the Helgi story, and the Sigurth story, the last of these three being by far the most extensive, and suggesting an almost limitless amount of further subdivision. With the Volsung-Sigmund-Sinfjotli story the Sigurth legend is connected only by the fact that Sigurth appears as Sigmund's son by his last wife, Hjordis; with the Helgi legend it is not connected directly at all. Aside from the fact that Helgi appears as Sigmund's son by his first wife, Borghild, the only link between the Volsung story proper and that of Helgi is the appearance of Sinfjotli in two of the Helgi poems. Originally it is altogether probable that the three stories, or sets of stories, were entirely distinct, and that Sigurth (the familiar Siegfried) had little or nothing more to do with the Volsungs of northern mythological-heroic tradition than he had with Helgi.

The annotator or compiler of the collection of poems preserved in the *Codex Regius*, having finished with the Helgi lays, had before him the task of setting down the fifteen complete or fragmentary poems dealing with the Sigurth story. Before doing this, however, he felt it incumbent on him to dispose of both Sigmund and Sinfjotli, the sole links with the two other sets of stories. He apparently knew of no poem or poems concerning the deaths of these two; perhaps there were none, though this is unlikely. Certainly the story of how Sinfjotli and Sigmund died was current in oral prose tradition, and this story the compiler set forth in the short prose passage entitled *Of Sinfjotli's Death* which, in *Regius*, immediately follows the second lay of Helgi Hundingsbane. The relation of this passage to the prose of the *Reginsmol* is discussed in the introductory note to that poem.

Sigmund, the son of Volsung, was a king in the land of the Franks; Sinfjotli was his eldest son, the second was Helgi, and the third Hamund. Borghild, Sigmund's wife, had a brother who was named -- ---. Sinfjotli, her stepson, and ----- both wooed the same woman, wherefore Sinfjotli slew him. And when he came home, Borghild bade him depart, but Sigmund offered her atonement-money, and this she had to accept. At the funeral feast Borghild brought in ale; she took poison, a great horn full, and brought it to Sinfjotli. But when he looked into the horn, he saw that it was poison, and said to Sigmund: "Muddy is the drink, Father!" Sigmund took the horn and drank therefrom. It is said that Sigmund was so hardy that poison might not harm him, either outside or in, but all his sons could withstand poison only without on their skin. Borghild bore another horn to Sinfjotli and bade him drink, and all happened as before. And yet a third time she brought him a horn, and spoke therewith scornful words of him if he should not drink from it. He spoke as before with Sigmund. The latter said: "Let it trickle through your beard, Son!" Sinfjotli drank, and straight way was dead. Sigmund bore him a long way in his arms, and came to a narrow and long fjord, and there was a little boat and a man in it. He offered to take Sigmund across the fjord. But when Sigmund had borne the corpse out into the boat, then the craft was full. The man told Sigmund to go round the inner end of the fjord. Then the man pushed the boat off, and disappeared.

King Sigmund dwelt long in Denmark in Borghild's kingdom after he had married her. Thereafter Sigmund went south into the land of the Franks, to the kingdom which he had there. There he married Hjordis, the daughter of King Eylimi; their son was Sigurth. King Sigmund fell in a battle with the sons of Hunding, and Hjordis then married Alf the son of King Hjalprek. There Sigurth grew up in his boyhood. Sigmund and all his sons were far above all other men in might and stature and courage and every kind of ability. Sigurth, however, was the fore most of all, and all men call him in the old tales the noblest of mankind and the mightiest leader.

[*Prose*. Regarding *Sigmund, Sinfjotli*, and *Volsung* see Introductory Note. *The Franks*: although the Sigurth story had reached the North as early as the sixth or seventh century, it never lost all the marks of its Frankish origin. *Helgi* and *Hamund*: sons of Sigmund and Borghild; Helgi is, of course Helgi Hundingsbane; of Hamund nothing further is. recorded. *Borghild*: the manuscript leaves a blank for the name of her brother; evidently the compiler hoped some day to discover it and write it in, but never did. A few editions insert wholly unauthorized names from late paper manuscripts, such as Hroar, Gunnar, or Borgar. In the *Volsungasaga* Borghild bids Sinfjotli drink "if he has the courage of a Volsung." Sigmund gives his advice because "the king was very drunk, and that was why he spoke thus." Gering, on the other hand, gives Sigmund credit for having believed that the draught would deposit its poisonous [fp. 335] contents in Sinfjotli's beard, and thus do him no harm. *Boat*: the man who thus carries off the dead Sinfjotli in his boat is presumably Othin. *Denmark*: Borghild belongs to the Danish Helgi part of the story. The Franks: with this the Danish and Norse stories of Helgi and Sinfjotli come to an end, and the Frankish story of Sigurth begins. Sigmund's two kingdoms are an echo of the blended traditions. *Hjordis*: just where this name came from is not clear, for in the German story Siegfried's mother is Sigelint, but the name of the father of Hjordis, Eylimi, gives a clew, for Eylimi is the father of Svava, wife of Helgi Hjorvarthsson. [fp. 336] Doubtless the two men are not identical, but it seems likely that both Eylimi and Hjordis were introduced into the Sigmund-Sigurth story, the latter replacing Sigelint, from some version of the Helgi tradition. *Hunding*: in the Helgi lays the sons of Hunding are all killed, but they reappear here and in two of the poems (*Gripisspo*, 9, and *Reginsmol*, 13), and the *Volsungasaga* names Lyngvi as the son of Hunding who, as the rejected lover of Hjordis, kills Sigmund and his father-in-law, Eylimi, as well. The episode of Hunding and his sons belongs entirely to the Danish (Helgi) part of the story; the German legend knows nothing of it, and permits the elderly Sigmund to outlive his son. There was doubtless a poem on this battle, for the Volsungasaga quotes two lines spoken by the dying Sigmund to

Hjordis before he tells her to give the pieces of his broken sword to their unborn son. *Alf*: after the battle, according to the Volsungasaga, Lyngvi Hundingsson tried to capture Hjordis, but she was rescued by the sea-rover Alf, son of King Hjalprek of Denmark, who subsequently married her. Here is another trace of the Danish Helgi tradition. The *Nornageststhattr* briefly tells the same story.]

GRIPISSPO

Gripir's Prophecy

INTRODUCTORY NOTE

The *Gripisspo* immediately follows the prose *Fra Dautha Sinfjotla* in the *Codex Regius*, and is contained in no other early manuscript. It is unquestionably one of the latest of the poems in the Eddic collection; most critics agree in calling it the latest of all, dating it not much before the year 1200. Its author (for in this instance the word may be correctly used) was not only familiar with the other poems of the Sigurth cycle, but seems to have had actual written copies of them before him; it has, indeed, been suggested, and not without plausibility, that the *Gripisspo* may have been written by the very man who compiled and annotated the collection of poems preserved in the *Codex Regius*.

In form the poem is a dialogue between the youthful Sigurth and his uncle, Gripir, but in substance it is a condensed outline of Sigurth's whole career as told piecemeal in the older poems. The writer was sufficiently skillful in the handling of verse, but he was utterly without inspiration; his characters are devoid of vitality, and their speeches are full of conventional phrases, with little force or incisiveness. At the same time, the poem is of considerable interest as giving, in brief form, a summary of the story of Sigurth as it existed in Iceland (for the *Gripisspo* is almost certainly Icelandic) in the latter half of the twelfth century.

It is not desirable here to go in detail into the immensely complex question of the origin, growth, and spread of the story of Sigurth (Siegfried). The volume of critical literature on the subject is enormous, and although some of the more patently absurd theories have been eliminated, there are still wide divergencies of opinion regarding many important points. At the same time, a brief review of the chief facts is necessary in order to promote a clearer understanding of the poems which follow, and which make up more than a third of the Eddic collection.

That the story of Sigurth reached the North from Germany, having previously developed among the Franks of the Rhine country, is now universally recognized. How and when it spread from northwestern Germany into Scandinavia are less certainly known. It spread, indeed, in every direction, so that traces of it are found wherever Frankish influence was extensively felt; but it was clearly better known and more popular in Norway, and in the settlements established by Norwegians, than anywhere else. We have historical proof that there was considerable contact, commercial and otherwise, between the Franks of northwestern Germany and the Norwegians (but not the Swedes or the Danes) throughout the period from 600 to 800; coins of Charlemagne have been found in Norway, and there is other evidence showing a fairly extensive interchange of ideas as well as of goods. Presumably, then, the story of the Frankish hero found its way into Norway in the seventh century. While, at this stage of its development, it may conceivably have included a certain amount of verse, it is altogether probable that the story as it came into Norway in the seventh century was told largely in prose, and that, even after the poets had got hold of it, the legend continued to live among the people in the form of oral prose saga.

The complete lack of contemporary material makes it impossible for us to speak with certainty regarding the character and content of the Sigurth legend as it existed in the Rhine country in the seventh century. It is, however, important to remember the often overlooked fact that any popular traditional hero became a magnet for originally unrelated stories of every kind. It must also be remembered that in the early Middle Ages there existed no such distinction between fiction and history as we now make; a saga, for instance, might be anything from the most meticulously accurate history to the wildest of fairy tales, and a single saga might (and sometimes did) combine both elements. This was equally true of the Frankish traditions, and the two principles just stated account for most of the puzzling phenomena in the growth of the Sigurth story.

Of the origin of Sigurth himself we know absolutely nothing. No historical analogy can be made to fit in the slightest degree. If one believes in the possibility of resolving hero stories into nature myths, he may be explained in that fashion, but such a solution is not necessary. The fact remains that from very early days Sigurth (Sifrit) was a great traditional hero among the Franks. The tales of his strength and valor, of his winning of a great treasure, of his wooing a more or less supernatural bride, and of his death at the hands of his kinsmen, probably were early features of this legend.

The next step was the blending of this story with one which had a clear basis in history. In the year 437 the Burgundians, under their king, Gundicarius (so the Latin histories call him), were practically annihilated by the Huns. The story of this great battle soon became one of the foremost of Rhineland traditions; and though Attila was presumably not present in person, he was quite naturally introduced as the famous ruler of the invading hordes. The dramatic story of Attila's death in the year 453 was likewise added to the tradition, and during the sixth century the chain was completed by linking together the stories of Sigurth and those of the Burgundian slaughter. Gundicarius becomes the Gunther of the *Nibelungenlied* and the Gunnar of the Eddic poems; Attila becomes Etzel and Atli. A still further development came through the addition of another, and totally unrelated, set of historical traditions based on the career of Ermanarich, king of the Goths, who died about the year 376. Ermanarich figures largely in many stories unconnected with the Sigurth cycle, but, with the zeal of the medieval story-tellers for connecting their heroes, he was introduced as the husband of Sigurth's daughter, Svanhild, herself originally part of a separate narrative group, and as Jormunrek he plays a considerable part in a few of the Eddic poems.

Such, briefly, appears to have been the development of the legend before it came into Norway. Here it underwent many changes, though the clear marks of its southern origin were never obliterated. The names were given Scandinavian forms, and in some cases were completely changed (*e.g.*, Kriemhild becomes Guthrun). New figures, mostly of secondary importance, were introduced, and a large amount of purely Northern local color was added. Above all, the earlier part of the story was linked with Northern mythology in a way which seems to have had no counterpart among the southern Germanic peoples. The Volsungs become direct descendants of Othin; the gods are closely concerned with Fafnir's treasure, and so on. Above all, the Norse story-tellers and poets changed the figure of Brynhild. In making her a Valkyrie, sleeping on the flame-girt rock, they were never completely successful, as she persisted in remaining, to a considerable extent, the entirely human daughter of Buthli whom Sigurth woos for Gunnar. This confusion, intensified by a mixing of names (cf. *Sigrdrifumol*, introductory note), and much resembling that which existed in the parallel cases of Svava and Sigrun in the Helgi tradition, created difficulties which the Norse poets and story-tellers were never able to smooth out, and which have perplexed commentators ever since.

Those who read the Sigurth poems in the *Edda*, or the story told in the *Volsungasaga*, expecting to find a critically accurate biography of the hero, will, of course, be disappointed. If, how. ever, they will constantly keep in mind the general manner in which the legend grew, its accretions ranging all the way from the Danube to Iceland, they will find that most of the difficulties are simply the natural results of conflicting traditions. just as the Danish Helgi had to be "reborn" twice in order to enable three different men to kill him, so the story of Sigurth, as told in the Eddic poems, involves here and there inconsistencies explicable only when the historical development of the story is taken into consideration.

Gripir was the name of Eylimi's son, the brother of Hjordis; he ruled over lands and was of all men the wisest and most forward-seeing. Sigurth once was riding alone and came to Gripir's hall. Sigurth was easy to recognize; he found out in front of the hall a man whose name was Geitir. Then Sigurth questioned him and asked:

1. "Who is it has | this dwelling here,
Or what do men call | the people's king?"

Geitir spake:
"Gripir the name | of the chieftain good
Who holds the folk | and the firm-ruled land."

Sigurth spake:
2. "Is the king all-knowing | now within,
Will the monarch come | with me to speak?
A man unknown | his counsel needs,
And Gripir fain | I soon would find."

Geitir spake:
3. "The ruler glad | of Geitir will ask
Who seeks with Gripir | speech to have."

Sigurth spake:
"Sigurth am I, | and Sigmund's son,
And Hjordis the name | of the hero's mother."

4. Then Geitir went | and to Gripir spake:
"A stranger comes | and stands without;
Lofty he is | to look upon,
And, prince, thyself | he fain would see."

5. From the hall the ruler | of heroes went,
And greeted well | the warrior come:
"Sigurth, welcome | long since had been thine;
Now, Geitir, shalt thou | Grani take."

6. Then of many | things they talked,
When thus the men | so wise had met.

Sigurth spake:
"To me, if thou knowest, | my mother's brother,
Say what life | will Sigurth's be."

Gripir spake:
7. "Of men thou shalt be | on earth the mightiest,
And higher famed | than all the heroes;
Free of gold-giving, | slow to flee,
Noble to see, | and sage in speech."

Sigurth spake:
8. "Monarch wise, | now more I ask;
To Sigurth say, | if thou thinkest to see,
What first will chance | of my fortune fair,
When hence I go | from out thy home?"

Gripir spake:
9. "First shalt thou, prince, | thy father avenge,
And Eylimi, | their ills requiting;
The hardy sons | of Hunding thou
Soon shalt fell, | and victory find."

Sigurth spake:
10. "Noble king, | my kinsman, say
Thy meaning true, | for our minds we speak:
For Sigurth mighty | deeds dost see,
The highest beneath | the heavens all?"

Gripir spake:
IT. "The fiery dragon | alone thou shalt fight
That greedy lies | at Gnitaheith;
Thou shalt be of Regin | and Fafnir both
The slayer; truth | doth Gripir tell thee."

Sigurth spake:
12. "Rich shall I be | if battles I win
With such as these, | as now thou sayest;
Forward look, | and further tell:
What the life | that I shall lead?"

Gripir spake:
13. "Fafnir's den | thou then shalt find,
And all his treasure | fair shalt take;
Gold shalt heap | on Grani's back,
And, proved in fight, | to Gjuki fare."

Sigurth spake:
14. "To the warrior now | in words. so wise,
Monarch noble, | more shalt tell;
I am Gjuki's guest, | and thence I go:
What the life | that I shall lead?"

Gripir spake:
15. "On the rocks there sleeps | the ruler's daughter,
Fair in armor, | since Helgi fell;
Thou shalt cut | with keen-edged sword,
And cleave the byrnie | with Fafnir's killer."

Sigurth spake:
16. "The mail-coat is broken, | the maiden speaks,
The woman who | from sleep has wakened;
What says the maid | to Sigurth then
That happy fate | to the hero brings?"

Gripir spake:

17. "Runes to the warrior | will she tell,
All that men | may ever seek,
And teach thee to speak | in all men's tongues,
And life with health; | thou'rt happy, king!"

Sigurth spake:

18. "Now is it ended, | the knowledge is won,
And ready I am | forth thence to ride;
Forward look | and further tell:
What the life | that I shall lead?"

Gripir spake:

19. "Then to Heimir's | home thou comest,
And glad shalt be | the guest of the king;
Ended, Sigurth, | is all I see,
No further aught | of Gripir ask."

Sigurth spake:

20. "Sorrow brings me | the word thou sayest,
For, monarch, forward | further thou seest;
Sad the grief | for Sigurth thou knowest,
Yet nought to me, Gripir, | known wilt make."

Gripir spake:

21. "Before me lay | in clearest light
All of thy youth | for mine eyes to see;
Not rightly can I | wise be called,
Nor forward-seeing; | my wisdom is fled."

Sigurth spake:

22. "No man, Gripir, | on earth I know
Who sees the future | as far as thou;
Hide thou nought, | though hard it be,
And base the deeds | that I shall do."

Gripir spake:
2Z. "With baseness never | thy life is burdened,
Hero noble, | hold that sure;
Lofty as long | as the world shall live,
Battle-bringer, | thy name shall be."

Sigurth spake:
24. "Nought could seem worse, | but now must part
The prince and Sigurth, | since so it is,
My road I ask,-- | the future lies open,--
Mighty one, speak, | my mother's brother."

Gripir spake:
25. "Now to Sigurth | all shall I say,
For to this the warrior | bends my will;
Thou knowest well | that I will not lie,--
A day there is | when thy death is doomed."

Sigurth spake:
26. "No scorn I know | for the noble king,
But counsel good | from Gripir I seek;
Well will I know, | though evil awaits,
What Sigurth may | before him see."

Gripir spake:
27. "A maid in Heimir's | home there dwells,
Brynhild her name | to men is known,
Daughter of Buthli, | the doughty king,
And Heimir fosters | the fearless maid."

Sigurth spake:
28. "What is it to me, | though the maiden be
So fair, and of Heimir | the fosterling is?
Gripir, truth | to me shalt tell,
For all of fate | before me thou seest."

Gripir spake:
29. "Of many a joy | the maiden robs thee,
Fair to see, | whom Heimir fosters;
Sleep thou shalt find not, | feuds thou shalt end not,
Nor seek out men, | if the maid thou seest not."

Sigurth spake:
30. "What may be had | for Sigurth's healing?
Say now, Gripir, | if see thou canst;
May I buy the maid | with the marriage-price,
The daughter fair | of the chieftain famed?"

Gripir spake:
31. "Ye twain shall all | the oaths then swear
That bind full fast; | few shall ye keep;
One night when Gjuki's | guest thou hast been,
Will Heimir's fosterling | fade from thy mind."

Sigurth spake:
32. "What sayst thou, Gripir? | give me the truth,
Does fickleness hide | in the hero's heart?
Can it be that troth | I break with the maid,
With her I believed | I loved so dear?"

Gripir spake:
33. "Tricked by another, | prince, thou art,
And the price of Grimhild's | wiles thou must pay;
Fain of thee | for the fair-haired maid,
Her daughter, she is, | and she drags thee down."

Sigurth spake:
34. "Might I with Gunnar | kinship make,
And Guthrun win | to be my wife,
Well the hero | wedded would be,
If my treacherous deed | would trouble me not."

Gripir spake:
35. "Wholly Grimhild | thy heart deceives,
She will bid thee go | and Brynhild woo
For Gunnar's wife, | the lord of the Goths;
And the prince's mother | thy promise shall win."

Sigurth spake:
36. "Evil waits me, | well I see it,
And gone is Sigurth's | wisdom good,
If I shall woo | for another to win
The maiden fair | that so fondly I loved."

Gripir spake:
37. "Ye three shall | all the oaths then take,
Gunnar and Hogni, | and, hero, thou;
Your forms ye shall change, | as forth ye tare,
Gunnar and thou; | for Gripir lies not."

Sigurth spake:
38. "How meanest thou? | Why make we the change
Of shape and form | as forth we fare?
There must follow | another falsehood
Grim in all ways; | speak on, Gripir!"

Gripir spake:
39. "The form of Gunnar | and shape thou gettest,
But mind and voice | thine own remain;
The hand of the fosterling | noble of Heimir
Now dost thou win, | and none can prevent."

Sigurth spake:
40. "Most evil it seems, | and men will say
Base is Sigurth | that so he did;
Not of my will shall | I cheat with wiles
The heroes' maiden | whom noblest I hold."

Gripir spake:
41. "Thou dwellest, leader | lofty of men,
With the maid as if | thy mother she were;
Lofty as long | as the world shall live,
Ruler of men, | thy name shall remain."

Sigurth spake:
42. "Shall Gunnar have | a goodly wife,
Famed among men,-- | speak forth now, Gripir!
Although at my side | three nights she slept,
The warrior's bride? | Such ne'er has been."

Gripir spake:
43. "The marriage draught | will be drunk for both,
For Sigurth and Gunnar, | in Gjuki's hall;
Your forms ye change, | when home ye fare,
But the mind of each | to himself remains."

Sigurth spake:
44. "Shall the kinship new | thereafter come
To good among us? | Tell me, Gripir!
To Gunnar joy | shall it later give,
Or happiness send | for me myself?"

Gripir spake:
45. "Thine oaths remembering, | silent thou art,
And dwellest with Guthrun | in wedlock good;
But Brynhild shall deem | she is badly mated,
And wiles she seeks, | herself to avenge."

Sigurth spake:
46. "What may for the bride | requital be,
The wife we won | with subtle wiles?
From me she has | the oaths I made,
And kept not long; | they gladdened her little."

Gripir spake:

47. "To Gunnar soon | his bride will say
That ill didst thou | thine oath fulfill,
When the goodly king, | the son of Gjuki,
With all his heart | the hero trusted."

Sigurth spake:

48. "What sayst thou, Gripir? | give me the truth!
Am I guilty so | as now is said,
Or lies does the far-famed | queen put forth
Of me and herself? | Yet further speak."

Gripir spake:

49. "In wrath and grief | full little good
The noble bride | shall work thee now;
No shame thou gavest | the goodly one,
Though the monarch's wife | with wiles didst cheat."

Sigurth spake:

50. "Shall Gunnar the wise | to the woman's words,
And Gotthorm and Hogni, | then give heed?
Shall Gjuki's sons, | now tell me, Gripir,
Redden their blades | with their kinsman's blood?"

Gripir spake:

51. "Heavy it lies | on Guthrun's heart,
When her brothers all | shall bring thee death;
Never again | shall she happiness know,
The woman so fair; | 'tis Grimhild's work."

Sigurth spake:

52. "Now fare thee well! | our fates we shun not;
And well has Gripir | answered my wish;
More of joy | to me wouldst tell
Of my life to come | if so thou couldst."

312

Gripir spake:
53 "Ever remember, ruler of men,
That fortune lies in the hero's life;
A nobler man shall never live
Beneath the sun than Sigurth shall seem."

[*Prose.* The manuscript gives the poem no title. *Gripir*: this uncle of Sigurth's was probably a pure invention of the poet's. The *Volsungasaga* mentions him, but presumably only because of his appearance here. On *Eylimi* and *Hjordis* see *Fra Dautha Sinfjotla* and note. *Geitir*, the serving-man, is likewise apparently an invention of the poet's.

1. The manuscript does not indicate the speakers anywhere in the poem. Some editors have made separate stanzas out of the two-line speeches in stanzas 1, 3 and 6.]

[3. *Sigurth*: a few editions use in the verse the older form of this name, "Sigvorth," though the manuscript here keeps to the form used in this translation. The Old High German "Sigifrid" ("Peace-Bringer through Victory") became the Norse "Sigvorth" ("Victory-Guarder"), this, in turn, becoming "Sigurth."

4. Bugge thinks a stanza has been lost after stanza 4, in which Geitir tells Gripir who Sigurth is.]

[5. *Grani.* Sigurth's horse. According to the *Volsungasaga* his father was Sleipnir, Othin's eight-legged horse, and Othin him self gave him to Sigurth. The introductory note to the *Reginsmol* tells a different story.

9. *Thy father*: on The death of Sigmund and *Eylimi* at the hands of *Hunding's sons* see *Fra Dautha Sinfjotla* and note.]

[11. *The dragon*: Fafnir, brother of the dwarf Regin, who turns himself into a dragon to guard Andvari's hoard; cf. *Reginsmol* and *Fafnismol. Gnitaheith*: a relic of the German tradition; it has been identified as lying south of Paderborn.

13. *Gjuki*: the Norse form of the name Gibeche ("The Giver"). Gjuki is the father of Gunnar, Hogni, and Guthrun, the family which reflects most directly the Burgundian part of [fp. 343] the tradition (cf. Introductory Note). The statement

313

that Sigurth is to go direct from the slaying of Fafnir to Gjuki's hall involves one of the confusions resulting from the dual personality of Brynhild. In the older (and the original South Germanic) story, Sigurth becomes a guest of the Gjukungs before he has ever heard of Brynhild, and first sees her when, having changed forms with Gunnar, he goes to woo her for the latter. In an other version he finds Brynhild before he visits the Gjukungs, only to forget her as the result of the magic-draught administered by Guthrun's mother. Both these versions are represented in the poems of which the author of the *Gripisspo* made use, and he tried, rather clumsily, to combine them, by having Sigurth go to Gjuki's house, then find the unnamed Valkyrie, and then return to Gjuki, the false wooing following this second visit.]

[15. Basing his story on the *Sigrdrifumol*, the poet here tells of Sigurth's finding of the Valkyrie, whom he does not identify with Brynhild, daughter of Buthli (stanza 27), at all. His error in this respect is not surprising, in view of Brynhild's dual identity (cf. Introductory Note, and *Fafnismol*, 44 and note). [fp. 345] *Helgi*: according to *Helreith Brynhildar* (stanza 8), with which the author of the *Gripisspo* was almost certainly familiar, the hero for whose death Brynhild was punished was named Hjalmgunnar. Is Helgi here identical with Hjalmgunnar, or did the author make a mistake? Finnur Jonsson thinks the author regarded Sigurth's Valkyrie as a fourth incarnation of Svava Sigrun-Kara, and wrote Helgi's name in deliberately. Many editors, following Bugge, have tried to reconstruct line 2 so as to get rid of Helgi's name.]

[19. *Heimir*: the *Volsungasaga* says that Heimir was the husband of Brynhild's sister, Bekkhild. Brynhild's family connections [fp. 346] involve a queer mixture of northern and southern legend. Heimir and Bekkhild are purely of northern invention; neither of them is mentioned in any of the earlier poems, though Brynhild speaks of her "foster-father" in *Helreith Brynhildar*. In the older Norse poems Brynhild is a sister of Atli (Attila), a relationship wholly foreign to the southern stories, and the father of this strangely assorted pair is Buthli, who in the *Nibelungenlied* is apparently Etzel's grandfather. Add to this her role of Valkyrie, and it is small wonder that the annotator himself was puzzled.]

[27. *Brynhild* ("Armed Warrior"): on her and her family see introductory Note and note to stanza 19.]

[33. Most editions have no comma after line 3, and change the meaning to "Fain of thee | the fair-haired one / For her daughter is." *Grimhild*: in the northern form of the story Kriemhild, Gunther's sister and Siegfried's wife, becomes Grimhild, mother of Gunnar and Guthrun, the latter taking Kriemhild's place.
The *Volsungasaga* tells how Grimhild gave Sigurth a magic draught which made

314

him utterly forget Brynhild. Edzardi thinks two stanzas have been lost after stanza 33, their remains appearing in stanza 37.

35. In the *Volsungasaga* Grimhild merely advises Gunnar to seek Brynhild for his wife, and to have Sigurth ride with him. *Goths*: the historical Gunnar (Gundicarius, cf. Introductory Note) was not a Goth, but a Burgundian, but the word "Goth" was applied in the North without much discrimination to the southern Germanic peoples.]

[17. In the *Nibelungenlied* Siegfried merely makes himself invisible in order to lend Gunther his strength for the feats which must be performed in order to win the redoubtable bride. In the northern version Sigurth and Gunnar change forms, "as Grimhild had taught them how to do." The *Volsungasaga* tells how Sigurth and Gunnar came to Heimir, who told them that to win Brynhild one must ride through the ring of fire which surrounded her hall (cf. the hall of Mengloth in *Svipdagsmol*). Gunnar tries it, but his horse balks; then he mounts Grani, but Grani will not stir for him. So they change forms, and Sigurth rides Grani through the flames. *Oaths*: the blood-brotherhood sworn by Sigurth, Gunnar, and Hogni makes it impossible for the brothers to kill him themselves, but they finally get around the difficulty by inducing their half-brother, Gotthorm (cf. *Hyndluljoth*, 27 and note) to do it.]

[39. The last half of line 4 is obscure, and the reading is conjectural.

41. Something is clearly wrong with stanzas 41-43. in the manuscript the order is 41, 43, 42, which brings two of Gripir's answers together, followed by two of Sigurth's questions. Some editors have arranged the stanzas as in this translation, while others have interchanged 41 and 43. In any case, Sigurth in stanza 42 asks about the "three nights" which Gripir has never mentioned. I suspect that lines 3-4 of stanza 41, which are practically identical with lines 3-4 of stanza 23, got in here by mistake, replacing two lines which may have run thus: "With thy sword between, | three nights thou sleepest / With her thou winnest | for Gunnar's wife." The subsequent poems tell how Sigurth laid his sword Gram between himself and Brynhild.]

[45. The simultaneous weddings of Sigurth and Gunnar form a memorable feature of the German tradition as it appears in the *Nibelungenlied*, but in the *Volsungasaga* Sigurth marries Guthrun before he sets off with Gunnar to win Brynhild.

45. According to the *Volsungasaga*, Sigurth remembers his oaths to Brynhild almost immediately after his return to Gunnar's house. Brynhild, on the other

hand, knows nothing until the [fp. 353] famous quarrel between herself and Guthrun at the bath (an other reminiscence of the German story), when she taunts Guthrun with Sigurth's inferiority to Gunnar, and Guthrun retorts with the statement that it was Sigurth, and not Gunnar, who rode through the flames.]

[47. Brynhild tells Gunnar that Sigurth really possessed her during the three nights when he slept by her in Gunnar's form, thus violating his oath. Here again there is a confusion of two traditions. If Sigurth did not meet Brynhild until after his oath to Gunnar (cf. note on stanza 13), Brynhild's charge is entirely false, as she herself admits in *Helreith Brynhildar*. On the other hand, according to the version in which Sigurth finds Brynhild before he meets Gjuki's sons, their union was not only completed, but she had by him a daughter, Aslaug, whom she leaves in Heimir's charge before going to become Gunnar's wife. This is the *Volsungasaga* version, and thus the statement Brynhild makes to Gunnar, as a result of which Sigurth is slain, is quite true.]

[50. *Gotthorm*: Gunnar's half-brother, and slayer of Sigurth.

52. The manuscript has stanzas 52 and 53 in inverse order.]

REGINSMOL

The Ballad of Regin

INTRODUCTORY NOTE

The *Reginsmol* immediately follows the *Gripisspo* in the *Codex Regius*, and in addition stanzas 1, 2, 6, and 18 are quoted in the *Volsungasaga*, and stanzas 11-26 in the *Nornageststhattr*. In no instance is the title of the poem stated, and in *Regius* there stands before the introductory prose, very faintly written, what appears to be "Of Sigurth." As a result, various titles have been affixed to it, the two most often used being "the Ballad of Regin" and "the First Lay of Sigurth Fafnisbane."

As a matter of fact, it is by no means clear that the compiler of the Eddic collection regarded this or either of the two following poems, the *Fafnismol* and the *Sigrdrifumol*, as separate and distinct poems at all. There are no specific titles given, and the prose notes link the three poems in a fairly consecutive whole. Furthermore, the prose passage introducing the *Reginsmol* connects directly with *Fra Dautha Sinfjotla*, and only the insertion of the *Gripisspo* at this point, which may well have been done by some stupid copyist, breaks the continuity of the story. For convenience I have here followed the usual plan of dividing this material into distinct parts, or poems, but I greatly doubt if this division is logically sound. The compiler seems, rather, to have undertaken to set down the story of Sigurth in consecutive form, making use of all the verse with which he was familiar, and which, by any stretch of the imagination, could be made to fit, filling up the gaps with prose narrative notes based on the living oral tradition.

This view is supported by the fact that not one of the three poems in question, and least of all the *Reginsmol*, can possibly be regarded as a unit. For one thing, each of them includes both types of stanza

317

commonly used in the Eddic poems, and this, notwithstanding the efforts of Grundtvig and Müllenhoff to prove the contrary, is almost if not quite conclusive proof that each poem consists of material taken from more than one source. Furthermore, there is nowhere continuity within the verse itself for more than a very few stanzas. An analysis of the *Reginsmol* shows that stanzas 1-4, 6-10, and 12, all in Ljothahattr stanza form, seem to belong together as fragments of a poem dealing with Loki's (not Andvari's) curse on the gold taken by the gods from Andvari and paid to Hreithmar, together with Hreithmar's death at the hands of his son, Fafnir, as the first result of this curse. Stanza 5, in Fornyrthislag, is a curse on the gold, here ascribed to Andvari, but the only proper name in the stanza, Gust, is quite unidentifiable, and the stanza may originally have had to do with a totally different story. Stanza 11, likewise in Fornyrthislag, is merely a father's demand that his daughter rear a family to avenge his death; there is nothing in it to link it necessarily with the dying Hreithmar. Stanzas 13-18, all in Fornyrthislag, give Regin's welcome to Sigurth (stanzas 13,14), Sigurth's announcement that he will avenge his father's death on the sons of Hunding before he seeks any treasure (stanza 15), and a dialogue between a certain Hnikar, who is really Othin, and Regin, as the latter and Sigurth are on the point of being shipwrecked. This section (stanzas 13-19) bears a striking resemblance to the Helgi lays, and may well have come originally from that cycle. Next follows a passage in Ljothahattr form (stanzas 19-22 and 24-25) in which Hnikar-Othin gives some general advice as to lucky omens and good conduct in battle; the entire passage might equally well stand in the Hovamol, and I suspect that it originally came from just such a collection of wise saws. Inserted in this passage is stanza 23, in Fornyrthislag, likewise on the conduct of battle, with a bit of tactical advice included. The "poem" ends with a single stanza, in Fornyrthislag, simply stating that the bloody fight is over and that Sigurth fought well--a statement equally applicable to any part of the hero's career.

Finnur Jonsson has divided the *Reginsmol* into two poems, or rather into two sets of fragments, but this, as the foregoing analysis has indicated, does not appear to go nearly far enough. It accords much better with the facts to assume that the compiler of the collection represented by the *Codex Regius*, having set out to tell the story of Sigurth, took his verse fragments pretty much wherever he happened to find them. In this connection, it should be remembered that in the fluid state of oral tradition poems, fragments, and stanzas passed readily and frequently from one story to another. Tradition, never critical, doubtless connected with the Sigurth story much verse that never originated there.

If the entire passage beginning with the prose *Fra Dautha Sinfjotla*, and, except for the *Gripisspo*, including the *Reginsmol,Fafnismol*, and *Sigrdrifumol*, be regarded as a highly uncritical piece of compilation, rendered consecutive by the compiler's prose narrative, its difficulties are largely smoothed away; any other way of looking at it results in utterly inconclusive attempts to reconstruct poems some of which quite possibly never existed. The twenty-six stanzas and accompanying prose notes included under the heading of *Reginsmol* belong almost wholly to the northern part of the Sigurth legend; the mythological features have no counterpart in the southern stories, and only here and there is there any betrayal of the tradition's Frankish home. The story of Andvari, Loki, and Hreithmar is purely Norse, as is the concluding section containing Othin's counsels. If we assume that the passage dealing with the victory over Hunding's sons belongs to the Helgi cycle (cf. introductory notes to *Helgakvitha Hjorvarthssonar* and *Helgakvitha Hundingsbana I*), there is very little left to reflect the Sigurth tradition proper.

Regarding the general development of the story of Sigurth in the North, see the introductory note to the *Gripisspo*.

Sigurth went to Hjalprek's stud and chose for himself a horse, who thereafter was called Grani. At that time Regin, the son of

Hreithmar, was come to Hjalprek's home; he was more ingenious than all other men, and a dwarf in stature; he was wise, fierce and skilled in magic. Regin undertook Sigurth's bringing up and teaching, and loved him much. He told Sigurth of his forefathers, and also of this: that once Othin and Hönir and Loki had come to Andvari's waterfall, and in the fall were many fish. Andvari was a dwarf, who had dwelt long in the waterfall in the shape of a pike, and there he got his food. "Otr was the name of a brother of ours," said. Regin, "who often went into the fall in the shape of an otter; he had caught a salmon, and sat on the high bank eating it with his eyes shut. Loki threw a stone at him and killed him; the gods thought they bad had great good luck, and stripped the skin off the otter. That same evening they sought a night's lodging at Hreithmar's house, and showed their booty. Then we seized them, and told them, as ransom for their lives, to fill the otter skin with gold, and completely cover it outside as well with red gold. Then they sent Loki to get the gold; he went to Ron and got her net, and went then to Andvari's fall and cast the net in front of the pike, and the pike leaped into the net." Then Loki said:

1. "What is the fish | that runs in the flood,
And itself from ill cannot save?
If thy head thou wouldst | from hell redeem,
Find me the water's flame."

Andvari spake:
2. "Andvari am I, | and Oin my father,
In many a fall have I fared,
An evil Norn | in olden days
Doomed me In waters to dwell."

Loki spake:
3. "Andvari, say, | if thou seekest still
To live in the land of men,
What payment is set | for the sons of men
Who war with lying words?"

Andvari spake:
4. "A mighty payment | the men must make
Who in Valthgelmir's waters wade;
On a long road lead | the lying words
That one to another utters."

Loki saw all the gold that Andvari had. But when he had brought
forth all the gold, he held back one ring, and Loki took this from
him. The dwarf went into his rocky hole and said:

5. "Now shall the gold | that Gust once had
Bring their death | to brothers twain,
And evil be | for heroes eight;
joy of my wealth | shall no man win."

The gods gave Hreithmar the gold, and filled up the otter-skin, and
stood it on its feet. Then the gods had to heap up gold and hide it.
And when that was done, Hreithmar came forward and saw a single
whisker, and bade them cover it. Then Othin brought out the ring
Andvaranaut and covered the hair. Then Loki said:

6. "The gold is given, | and great the price
Thou hast my head to save;
But fortune thy sons | shall find not there,
The bane of ye both it is."

Hreithmar spake:
7. "Gifts ye gave, | but ye gave not kindly,
Gave not with hearts that were whole;
Your lives ere this | should ye all have lost,
If sooner this fate I had seen."

Loki spake:
8. "Worse is this | that methinks I see,
For a maid shall kinsmen clash;

Heroes unborn | thereby shall be,
I deem, to hatred doomed."

Hreithmar spake:
9. "The gold so red | shall I rule, methinks,
So long as I shall live;
Nought of fear | for thy threats I feel,
So get ye hence to your homes."

Fafnir and Regin asked Hreithmar for a share of the wealth that was
paid for the slaying of their brother, Otr. This he refused, and Fafnir
thrust his sword through the

body of his father, Hreithmar, while he was sleeping. Hreithmar
called to his daughters:

10. "Lyngheith and Lofnheith, | fled is my life,
And mighty now is my need!"

Lyngheith spake:
"Though a sister loses | her father, seldom
Revenge on her brother she brings."

Hreithmar spake:
11. "A daughter, woman | with wolf's heart, bear,
If thou hast no son | with the hero brave;
If one weds the maid, | for the need is mighty,
Their son for thy hurt | may vengeance seek."

Then Hreithmar died, and Fafnir took all the gold. Thereupon Regin
asked to have his inheritance from his father, but Fafnir refused this.
Then Regin asked counsel of Lyngheith, his sister, how he should
win his inheritance. She said:

12. "In friendly wise | the wealth shalt thou ask
Of thy brother, and better will;

Not seemly is it | to seek with the sword
Fafnir's treasure to take."

All these happenings did Regin tell to Sigurth.

One day, when he came to Regin's house, he was gladly welcomed.
Regin said:

13. "Hither the son | of Sigmund is come,
The hero eager, | here to our hall;
His courage is more | than an ancient man's,
And battle I hope | from the hardy wolf.

14. "Here shall I foster | the fearless prince,
Now Yngvi's heir | to us is come;
The noblest hero | beneath the sun,
The threads of his fate | all lands enfold."

Sigurth was there continually with Regin, who said to Sigurth that
Fafnir lay at Gnitaheith, and was in the shape of a dragon. He had a
fear-helm, of which all living creatures were terrified. Regin made
Sigurth the sword which was called Gram; it was so sharp that when
he thrust it down into the Rhine, and let a strand of wool drift
against it with the stream, it cleft the strand asunder as if it were
water. With this sword Sigurth cleft asunder Regin's anvil. After that
Regin egged Sigurth on to slay Fafnir, but he said:

15. "Loud will the sons | of Hunding laugh,
Who low did Eylimi | lay in death,
If the hero sooner | seeks the red
Rings to find | than his father's vengeance."

King Hjalprek gave Sigurth a fleet for the avenging of his father.
They ran into a great storm, and were off a certain headland. A man
stood on the mountain, and said:

16. "Who yonder rides | on Rævil's steeds,
O'er towering waves | and waters wild?
The sail-horses all | with sweat are dripping,
Nor can the sea-steeds | the gale withstand."

Regin answered:
17. "On the sea-trees here | are Sigurth and I,
The storm wind drives us | on to our death;
The waves crash down | on the forward deck,
And the roller-steeds sink; | who seeks our names?"

The Man spake:
18. "Hnikar I was | when Volsung once
Gladdened the ravens | and battle gave;
Call me the Man | from the Mountain now,
Feng or Fjolnir; | with you will I fare."

They sailed to the land, and the man went on board the ship, and the storm subsided. Sigurth spake:

19. "Hnikar, say, | for thou seest the fate
That to gods and men is given;
What sign is fairest | for him who fights,
And best for the swinging of swords?"

Hnikar spake:
20. "Many the signs, | if men but knew,
That are good for the swinging of swords;
It is well, methinks, | if the warrior meets
A raven black on his road.

21. "Another it is | if out thou art come,
And art ready forth to fare,
To behold on the path | before thy house
Two fighters greedy of fame.

22. "Third it is well | if a howling wolf
Thou hearest under the ash;
And fortune comes | if thy foe thou seest
Ere thee the hero beholds.

23. "A man shall fight not | when he must face
The moon's bright sister setting late;
Win he shall | who well can see,
And wedge-like forms | his men for the fray.

24. "Foul is the sign | if thy foot shall stumble
As thou goest forth to fight;
Goddesses baneful | at both thy sides
Will that wounds thou shalt get.

25. "Combed and washed | shall the wise man go,
And a meal at morn shall take;
For unknown it is | where at eve he may be;
It is ill thy luck to lose."

Sigurth had a great battle with Lyngvi, the son of Hunding, and his brothers; there Lyngvi fell, and his two brothers with him. After the battle Regin said:

26. "Now the bloody eagle | with biting sword
Is carved on the back | of Sigmund's killer;
Few were more fierce | in fight than his son,
Who reddened the earth | and gladdened the ravens."

Sigurth went home to Hjalprek's house; thereupon Regin egged him on to fight with Fafnir.

[*Prose. Hjalprek*: father of Alf, Sigurth's step-father; cf. *Fra Dautha Sinfjotla*, and note. *Grani*: cf. *Gripisspo*, 5 and note. *Regin* ("Counsel-Giver"): undoubtedly he goes back to the smith of the German story; in the *Thithrekssaga* version he is called Mimir, while Regin is there the name of the dragon (here Regin's brother, Fafnir). The *Voluspo* (stanza 12) names a Regin among the dwarfs, and the name may have assisted in making Regin a dwarf here. *Hreithmar*: nothing is known of him outside of this story. Othin, Hönir and Loki: these same three gods appear in company in *Voluspo*, 17-18. Andvari's fall: according to Snorri, who tells this entire story in the *Skaldskaparmal*, Andvari's fall was in the world of the dark elves, while the one when Loki killed the otter was not; here, however, the two are considered identical. *With his eyes shut*: according to Snorri, Otr ate with his eyes shut because be was so greedy that he could not bear to see the food before him diminishing. *Ron*: wife of the sea-god Ægir, who draws down drowning men with her net; cf. *Helgakvitha Hjorvarthssonar*, 18 and note. Snorri says that Loki caught the pike with his hands.

1. Snorri quotes this stanza. *Water's game*: gold, so called because Ægir, the sea-god, was wont to light his hall with gold.]

[2. Snorri quotes this stanza. The name of the speaker is not given in the manuscripts. Oin: nothing further is known of Andvari's father. *Norn*: cf. *Voluspo*, 20.

3. Stanzas 3-4 may well be fragments of some other poem. Certainly Loki's question does not fit the situation, and the passage looks like an extract from some such poem as *Vafthruthnismol*. In *Regius* the phrase "Loki spake" stands in the middle of line 1.

4. The manuscript does not name the speaker. *Vathgelmir* ("Raging to Wade"): a river not elsewhere mentioned, but cf. *Voluspo*, 39.

Prose. Snorri says Andvari's ring had the power to create new gold. In this it resembled Baldr's ring, Draupnir; c.f. *Skirnismol*, 21 and note.]

[5. This stanza apparently comes from a different source from stanzas 1-4 (or 1-2 if 3-4 are interpolated) and 6-10; cf. *Introductory Note*. In the *Volsungasaga* Andvari lays his curse particularly on the ring. *Gust*: possibly a name for Andvari himself, or for an earlier possessor of the treasure. *Brothers twain*: Fafnir and Regin. *Heroes eight*: the word "eight" may easily have been substituted for something like "all" to make the stanza fit the case; the "eight" in question are presumably Sigurth, Gotthorm, Gunnar, Hogni, Atli, Erp, Sorli and Hamther, all of whom are slain in the course of the story. But the stanza may originally not have referred to Andvari's treasure at all.

Prose. Andvaranaut: "Andvari's Gem."

6. Snorri quotes this stanza, introducing it, as here, with "Then Loki said" in the prose. *Regius* omits this phrase, but inserts "said Loki" in line 1.]

[8. The word translated "maid" in line 2 is obscure, and "gold" may be meant. Apparently, however, the reference is to the fight between Sigurth and the sons of Gjuki over Brynhild. The manuscript does not name the speaker, and many editions assign this stanza to Hreithmar.

9. The manuscript includes "said Hreithmar" (abbreviated) in the middle of line 1, and some editors have followed this.]

[10. Hreithmar's daughters do not appear elsewhere. It has been suggested that originally stanza 10 was followed by one in which Lofnheith lamented her inability to avenge her father, as she was married and had no son.

11. Apparently an interpolation (cf. Introductory Note). Vigfusson tries to reconstruct lines 2 and 4 to fit the Ljothahattr rhythm, but without much success. Hreithmar urges his daughter, as she has no sons, to bear a daughter who, in turn, will have a son to avenge his great-grandfather. Grundtvig worked out an ingenious theory to fit this stanza, making Sigurth's grand-father, Eylimi, the husband of Lyngheith's daughter, but there is absolutely no evidence to support this. The stanza may have nothing to do with Hreithmar.]

[13. This and the following stanza may be out of place here, really belonging, together with their introductory prose sentence, in the opening prose passage, following the first sentence describing Regin. Certainly they seem to relate to Regin's first meeting with Sigurth. Stanzas 13-26, interspersed with prose, are quoted in the *Nornageststhattr*. Stanzas 13-18 may be the remnants of a lost poem belonging to the Helgi cycle (cf. Introductory Note). *Hardy wolf*: warrior, i. e., Sigurth.

14. *Yngvi's heir*: Yngvi was one of the sons of the Danish king Halfdan the Old, and traditionally an ancestor of Helgi (cf. *Helgakvitha Hundingsbana I*, 57 and note). Calling Sigurth [fp. 365] a descendant of Yngvi is, of course, absurd, and the use of this phrase is one of the many reasons for believing that stanzas 13-18 belonged originally to the Helgi cycle. *The threads*, etc.: another link with Helgi; cf. *Helgakvitha Hundingsbana I*, 3-4. As Helgi was likewise regarded as a son of Sigmund, stanzas 15-14 would fit him just as well as Sigurth.]

[*Prose. Gnitaheith*: cf. *Gripisspo*, 11 and note. *Fear-helm*: the word "ægis-hjalmr," which occurs both here and in *Fafnismol*, suggests an extraordinarily interesting, and still disputed, question of etymology. *Gram*: according to

327

the *Volsungasaga* Regin forged this sword from the fragments of the sword given by Othin to Sigmund (cf. *Fra Dautha Sinfjotla* and note).

15. Regarding the sons of Hunding and Eylimi, father of Sigurth's mother, all of whom belong to the Helgi-tradition, cf. *Fra Dautha Sinfjotla*and note.

Prose. The fleet, and the subsequent storm, are also reminiscent [fp. 366] of the Helgi cycle; cf. *Helgakvitha Hundingsbana I*, 29-31, and 11, prose after stanza 16. *A man*: Othin.]

[16. *Rævil's steeds* (Rævil was a sea-king, possibly the grandson of Ragnar Lothbrok mentioned in the *Hervararsaga*), sail-horses and sea-steeds all mean "ships."

17. *Sea-trees* and *roller-steeds* (the latter because ships were pulled up on shore by means of rollers) both mean "ships."

18. The *Volsungasaga* quotes this stanza. *Hnikar* and *Fjolnir*: Othin gives himself both these names in *Grimnismol*, 47; *Feng* ("The Seizer") does not appear elsewhere. According to the *Volsungasaga*, no one knew Othin's name when he came to Volsung's house and left the sword there for Sigmund.]

[19. This and the following stanzas are strongly suggestive of the *Hovamol*, and probably came originally from some such collection.

23. This stanza is clearly an interpolation, drawn in by the [fp. 368] common-sense advice, as distinct from omens, given in the last lines of stanza 22. *Moon's sister*: the sun; cf. *Vafthruthnismol*, 23 and note. *Wedge-like*: the wedge formation (prescribed anew in 1920 for the United States Army under certain circumstances) was said to have been invented by Othin himself, and taught by him only to the most favored warriors.]

[24. *Goddesses*: Norse mythology included an almost limitless number of minor deities, the female ones, both kind and unkind, being generally classed among the lesser Norns.

25. This stanza almost certainly had nothing originally to do with the others in this passage; it may have been taken from a longer version of the *Hovamol* itself.

Prose. Lyngvi: the son of Hunding who killed Sigmund in jealousy of his marriage with Hjordis; cf. *Fra Dautha Sinfjotla* and note. The*Volsungasaga* names one

328

brother who was with Lyngvi in the battle, Hjorvarth, and Sigurth kills him as readily as if he had not already been killed long before by Helgi. But, as has been seen, it was nothing for a man to be killed in two or three different ways.]

[26. *Bloody eagle*, etc.: the *Nornageststhattr* describes the manner in which the captured Lyngvi was put to death. "Regin advised that they should carve the bloody eagle on his back. So Regin took his sword and cleft Lyngvi's back so that he severed his back from his ribs, and then drew out his lungs. So died Lyngvi with great courage."

Prose. In *Regius* there is no break of any kind between this prose passage and the prose introduction to the *Fafnismol* (cf. Introductory Note).]

FAFNISMOL

The Ballad of Fafnir

INTRODUCTORY NOTE

The so-called *Fafnismol*, contained in full in the *Codex Regius*, where it immediately follows the *Reginsmol* without any indication of a break, is quoted by Snorri in the *Gylfaginning* (stanza 13) and the *Skaldskaparmal* (stanzas 32 and 33), and stanzas 6, 3, and 4 appear in the *Sverrissaga*. Although the *Volsungasaga* does not actually quote any of the stanzas, it gives a very close prose parallel to the whole poem in chapters 18 and 19.

The general character of the *Fafnismol*, and its probable relation to the *Reginsmol* and the *Sigrdrifumol*, have been discussed in the introductory note to the *Reginsmol*. While it is far more nearly a unit than the *Reginsmol*, it shows many of the same characteristics. It has the same mixture of stanza forms, although in this case only nine stanzas (32-33, 35-36 and 40-44) vary from the normal Ljothahattr measure. It shows, though to a much less marked extent, the same tendency to introduce passages from extraneous sources, such as the question-and-answer passage in stanzas 11-15. At the same time, in this instance it is quite clear that one distinct poem, including probably stanzas 1-10, 16-23, 25-31, and 34-39, underlay the compilation which we here have. This may, perhaps, have been a long poem (not, however, the "Lone' Sigurth Lay; see introductory note to *Brot af Sigurtharkvithu*) dealing with the Regin-Fafnir-Sigurth-Brynhild story, and including, besides most of the *Fafnismol*, stanzas 1-4 and 6-11 of the *Reginsmol* and part of the so-called *Sigrdrifumol*, together with much that has been lost. The original poem may, on the other hand, have confined itself to the Fafnir episode. In any case, and while the extant *Fafnismol* can be spoken of as a distinct poem far more justly than the *Reginsmol*, there is still no indication that the compiler regarded it as a poem by itself. His prose notes run on without a break, and the verses simply cover a dramatic episode in Sigurth's early life. The fact that the work of compilation has been done more intelligently than in the case of the *Reginsmol* seems to have resulted chiefly from the compiler's having been familiar with longer consecutive verse passages dealing with the Fafnir episode.

The *Reginsmol* is little more than a clumsy mosaic, but in the *Fafnismol* it is possible to distinguish between the main substance of the poem and the interpolations.

Here, as in the *Reginsmol*, there is very little that bespeaks the German origin of the Sigurth story. Sigurth's winning of the treasure is in itself undoubtedly a part of the earlier southern legend, but the manner in which he does it is thoroughly Norse. Moreover, the concluding section, which points toward the finding of the sleeping Brynhild, relates entirely to the northern Valkyrie, the warrior-maiden punished by Othin, and not at all to the southern Brynhild the daughter of Buthli. The *Fafnismol* is, however, sharply distinguished from the *Reginsmol* by showing no clear traces of the Helgi tradition, although a part of the bird song (stanzas 40-44, in Fornyrthislag form, as distinct from the body of the poem) sounds suspiciously like the bird passage in the beginning of the *Helgakvitha Hjorvarthssonar*. Regarding the general relations of the various sets of traditions in shaping the story of Sigurth, see the introductory note to *Gripisspo*.

The *Fafnismol*, together with a part of the *Sigrdrifumol*, has indirectly become the best known of all the Eddic poems, for the reason that Wagner used it, with remarkably little change of outline, as the basis for his "Siegfried."

Sigurth and Regin went up to the Gnitaheith, and found there the track that Fafnir made when he crawled to water. Then Sigurth made a great trench across the path, and took his place therein. When Fafnir crawled from his gold, he blew out venom, and it ran down from above on Sigurth's head. But when Fafnir crawled over the trench, then Sigurth thrust his sword into his body to the heart. Fafnir writhed and struck out with his head and tail. Sigurth leaped from the trench, and each looked at the other. Fafnir said:

1. "Youth, oh, youth! | of whom then, youth, art thou born?
Say whose son thou art,
Who in Fafnir's blood | thy bright blade reddened,
And struck thy sword to my heart."

Sigurth concealed his name because it was believed in olden times that the word of a dying man might have great power if he cursed his foe by his name. He said:

2. "The Noble Hart | my name, and I go
A motherless man abroad;
Father I had not, | as others have,
And lonely ever I live."

Fafnir spake:
3. "If father thou hadst not, | as others have,
By what wonder wast thou born?
(Though thy name on the day | of my death thou hidest,
Thou knowest now thou dost lie.)"

Sigurth spake:
4. "My race, methinks, | is unknown to thee,
And so am I myself;
Sigurth my name, | and Sigmund's son,
Who smote thee thus with the sword."

Fafnir spake:
5. "Who drove thee on? | why wert thou driven
My life to make me lose?

A father brave | had the bright-eyed youth,
For bold in boyhood thou art."

Sigurth spake:
6. "My heart did drive me, | my hand fulfilled,
And my shining sword so sharp;
Few are keen | when old age comes,
Who timid in boyhood be."

Fafnir spake:
7. "If thou mightest grow | thy friends among,
One might see thee fiercely fight;
But bound thou art, | and in battle taken,
And to fear are prisoners prone."

Sigurth spake:
8. "Thou blamest me, Fafnir, | that I see from afar
The wealth that my father's was;
Not bound am I, | though in battle taken,
Thou hast found that free I live."

Fafnir spake:
9. "In all I say | dost thou hatred see,
Yet truth alone do I tell;
The sounding gold, | the glow-red wealth,
And the rings thy bane shall be."

Sigurth spake:
10. "Some one the hoard | shall ever hold,
Till the destined day shall come;
For a time there is | when every man
Shall journey hence to hell."

Fafnir spake:
11. "The fate of the Norns | before the headland
Thou findest, and doom of a fool;

In the water shalt drown | if thou row 'gainst the wind,
All danger is near to death."

Sigurth spake:
12. "Tell me then, Fafnir, | for wise thou art famed,
And much thou knowest now:
Who are the Norns | who are helpful in need,
And the babe from the mother bring?"

Fafnir spake:
13. "Of many births | the Norns must be,
Nor one in race they were;
Some to gods, others | to elves are kin,
And Dvalin's daughters some."

Sigurth spake:
14. "Tell me then, Fafnir, | for wise thou art famed,
And much thou knowest now:
How call they the isle | where all the gods
And Surt shall sword-sweat mingle?"

Fafnir spake:
15. "Oskopnir is it, | where all the gods
Shall seek the play of swords;
Bilrost breaks | when they cross the bridge,
And the steeds shall swim in the flood.

16. "The fear-helm I wore | to affright mankind,
While guarding my gold I lay;
Mightier seemed I | than any man,
For a fiercer never I found."

Sigurth spake:
17. "The fear-helm surely | no man shields
When he faces a valiant foe;

Oft one finds, | when the foe he meets,
That he is not the bravest of all."

Fafnir spake:
18. "Venom I breathed | when bright I lay
By the hoard my father had;
 (There was none so mighty | as dared to meet me,
And weapons nor wiles I feared.)"

Sigurth spake:
19. "Glittering worm, | thy hissing was great,
And hard didst show thy heart;
But hatred more | have the sons of men
For him who owns the helm."

Fafnir spake:
20. "I counsel thee, Sigurth, | heed my speech,
And ride thou homeward hence,
The sounding gold, | the glow-red wealth,
And the rings thy bane shall be."

Sigurth spake:
21. "Thy counsel is given, | but go I shall
To the gold in the heather hidden;
And, Fafnir, thou | with death dost fight,
Lying where Hel shall have thee."

Fafnir spake:
22. "Regin betrayed me, | and thee will betray,
Us both to death will he bring;
His life, methinks, | must Fafnir lose,
For the mightier man wast thou."

Regin had gone to a distance while Sigurth fought Fafnir, and came
back while Sigurth was wiping the blood from his sword. Regin
said:

23. "Hail to thee, Sigurth! | Thou victory hast,
And Fafnir in fight hast slain;
Of all the men | who tread the earth,
Most fearless art thou, methinks."

Sigurth spake:
24. "Unknown it is, | when all are together,
(The sons of the glorious gods,)
Who bravest born shall seem;
Some are valiant | who redden no sword
In the blood of a foeman's breast."

Regin spake:
25. "Glad art thou, Sigurth, | of battle gained,
As Gram with grass thou cleansest;
My brother fierce | in fight hast slain,
And somewhat I did myself."

Sigurth spake:
26. "Afar didst thou go | while Fafnir reddened
With his blood my blade so keen;
With the might of the dragon | my strength I matched,
While thou in the heather didst hide."

Regin spake:
27. "Longer wouldst thou | in the heather have let
Yon hoary giant hide,
Had the weapon availed not | that once I forged,
The keen-edged blade thou didst bear."

Sigurth spake:
28. "Better is heart | than a mighty blade
For him who shall fiercely fight;
The brave man well | shall fight and win,
Though dull his blade may be.

29. "Brave men better | than cowards be,
When the clash of battle comes;
And better the glad | than the gloomy man
Shall face what before him lies.

30. "Thy rede it was | that I should ride
Hither o'er mountains high;
The glittering worm | would have wealth and life
If thou hadst not mocked at my might."

Then Regin went up to Fafnir and cut out his heart with his sword, that was named Rithil, and then he drank blood from the wounds. Regin said:

31. "Sit now, Sigurth, | for sleep will I,
Hold Fafnir's heart to the fire;
For all his heart | shall eaten be,
Since deep of blood I have drunk."

Sigurth took Fafnir's heart and cooked it on a spit. When he thought that it was fully cooked, and the blood foamed out of the heart, then he tried it with his finger to see whether it was fully cooked. He burned his finger, and put it in his mouth. But when Fafnir's heart's-blood came on his tongue, he understood the speech of birds. He heard nut-hatches chattering in the thickets. A nut hatch said:

32. "There sits Sigurth, | sprinkled with blood,
And Fafnir's heart | with fire he cooks;
Wise were the breaker | of rings, I ween,
To eat the life-muscles | all so bright."

A second spake:
33. "There Regin lies, | and plans he lays
The youth to betray | who trusts him well;
Lying words | with wiles will he speak,
Till his brother the maker | of mischief avenges."

A third spake:

34. "Less by a head | let the chatterer hoary
Go from here to hell;
Then all of the wealth | he alone can wield,
The gold that Fafnir guarded."

A fourth spake:

35. "Wise would he seem | if so he would heed
The counsel good | we sisters give;
Thought he would give, | and the ravens gladden,
There is ever a wolf | where his ears I spy."

A fifth spake:

36. "Less wise must be | the tree of battle
Than to me would seem | the leader of men,
If forth he lets | one brother fare,
When he of the other | the slayer is."

A sixth spake:

37. "Most foolish he seems | if he shall spare
His foe, the bane of the folk,
There Regin lies, | who hath wronged him so,
Yet falsehood knows he not."

A seventh spake:

38. "Let the head from the frost-cold | giant be hewed,
And let him of rings be robbed;
Then all the wealth | which Fafnir's was
Shall belong to thee alone."

Sigurth spake:

39. "Not so rich a fate | shall Regin have
As the tale of my death to tell;
For soon the brothers | both shall die,
And hence to hell shall go."

338

Sigurth hewed off Regin's head, and then he ate Fafnir's heart, and drank the blood of both Regin and Fafnir. Then Sigurth heard what the nut-hatch said:

40. "Bind, Sigurth, the golden | rings together,
Not kingly is it | aught to fear;
I know a maid, | there is none so fair,
Rich in gold, | if thou mightest get her.

41. "Green the paths | that to Gjuki lead,
And his fate the way | to the wanderer shows;
The doughty king | a daughter has,
That thou as a bride | mayst, Sigurth, buy."

Another spake:
42. "A hall stands high | on Hindarfjoll,
All with flame | is it ringed without;
Warriors wise | did make it once
Out of the flaming | light of the flood.

43. "On the mountain sleeps | a battle-maid,
And about her plays | the bane of the wood;
Ygg with the thorn | hath smitten her thus,
For she felled the fighter | he fain would save.

44. "There mayst thou behold | the maiden helmed,
Who forth on Vingskornir | rode from the fight;
The victory-bringer | her sleep shall break not,
Thou heroes' son, | so the Norns have set."

Sigurth rode along Fafnir's trail to his lair, and found it open. The gate-posts were of iron, and the gates; of iron, too, were all the beams in the house, which was dug down into the earth. There Sigurth found a mighty store of gold, and he filled two chests full thereof; he took the fear-helm and a golden mail-coat and the sword Hrotti, and many other precious things, and loaded Grani with them, but the horse would not go forward until Sigurth mounted on his back.

[*Prose*. The prose follows the concluding prose passage of the *Reginsmol* without any interruption; the heading "Of Fafnir's Death" is written in the manuscript very faintly just before stanza 1. *Gnitaheith*: cf. *Gripisspo*, ii and note. *Fafnir*: Regin's brother: cf. *Reginsmol*, prose after stanza 14. *Venom*: in the *Volsungasaga* [fp. 371] it was the blood, and not the venom, that poured down on Sigurth's head. Sigurth was much worried about this danger, and before he dug the trench asked Regin what would happen if the dragon's blood overcame him. Regin thereupon taunted him with cowardice (Sigurth refers to this taunt in stanza 30, but the stanza embodying it has disappeared). After Sigurth had dug his trench, an old man (Othin, of course) appeared and advised him to dig other trenches to carry off the blood, which he did, thereby escaping harm.]

[1. The first line in the original, as here, is unusually long, but dramatically very effective on that account.

3. The names of the speakers do not appear in the manuscript, though they seem originally to have been indicated in the [fp. 373] margin for stanzas 3-30. The last two lines of stanza 3 are missing in the manuscript, with no gap indicated, but the *Volsungasaga* prose paraphrase indicates that something was omitted, and the lines here given are conjecturally reconstructed from this paraphrase.]

[4. The manuscript marks line 3 as the beginning of a stanza.

5. Line 4, utterly obscure in the manuscript, is guesswork.]

[7. Fafnir here refers to the fact that Hjordis, mother of the still unborn Sigurth, was captured by Alf after Sigmund's death; cf. *Fra Dautha Sinfjotla*, note.

11. Stanzas 11-15 are probably interpolated, and come from [fp. 375] a poem similar to *Vafthruthnismol*. *The headland*: Fafnir is apparently quoting proverbs; this one seems to mean that disaster ("the fate of the Norns") awaits when one rounds the first headland (i. e., at the beginning of life's voyage, in youth). The third line is a commentary on obstinate rashness. The *Volsungasaga* paraphrases stanzas 11 15 throughout.]

[12. *Norns*: cf. stanza 13 and note. Sigurth has no possible interest in knowing what Norns are helpful in childbirth, but interpolations were seldom logical.

13. Snorri quotes this stanza. There were minor Norns, or fates, in addition to the three great Norns, regarding whom cf. *Voluspo*, 20. *Dvalin*: chief of the dwarfs; cf. *Voluspo*, 14.]

[14. *Surt*: ruler of the fire world; the reference is to the last great battle. *Sword-sweat*: blood.

15. *Oskopnir* ("Not-Made"): apparently another name for Vigrith, which is named in *Vafthruthnismol*, 19, as the final battle-ground. *Bilrost* (or *Bifrost*): the rainbow bridge which breaks beneath Surt's followers; cf. *Grimnismol*, 29 and note.

16. With this stanza Fafnir returns to the situation. *Fear-helm*: regarding the "ægis-hjalmr" cf. *Reginsmol*, prose after stanza 14 and note.]

[18. Lines 3-4 do not appear in the manuscript and no gap is indicated; they are here conjecturally paraphrased from the prose passage in the *Volsungasaga*.

20. It has been suggested that this stanza is spurious, and that stanza 21 ought to follow stanza 22. Lines 3-4, abbreviated in the manuscript, are identical with lines 3-4 of stanza 9. The *Volsungasaga* paraphrase in place of these two lines makes [fp. 378] Fafnir say: "For it often happens that he who gets a deadly wound yet avenges himself." It is quite likely that two stanzas have been lost.]

[22. The *Volsungasaga* places its paraphrase of this stanza between those of stanzas 15 and 16.

24. Line 2 is probably spurious, but it is a phrase typical of such poems as *Grimnismol* or *Vafthruthnismol*.

25. *Grain*: Sigurth's sword; cf. *Reginsmol*, prose after 14.]

[26. In the manuscript stanzas 26-29 stand after stanza 31, which fails to make clear sense; they are here rearranged in accordance with the *Volsungasaga* paraphrase.

28-29. Almost certainly interpolated from some such poem as the *Hovamol*. Even the faithful *Volsungasaga* fails to paraphrase stanza 29.]

[30. Something has evidently been lost before this stanza. Sigurth clearly refers to Regin's reproach when he was digging the trench (cf. note on introductory prose), but the poem does not give such a passage.

Prose. Rithil ("Swift-Moving"): Snorri calls the sword Refil ("Serpent").

32. That the birds' stanzas come from more than one source [fp. 381] is fairly apparent, but whether from two or from three or more is uncertain. It is also far from clear how many birds are speaking. The manuscript numbers II, III, and IV in the margin with numerals; the *Volsungasaga* makes a different bird speak each time. There are almost as many guesses as there are editions. I suspect that in the original poem there was one bird, speaking stanzas 34 and 37. Stanza 38 is little more, than a repetition of stanza 34, and may well have been a later addition. As for the stanzas in Fornyrthislag (32-53 and 35-36), they apparently come from another poem, in which several birds speak (cf. "we sisters" in stanza 35). This may be the same poem from which stanzas 40-44 were taken, as well as some of the Fornyrthislag stanzas in the *Sigrdrifumol*.]

[34. Some editions turn this speech from the third person into the second, but the manuscript is clear enough.]

[35. *Wolf*, etc.: the phrase is nearly equivalent to "there must be fire where there is smoke." The proverb appears else where in Old Norse.

36. *Tree of battle*: warrior.

37. Here, as in stanza 34, some editions turn the speech from the third person into the second.

38. *Giant*: Regin was certainly not a frost-giant, and the whole stanza looks like some copyist's blundering reproduction of stanza 34.]

[40. Neither the manuscript nor any of the editions suggest the existence of more than one bird in stanzas 40-44. it seems to me, however, that there are not only two birds, but two distinct stories. Stanzas 40-41 apply solely to Guthrun, and suggest that Sigurth will go straight to Gunnar's hall. Stanzas 42-44, on the other hand, apply solely to Brynhild, and indicate that Sigurth will find her before he visits the Gjukungs. The confusion which existed between these two versions of the story, and which involved a fundamental difference in the final working out of Brynhild's revenge, is commented on in the note on *Gripisspo*, 13. In the present passage it is possible that two birds are speaking, each reflecting one version of the story; it seems even more likely that one speech or the other (40-41 or 42-44) reflects the original form of the narrative, the other having been added, either later or from another poem. In the *Volsungasaga* the whole passage is condensed into a few words by one bird: "Wiser were it if he should then ride up on Hindarfjoll, where Brynhild sleeps, and there would he get much wisdom." The Guthrun-bird does not appear at all.

41. *Gjuki*: father of Gunnar and Guthrun: cf. *Gripisspo*, 13 and note.]

[42. *Hindarfjoll*: "Mountain of the Hind." *Light of the flood*: gold; cf. *Reginsmol*, 1 and note.

43. *Battle-maid*: Brynhild, here clearly defined as a Valkyrie. *Bane of the wood*: fire. *Ygg*: Othin; cf. *Grimnismol*, 53. *The thorn*: a prose note in *Sigrdrifumol* calls it "sleep-thorn." *The fighter*: the story of the reason for Brynhild's punishment is told in the prose following stanza 4 of *Sigrdrifumol*.

44. *Vingskornir*: Brynhild's horse, not elsewhere mentioned. *Victory-bringer*: the word thus translated is in the original "sigrdrifa." The compiler of the collection, not being familiar with this word, assumed that it was a proper name, and in the prose following stanza 4 of the *Sigrdrifumol* he specifically states that this was the Valkyrie's name. Editors, until recently, [fp. 385] have followed him in this error, failing to recognize that "sigrdrifa" was simply an epithet for Brynhild. It is from this blunder that the so-called *Sigrdrifumol* takes its name. Brynhild's dual personality as a Valkyrie and as the daughter of Buthli has made plenty of trouble, but the addition of a second Valkyrie in the person of the supposed "Sigrdrifa" has made still more.]

[*Prose*. There is no break in the manuscript between the end of this prose passage and the beginning of the one introducing the *Sigrdrifumol*: some editors include the entire prose passage with one poem or the other. *Hrotti*: "Thruster."]

SIGRDRIFUMOL˙

The Ballad of The Victory-Bringer

INTRODUCTORY NOTE

The so-called *Sigrdrifumol,* which immediately follows the *Fafnismol* in the *Codex Regius* without any indication of a break, and without separate title, is unquestionably the most chaotic of all the poems in the Eddic collection. The end of it has been entirely lost, for the fifth folio of eight sheets is missing from *Regius*, the gap coming after the first line of stanza 29 of this poem. That stanza has been completed, and eight more have been added, from much later paper manuscripts, but even so the conclusion of the poem is in obscurity.

Properly speaking, however, the strange conglomeration of stanzas which the compiler of the collection has left for us, and which, in much the same general form, seems to have lain before the authors of the *Volsungasaga*, in which eighteen of its stanzas are quoted, is not a poem at all. Even its customary title is an absurd error. The mistake made by the annotator in thinking that the epithet "sigrdrifa," rightly applied to Brynhild as a "bringer of victory," was a proper name has already been explained and commented on (note on *Fafnismol*, 44). Even if the collection of stanzas were in any real sense a poem, which it emphatically is not, it is certainly not the "Ballad of Sigrdrifa" which it is commonly called. "Ballad of Brynhild" would be a sufficiently suitable title, and I have here brought the established name "Sigrdrifumol" into accord with this by translating the epithet instead of treating it as a proper name.

Even apart from the title, however, the *Sigrdrifumol* has little claim to be regarded as a distinct poem, nor is there any indication that the compiler did so regard it. Handicapped as we are by the loss of the concluding section, and of the material which followed it on those

344

missing pages, we can yet see that the process which began with the prose *Fra Dautha Sinfjotla*, and which, interrupted by the insertion of the *Gripisspo*, went on through the *Reginsmol* and the *Fafnismol*, continued through as much of the *Sigrdrifumol* as is left to us. In other words, the compiler told the story of Sigurth in mixed prose and verse, using whatever verse he could find without much questioning as to its origin, and filling in the gaps with hii own prose. *Fra Dautha Sinfjotla*, *Reginsmol*, *Fafnismol*, and *Sigrdrifumol* are essentially a coherent unit, but one of the compiler's making only; they represent neither one poem nor three distinct poems, and the divisions and titles which have been almost universally adopted by editors are both arbitrary and misleading.

The *Sigrdrifumol* section as we now have it is an extraordinary piece of patchwork. It is most unlikely that the compiler himself brought all these fragments together for the first time; little by little, through a process of accretion and also, unluckily, through one of elimination, the material grew into its present shape. Certainly the basis of it is a poem dealing with the finding of Brynhild by Sigurth, but of this original poem only five stanzas (2-4 and 20-21) can be identified with any degree of confidence. To these five stanzas should probably, however, be added some, if not all, of the passage (stanzas 6-12) in which Brynhild teaches Sigurth the magic runes. These stanzas of rune-lore attracted sundry similar passages from other sources, including stanza 5, in which a magic draught is administered (not necessarily by Brynhild or to Sigurth), the curious rune-chant in stanzas 15-17, and stanzas 13-14 and 18-19. Beginning with stanza 22, and running to the end of the fragment (stanza 37), is a set of numbered counsels closely resembling the *Loddfafnismol* (*Hovamol*, stanzas 111-138), which manifestly has nothing whatever to do with Brynhild. Even in this passage there are probably interpolations (stanzas 25, 27, 30, 54, and 36). Finally, and bespeaking the existence at some earlier time of another Sigurth-Brynhild poem, is stanza 1, sharply distinguished by its metrical form from stanzas 2-4 and 20-21. Many critics argue that stanzas 6-10 of *Helreith Brynildar* belonged originally to the same poem as stanza 1 of the *Sigrdrifumol*.

The *Sigrdrifumol*, then, must be regarded simply as a collection of fragments, most of them originally having no relation to the main subject. All of the story, the dialogue and the characterization are embodied in stanzas 1-4 and 20-21 and in the prose notes accompanying the first four stanzas; all of the rest might equally well (or better) be transferred to the *Hovamol*, where its character entitles it to a place. Yet stanzas 2-4 are as fine as anything in Old Norse poetry, and it is out of the scanty material of these three stanzas that Wagner constructed much of the third act of "Siegfried."

The *Sigrdrifumol* represents almost exclusively the contributions of the North to the Sigurth tradition (cf. introductory note to the *Gripisspo*). Brynhild, here disguised by the annotator as "Sigrdrifa," appears simply as a battle-maid and supernatural dispenser of wisdom; there is no trace of the daughter of Buthli and the rival of Guthrun. There is, however, so little of the "poem" which can definitely be assigned to the Sigurth cycle that it is impossible to trace back any of the underlying narrative substance.

The nature and condition of the material have made editorial conjectures and emendations very numerous, and as most of the guesses are neither conclusive nor particularly important, only a few of them are mentioned in the notes.

Sigurth rode up on Hindarfjoll and turned southward toward the land of the Franks. On the mountain he saw a great light, as if fire were burning, and the glow reached up to heaven. And when he came thither, there stood a tower of shields, and above it was a banner. Sigurth went into the shield-tower, and saw that a man lay there sleeping with all his war-weapons. First he took the helm from his head, and then he saw that it was a woman. The mail-coat was as fast as if it had grown to the flesh. Then he cut the mail-coat from the head-opening downward, and out to both the arm-holes. Then he took the mail-coat from her, and she awoke, and sat up and saw Sigurth, and said:

1. "What bit through the byrnie? | how was broken my sleep?
Who made me free | of the fetters pale?"

He answered:
"Sigmund's son, | with Sigurth's sword,
That late with flesh | hath fed the ravens."

Sigurth sat beside her and asked her name. She took a horn full of mead and gave him a memory-draught.

2. "Hail, day! | Hail, sons of day!
And night and her daughter now!
Look on us here | with loving eyes,
That waiting we victory win.

3. "Hail to the gods! | Ye goddesses, hail,
And all the generous earth!
Give to us wisdom | and goodly speech,
And healing hands, life-long.

4. "Long did I sleep, | my slumber was long,
And long are the griefs of life;
Othin decreed | that I could not break
The heavy spells of sleep."

Her name was Sigrdrifa, and she was a Valkyrie. She said that two kings fought in battle; one was called Hjalmgunnar, an old man but a mighty warrior, and Othin had promised him the victory, and

The other was Agnar, | brother of Autha,
None he found | who fain would shield him.

347

Sigrdrifa, slew Hjalmgunnar in the battle, and Othin pricked her with the sleep-thorn in punishment for this, and said that she should never thereafter win victory in battle, but that she should be wedded. "And I said to him that I had made a vow in my turn, that I would never marry a man who knew the meaning of fear." Sigurth answered and asked her to teach him wisdom, if she knew of what took place in all the worlds. Sigrdrifa said:

5. "Beer I bring thee, | tree of battle,
Mingled of strength | and mighty fame;
Charms it holds | and healing signs,
Spells full good, | and gladness-runes."

* * * * * *

6. Winning-runes learn, | if thou longest to win,
And the runes on thy sword-hilt write;
Some on the furrow, | and some on the flat,
And twice shalt thou call on Tyr.

7. Ale-runes learn, | that with lies the wife
Of another betray not thy trust;
On the horn thou shalt write, | and the backs of thy hands,
And Need shalt mark on thy nails.
Thou shalt bless the draught, | and danger escape,
And cast a leek in the cup;
(For so I know | thou never shalt see
Thy mead with evil mixed.)

8. Birth-runes learn, | if help thou wilt lend,
The babe from the mother to bring;
On thy palms shalt write them, | and round thy joints,
And ask the fates to aid.

9. Wave-runes learn, | if well thou wouldst shelter
The sail-steeds out on the sea;

On the stem shalt thou write, | and the steering blade,
And burn them into the oars;
Though high be the breakers, | and black the waves,
Thou shalt safe the harbor seek.

10. Branch-runes learn, | if a healer wouldst be,
And cure for wounds wouldst work;
On the bark shalt thou write, | and on trees that be
With boughs to the eastward bent.

11. Speech-runes learn, | that none may seek
To answer harm with hate;
Well he winds | and weaves them all,
And sets them side by side,
At the judgment-place, | when justice there
The folk shall fairly win.

12. Thought-runes learn, | if all shall think
Thou art keenest minded of men.

* * * * * *

13. Them Hropt arranged, | and them he wrote,
And them in thought he made,
Out of the draught | that down had dropped
From the head of Heithdraupnir,
And the horn of Hoddrofnir.

14. On the mountain he stood | with Brimir's sword,
On his head the helm he bore;
Then first the head | of Mim spoke forth,
And words of truth it told.

* * * * * *

15. He bade write on the shield | before the shining goddess,
On Arvak's ear, | and on Alsvith's hoof,
On the wheel of the car | of Hrungnir's killer,
On Sleipnir's teeth, | and the straps of the sledge.

16. On the paws of the bear, | and on Bragi's tongue,
On the wolf's claws bared, | and the eagle's beak,
On bloody wings, | and bridge's end,
On freeing hands | and helping foot-prints.

17. On glass and on gold, | and on goodly charms,
In wine and in beer, | and on well-loved seats,
On Gungnir's point, | and on Grani's breast,
On the nails of Norns, | and the night-owl's beak.

* * * * * *

18. Shaved off were the runes | that of old were written,
And mixed with the holy mead,
And sent on ways so wide;
So the gods had them, | so the elves got them,
And some for the Wanes so wise,
And some for mortal men.

19. Beech-runes are there, | birth-runes are there,
And all the runes of ale,
And the magic runes of might;
Who knows them rightly | and reads them true,
Has them himself to help;
Ever they aid,
Till the gods are gone.

* * * * * *

Brynhild spake:
20. "Now shalt thou choose, | for the choice is given,

Thou tree of the biting blade;
Speech or silence, | 'tis thine to say,
Our evil is destined all."

Sigurth spake:
21. "I shall not flee, | though my fate be near,
I was born not a coward to be;
Thy loving word | for mine will I win,
As long as I shall live."

22. Then first I rede thee, | that free of guilt
Toward kinsmen ever thou art;
No vengeance have, | though they work thee harm,
Reward after death thou shalt win.

23. Then second I rede thee, | to swear no oath
If true thou knowest it not;
Bitter the fate | of the breaker of troth,
And poor is the wolf of his word.

24. Then third I rede thee, | that thou at the Thing
Shalt fight not in words with fools;
For the man unwise | a worser word
Than he thinks doth utter oft.

25. Ill it is | if silent thou art,
A coward born men call thee,
And truth mayhap they tell;
Seldom safe is fame,
Unless wide renown be won;
On the day thereafter | send him to death,
Let him pay the price of his lies.

26. Then fourth I rede thee, | if thou shalt find
A wily witch on thy road,

It is better to go | than her guest to be,
Though night enfold thee fast.

27. Eyes that see | need the sons of men
Who fight in battle fierce;
Oft witches evil | sit by the way,
Who blade and courage blunt.

28. Then fifth I rede thee, | though maidens fair
Thou seest on benches sitting,
Let the silver of kinship | not rob thee of sleep,
And the kissing of women beware.

29. Then sixth I rede thee, | if men shall wrangle,
And ale-talk rise to wrath,
No words with a drunken | warrior have,
For wine steals many men's wits.

30. Brawls and ale | full oft have been
An ill to many a man,
Death for some, | and sorrow for some;
Full many the woes of men.

31. Then seventh I rede thee, | if battle thou seekest
With a foe that is full of might;
It is better to fight | than to burn alive
In the hall of the hero rich.

32. Then eighth I rede thee, | that evil thou shun,
And beware of lying words;
Take not a maid, | nor the wife of a man,
Nor lure them on to lust.

33. Then ninth I rede thee: | burial render
If thou findest a fallen corpse,

Of sickness dead, | or dead in the sea,
Or dead of weapons' wounds.

34. A bath shalt thou give them | who corpses be,
And hands and head shalt wash;
Wipe them and comb, | ere they go in the coffin,
And pray that they sleep in peace.

35. Then tenth I rede thee, | that never thou trust
The word of the race of wolves,
(If his brother thou broughtest to death,
Or his father thou didst fell;)
Often a wolf | in a son there is,
Though gold he gladly takes.

36. Battle and hate | and harm, methinks,
Full seldom fall asleep;
Wits and weapons | the warrior needs
If boldest of men he would be.

37. Then eleventh I rede thee, | that wrath thou shun,
And treachery false with thy friends;
Not long the leader's | life shall be,
For great are the foes he faces.

[*Prose.* The introductory prose follows without break the prose concluding
the *Fafnismol*, the point of division being arbitrary and not agreed upon by all
editors. *Hindarfjoll*: cf. *Fafnismol*, 42 and note. *Franks*: this does not necessarily
mean that Sigurth was on his way to the Gjukungs' home, for Sigmund had a
kingdom in the land of the Franks (cf. *Fra Dautha Sinfjotla*). *Shields*: the
annotator probably drew the notion of the shield-tower from the reference
in *Helreith Brynhildar*, 9. The flame-girt tower was not uncommon; cf.
Mengloth's hall in*Svipdagsmol*.]

353

[1. This stanza, and the two lines included in the prose after stanza 4, and possibly stanza 5 as well, evidently come from a different poem from stanzas 2-4. Lines 3-4 in the original are obscure, though the general meaning is clear.

Prose (after stanza 1). In the manuscript stanza 4 stands before this prose note and stanzas 2-3. The best arrangement of the stanzas seems to be the one here given, following Müllenhoff's suggestion, but the prose note is out of place anywhere. The first sentence of it ought to follow stanza 4 and immediately precede the next prose note; the second sentence ought to precede stanza 5.

2. *Sons of day*: the spirits of light. *The daughter of night* (Not), according to Snorri, was Jorth (Earth).]

[*Prose* (after stanza 4). *Sigrdrifa*: on the error whereby this epithet, "victory-bringer," became a proper name cf. *Fafnismol*, 44 and note.*Hjalmgunnar*: in *Helreith Brynhildar* (stanza 8) he is called a king of the Goths, which means little; of him and his adversary, *Agnar*, we know, nothing beyond what is told here. The two lines quoted apparently come from the same poem as stanza 1; the two first lines of the stanza have been reconstructed from the prose thus: "Hjalmgunnar was one, | the hoary king, / And triumph to him | had Heerfather promised." A few editions insert in this prose passage stanzas 7-10 of *Helreith Brynhildar*, which may or may not have be longed originally to this poem.]

[5. This stanza is perhaps, but by no means surely, from the same poem as stanza 1. *Tree of battle*: warrior. *Runes*: the earliest runes were not letters, but simply signs supposed to possess magic power; out of them developed the "runic alphabet."

6. Stanzas 6-12 give a list of runes which probably had no original connection with the Brynhild-Sigurth story. *Tyr*: the sword-god (cf. Hymiskvitha, 4 and note); "tyr" is also the name of a rune which became "T."

7. *Reglus* gives only lines 1-6; lines 7-8 are added from *Volsungasaga*. *Lies*, etc.: a guest on his arrival received a draught of ale from the hands of his host's wife, and it was to prevent this draught from bewitching him that the runes were recommended. *Need*: the word "nauth," meaning "need," is also the name of the rune which became "N." *Leek*: leeks were long supposed to have the power of counteracting poison or witchcraft.]

[9. *Sail-steeds*: ships.

10. *Branch-runes*: runes cut in the bark of trees. Such runes were believed to transfer sickness from the invalid to the tree. Some editors, however, have changed "limrunar" ("branch runes") to "lifrunar" ("life-runes").]

[11. Lines 3-6 look like an accidental addition, replacing two lines now lost. They mean, apparently, that the man who interweaves his speech with "speech-runes" when he pleads his case at the "Thing," or popular tribunal, will not unduly enrage his adversary in the argument of the case.

12. Here the list of runes breaks off, though the manuscript indicates no gap, and three short passages of a different type, though all dealing with runes, follow.

13. Stanzas 13-14 appear to have come from a passage regarding Othin's getting of the runes similar to *Hovamol*, 139-146. Editors have tried various combinations of the lines in stanzas 12-14. *Hropt*: Othin; cf. *Voluspo*, 62. *The draught*, etc.: apparently the reference is to the head of Mim, from which Othin derived his wisdom in magic (cf. *Voluspo*, 47 and note); *Heithdraupnir* ("Light-Dropper") and *Hoddrofnir* ("Treasure-Opener") seem to be names for Mim.]

[14. This stanza is clearly in bad shape; perhaps, as the manuscript indicates, a new stanza, of which most has been lost, should begin with line 3. *Brimir*: a giant (cf. *Voluspo*, 9 and 37); why Othin should have his sword is unknown.

15. Stanzas 15-17 constitute a wholly distinct rune-chant. Line 1 is unusually long in the original, as here. *Shield*: the shield Svalin ("Cooling") that stands in front of the sun; cf. *Grimnismol*, 38. *Arvak* ("Early Waker"') and *Alsvith* ("All Swift"): the horses that draw the sun's car; cf.*Grimnismol*, 37, *Hrungnir*: the slayer of the giant Hrungnir was Thor (cf. *Harbarthsljoth*, 14 and note), but the line is in bad shape; the name may not be Hrungnir, and "killer" is 2 conjectural addition. *Sleipnir*: Othin's eight-legged horse; cf. *Grimnismol*, 44 and note. *Sledge*: perhaps the one mentioned in *Grimnismol*, 49- 16. Bragi: the god of poetry; cf. *Grimnismol*, 44 and note.]

[17. *Charms*: the wearing of amulets was very common. *Gungnir*: Othin's spear, made by the dwarfs, which he occasionally lent to heroes to whom he granted victory. *Grani*: Sigurth's horse; the *Volsungasaga* has "giantesses'."

19. Stanzas 18-19, which editors have freely rearranged, apparently come from another source than any of the rest. *Shaved off*: the runes were shaved off by Othin from the wood on which they were carved, and the shavings bearing them were put into the magic mead. *Wanes*: cf.*Voluspo*, 21, note.

19. Lines 3, 6, and 7 look like spurious additions, but the whole stanza is chaotic. *Beech-runes*: runes carved on beech trees.]

[20. Stanzas 20-21 are all that remains of the dialogue between Brynhild and Sigurth from the poem to which stanzas 2-4 belong; cf. Introductory Note. In the intervening lost stanzas Brynhild has evidently warned Sigurth of the perils that will follow if he swears loyalty to her; hence the choice to which she here refers. *Tree*, etc.: warrior. The manuscript does not indicate the speaker of either this or the following stanza; the *Volsungasaga* names Sigurth before stanza 21.

21. It is quite possible that the original poem concluded with two stanzas after this, paraphrased thus in the *Volsungasaga*: "Sigurth said: 'Nowhere is to be found any one wiser than thou, and this I swear, that I shall have thee for mine, and that thou art after my heart's desire.' She answered: 'I would rather have thee though I might choose among all men.' And this they bound between them with oaths." Stanzas 22-37, which the *Volsungasaga* paraphrases, may have been introduced at a relatively early time, but can hardly have formed part of the original poem.]

[22. With this stanza begins the list of numbered counsels, closely resembling the *Loddfafnismol* (*Hovamol*, 111-138), here attributed to Brynhild. That the section originally had anything to do with Brynhild is more than improbable.

23. *Wolf of his word*: oath-destroyer, oath-breaker.

25. This chaotic and obscure jumble of lines has been unsuccessfully "improved" by various editors. It is clearly an interpolation, meaning, in substance: "It is dangerous to keep silent too long, as men may think you a coward; but if any one taunts [fp. 398] you falsely because of your silence, do not argue with him, but the next morning kill him as proof that he is a liar."]

[27. Probably another interpolation.

28. *Silver of kinship*: the passage is doubtful, but apparently it means the "marriage-price" for which a bride was "bought."

29. Line 1 comes at the end of the thirty-second leaf of *Regius*, and whatever further was contained in that manuscript has vanished [fp. 399] with the lost eight-leaf folio (cf. Introductory Note). The rest of stanza 29, and stanzas 50-37, are added from later paper manuscripts, which were undoubtedly copied from an old parchment, though probably not from the complete *Regius*. The *Volsungasaga* paraphrases these additional stanzas.]

[30. Probably an interpolation.

31. The meaning is that it is better to go forth to battle than to stay at home and be burned to death. Many a Norse warrior met his death in this latter way; the burning of the house in the *Njalssaga* is the most famous instance.

34. Probably an interpolation.]

[35. Lines 3-4 are probably interpolated. *Race of wolves*: family of a slain foe.

36. Probably an interpolation.

37. Lines 3-4 may well have come from the old Sigurth-Brynhild poem, like stanzas 2-4 and 20-21, being inserted here, where they do not fit particularly well, in place of the two lines with which the eleventh counsel originally ended. Perhaps they formed part of the stanza of warning which evidently preceded Brynhild's speech in stanza 20. In the *Volsungasaga* they are paraphrased at the end of Brynhild's long speech of advice (stanzas 20-37), and are immediately followed by the prose passage given in the note on stanza 21. It seems likely, therefore, [fp. 401] that the paper manuscripts have preserved all of the so-called *Sigrdrifumol* which was contained in the lost section of *Regius*, with the possible exception of these two concluding stanzas, and these may very well have been given only in the form of a prose note, though it is practically certain that at one time they existed in verse form.]

BROT AF SIGURTHARKVITHU

Fragment of a Sigurth Lay

INTRODUCTORY NOTE

The gap of eight leaves in the *Codex Regius* (cf. introductory note to the *Sigrdrifumol*) is followed by a passage of twenty stanzas which is evidently the end of a longer poem, the greater part of it having been contained in the lost section of the manuscript. There is here little question of such a compilation as made up the so-called *Reginsmol, Fafnismol,* and*Sigrdrifumol*; the extant fragment shows every sign of being part of a poem which, as it stood in the manuscript, was a complete and definite unit. The end is clearly marked; the following poem, *Guthrunarkvitha* I, carries a specific heading in the manuscript, so that there is no uncertainty as to where the fragment closes.

It seems altogether likely that the twenty stanzas thus remaining are the end of a poem entitled *Sigurtharkvitha* (Lay of Sigurth), and, more specifically, the "Long" Lay of Sigurth. The extant and complete Sigurth lay, a relatively late work, is referred to by the annotator as the "Short" Lay of Sigurth, which, of course, presupposes the existence of a longer poem with the same title. As the "short" lay is one of the longest poems in the whole collection (seventy stanzas), it follows that the other one must have been considerably more extensive in order to have been thus distinguished by its length. It may be guessed, then, that not less than eighty or a hundred stanzas, and possibly more, of the "Long" Lay of Sigurth have been lost with the missing pages of *Regius*.

The narrative, from the point at which the so-called *Sigrdrifumol* breaks off to that at which the *Brot* takes it up, is

358

given with considerable detail in the Volsungasaga. In this prose narrative four stanzas are quoted, and one of them is specifically introduced with the phrase: "as is told in the Lay of Sigurth." It is possible, but most unlikely, that the entire passage paraphrases this poem alone; such an assumption would give the Lay of Sigurth not less than two hundred and fifty stanzas (allowing about fifteen stanzas to each of the missing pages), and moreover there are inconsistencies in the *Volsungasaga* narrative suggesting that different and more or less conflicting poems were used as sources. The chances are that the "Long" Lay of Sigurth filled approximately the latter half of the lost section of the manuscript, the first half including poems of which the only trace is to be found in the *Volsungasaga* prose paraphrase and in two of the stanzas therein quoted.

The course of the *Volsungasaga's* story from the *Sigrdrifumol* to the *Brot* is, briefly, as follows. After leaving the Valkyrie, Sigurth comes to the dwelling of Heimir, Brynhild's brother-in-law, where he meets Brynhild and they swear oaths of fidelity anew (the *Volsungasaga* is no more lucid with regard to the Brynhild-Sigrdrifa confusion than was the annotator of the poems). Then the scene shifts to the home of the Gjukungs. Guthrun, Gjuki's daughter, has a terrifying dream, and visits Brynhild to have it explained, which the latter does by foretelling pretty much everything that is going to happen; this episode was presumably the subject of a separate poem in the lost section of the manuscript. Guthrun returns home, and Sigurth soon arrives, to be made enthusiastically welcome. Grimhild, mother of Gunnar and Guthrun, gives him a magic draught which makes him forget all about Brynhild, and shortly thereafter he marries Guthrun.

Then follows the episode of the winning of Brynhild for Gunnar (cf. *Gripisspo*, 97 and note). This was certainly the subject of a poem, possibly of the first part of the "Long" Lay of Sigurth, although it seems more likely that the episode was dealt with in a separate poem. The *Volsungasaga* quotes two stanzas describing

Sigurth's triumphant passing through the flames after Gunnar has failed and the two have changed forms. They run thus:

The fire raged, | the earth was rocked,
The flames leaped high | to heaven itself;
Few were the hardy | heroes would dare
To ride or leap | the raging flames.

Sigurth urged Grani | then with his sword,
The fire slackened | before the hero,
The flames sank low | for the greedy of fame,
The armor flashed | that Regin had fashioned.

After Sigurth has spent three nights with Brynhild, laying his sword between them (cf. *Gripisspo*, 41 and note), he and Gunnar return home, while Brynhild goes to the dwelling of her brother-in-law, Heimir, and makes ready for her marriage with Gunnar, directing Heimir to care for her daughter by Sigurth, Aslaug. The wedding takes place, to be followed soon after by the quarrel between Guthrun and Brynhild, in which the former betrays the fact that it was Sigurth, and not Gunnar, who rode through the flames. Brynhild speaks with contempt of Guthrun and her whole family, and the following stanza, which presumably be longs to the same Sigurth lay as the Brot, is quoted at this point:

Sigurth the dragon | slew, and that
Will men recall | while the world remains;
But little boldness | thy brother had
To ride or leap | the raging flames.

Gunnar and Sigurth alike try to appease the angry Brynhild, but in vain. After Sigurth has talked with her, his leaving her hall is described in the following stanza, introduced by the specific phrase: "as is said in the Lay of Sigurth":

Forth went Sigurth, | and speech he sought not,
The friend of heroes, | his head bowed down;
Such was his grief | that asunder burst
His mail-coat all | of iron wrought.

Brynhild then tells Gunnar that she had given herself wholly to
Sigurth before she had become Gunnar's wife (the confusion
between the two stories is commented on in the note to *Gripisspo*,
47), and Gunnar discusses plans of vengance with his brother,
Hogni. It is at this point that the action of the *Brot* begins. Beginning
with this poem, and thence to the end of the cycle, the German
features of the narrative predominate (cf. introductory note
to *Gripisspo*).

Hogni spake:
1. "(What evil deed | has Sigurth) done,
That the hero's life | thou fain wouldst have?"

Gunnar spake:
2. "Sigurth oaths | to me hath sworn,
Oaths hath sworn, | and all hath broken;
He betrayed me there | where truest all
His oaths, methinks, | he ought to have kept."

Hogni spake:
3. "Thy heart hath Brynhild | whetted to hate,
Evil to work | and harm to win,
She grudges the honor | that Guthrun has,
And that joy of herself | thou still dost have."

4. They cooked a wolf, | they cut up a snake,
They gave to Gotthorm | the greedy one's flesh,
Before the men, | to murder minded,
Laid their hands | on the hero bold.

361

5. Slain was Sigurth | south of the Rhine;
From a limb a raven | called full loud:
"Your blood shall redden | Atli's blade,
And your oaths shall bind | you both in chains."

6. Without stood Guthrun, | Gjuki's daughter,
Hear now the speech | that first she spake:
"Where is Sigurth now, | the noble king,
That my kinsmen riding | before him come?"

7. Only this | did Hogni answer:
"Sigurth we | with our swords have slain;
The gray horse mourns | by his master dead."

8. Then Brynhild spake, | the daughter of Buthli:
"Well shall ye joy | in weapons and lands;
Sigurth alone | of all had been lord,
If a little longer | his life had been.

9. "Right were it not | that so he should rule
O'er Gjuki's wealth | and the race of the Goths;
Five are the sons | for ruling the folk,
And greedy of fight, | that he hath fathered."

10. Then Brynhild laughed-- | and the building echoed--
Only once, | with all her heart;
"Long shall ye joy | in lands and men,
Now ye have slain | the hero noble."

11. Then Guthrun spake, | the daughter of Gjuki:
"Much thou speakest | in evil speech;
Accursed be Gunnar, | Sigurth's killer,
Vengeance shall come | for his cruel heart."

12. Early came evening, | and ale was drunk,
And among them long | and loud they talked.;

They slumbered all | when their beds they sought,
But Gunnar alone | was long awake.

13. His feet were tossing, | he talked to himself,
And the slayer of hosts | began to heed
What the twain from the tree | had told him then,
The raven and eagle, | as home they rode.

14. Brynhild awoke, | the daughter of Buthli,
The warrior's daughter, | ere dawn of day:
"Love me or hate me, | the harm is done,
And my grief cries out, | or else I die."

15. Silent were all | who heard her speak,
And nought of the heart | of the queen they knew,
Who wept such tears | the thing to tell
That laughing once | of the men she had won.

Brynhild spake:
16. "Gunnar, I dreamed | a dream full grim:
In the hall were corpses; | cold was my bed;
And, ruler, thou | didst joyless ride,
With fetters bound | in the foemen's throng.

17. ".   .   .   .   .

.   .   .   .
Utterly now your | Niflung race
All shall die; | your oaths ye have broken.

18. "Thou hast, Gunnar, | the deed forgot,
When blood in your footprints | both ye mingled;
All to him | hast repaid with ill
Who fain had made thee | the foremost of kings.

19. "Well did he prove, | when proud he rode
To win me then | thy wife to be,

How true the host-slayer | ever had held
The oaths he had made | with the monarch young.

20. "The wound-staff then, | all wound with gold,
The hero let | between us lie;
With fire the edge | was forged full keen,
And with drops of venom | the blade was damp."

Here it is told in this poem about the death of Sigurth, and the story goes here that they slew him out of doors, but some say that they slew him in the house, on his bed while he was sleeping. But German men say that they killed him out of doors in the forest; and so it is told in the old Guthrun lay, that Sigurth and Gjuki's sons had ridden to the council-place, and that he was slain there. But in this they are all agreed, that they deceived him in his trust of them, and fell upon him when he was lying down and unprepared.

[1. The fragment begins with the last words of line I (probably line 3 of the stanza). A few editors ascribe this speech to Gunnar and the next to Brynhild; one reconstruction of lines 1-2 on this probably false assumption runs: "Why art thou, Brynhild, | [fp. 405] daughter of Buthli, / Scheming ill | with evil counsel?" *Hogni* (German Hagene): brother of Gunnar and Guthrun.]

[2. A few editors ascribe this speech to Brynhild. Gunnar, if the stanza is his, has believed Brynhild's statement regarding Sigurth's disloyalty to his blood-brother.

4. The *Volsungasaga* quotes a somewhat different version of this stanza, in which the snake is called "wood-fish" and the third line adds "beer and many things." Eating snakes and the flesh of beasts of prey was commonly supposed to induce ferocity. *Gotthorm*: Grimhild's son, half-brother to Gunnar. He it is who, not having sworn brotherhood with Sigurth, does the killing.

5. In the manuscript this stanza stands between stanzas 11 and 12; most editions have made the change here indicated. [fp. 406] *South of the Rhine*: the definite localization of the action shows how clearly all this part of the story was recognized in the North as of German origin. *Atli*(Attila; cf. introductory note to *Gripisspo*): the Northern version of the story makes him Brynhild's brother. His

marriage with Guthrun, and his slaying of hex brothers, are told in the Atli poems. Regarding the manner of Sigurth's death cf. concluding prose passage and note. Stanza 13 indicates that after stanza 5 a stanza containing the words of an eagle has been lost.]

[7. One line of this stanza, but it is not clear which, seems to have been lost. *The gray horse*: Grani.

8. Some editions set stanzas 8 and 9 after stanza 11; Sijmons marks them as spurious. *Buthli*: cf. *Gripisspo*, 19, note.

9. *Goths*: a generic term for any German race; cf. Gripisspo, [fp. 407] 35 and note. *Five sons*: according to the *Volsungasaga* Sigurth had only one son, named Sigmund, who was killed at Brynhild's behest. *Sigurtharkvitha en skamma* and *Guthrunarkvitha II* like wise mention only one son. The daughter of Sigurth and Guthrun, Svanhild, marries Jormunrek (Ermanarich).]

[12. The manuscript marks line 4 as the beginning of a new stanza, and a few editions combine it with stanza 13.

13. *Slayer of hosts*: warrior (Gunnar). *Raven and eagle*: cf. note on stanza 5.]

[16. Mogk regards stanzas 16 and 17 as interpolated, but on not very satisfactory grounds. On the death of Gunnar cf. *Drap Niflunga*.

17. No gap is indicated in the manuscript, and some editions attach these two lines to stanza 16. *Niflungs*: this name (German Nibelungen), meaning "sons of the mist," seems to have belonged originally to the race of supernatural beings to which the treasure belonged in the German version. It was subsequently ex tended to include the Gjukungs and their Burgundians. This question, of minor importance in the Norse poems, has evoked an enormous amount of learned discussion in connection with the *Nibelungenlied.*]

[19. *Footprints*: the actual mingling of blood in one another's footprints was a part of the ceremony of swearing blood-brother hood, the oath which Gunnar and Sigurth had taken. The fourth line refers to the fact that Sigurth had won many battles for Gunnar.

20. Regarding the sword episode cf. *Gripisspo*, 41 and note. *Wound-staff*: sword.

Prose. This prose passage has in the manuscript, written in red, the phrase "Of Sigurth's Death" as a heading; there is no break between it and the prose introducing *Guthrunarkvitha I*, the heading for that poem coming just before stanza 1. This note is of special interest as an effort at real criticism. The annotator, troubled by the two versions of the story of Sigurth's death, feels it incumbent on him not only to point the fact out, but to cite the authority of "German men" for the form which appears [fp. 410] in this poem. The alternative version, wherein Sigurth is slain in bed, appears in *Sigurtharkvitha en skamma*, *Guthrunarhvot*, and *Hamthesmol*, and also in the *Volsungasaga*, which tells how Gotthorm tried twice to kill Sigurth but was terrified by the brightness of his eyes, and succeeded only after the hero had fallen asleep, That the annotator was correct in citing German authority for the slaying of Sigurth in the forest is shown by the *Nibelungenlied* and the*Thithrekssaga*. The "old" Guthrun lay is unquestionably *Guthrunarkvitha II*.]

GUTHRUNARKVITHA I

The First Lay of Guthrun

INTRODUCTORY NOTE

The *First Lay of Guthrun*, entitled in the *Codex Regius* simply *Guthrunarkvitha*, immediately follows the remaining fragment of the "long" Sigurth lay in that manuscript. Unlike the poems dealing with the earlier part of the Sigurth cycle, the so-called *Reginsmol*, *Fafnismol*, and *Sigrdrifumol*, it is a clear and distinct unit, apparently complete and with few and minor interpolations. It is also one of the finest poems in the entire collection, with an extraordinary emotional intensity and dramatic force. None of its stanzas are quoted elsewhere, and it is altogether probable that the compilers of the *Volsungasaga* were unfamiliar with it, for they do not mention the sister and daughter of Gjuki who appear in this poem, or Herborg, "queen of the Huns" (stanza 6).

The lament of Guthrun (Kriemhild) is almost certainly among the oldest parts of the story. The lament was one of the earliest forms of poetry to develop among the Germanic peoples, and I suspect, though the matter is not susceptible of proof, that the lament of Sigurth's wife had assumed lyric form as early as the seventh century, and reached the North in that shape rather than in prose tradition (cf. *Guthrunarkvitha II*, introductory note). We find traces of it in the seventeenth Aventiure of the *Nibelungenlied*, and in the poems of the *Edda* it dominates every appearance of Guthrun. The two first Guthrun lays (I and II) are both laments, one for Sigurth's death and the other including both that and the lament over the slaying of her brothers; the lament theme is apparent in the third Guthrun lay and in the *Guthrunarhvot*.

In their present forms the second Guthrun lay is undoubtedly older than he first; in the prose following the *Brot* the annotator refers to the "old" Guthrun lay in terms which can apply only to the second one in the collection. The shorter and "first" lay, therefore, can scarcely have been composed much before the year 1000, and may be somewhat later. The poet appears to have known and made use of the older lament; stanza 17, for example, is a close parallel to stanza 2 of the earlier poem; but whatever material he used he fitted into a definite poetic scheme of his own. And while this particular poem is, as critics have generally agreed, one of the latest of the collection, it probably represents one of the earliest parts of the entire Sigurth cycle to take on verse form.

Guthrunarkvitha I, so far as the narrative underlying it is concerned, shows very little northern addition to the basic German tradition. Brynhild appears only as Guthrun's enemy and the cause of Sigurth's death; the three women who attempt to comfort Guthrun, though unknown to the southern stories, seem to have been rather distinct creations of the poet's than traditional additions to the legend. Regarding the relations of the various elements in the Sigurth cycle, cf. introductory note to *Gripisspo*.

Guthrun sat by the dead Sigurth; she did not weep as other women, but her heart was near to bursting with grief. The men and women came to her to console her, but that was not easy to do. It is told of men that Guthrun had eaten of Fafnir's heart, and that she under stood the speech of birds. This is a poem about Guthrun.

1. Then did Guthrun | think to die,
When she by Sigurth | sorrowing sat;
Tears she had not, | nor wrung her hands,
Nor ever wailed, | as other women.

2. To her the warriors | wise there came,
Longing her heavy | woe to lighten;

Grieving could not | Guthrun weep,
So sad her heart, | it seemed, would break.

3. Then the wives | of the warriors came,
Gold-adorned, | and Guthrun sought;
Each one then | of her own grief spoke,
The bitterest pain | she had ever borne.

4. Then spake Gjaflaug, | Gjuki's sister:
"Most joyless of all | on earth am I;
Husbands five | were from me taken,
(Two daughters then, | and sisters three,)
Brothers eight, | yet I have lived."

5. Grieving could not | Guthrun weep,
Such grief she had | for her husband dead,
And so grim her heart | by the hero's body.

6. Then Herborg spake, | the queen of the Huns:
"I have a greater | grief to tell;
My seven sons | in the southern land,
And my husband, fell | in fight all eight.
(Father and mother | and brothers four
Amid the waves | the wind once smote,
And the seas crashed through | the sides of the ship.)

7. "The bodies all | with my own hands then
I decked for the grave, | and the dead I buried;
A half-year brought me | this to bear;
And no one came | to comfort me.

8. "Then bound I was, | and taken in war,
A sorrow yet | in the same half-year;
They bade me deck | and bind the shoes
Of the wife of the monarch | every morn.

9. "In jealous rage | her wrath she spake,
And beat me oft | with heavy blows;
Never a better | lord I knew,
And never a woman | worse I found."

10. Grieving could not | Guthrun weep,
Such grief she had | for her husband dead,
And so grim her heart | by the hero's body.

11. Then spake Gollrond, | Gjuki's daughter:
"Thy wisdom finds not, | my foster-mother,
The way to comfort | the wife so young."
She bade them uncover | the warrior's corpse.

12. The shroud she lifted | from Sigurth, laying
His well-loved head | on the knees of his wife:
"Look on thy loved one, | and lay thy lips
To his as if yet | the hero lived."

13. Once alone did | Guthrun look;
His hair all clotted | with blood beheld,
The blinded eyes | that once shone bright,
The hero's breast | that the blade had pierced.

14. Then Guthrun bent, | on her pillow bowed,
Her hair was loosened, | her cheek was hot,
And the tears like raindrops | downward ran.

15. Then Guthrun, daughter | of Gjuki, wept,
And through her tresses | flowed the tears;
And from the court | came the cry of geese,
The birds so fair | of the hero's bride.

16. Then Gollrond spake, | the daughter of Gjuki:
"Never a greater | love I knew
Than yours among | all men on earth;

Nowhere wast happy, | at home or abroad,
Sister mine, | with Sigurth away."

Guthrun spake:
17. "So was my Sigurth | o'er Gjuki's sons
As the spear-leek grown | above the grass,
Or the jewel bright | borne on the band,
The precious stone | that princes wear.

18. "To the leader of men | I loftier seemed
And higher than all | of Herjan's maids;
As little now | as the leaf I am
On the willow hanging; | my hero is dead.

19. "In his seat, in his bed, | I see no more
My heart's true friend; | the fault is theirs,
The sons of Gjuki, | for all my grief,
That so their sister | sorely weeps.

20. "So shall your land | its people lose
As ye have kept | your oaths of yore;
Gunnar, no joy | the gold shall give thee,
(The rings shall soon | thy slayers be,)
Who swarest oaths | with Sigurth once.

21. "In the court was greater | gladness then
The day my Sigurth | Grani saddled,
And went forth Brynhild's | hand to win,
That woman ill, | in an evil hour."

22. Then Brynhild spake, | the daughter of Buthli:
"May the witch now husband | and children want
Who, Guthrun, loosed | thy tears at last,
And with magic today | hath made thee speak."

23. Then Gollrond, daughter | of Gjuki, spake:
"Speak not such words, | thou hated woman;
Bane of the noble | thou e'er hast been,
(Borne thou art | on an evil wave,
Sorrow hast brought | to seven kings,)
And many a woman | hast loveless made."

24. Then Brynhild, daughter | of Buthli, spake:
"Atli is guilty | of all the sorrow,
(Son of Buthli | and brother of mine,)
When we saw in the hall | of the Hunnish race
The flame of the snake's bed | flash round the hero;
(For the journey since | full sore have I paid,
And ever I seek | the sight to forget.)"

25. By the pillars she stood, | and gathered her strength,
From the eyes of Brynhild, | Buthli's daughter,
Fire there burned, | and venom she breathed,
When the wounds she saw | on Sigurth then.

Guthrun went thence away to a forest in the waste, and journeyed all the way to Denmark, and was there seven half-years with Thora, daughter of Hokon. Brynhild would not live after Sigurth. She had eight of her thralls slain and five serving-women. Then she killed her self with a sword, as is told in the Short Lay of Sigurth.

[*Prose.* The prose follows the concluding prose of the *Brot* without indication of a break, the heading standing immediately before stanza 1. *Fafnir's heart*: this bit of information is here quite without point, and it is nowhere else stated that Guthrun understood the speech of birds. In the *Volsungasaga* it is stated that Sigurth gave Guthrun some of Fafnir's heart to eat, "and thereafter she was much grimmer than before, and wiser."

1. This stanza seems to be based on Guthrunarkvitha II, 11-12.]

[4. *Gjaflaug*: nothing further is known of this aunt of Guthrun, or of the many relatives whom she has lost. Very likely she is an invention of the poet's, for it seems improbable that other wise all further trace of her should have been lost. Line 4 has been marked by many editors as spurious.

5. Some editors assume the loss of a line, after either line 1 or line 3. I prefer to believe that here and in stanza 10 the poet knew exactly what he was doing, and that both stanzas are correct.

6. *Herborg*: neither she nor her sorrows are elsewhere mentioned, [fp. 415] nor is it clear what a "queen of the Huns" is doing in Gunnar's home, but the word "Hun" has little definiteness of meaning in the poems, and is frequently applied to Sigurth himself (cf. note on stanza 24). Herborg appears from stanza 11 to have been the foster-mother of Gollrond, Guthrun's sister. Lines 5-7 may be interpolations, or may form a separate stanza.]

[7. Lines 1 and 2 stand in reversed order in the manuscript; I have followed Gering's conjectural transposition.

9. Herborg implies that the queen's jealousy was not altogether misplaced.]

[10. Cf. stanza 5 and note. The manuscript abbreviates to first letters.

11. *Gollrond*: not elsewhere mentioned. Line 4 looks like an interpolation replacing a line previously lost.

12. The manuscript indicates line 3 as the beginning of a stanza. and some editors have attempted to follow this arrangement. Many editors assume the loss of a line from this stanza.]

[15. The word here translated "tresses" is sheer guesswork. The detail of the geese is taken from *Sigurtharkvitha en skamma*, 29, line 3 here being identical with line 4 of that stanza.

16. Line 1, abbreviated in the manuscript, very likely should be simply "Gollrond spake."

17. Cf. *Guthrunarkvitha II*, 2. The manuscript does not name the speaker, and some editions have a first line, "Then Guthrun spake, the daughter of Gjuki."

18. *Herjan*: Othin; his maids are the Valkyries; cf. *Voluspo*, 31, where the same phrase is used.]

[20. Line 4 looks like an interpolation (cf. *Fafnismol*, 9, line 4), but some editors instead have queried line 5. How Guthrun's curse is fulfilled is told in the subsequent poems. That desire for Sigurth's treasure (the gold cursed by Andvari and Loki) was one of the motives for his murder is indicated in *Sigurtharkvitha en skamma* (stanza 16), and was clearly a part of the German tradition, as it appears in the *Nibelungenlied*.

21. Cf. *Gripisspo*, 35 and note.

22. Line 1 is abbreviated in the manuscript.]

[23. Editors are agreed that this stanza shows interpolations, but differ as to the lines to reject. Line 4 (literally "every wave of ill-doing drives thee") is substantially a proverb, and line 5, with its apparently meaningless reference to "seven" kings, may easily have come from some other source.

24. The stanza is obviously in bad shape; perhaps it represents two separate stanzas, or perhaps three of the lines are later additions. *Atli*: Brynhild here blames her brother, following the frequent custom of transferring the responsibility for a murder (cf. *Helgakvitha Hundingsbana II*, 33), because he compelled her to marry Gunnar against her will, an idea which the poet seems to have gained from *Sigurtharkvitha en skamma*, 32-39. These stanzas represent an entirely different version of the story, wherein Atli, attacked by Gunnar and Sigurth, buys them off by giving Gunnar his sister, Brynhild, as wife. He seems to have induced the latter to marry Gunnar by falsely telling her that Gunnar was Sigurth (a rationalistic explanation of the interchange of forms described in the *Volsungasaga* and *Gripisspo*, 37-39). In the present stanza Atli is made to do this out of desire for Sigurth's treasure. *Hunnish race*: this may be [fp. 419] merely an error (neither Gunnar nor Sigurth could properly have been connected in any way with Atli and his Huns), based on *Sigurtharkvitha en skamma*, wherein Sigurth appears more than once as the "Hunnish king." The North was very much in the dark as to the differences between Germans, Burgundians, Franks, Goths, and Huns, and used the words without much discrimination. On the other hand, it may refer to Sigurth's appearance when, adorned with gold, he came with Gunnar to besiege Atli, in the alternative version of the story just cited (cf. *Sigurtharkvitha en skamma*, 36). *Flame of the snake's bed*: gold, so called because serpents and dragons were the' traditional guardians of treasure, on which they lay.]

[*Prose*. The manuscript has "Gunnar" in place of "Guthrun," but this is an obvious mistake; the entire prose passage is based on *Guthrunarkvitha II*, 14.
The *Volsungasaga* likewise merely paraphrases *Guthrunarkvitha II*, and nothing further is known of Thora or her father, Hokon, though many inconclusive

attempts have been made to identify the latter. *Brynhild*: the story of her death is told in great detail in the latter part of *Sigurtharkvitha en skamma*.]

SIGURTHARKVITHA EN SKAMMA

The Short Lay of Sigurth

INTRODUCTORY NOTE

Guthrunarkvitha I is immediately followed in the *Codex Regius* by a long poem which in the manuscript bears the heading "Sigurtharkvitha," but which is clearly referred to in the prose link between it and *Guthrunarkvitha I* as the "short" Lay of Sigurth. The discrepancy between this reference and the obvious length of the poem has led to many conjectures, but the explanation seems to be that the "long" Sigurth lay, of which the *Brot* is presumably a part, was materially longer even than this poem. The efforts to reduce the "short" Sigurth lay to dimensions which would justify the appellation in comparison with other poems in the collection, either by separating it into two poems or by the rejection of many stanzas as interpolations, have been utterly inconclusive.

Although there are probably several interpolated passages, and indications of omissions are not lacking, the poem as we now have it seems to be a distinct and coherent unit. From the narrative point of view it leaves a good deal to be desired, for the reason that the poet's object was by no means to tell a story, with which his hearers were quite familiar, but to use the narrative simply as the background for vivid and powerful characterization. The lyric element, as Mogk points out, overshadows the epic throughout, and the fact that there are frequent confusions of narrative tradition does not trouble the poet at all.

The material on which the poem was based seems to have existed in both prose and verse form; the poet was almost certainly familiar with some of the other poems in the Eddic collection, with poems

376

which have since been lost, and with the narrative prose traditions which never fully assumed verse form. The fact that he seems to have known and used the *Oddrunargratr*, which can hardly have been composed before 1050, and that in any case he introduces the figure of Oddrun, a relatively late addition to the story, dates the poem as late as the end of the eleventh century, or even the first half of the twelfth. There has been much discussion as to where it was composed, the debate centering chiefly on the reference to glaciers (stanza 8). There is something to be said in favor of Greenland as the original home of the poem (cf. introductory note to *Atlakvitha*), but the arguments for Iceland are even stronger; Norway in this case is practically out of the question.

The narrative features of the poem are based on the German rather than the Norse elements of the story (cf. introductory note to *Gripisspo*), but the poet has taken whatever material he wanted without much discrimination as to its source. By the year 1100 the story of Sigurth, with its allied legends, existed through out the North in many and varied forms, and the poem shows traces of variants of the main story which do not appear elsewhere.

1. Of old did Sigurth | Gjuki seek,
The Volsung young, | in battles victor;
Well he trusted | the brothers twain,
With mighty oaths | among them sworn.

2. A maid they gave him, | and jewels many,
Guthrun the young, | the daughter of Gjuki;
They drank and spake | full many a day,
Sigurth the young | and Gjuki's sons.

3. Thereafter went they | Brynhild to woo,
And so with them | did Sigurth ride,
The Volsung young, | in battle valiant,--
Himself would have had her | if all he had seen.

4. The southern hero | his naked sword,
Fair-flashing, let | between them lie;
(Nor would he come | the maid to kiss;)
The Hunnish king | in his arms ne'er held
The maiden he gave | to Gjuki's sons.

5. Ill she had known not | in all her life,
And nought of the sorrows | of men she knew;
Blame she had not, | nor dreamed she should bear it,
But cruel the fates | that among them came.

6. By herself at the end | of day she sat,
And in open words | her heart she uttered:
"I shall Sigurth have, | the hero young,
E'en though within | my arms he die.

7. "The word I have spoken; | soon shall I rue it,
His wife is Guthrun, | and Gunnar's am I;
Ill Norns set for me | long desire."

8. Oft did she go | with grieving heart
On the glacier's ice | at even-tide,
When Guthrun then | to her bed was gone,
And the bedclothes Sigurth | about her laid.

9. " (Now Gjuki's child | to her lover goes,)
And the Hunnish king | with his wife is happy;
Joyless I am | and mateless ever,
Till cries from my heavy | heart burst forth."

10. In her wrath to battle | she roused herself:
"Gunnar, now | thou needs must lose
Lands of mine | and me myself,
No joy shall I have | with the hero ever.

11. "Back shall I fare | where first I dwelt,
Among the kin | that come of my race,
To wait there, sleeping | my life away,
If Sigurth's death | thou shalt not dare,
(And best of heroes | thou shalt not be.)

12. "The son shall fare | with his father hence,
And let not long | the wolf-cub live;
Lighter to pay | is the vengeance-price
After the deed | if the son is dead."

13. Sad was Gunnar, | and bowed with grief,
Deep in thought | the whole day through;
Yet from his heart | it was ever hid
What deed most fitting | he should find,
(Or what thing best | for him should be,
Or if he should seek | the Volsung to slay,
For with mighty longing | Sigurth he loved.)

14. Much he pondered | for many an hour;
Never before | was the wonder known
That a queen should thus | her kingdom leave;
In counsel then | did he Hogni call,
(For him in truest | trust he held.)

15. "More than all | to me is Brynhild,
Buthli's child, | the best of women;
My very life | would I sooner lose
Than yield the love | of yonder maid.

16. "Wilt thou the hero | for wealth betray?
'Twere good to have | the gold of the Rhine,
And all the hoard | in peace to hold,
And waiting fortune | thus to win."

17. Few the words | of Hogni were:
"Us it beseems not | so to do,
To cleave with swords | the oaths we swore,
The oaths we swore | and all our vows.

18. "We know no mightier | men on earth
The while we four | o'er the folk hold sway,
And while the Hunnish | hero lives,
Nor higher kinship | the world doth hold.

19. "If sons we five | shall soon beget,
Great, methinks, | our race shall grow;
Well I see | whence lead the ways;
Too bitter far | is Brynhild's hate."

Gunnar spake:
20. "Gotthorm to wrath | we needs must rouse,
Our younger brother, | in rashness blind;
He entered not | in the oaths we swore,
The oaths we swore | and all our vows."

21. It was easy to rouse | the reckless one.
.   .   .   .
The sword in the heart | of Sigurth stood.

22. In vengeance the hero | rose in the hall,
And hurled his sword | at the slayer bold;
At Gotthorm flew | the glittering steel
Of Gram full hard | from the hand of the king.

23. The foeman cleft | asunder fell,
Forward hands | and head did sink,
And legs and feet | did backward fall.

24. Guthrun soft | in her bed had slept,
Safe from care | at Sigurth's side;

She woke to find | her joy had fled,
In the blood of the friend | of Freyr she lay.

25. So hard she smote | her hands together
That the hero rose up, | iron-hearted:
"Weep not, Guthrun, | grievous tears,
Bride so young, | for thy brothers live.

26. "Too young, methinks, | is my son as yet,
He cannot flee | from the home of his foes;
Fearful and deadly | the plan they found,
The counsel new | that now they have heeded.

27. "No son will ride, | though seven thou hast,
To the Thing as the son | of their sister rides;
Well I see | who the ill has worked,
On Brynhild alone | lies the blame for all.

28. "Above all men | the maiden loved me,
Yet false to Gunnar | I ne'er was found;
I kept the oaths | and the kinship I swore;
Of his queen the lover | none may call me.

29. In a swoon she sank | when Sigurth died;
So hard she smote | her hands together
That all the cups | in the cupboard rang,
And loud in the courtyard | cried the geese.

30. Then Brynhild, daughter | of Buthli, laughed,
Only once, | with all her heart,
When as she lay | full loud she heard
The grievous wail | of Gjuki's daughter.

31. Then Gunnar, monarch | of men, spake forth:
"Thou dost not laugh, | thou lover of hate,
In gladness there, | or for aught of good;

Why has thy face | so white a hue,
Mother of ill? | Foredoomed thou art.

32. "A worthier woman | wouldst thou have been
If before thine eyes | we had Atli slain;
If thy brother's bleeding | body hadst seen
And the bloody wounds | that thou shouldst End."

Brynhild spake:
33. "None mock thee, Gunnar! | thou hast mightily fought,
But thy hatred little | doth Atli heed;
Longer than thou, | methinks, shall he live,

34. "To thee I say, | and thyself thou knowest,
That all these ills | thou didst early shape;
No bonds I knew, | nor sorrow bore,
And wealth I had | in my brother's home.

35. "Never a husband | sought I to have,
Before the Gjukungs | fared to our land;
Three were the kings | on steeds that came,--
Need of their journey | never there was.

36. "To the hero great | my troth I gave
Who gold-decked sat | on Grani's back;
Not like to thine | was the light of his eyes,
(Nor like in form | and face are ye,)
Though kingly both | ye seemed to be.

37. "And so to me | did Atli say
That share in our wealth | I should not have,
And greater in might | shall he ever remain.
Of gold or lands, | if my hand I gave not;
(More evil yet, | the wealth I should yield,)
The gold that he | in my childhood gave me,
(The wealth from him | in my youth I had.)

38. "Oft in my mind | I pondered much
If still I should fight, | and warriors fell,
Brave in my byrnie, | my brother defying;
That would wide | in the world be known,
And sorrow for many | a man would make.

39. "But the bond at last | I let be made,
For more the hoard | I longed to have,
The rings that the son | of Sigmund won;
No other's treasure | e'er I sought.

40. "One-alone | of all I loved,
Nor changing heart | I ever had;
All in the end | shall Atli know,
When he hears I have gone | on the death-road hence."

*   *   *   *   *   *

41. "Never a wife | of fickle will
Yet to another | man should yield.
.   .   .   .
So vengence for all | my ills shall come."

42, Up rose Gunnar, | the people's ruler,
And flung his arms | round her neck so fair;
And all who came, | of every kind,
Sought to hold her | with all their hearts.

43. But back she cast | all those who came,
Nor from the long road | let them hold her;
In counsel then | did he Hogni call:
"Of wisdom now | full great is our need.

44. "Let the warriors here | in the hall come forth,
Thine and mine, | for the need is mighty,

If haply the queen | from death they may hold,
Till her fearful thoughts | with time shall fade."

45. (Few the words | of Hogni were:)
"From the long road now | shall ye hold her not,
That born again | she may never be!
Foul she came | from her mother forth,
And born she was | for wicked deeds,
(Sorrow to many | a man to bring.)"

46. From the speaker gloomily | Gunnar turned,
For the jewel-bearer | her gems was dividing;
On all her wealth | her eyes were gazing,
On the bond-women slain | and the slaughtered slaves.

47. Her byrnie of gold | she donned, and grim
Was her heart ere the point | of her sword had pierced it;
On the pillow at last | her head she laid,
And, wounded, her plan | she pondered o'er.

48. "Hither I will | that my women come
Who gold are fain | from me to get;
Necklaces fashioned | fair to each
Shall I give, and cloth, | and garments bright."

49. Silent were all | as so she spake,
And all together | answer made:
"Slain are enough; | we seek to live,
Not thus thy women | shall honor win."

50. Long the woman, | linen-decked, pondered,--
--Young she was,-- | and weighed her words:
"For my sake now | shall none unwilling
Or loath to die | her life lay down.

51. "But little of gems | to gleam on your limbs
Ye then shall find | when forth ye fare
To follow me, | or of Menja's wealth.

. . . .

52. "Sit now, Gunnar! | for I shall speak
Of thy bride so fair | and so fain to die;
Thy ship in harbor | home thou hast not,
Although my life | I now have lost.

53. "Thou shalt Guthrun requite | more quick than thou thinkest,
. . . .
Though sadly mourns | the maiden wise
Who dwells with the king, | o'er her husband dead.

54. "A maid shall then | the mother bear;
Brighter far | than the fairest day
Svanhild shall be, | or the beams of the sun.

55. "Guthrun a noble | husband thou givest,
Yet to many a warrior | woe will she bring,
Not happily wedded | she holds herself;
Her shall Atli | hither seek,
(Buthli's son, | and brother of mine.)

56. "Well I remember | how me ye treated
When ye betrayed me | with treacherous wiles;
. . . .
Lost was my joy | as long as I lived.

57. "Oddrun as wife | thou fain wouldst win,
But Atli this | from thee withholds;
Yet in secret tryst | ye twain shall love;
She shall hold thee dear, | as I had done
If kindly fate | to us had fallen.

58. "Ill to thee | shall Atli bring,
When he casts thee down | in the den of snakes.

59. "But soon thereafter | Atli too
His life, methinks, | as thou shalt lose,
(His fortune lose | and the lives of his sons;)
Him shall Guthrun, | grim of heart,
With the biting blade | in his bed destroy.

60. "It would better beseem | thy sister fair
To follow her husband | first in death,
If counsel good | to her were given,
Or a heart akin | to mine she had.

61. "Slowly I speak,-- | but for my sake
Her life, methinks, | she shall not lose;
She shall wander over | the tossing waves,
To where Jonak rules | his father's realm.

62. "Sons to him | she soon shall bear,
Heirs therewith | of Jonak's wealth;
But Svanhild far | away is sent,
The child she bore | to Sigurth brave.

63. "Bikki's word | her death shall be,
For dreadful the wrath | of Jormunrek;
So slain is all | of Sigurth's race,
And greater the woe | of Guthrun grows.

64. "Yet one boon | I beg of thee,
The last of boons | in my life it is:
Let the pyre be built | so broad in the field
That room for us all | will ample be,
(For us who slain | with Sigurth are.)

65. "With shields and carpets | cover the pyre,
. . . .
Shrouds full fair, | and fallen slaves,
And besides the Hunnish | hero burn me.

66. "Besides the Hunnish | hero there
Slaves shall burn, | full bravely decked,
Two at his head | and two at his feet,
A brace of hounds | and a pair of hawks,
For so shall all | be seemly done.

67. "Let between us | lie once more
The steel so keen, | as so it lay
When both within | one bed we were,
And wedded mates | by men were called.

68. "The door of the hall | shall strike not the heel
Of the hero fair | with flashing rings,
If hence my following | goes with him;
Not mean our faring | forth shall be.

69. "Bond-women five | shall follow him,
And eight of my thralls, | well-born are they,
Children with me, | and mine they were
As gifts that Buthli | his daughter gave.

70. "Much have I told thee, | and more would say
If fate more space | for speech had given;
My voice grows weak, | my wounds are swelling;
Truth I have said, | and so I die."

[1. *Gjuki*: father of the brothers twain, Gunnar and Hogni, and of Guthrun. In this
version of the story Sigurth goes straight to the home of the Gjukungs after his
victory over the dragon Fafnir, without meeting Brynhild on the way

(cf. *Gripisspo*, 13 and note). *Volsung*: Sigurth's grandfather was Volsung; cf. *Fra Dautha Sinfjotla* and note. *Oaths*: regarding the blood-brother hood sworn by Sigurth, Gunnar, and Hogni cf. *Brot*, 18 and note.

3. Brynhild: on the winning of Brynhild by Sigurth in Gunnar's shape cf. *Gripisspo*, 37 and note. The poet here omits details, [fp. 422] and in stanzas 32-39 appears a quite different tradition regarding the winning of Brynhild, which I suspect he had in mind throughout the poem.]

[4. *Southern hero*: Sigurth, whose Frankish origin is seldom wholly lost sight of in the Norse versions of the story. On the episode of the sword cf. *Gripisspo*, 41 and note. Line 3 may well be an interpolation; both lines 4 and 5 have also been questioned, and some editions combine line 5 with lines 1-3 of stanza 5. *Hunnish king*: Sigurth, who was, of course, not a king of the Huns, but was occasionally so called in the later poems owing to the lack of ethnological distinction made by the Norse poets (cf. *Guthrunarkvitha I*, 24 and note).

5. This stanza may refer, as Gering thinks, merely to the fact that Brynhild lived happy and unsuspecting as Gunnar's wife until the fatal quarrel with Guthrun (cf. *Gripisspo*, 45 and note) revealed to her the deceit whereby she had been won, or it may refer to the version of the story which appears in stanzas 32-39, wherein Brynhild lived happily with Atli, her brother, until he was attacked by Gunnar and Sigurth, and was compelled to give his sister to Gunnar, winning her consent thereto by representing [fp. 432] Gunnar as Sigurth, her chosen hero (cf.*Guthrunarkvitha I*, 24 and note). The manuscript marks line 4 as the beginning of a new stanza, and many editors combine it with stanza 6.]

[6. Brynhild has now discovered the deceit that has been practised on her. That she had loved Sigurth from the outset (cf. stanza 40) fits well with the version of the story wherein Sigurth meets her before he comes to Gunnar's home (the version not used in this poem), or the one outlined in the note on stanza 5, but does not accord with the story of Sigurth's first meeting Brynhild in Gunnar's form-an added reason for believing that the poet in stanzas 5-6 had in mind the story represented by stanzas 32-39. *The hero*: the manuscript originally had the phrase thus, then corrected it to "though I die," and finally crossed out the correction. Many editions have "I."

7. Perhaps a line is missing after line 3.

8. *Glacier*: a bit of Icelandic (or Greenland) local color.

9. Line 1 does not appear in the manuscript, and is based on [fp. 424] a conjecture by Bugge. Some editions add line 2 to stanza 8. The manuscript indicates line 3 as the beginning of a stanza, and some editors assume a gap of two lines after line 4. *Hunnish king*: cf. stanza 4.]

[10. *Lands*: Brynhild's wealth again points to the story represented by stanzas 32-39; elsewhere she is not spoken of as bringing wealth to Gunnar.

11. Line 5, or perhaps line 3, may be interpolated.

12. *The son*: the three-year-old son of Sigurth and Guthrun, Sigmund, who was killed at Brynhild's behest.]

[13. This stanza has been the subject of many conjectural emendations. Some editions assume a gap after line 2, and make a separate stanza of lines 3-7; others mark lines 5-7 as spurious. The stanza seems to have been expanded by repetition. *Grief* (line 1): the manuscript has "wrath," involving a metrical error.

14. Bugge and Gering transfer lines 4-5 to the beginning of stanza 16, on the basis of the *Volsungasaga* paraphrase, and assume a gap of one line after line 3. Line 5, which is in the nature of a stereotyped clause, may well be interpolated.

15. After "Buthli" in line 2 the manuscript has "my brother," apparently a scribal error. In line 4 the manuscript has "wealth" instead of "love," apparently with stanza 10, in mind, but the *Volsungasaga* paraphrase has "love," and many editors have suspected an error.

16. Cf. note on stanza 14. After thus adding lines 4-5 of [fp. 426] stanza 14 at the beginning of stanza 16, Gering marks line 4 as probably spurious; others reject both lines 3 and 4 as mere repetitions. *Rhine*: the Rhine, the sands of which traditionally contained gold, was apparently the original home of the treasure of the Nibelungs, converted in the North to Andvari's treasure (cf. *Reginsmol*, 1-9). That greed for Sigurth's wealth was one of the motives for his slaying is indicated likewise in *Guthrunarkvitha I*, 20, and in the German versions of the story.]

[18. *We four*: if line 1 of stanza 19 is spurious, or the reference therein to "five" is a blunder, as may well be the case, then the "four" are Sigurth and the three brothers, Gunnar, Hogni, and Gotthorm. But it may be that the poet had in mind a tradition which, as in the *Thithrekssaga*, gave Gjuki a fourth son, in which case the "four" refers only to the four Gjukungs. *Hunnish hero*: Sigurth; cf. stanza 4 and note. Some editions put line 4 between lines 1 and 2. Some add lines 1-2 of stanza 19 to stanza 18, marking them as spurious.

19. *We five*: see note on preceding stanza. Some editors mark [fp. 427] lines 1-2 as spurious, and either assume a gap of two lines after line 4 or combine lines 5-4 with stanza 20. *Whence lead the ways*: a proverbial expression signifying "whence the trouble comes."]

[20. The manuscript does not name the speaker. *Gotthorm* (the name is variously spelt): half-brother of Gunnar and Hogni (cf. *Hyndluljoth*, 27 and note, and *Brot*, 4 and note). The name is the northern form of Gundomar; a prince of this name is mentioned in the *Lex Burgundionum*, apparently as a brother of Gundahari (Gundicarius). In the *Nibelungenlied* the third brother is called Gernot.

21. No gap is indicated in the manuscript, and many editors combine stanza 21 with stanza 22, but it seems likely that not only two lines, but one or more stanzas in addition, have been lost; cf. *Brot*, 4, and also the detailed account of the slaying of Sigurth in the *Volsungasaga*, wherein, as here, Sigurth is killed in his bed (cf. stanza 24) and not in the forest.

22. Some editions combine lines 3-4 with stanza 23. *Gram*: {footnote p,.

428 Sigurth's sword (cf. *Reginsmol*, prose after stanza 14); the word here, however, may not be a proper name, but may mean "the hero."]}

[23. A line may well have been lost from this stanza.

24. *Freyr*: if the phrase "the friend of Freyr" means any thing more than "king" (cf. *Rigsthula*, 46 etc.), which I doubt, it has reference to the late tradition that Freyr, and not Othin, was the ancestor of the Volsungs (cf. *Helgakvitha Hundingsbana I*, 57 and note).

25. Müllenhoff thinks this stanza, or at any rate lines 1-2, a later addition based on stanza 29.

26. *My son*: Sigmund; cf. stanza 12 and note, and also *Brot*, 9 and note.]

[27. Sigurth means that although Guthrun may have seven sons by a later marriage, none of them will equal Sigmund, "son of their (i.e., Gunnar's and Hogni's) sister." *Thing*: council.

28. Sigurth's protestation of guiltlessness fits perfectly with the story of his relations with Brynhild used in this poem, but not, of course, with the alternative version, used in the *Gripisspo* and elsewhere, wherein Sigurth meets Brynhild before he woos her for Gunnar, and they have a daughter, Aslaug.

29. Cf. *Guthrunarkvitha I*, 115.

30. Cf. *Brot*, 10.]

[31. Line 1 may well be a mere expansion of "Gunnar spake." The manuscript marks line 4 as the beginning of a new stanza, and some editions combine lines 4-5 with stanza 32.

32. This stanza, which all editors have accepted as an integral part of the poem, apparently refers to the same story represented by stanzas 37-39, which most editors have (I believe mistakenly) marked as interpolated. As is pointed out in the notes on stanzas 3, 5, 6 and 10, the poet throughout seems to have accepted the version of the story wherein Gunnar and Sigurth besiege Atli, and are bought off by the gift of Atli's sister, Brynhild, to Gunnar as wife, her consent being won by Atli's representation that Gunnar is Sigurth (cf. also *Guthrunarkvitha I*, 24 and note).

33. The manuscript does not name the speaker, and some editions add a first line: "Then Brynhild, daughter | of Buthli, spake."]

[34. Cf. stanza 5.

35. *Three kings*: Gunnar, Hogni, and Sigurth.

36. Some editions place this stanza after stanza 39, on the theory that stanzas 37-39 are interpolated. Line 4, as virtually a repetition of line 3, has generally been marked as spurious. In this version of the winning of Brynhild it appears that Atli pointed out Sigurth as Gunnar, and Brynhild promptly fell in love with the hero whom, as he rode on *Grani* and was decked with some of the spoils taken from Fafnir, she recognized as the dragon's slayer. Thus no change of form between Sigurth and Gunnar was necessary. The oath to marry Gunnar had to be carried out even after Brynhild had discovered the deception.

37. Most editors mark stanzas 37-39 as interpolated, but cf. note on stanza 32. Stanza 37 has been variously emended. Lines 4 and 6 look like interpolated repetitions, but many editors make [fp. 432] two stanzas, following the manuscript in beginning a new stanza with line 4. After line I Grundtvig adds: "Son of Buthli, | and brother of mine." After line 6 Bugge adds: "Not thou was it, Gunnar, | who Grani rode, / Though thou my brother | with rings didst buy." Regarding Brynhild's wealth cf. stanza 10 and note.]

[38. Brynhild here again appears as a Valkyrie. The manuscript marks line 4 as the beginning of a new stanza. Any one of the last three lines may be spurious.

39. Some editions combine this stanza with lines 4-5 of stanza 38, with lines 1-2 of stanza 40, or with the whole of stanza 40. *The bond*: Brynhild thought she was marrying Sigurth, owner of the treasure, whereas she was being tricked into marrying Gunnar.]

[41. At this point there seem to be several emissions. Brynhild's statement in lines 1-2 seems to refer to the episode, not here mentioned but told in detail in the *Volsungasaga*, of Sigurth's effort to repair the wrong that has been done her by himself giving up Guthrun in her favor, an offer which she refuses. The lacuna here suggested, which is not indicated in the manuscript, may be simply a single line (line 1) or a stanza or more. After line 2 there is almost certainly a gap of at least one stanza, and possibly more, in which Brynhild states her determination to die.

42. Hardly any two editions agree as to the arrangement of the lines in stanzas 42-44. I have followed the manuscript except in transposing line 4 of stanza 43 to this position from the place it holds in the manuscript after line 4 of stanza 14. All the other involve the rejection of two or more lines as spurious and the assumption of various gaps. Gering and Sijmons both arrange the lines thus: 42, 1-2; two-line gap; 43, 3 [fp. 434] (marked probably spurious); 44, 1-4; 43-4 (marked probably spurious); 42, 3-4; 43, 1-2.]

[43. Cf. note on preceding stanza.

44. Cf. note on stanza 42.

45. Perhaps the remains of two stanzas; the manuscript marks line 4 as the beginning of a new stanza, and after line 4 an added line has been suggested: "She was ever known for evil thoughts." On the other hand, line 1, identical with line 31 of stanza 17, may well be a mere expansion of "Hogni spake," and line 6 may have been introduced, with a slight variation, from line 5 of stanza 38. *Born again*: this looks like a trace of Christian influence (the poem was composed well after the coming of Christianity to Iceland) in the assumption that if Brynhild killed herself she could not be "born again" (cf. concluding prose to *Helgakvitha Hundingsbana II*).

46. The manuscript marks line 3 as beginning a stanza; some [fp. 435] editions treat lines 1-2 as a separate stanza, and combine lines 3-4 with lines 1-2 of stanza 47. *Jewel-bearer* (literally "land of jewels"): woman, here Brynhild. *Bond-women*,

etc.: in stanza 69 we learn that five female slaves and eight serfs were killed to be burned on the funeral pyre, and thus to follow Sigurth in death.]

[47. The manuscript marks line 3, and not line 1, as beginning a stanza, and some editions treat lines 3-4 as a separate stanza, or combine them with stanza 48.

48. Brynhild means, as stanzas 49-51 show, that those of her women who wish to win rewards must be ready to follow her in death. The word translated "women" in line 1 is conjectural, but the general meaning is clear enough.

49. In place of "as so she spake" in line 1 the manuscript has [fp. 436]"of their plans they thought," which involves a metrical error.]

[51. No gap indicated in the manuscript; many editions place it between lines 3 and 4. *Menja's wealth*: gold; the story of the mill Grotti, whereby the giantesses Menja and Fenja ground gold for King Frothi, is told in the *Grottasongr*.

52. With this stanza begins Brynhild's prophesy of what is to befall Gunnar, Guthrun, Atli, and the many others involved in their fate. Line 3 is a proverbial expression meaning simply "your troubles are not at an end."

53. No gap is indicated in the manuscript; one suggestion for line 2 runs: "Grimhild shall make her | to laugh once [fp. 437] more." Gering: suggests a loss of three lines, and joins lines 3-4 with stanza 54.]

[54. Probably a line has been lost from this stanza. Grundtvig adds as a new first line: "Her shalt thou find in the hall of Half." Some editions query line 3 as possibly spurious. *Svanhild*: the figure of Svanhild is exceedingly old. The name means "Swan-Maiden-Warrior," applying to just such mixtures of swan-maiden and Valkyrie as appear in the *Völundarkvitha*. Originally part of a separate tradition, Svanhild appears first to have been incorporated in the Jormunrek (Ermanarich) story as the unhappy wife of that monarch, and much later to have been identified as the daughter of Sigurth and Guthrun, thus linking the two sets of legends.

55. Line 2 in the original is almost totally obscure. Line 4 should very possibly precede line 2, while line 5 looks like an unwarranted addition.

56. This stanza probably ought to follow stanza 52, as it refers solely to) the winning of Brynhild by Gunnar and Sigurth. Müllenhoff regards stanzas 53-55 as interpolated. The manuscript indicates no gap after line 3.]

[57. Stanzas 57-58 seem to be the remains of two stanzas, but the *Volsungasaga* paraphrase follows closely the form here given. Line 3 may well be spurious; line 5 has likewise been questioned. *Oddrun*: this sister of Atli and Brynhild, known mainly through the *Oddrunargratr*, is a purely northern addition to the cycle, and apparently one of a relatively late date. She figures solely by reason of her love affair with Gunnar.

58. Possibly two lines have been lost; many editions combine the two remaining lines with lines 1-3 of stanza 59. Concerning the manner of Gunnar's death cf. *Drap Niflunga*.

59. Line 3 may well be spurious, as it is largely repetition. The manuscript has "sofa" ("sleep") in place of "sona" ("sons"), but the *Volsungasaga* paraphrase says clearly "sons." The slaying of Atli by Guthrun in revenge for his killing of her brothers is told in the two Atli lays. The manuscript marks line 4 as the beginning of a new stanza, and some editions make a separate stanza out of lines 4-5, or else combine them with stanza 60.

60. *To follow in death*: this phrase is not in *Regius*, but is [fp. 439] included in late paper manuscripts, and has been added in most editions.]

[61. *Jonak*: this king, known only through the *Hamthesmol* and the stories which, like this one, are based thereon, is another purely northern addition to the legend. The name is apparently of Slavic origin. He appears solely as Guthrun's third husband and the father of Hamther, Sorli, and Erp (cf. introductory prose to *Guthrunarhvot*).

62. *Svanhild*: cf. stanza 54 and note.

63. *Bikki*: Svanhild is married to the aged Jormunrek (Ermanarich), but Bikki, one of his followers, suggests that she is unduly intimate with Jormunrek's son, Randver. Thereupon Jormunrek has Randver hanged, and Svanhild torn to pieces by wild horses. Ermanarich's cruelty and his barbarous slaying of his wife and son were familiar traditions long before they be [fp. 440] came in any way connected with the Sigurth cycle (cf. introductory note to *Gripisspo*).]

[64. Line 5 is very probably spurious.

65. The manuscript indicates no gap; a suggested addition runs "Gold let there be, and jewels bright." *Fallen slaves*: cf. stanzas 66 and 69. *Hunnish hero*: cf. stanza 4 and note.

66. In place of lines 3-4 the manuscript has one line "Two at his head, and a pair of hawks"; the addition is made from the *Volsungasaga*paraphrase. The burning or burying of slaves or beasts to accompany their masters in death was a general custom in the North. The number of slaves indicated in this stanza does not tally with the one given in stanza 69, wherefore Vigfusson rejects most of this stanza.]

[67. Cf. *Gripisspo*, 41 and note. After line I the manuscript adds the phrase "bright, ring-decked," referring to the sword, but it is metrically impossible, and many editions omit it.

68. *The door*: The gate of Hel's domain, like that of Mengloth's house (cf. *Svipdagsmol*, 26 and note), closes so fast as to catch any one attempting to pass through. Apparently the poet here assumes that the gate of Valhall does likewise, but that it will be kept open for Sigurth's retinue.

69. Cf. stanza 66.]

HELREITH BRYNHILDAR

Brynhild's Hell-Ride

INTRODUCTORY NOTE

The little *Helreith Brynhildar* immediately follows the "short" Sigurth lay in the *Codex Regius*, being linked to it by the brief prose note; the heading, "Brynhild's Ride on Hel-Way," stands just before the first stanza. The entire poem, with the exception of stanza. 6, is likewise quoted in the *Nornageststhattr*. Outside of one stanza (No. 11), which is a fairly obvious interpolation, the poem possesses an extraordinary degree of dramatic unity, and, certain pedantic commentators notwithstanding, it is one of the most vivid and powerful in the whole collection. None the less, it has been extensively argued that parts of it belonged originally to the so-called *Sigrdrifumol*. That it stands in close relation to this poem is evident enough, but it is difficult to believe that such a masterpiece of dramatic poetry was ever the result of mere compilation. It seems more reasonable to regard the *Helreith*, with the exception of stanza 11 and allowing for the loss of two lines from stanza 6, as a complete and carefully constructed unit, based undoubtedly on older poems, but none the less an artistic creation in itself.

The poem is generally dated as late as the eleventh century, and the concluding stanza betrays Christian influence almost unmistakably. It shows the confusion of traditions manifest in all the later poems; for example, Brynhild is here not only a Valkyrie but also a swan-maiden. Only three stanzas have any reference to the Guthrun-Gunnar part of the story; otherwise the poem is concerned solely with the episode of Sigurth's finding the sleeping Valkyrie. Late as it is, therefore, it is essentially a Norse creation, involving very few of the details of the German cycle (cf. introductory note to *Gripisspo*).

After the death of Brynhild there were made two bale-fires, the one for Sigurth, and that burned first, and on the other was Brynhild burned, and she was on a wagon which was covered with a rich cloth. Thus it is told, that Brynhild went in the wagon on Hel-way, and passed by a house where dwelt a certain giantess. The giantess spake:

1. "Thou shalt not further | forward fare,
My dwelling ribbed | with rocks across;
More seemly it were | at thy weaving to stay,
Than another's husband | here to follow.

2. "What wouldst thou have | from Valland here,
Fickle of heart, | in this my house?
Gold-goddess, now, | if thou wouldst know,
Heroes' blood | from thy hands hast washed."

Brynhild spake:
3. "Chide me not, woman | from rocky walls,
Though to battle once | I was wont to go;
Better than thou | I shall seem to be,
When men us two | shall truly know."

The giantess spake:
4. "Thou wast, Brynhild, | Buthli's daughter,
For the worst of evils | born in the world;
To death thou hast given | Gjuki's children,
And laid their lofty | house full low."

Brynhild spake:
5. "Truth from the wagon | here I tell thee,
Witless one, | if know thou wilt

How the heirs of Gjuki | gave me to be
joyless ever, | a breaker of oaths.

6. "Hild the helmed | in Hlymdalir
They named me of old, | all they who knew me.

. . . .

. . . .

7. "The monarch bold | the swan-robes bore
Of the sisters eight | beneath an oak;
Twelve winters I was, | if know thou wilt,
When oaths I yielded | the king so young.

8. "Next I let | the leader of Goths,
Hjalmgunnar the old, | go down to hell,
And victory brought | to Autha's brother;
For this was Othin's | anger mighty.

9. "He beset me with shields | in Skatalund,
Red and white, | their rims o'erlapped;
He bade that my sleep | should broken be
By him who fear | had nowhere found.

10. "He let round my hall, | that southward looked,   .
The branches' foe | high-leaping burn;
Across it he bade | the hero come
Who brought me the gold | that Fafnir guarded

11. On Grani rode | the giver of gold,
Where my foster-father | ruled his folk;
Best of all | he seemed to be,
The prince of the Danes, | when the people met.

12. "Happy we slept, | one bed we had,
As he my brother | born had been;

Eight were the nights | when neither there
Loving hand | on the other laid.

13. "Yet Guthrun reproached me, | Gjuki's daughter,
That I in Sigurth's | arms had slept;
Then did I hear | what I would were hid,
That they had betrayed me | in taking a mate.

14. "Ever with grief | and all too long
Are men and women | born in the world;
But yet we shall live | our lives together,
Sigurth and I. | Sink down, Giantess!"

[*Prose.* The prose follows the last stanza of *Sigurtharkvitha en skamma* without break. *Two bale-fires*: this contradicts the statement made in the concluding stanzas of *Sigurtharkvitha en skamma*, that Sigurth and Brynhild were burned on the same pyre; there is no evidence that the annotator here had anything but his own mistaken imagination to go on.

2. *Valland*: this name ("Land of Slaughter") is used else where of mythical places; cf. *Harbarthsljoth*, 24, and prose introduction to *Völundarkvitha*; it may here not be a proper name at all, *Gold-goddess*: poetic circumlocution for "woman."]

[6. In *Regius* these two lines stand after stanza 7, but most editions; place them as here. They are not quoted in the *Nornageststhattr*. Presumably two lines, and perhaps more, have been lost. It has frequently been argued that all or part of the passage from stanza 6 through stanza 10 (6-10, 7-10 or 8-10) comes originally from the so-called *Sigrdrifumol*, where it would undoubtedly fit exceedingly well. *Hild*: a Valkyrie name meaning "Fighter" (cf. *Voluspo*, 31). in such compound names as Brynhild ("Fighter in Armor") the first element was occasionally omitted. *Hlymdalir* ("Tumult-Dale"): a mythical name, merely signifying the place of battle as the home of Valkyries.

7. Regarding the identification of swan-maidens with Valkyries, and the manner in which men could get them in their power by stealing their swan-garments, cf. *Völundarkvitha*, introductory prose and note, where the same thing happens. *The monarch*: perhaps Agnar, brother of Autha, mentioned in

Sigrdrifumol (prose and quoted verse following stanza 4) as the warrior for [fp. 445] whose sake Brynhild defied Othin in slaying Hjalmgunnar. *Eight*: the *Nornageststhattr* manuscripts have "sisters of Atli" instead of "sisters eight."]

[8. *Hjalmgunnar*: regarding this king of the Goths (the phrase means little) and his battle with Agnar, brother of *Autha* cf. *Sigrdrifumol*, prose after stanza 4. One *Nornageststhattr* manuscript has "brother of the giantess" in place of "leader of Goths."

9. Cf. *Sigrdrifumol*, prose introduction. *Skatalund* ("Warriors' Grove"): a mythical name; elsewhere the place where Brynhild lay is called Hindarfjoll.

10. *Branches' foe*: fire. Regarding the treasure cf. *Fafnismol*.

11. This stanza is presumably an interpolation, reflecting a different version of the story, wherein Sigurth meets Brynhild at the home of her brother-in-law and foster-father, Heimir (cf. [fp 446] *Gripisspo*, 19 and 27). *Grani*: Sigurth's horse. *Danes*: nowhere else does Sigurth appear in this capacity. Perhaps this is a curious relic of the Helgi tradition.]

[12. *Eight nights*: elsewhere (cf. *Gripisspo*, 4.2) the time is stated as three nights, not eight. There is a confusion of traditions here, as in*Gripisspo*. In the version of the story wherein Sigurth met Brynhild before he encountered the Gjukungs, Sigurth was bound by no oaths, and the union was completed; it is only in the alternative version that the episode of the sword laid between the two occurs.

14. The idea apparently conveyed in the concluding lines, that Sigurth and Brynhild will be together in some future life, is utterly out of keeping with the Norse pagan traditions, and the whole stanza indicates the influence of Christianity.]

DRAP NIFLUNGA

The Slaying of The Niflungs

INTRODUCTORY NOTE

It has been already pointed out (introductory note to *Reginsmol*) that the compiler of the Eddic collection had clearly undertaken to formulate a coherent narrative of the entire Sigurth cycle, piecing together the various poems by means of prose narrative links. To some extent these links were based on traditions existing outside of the lays themselves, but in the main the material was gathered from the contents of the poems. The short prose passage entitled *Drap Niflunga*, which in the *Codex Regius* immediately follows the *Helreith Brynhildar*, is just such a narrative link, and scarcely deserves a special heading, but as nearly all editions separate it from the preceding and following poems, I have followed their example.

With Sigurth and Brynhild both dead, the story turns to the slaying of the sons of Gjuki by Atli, Guthrun's second husband, and to a few subsequent incidents, mostly late incorporations from other narrative cycles, including the tragic death of Svanhild, daughter of Sigurth and Guthrun and wife of Jormunrek (Ermanarich), and the exploits of Hamther, son of Guthrun and her third husband, Jonak. These stories are told, or outlined, in the two Atli lays, the second and third Guthrun lays, the*Oddrunargratr*, the *Guthrunarhvot*, and the *Hamthesmol*. Had the compiler seen fit to put the Atli lays immediately after the *Helreith Brynhildar*, he would have needed only a very brief transitional note to make the course of the story clear, but as the second Guthrun lay, the next poem in the collection, is a lament following the death of Guthrun's brothers, some sort of a narrative bridge was manifestly needed.

Drap Niflunga is based entirely on the poems which follow it in the collection, with no use of extraneous material. The part of the story which it summarizes belongs to the semi-historical Burgundian tradition (cf. introductory note to *Gripisspo*), in many respects parallel to the familiar narrative of the Nibelungenlied, and, except in minor details, showing few essentially Northern additions. Sigurth is scarcely mentioned, and the outstanding episode is the slaying of Gunnar and Hogni, following their journey to Atli's home.

Gunnar and Hogni then took all the gold that Fafnir had had. There was strife between the Gjukungs and Atli, for he held the Gjukungs guilty of Brynhild's death. It was agreed that they should give him Guthrun as wife, and they gave her a draught of forgetfulness to drink before she would consent to be wedded to Atli. The sons of Atli were Erp and Eitil, and Svanhild was the daughter of Sigurth and Guthrun. King Atli invited Gunnar and Hogni to come to him, and sent as messenger Vingi or Knefröth. Guthrun was aware of treachery, and sent with him a message in runes that they should not come, and as a token she sent to Hogni the ring Andvaranaut and tied a wolf's hair in it. Gunnar had sought Oddrun, Atli's sister, for his wife, but had her not; then he married Glaumvor, and Hogni's wife was Kostbera; their sons were Solar and Snævar and Gjuki. And when the Gjukungs came to Atli, then Guthrun be sought her sons to plead for the lives of both the Gjukungs, but they would not do it. Hogni's heart was cut out, and Gunnar was cast into the serpent's den. He smote on the harp and put the serpents to sleep, but an adder stung him in the liver.

[*Prose. Niflungs*: regarding the mistaken application of this name to the sons of Gjuki, who were Burgundians, cf. *Brot*, 17 and note. *Draught of forgetfulness*: according to the *Volsungasaga* Grimhild, Guthrun's mother, administered this, just as she did the similar draught which made Sigurth forget Brynhild. *Erp and Eitil*: Guthrun kills her two sons by Atli as part of her revenge; the annotator here explains her act further by saying that Guthrun asked her sons to intercede with their father in favor of Guthrun's brothers, but that they refused, a detail which he appears to have invented, as it is found nowhere else. *Svanhild*: cf. *Sigurtharkvitha en skamma*, 54 and note. *Vingi* or *Knefröth*: *Atlakvitha* (stanza 1) calls the messenger Knefröth; *Atlamol* (stanza 4) speaks of two messengers, but

402

names only one of them, Vingi. The annotator has here tried, unsuccessfully, to combine the two accounts. *Andvaranaut*: regarding the origin of Andvari's ring cf. *Reginsmol*, prose after stanzas 4 and 5 and notes; Sigurth gave the ring to Guthrun. Here again the annotator is combining two stories; in *Atlakvitha* (stanza 8) Guthrun sends a ring (not Andvaranaut) with a wolf's hair; in *Atlamol* (stanza 4) she sends a message written [fp. 449] in runes. The messenger obscures these runes, and Kostbera, Hogni's wife, who attempts to decipher them, is not clear as to their meaning, though she suspects danger. *Oddrun*: cf. *Sigurtharkvitha en skamma*, 57 and note. *Glaumvor*: almost nothing is told of Gunnar's second wife, though she appears frequently in the *Atlamol*. *Kostbera* (or Bera), Hogni's wife, is known only as skilled in runes. Her brother was Orkning. The sons of Hogni and Kostbera, according to the *Atlamol* (stanza 28), were *Solar* and *Snævar*; the third son, *Gjuki*, named after his grandfather, seems to be an invention of the annotator's. *Adder*: according to *Oddrunargratr* (stanza 30) Atli's mother assumed this form in order to complete her son's vengeance.]

GUTHRUNARKVITHA II, EN FORNA

The Second, or Old, Lay of Guthrun

INTRODUCTORY NOTE

It has already been pointed out (introductory note to *Guthrunarkvitha I*) that the tradition of Guthrun's lament was known wherever the Sigurth story existed, and that this lament was probably one of the earliest parts of the legend to assume verse form. Whether it reached the North as verse cannot, of course, be determined, but it is at least possible that this was the case, and in any event it is clear that by the tenth and eleventh centuries there were a number of Norse poems with Guthrun's lament as the central theme. Two of these are included in the Eddic collection, the second one being unquestionably much the older. It is evidently the poem referred to by the annotator in the prose note following the *Brot* as "the old Guthrun lay," and its character and state of preservation have combined to lead most commentators to date it as early as the first half of the tenth century, whereas *Guthrunarkvitha I* belongs a hundred years later.

The poem has evidently been preserved in rather bad shape, with a number of serious omissions and some interpolations, but in just this form it lay before the compilers of the *Volsungasaga*, who paraphrased it faithfully, and quoted five of its stanzas. The interpolations are on the whole unimportant; the omissions, while they obscure the sense of certain passages, do not destroy the essential continuity of the poem, in which Guthrun reviews her sorrows from the death of Sigurth through the slaying of her brothers to Atli's dreams foretelling the death of their sons. It is, indeed, the only Norse poem of the Sigurth cycle antedating the year 1000 which has come down to us in anything approaching complete form; the *Reginsmol*,*Fafnismol*, and *Sigrdrifumol* are all collections of fragments, only a short bit of the "long" Sigurth lay remains, and the others--*Gripisspo*, *Guthrunarkvitha I* and *III*, *Sigurtharkvitha en skamma*, *Helreith Brynhildar*, *Oddrunargratr*,*Guthrunarhvot*, *Hamthesmol*, and the two Atli lays--are all generally dated from the eleventh and even the twelfth centuries.

An added reason for believing that *Guthrunarkvitha II* traces its origin back to a lament which reached the North from Germany in verse form is the absence of most characteristic Norse additions to the narrative, except in minor details. Sigurth is slain in the forest, as "German men say" (cf. *Brot*, concluding prose); the urging of Guthrun by her mother 2nd brothers to become Atli's wife, the slaying of the Gjukungs (here only intimated, for at that point something seems to have been lost), and Guthrun's prospective revenge on Atli, all belong directly to the German tradition (cf. introductory note to*Gripisspo*).

In the *Codex Regius* the poem is entitled simply *Guthrunarkvitha*; the numeral has been added in nearly all editions to distinguish this poem from the other two Guthrun lays, and the phrase "the old" is borrowed from the annotator's comment in the prose note at the end of the *Brot*.

King Thjothrek was with Atli, and had lost most of his men. Thjothrek and Guthrun lamented their griefs together. She spoke to him, saying:

1. A maid of maids | my mother bore me,
Bright in my bower, | my brothers I loved,
Till Gjuki dowered | me with gold,
Dowered with gold, | and to Sigurth gave me.

2. So Sigurth rose | o'er Gjuki's sons
As the leek grows green | above the grass,
Or the stag o'er all | the beasts doth stand,
Or as glow-red gold | above silver gray.

3. Till my brothers let me | no longer have
The best of heroes | my husband to be;
Sleep they could not, | or quarrels settle,
Till Sigurth they | at last had slain.

4. From the Thing ran Grani | with thundering feet,
But thence did Sigurth | himself come never;
Covered with sweat | was the saddle-bearer,
Wont the warrior's | weight to bear.

5. Weeping I sought | with Grani to speak,
With tear-wet cheeks | for the tale I asked;
The head of Grani | was bowed to the grass,
The steed knew well | his master was slain.

6. Long I waited | and pondered well
Ere ever the king | for tidings I asked.

. . . .

7. His head bowed Gunnar, | but Hogni told
The news full sore | of Sigurth slain:
"Hewed to death | at our hands he lies,
Gotthorm's slayer, | given to wolves.

8. "On the southern road | thou shalt Sigurth see,
Where hear thou canst | the ravens cry;
The eagles cry | as food they crave,
And about thy husband | wolves are howling."

9. "Why dost thou, Hogni, | such a horror
Let me hear, | all joyless left?

Ravens yet | thy heart shall rend
In a land that never | thou hast known."

10. Few the words | of Hogni were,
Bitter his heart | from heavy sorrow:
"Greater, Guthrun, | thy grief shall be
If the ravens so | my heart shall rend."

11. From him who spake | I turned me soon,
In the woods to find | what the wolves had left;
Tears I had not, | nor wrung my bands,
Nor wailing went, | as other women,
(When by Sigurth | slain I sat).

12. Never so black | had seemed the night
As when in sorrow | by Sigurth I sat;
The wolves .   .   .   .

13. .   .   .   .
Best of all | methought 'twould be
If I my life | could only lose,
Or like to birch-wood | burned might be.

14. From the mountain forth | five days I fared,
Till Hoalf's hall | so high I saw;
Seven half-years | with Thora I stayed,
Hokon's daughter, | in Denmark then.

15. With gold she broidered, | to bring me joy,
Southern halls | and Danish swans;
On the tapestry wove we | warrior's deeds,
And the hero's thanes | on our handiwork;
(Flashing shields | and fighters armed,
Sword-throng, helm-throng, | the host of the king).

16. Sigmund's ship | by the land was sailing,
Golden the figure-head, | gay the beaks;
On board we wove | the warriors faring,
Sigar and Siggeir, | south to Fjon.

17. Then Grimhild asked, | the Gothic queen,
Whether willingly would I   .   .   .   .   .

.   .   .   .

18. Her needlework cast she | aside, and called
Her sons to ask, | with stern resolve,
Who amends to their sister | would make for her son,
Or the wife requite | for her husband killed.

19. Ready was Gunnar | gold to give,
Amends for my hurt, | and Hogni too;
Then would she know | who now would go,
The horse to saddle, | the wagon to harness,
(The horse to ride, | the hawk to fly,
And shafts from bows | of yew to shoot).

20. (Valdar, king | of the Danes, was come,
With Jarizleif, Eymoth, | and Jarizskar).
In like princes | came they all,
The long-beard men, | with mantles red,
Short their mail-coats, | mighty their helms,
Swords at their belts, | and brown their hair.

21. Each to give me | gifts was fain,
Gifts to give, | and goodly speech,
Comfort so | for my sorrows great
To bring they tried, | but I trusted them not.

22. A draught did Grimhild | give me to drink,
Bitter and cold; | I forgot my cares;

For mingled therein was magic earth,
Ice-cold sea, and the blood of swine.

23. In the cup were runes of every kind,
Written and reddened, I could not read them;
A heather-fish from the Haddings' land,
An ear uncut, and the entrails of beasts.

24. Much evil was brewed within the beer,
Blossoms of trees, and acorns burned,
Dew of the hearth, and holy entrails,
The liver of swine,-- all grief to allay.

25. Then I forgot, when the draught they gave me,
There in the hall, my husband's slaying;
On their knees the kings all three did kneel,
Ere she herself to speak began:

26. "Guthrun, gold | to thee I give,
The wealth that once | thy father's was,
Rings to have, | and Hlothver's halls,
And the hangings all | that the monarch had.

27. "Hunnish women, | skilled in weaving,
Who gold make fair | to give thee joy,
And the wealth of Buthli | thine shall be,
Gold-decked one, | as Atli's wife."

Guthrun spake:
28. "A husband now | I will not have,
Nor wife of Brynhild's | brother be;
It beseems me not | with Buthli's son
Happy to be, | and heirs to bear."

Grimhild spake:
29. "Seek not on men | to avenge thy sorrows,

Though the blame at first | with us hath been;
Happy shalt be | as if both still lived,
Sigurth and Sigmund, | if sons thou bearest."

Guthrun spake:
30. "Grimhild, I may not | gladness find,
Nor hold forth hopes | to heroes now,
Since once the raven | and ravening wolf
Sigurth's heart's-blood | hungrily lapped."

Grimhild spake:
31. "Noblest of birth | is the ruler now
I have found for thee, | and foremost of all;
Him shalt thou have | while life thou hast,
Or husbandless be | if him thou wilt choose not."

Guthrun spake:
32. "Seek not so eagerly | me to send
To be a bride | of yon baneful race;
On Gunnar first | his wrath shall fall,
And the heart will he tear | from Hogni's breast."

33. Weeping Grimhild | heard the words
That fate full sore | for her sons foretold,
(And mighty woe | for them should work;)
"Lands I give thee, | with all that live there,
(Vinbjorg is thine, | and Valbjorg too,)
Have them forever, | but hear me, daughter."

34. So must I do | as the kings besought,
And against my will | for my kinsmen wed,
Ne'er with my husband | joy I had,
And my sons by my brothers' | fate were saved not.

35. .   .   .   .
I could not rest | till of life I had robbed
The warrior bold, | the maker of battles.

36. Soon on horseback | each hero was,
And the foreign women | in wagons faring;
A week through lands | so cold we went,
And a second week | the waves we smote,
(And a third through lands | that water lacked).

37. The warders now | on the lofty walls
Opened the gates, | and in we rode.

*   *   *   *   *   *

38. Atli woke me, | for ever I seemed
Of bitterness full | for my brothers' death.

Atli spake:
39. "Now from sleep | the Norris have waked me
With visions of terror,-- | to thee will I tell them;
Methought thou, Guthrun, | Gjuki's daughter,
With poisoned blade | didst pierce my body."

Guthrun spake:
40. "Fire a dream | of steel shall follow
And willful pride | one of woman's wrath;
A baneful sore | I shall burn from thee,
And tend and heal thee, | though hated thou am"

Atli spake:
41. "Of plants I dreamed, | in the garden drooping,
That fain would I have | full high to grow;
Plucked by the roots, | and red with blood,
They brought them hither, | and bade me eat.

411

42. "I dreamed my hawks | from my hand had flown,
Eager for food, | to an evil house;
I dreamed their hearts | with honey I ate,
Soaked in blood, | and heavy my sorrow.

43. "Hounds I dreamed | from my hand I loosed,
Loud in hunger | and pain they howled;
Their flesh methought | was eagles' food,
And their bodies now | I needs must eat."

Guthrun spake:
44. "Men shall soon | of sacrifice speak,
And off the heads | of beasts shall hew
Die they shall | ere day has dawned,
A few nights hence, | and the folk shall have them."

Atli spake:
45. "On my bed I sank, | nor slumber sought,
Weary with woe,-- | full well I remember.
.   .   .   .

[*Prose. Thjothrek*: the famous Theoderich, king of the Ostrogoths, who became
renowned in German story as Dietrich von Bern. The German tradition early
accepted the anachronism of bringing together Attila (Etzel, Atli), who died in
453, and Theoderich, who was born about 455, and adding thereto Ermanarich
(Jormunrek), king of the Goths, who died about 376. Ermanarich, in German
tradition, replaced Theoderich's actual enemy, Odovakar, and it was in battle with
Jormunrek (i. e., Odovakar) that Thjothrek is here said to have lost most WE his
men. The annotator found the material for this note in *Guthrunarkvitha III*, in
which Guthrun is accused of having Thjothrek as her lover. At the time
when *Guthrunarkvitha II* [fp. 452] was composed (early tenth century) it is
probable that the story of Theoderich had not reached the North at all, and the
annotator is consequently wrong in giving the poem its setting.]

[2. Cf. *Guthrunarkvitha I*, 17.

4. Regarding the varying accounts of the manner of Sigurth's death cf. *Brot*, concluding prose and note. *Grani*: cf. *Brot*, 7.

6. No gap indicated in the manuscript. Some editions combine these two lines with either stanza 5 or stanza 7.]

[7. *Gotthorm*: from this it appears that in both versions of the death of Sigurth the mortally wounded hero killed his murderer, the younger brother of Gunnar and Hogni. The story of how Gotthorm, was slain after killing Sigurth in his bed is told in *Sigurtharkvitha en skamma*, 22-23, and in the *Volsungasaga*.

11. On lines 3-4 cf. *Guthrunarkvitha I*, 1. Line 5 is probably spurious.]

[12. Many editions make one stanza of stanzas 12 and 13, reconstructing line 3; the manuscript shows no gap. Bugge fills out the stanza thus: "The wolves were howling | on all the ways, / The eagles cried as their food they craved."

13. Cf. note on preceding stanza. Grundtvig suggests as a first line: "Long did I bide, | my brothers awaiting." Many editors reject line 4.

14. The manuscript marks line 3 as beginning a stanza, and many editions combine lines 3-4 with lines 1-2 of stanza 15 Hoalf (or Half): Gering thinks this Danish king may be identical with Alf, son of King Hjalprek, and second husband of Hjordis, Sigurth's mother (cf. *Fra Dautha Sinfjotla* and note), but the name was a common one. *Thora* and *Hokon* have not been identified (cf. *Guthrunarkvitha I*, concluding prose, which is clearly based on this stanza). A Thora appears in *Hyndluljoth*, 18, as the wife of Dag, one of the sons of Halfdan the Old, the most famous of Denmark's mythical kings, and one of her sons is Alf (Hoalf?).]

[15. The manuscript marks line 3 as the beginning of a stanza. Some editors combine lines 5-6 with lines 1-2 of stanza 16, while others mark them as interpolated.

16. Some editions combine lines 3-4 with stanza 17. *Sigmund*: Sigurth's father, who here appears as a sea-rover in Guthrun's tapestry. *Sigar*: named in *Fornaldar sögur II*, 10, as the father of *Siggeir*, the latter being the husband of Sigmund's twin sister, Signy (cf. *Fra Dautha Sinfjotla*). *Fjon*: this name, referring to the Danish island of Fünen, is taken from the *Volsungasaga* paraphrase as better fitting the Danish setting of the stanza than the name in *Regius*, which is "Fife" (Scotland).

17. No gap is indicated in the manuscript, and most editions combine these two lines either with lines 3-4 of stanza 16, with lines 1-2 of stanza 18, or with the whole of stanza 18. Line 2 [fp. 456] has been filled out in various ways.
The *Volsungasaga* paraphrase indicates that these two lines are the remains of a full stanza, the prose passage running: "Now Guthrun was some what comforted of her sorrows. Then Grimhild learned where Guthrun was now dwelling." The first two lines may be the ones missing. *Gothic*: the term "Goth" was used in the North without much discrimination to apply to all south-Germanic peoples. In *Gripisspo*, 35, Gunnar, Grimhild's son, appears as "lord of the Goths."]

[18. The manuscript marks line 3 as the beginning of a stanza. Grimhild is eager to have amends made to Guthrun for the slaying of Sigurth and their son, Sigmund, because Atli has threatened war if he cannot have Guthrun for his wife.

19. Lines 5-6 are almost certainly interpolations, made by a scribe with a very vague understanding of the meaning of the stanza, which refers simply to the journey of the Gjukungs to bring their sister home from Denmark.

20. Lines 1-2 are probably interpolated, though the *Volsungasaga* includes the names. Some one apparently attempted to [fp. 457] supply the names of Atli's messengers, the "long-beard men" of line 4, who have come to ask for Guthrun's hand. Some commentators assume, as the Volsungasaga does, that these messengers went with the Gjukungs to Denmark in search of Guthrun, but it seems more likely that a transitional stanza has dropped out after stanza 19, and that Guthrun received Atli's emissaries in her brothers' home. *Long-beards*: the word may actually mean Langobards or Lombards, but, if it does, it is presumably without any specific significance here. Certainly the names in the interpolated two lines do not fit either Lombards or Huns, for Valdar is identified as a Dane, and Jarizleif and Jarizskar are apparently Slavic. The manuscript indicates line 5 as beginning a new stanza.]

[21. *Each*: the reference is presumably to Gunnar and Hogni, and perhaps also Grimhild. I suspect that this stanza belongs before stanza 20.

22. Stanzas 22-25 describe the draught of forgetfulness which Grimhild gives Guthrun, just as she gave one to Sigurth (in one version of the story) to make him forget Brynhild. The draught does not seem to work despite Guthrun's statement in stanza 25 (cf. stanza 30), for which reason Vigfusson, not unwisely, places stanzas 22-25 after stanza 34. *Blood of swine*: cf. *Hyndluljoth*, 39 and note.]

[23. The *Volsungasaga* quotes stanzas 23-24. *Heather-fish*: a snake. *Haddings' land*: the world of the dead, so called because, according to Saxo Grammaticus, the Danish king Hadingus once visited it. It is possible that the comma should follow "heather fish," making the "ear uncut" (of grain) come from the world of the dead.

24. *Dew of the hearth*: soot.

25. In the manuscript, and in some editions, the first line is in the third person plural: "Then they forgot, when the draught they had drunk." The second line in the original is manifestly in bad shape, and has been variously emended. I forgot: this emendation is doubtful, in view of stanza 30, but cf. note to stanza 22. The kings all three: probably Atli's emissaries, though the interpolated lines of stanza 20 name four of them. I suspect that line 4 is wrong, and should read: "Ere he himself (Atli) to speak began." Certainly stanzas 26-27 [fp. 459] fit Atli much better than they do Grimhild, and there is nothing unreasonable in Atli's having come in person, along with his tributary kings, to seek Guthrun's hand. However, the "three kings" may not be Atli's followers at all, but Gunnar, Hogni, and the unnamed third brother possibly referred to in*Sigurtharkvitha en skamma*, 18.]

[26. *Thy father's*: So the manuscript, in which case the reference is obviously to Gjuki. But some editions omit the "thy," and if Atli, and not Grimhild, is speaking (cf. note on stanza 25), the reference may be, as in line 3 of stanza 27, to the wealth of Atli's father, Buthli. *Hlothver*: the northern form of the Frankish name Chlodowech (Ludwig), but who this Hlothver was, beyond the fact that he was evidently a Frankish king, is uncertain. If Atli is speaking, he is presumably a Frankish ruler whose land Atli and his Huns have conquered.

27. Cf. note on stanza 25 as to the probable speaker.

28. In stanzas 28-32 the dialogue, in alternate stanzas, is clearly between Guthrun and her mother, Grimhild, though the manuscript does not indicate the speakers.]

[29. *Sigmund*: son of Sigurth and Guthrun, killed at Brynhild's behest.

30. This stanza presents a strong argument for transposing the description of the draught of forgetfulness (stanzas 22-24 and lines 1-2 of stanza 25) to follow stanza 33. *Raven*, etc.: the original is somewhat obscure, and the line may refer simply to the "corpse-eating raven." 32. In the manuscript this stanza is immediately followed by the two lines which here, following Bugge's suggestion, appear [fp. 461] as stanza 35. In lines 5-4 Guthrun foretells what will (and actually does) happen if she is forced to become Atli's wife. If stanza 35 really belongs here, it continues the prophesy to the effect that Guthrun will have no rest till she has avenged her brothers' death.]

[33. Very likely the remains of two stanzas; the manuscript marks line 4 as beginning a new stanza. On the other band, lines 3 and 5 may be interpolations. *Vinbjorg* and *Valbjorg*: apparently imaginary place-names.

34. *The kings*: presumably Gunnar and Hogni. *My sons*: regarding Guthrun's slaying of her two sons by Atli, Erp and Eitil, cf. *Drap Niflunga*, note.

35. In the manuscript this stanza follows stanza 32. The loss of two lines, to the effect that "Ill was that marriage for my brothers, and ill for Atli himself," and the transposition of the remaining two lines to this point, are indicated in a number of editions. *The warrior*, etc.: Atli, whom Guthrun kills.]

[36. The stanza describes the journey to Atli's home, and sundry unsuccessful efforts have been made to follow the travellers through Germany and down the Danube. *Foreign women*: slaves. Line 5, which the manuscript marks as beginning a stanza, is probably spurious.

37. After these two lines there appears to be a considerable gap, the lost stanzas giving Guthrun's story of the slaying of her brothers. It is possible that stanzas 38-45 came originally from another poem, dealing with Atli's dream, and were here substituted for the original conclusion of Guthrun's lament. Many editions combine stanzas 37 and 38, or combine stanza 38 (the manuscript marks line I as beginning a stanza) with lines 1-2 of stanza 39.

39. The manuscript indicates line 3 as the beginning of a stanza. The manuscript and most editions do not indicate the speakers in this and the following stanzas.]

[40. Guthrun, somewhat obscurely, interprets Atli's first dream (stanza 39) to mean that she will cure him of an abscess by cauterizing it. Her interpretation is, of course, intended merely to blind him to her purpose.

41. In stanzas 41-43 Atli's dreams forecast the death of his two sons, whose flesh Guthrun gives him to eat (cf. *Atlakvitha*, 39, and *Atlamol*, 78).

44. This stanza is evidently Guthrun's intentionally cryptic [fp. 464] interpretation of Atli's dreams, but the meaning of the original is more than doubtful. The word here rendered "sacrifice" may mean "sea-catch," and the one rendered "beasts" may mean "whales." None of the attempted emendations have rendered the stanza really intelligible, but it appears to mean that Atli will soon make a sacrifice of beasts at night, and give their bodies to the people. Guthrun of course has in mind the slaying of his two sons.]

[45. With these two lines the poem abruptly ends; some editors assign the speech to Atli (I think rightly), others to Guthrun. Ettmüller combines the lines with stanza 38. Whether stanzas 38-45 originally belonged to Guthrun's lament, or were interpolated here in place of the lost conclusion of that poem from another one dealing with Atli's dreams (cf. note on stanza 37), it is clear that the end has been lost.]

GUTHRUNARKVITHA III

The Third Lay of Guthrun

INTRODUCTORY NOTE

The short *Guthrunarkvitha III*, entitled in the manuscript simply Guthrunarkvitha, but so numbered in most editions to distinguish it from the first and second Guthrun lays, appears only in the *Codex Regius*. It is neither quoted nor paraphrased in the *Volsungasaga*, the compilers of which appear not to have known the story with which it deals. The poem as we have it is evidently complete and free from serious interpolations. It can safely be dated from the first half of the eleventh century, for the ordeal by boiling water, with which it is chiefly concerned, was first introduced into Norway by St. Olaf, who died in 1030, and the poem speaks of it in stanza 7 as still of foreign origin.

The material for the poem evidently came from North Germany, but there is little indication that the poet was working on the basis of a narrative legend already fully formed. The story of the wife accused of faithlessness who proves her innocence by the test of boiling water had long been current in Germany, as elsewhere, and had attached itself to various women of legendary fame, but not except in this poem, so far as we can judge, to Guthrun (Kriemhild). The introduction of Thjothrek (Theoderich, Dietrich, Thithrek) is another indication of relative lateness, for the legends of Theoderich do not appear to have reached the North materially before the year 1000. On the anachronism of bringing Thjothrek to Atli's court cf.*Guthrunarkvitha II*, introductory prose, note, in which the development of the Theoderich tradition in its relation to that of Atli is briefly outlined.

Guthrunarkvitha III is, then, little more than a dramatic German story made into a narrative lay by a Norse poet, with the names of

418

Guthrun, Atli, Thjothrek, and Herkja incorporated for the sake of greater effectiveness. Its story probably nowhere formed a part of the living tradition c)f Sigurth and Atli, but the poem has so little distinctively Norse coloring that it may Possibly have been based on a story or even a poem which its composer heard in Germany or from the lips of a German narrator.

Herkja was the name of a serving-woman of Atli's; she had been his concubine. She told Atli that she had seen Thjothrek and Guthrun both together. Atli was greatly angered thereby. Then Guthrun said:

1. "What thy sorrow, Atli, | Buthli's son?
Is thy heart heavy-laden? | Why laughest thou never?
It would better befit | the warrior far
To speak with men, | and me to look on."

Atli spake:
2. "It troubles me, Guthrun, | Gjuki's daughter,
What Herkja here | in the hall hath told me,
That thou in the bed | with Thjothrek liest,
Beneath the linen | in lovers' guise."

Guthrun spake:
3. "This shall I | with oaths now swear,
Swear by the sacred | stone so white,
That nought was there | with Thjothmar's son
That man or woman | may not know.

4. "Nor ever once | did my arms embrace
The hero brave, | the leader of hosts;
In another manner | our meeting was,
When our sorrows we | in secret told.

419

5. "With thirty warriors | Thjothrek came,
Nor of all his men | doth one remain;
Thou hast murdered my brothers | and mail-clad men,
Thou hast murdered all | the men of my race.

6. "Gunnar comes not, | Hogni I greet not,
No longer I see | my brothers loved;
My sorrow would Hogni | avenge with the sword,
Now myself for my woes | I shall payment win.

7. "Summon Saxi, | the southrons' king,
For be the boiling | kettle can hallow."
Seven hundred | there were in the hall,
Ere the queen her hand | in the kettle thrust.

8. To the bottom she reached | with hand so bright,
And forth she brought | the flashing stones:
"Behold, ye warriors, | well am I cleared
Of sin by the kettle's | sacred boiling."

9. Then Atli's heart | in happiness laughed,
When Guthrun's hand | unhurt he saw;
"Now Herkja shall come | the kettle to try,
She who grief | for Guthrun planned."

10. Ne'er saw man sight | more sad than this,
How burned were the hands | of Herkja then;
In a bog so foul | the maid they flung,
And so was Guthrun's | grief requited.

[*Prose.* The annotator derived all the material for this note from the poem itself,
except for the reference to Herkja as Atli's former concubine. *Herkja*: the historical
Kreka and the Helche of the *Nibelungenlied*, who there appears as Etzel's (Attila's)
first wife. *Thjothrek*: cf. Introductory Note.

2. The manuscript omits the names of the speakers through out.

3. *Holy stone*: just what this refers to is uncertain; it may be identical with the "ice-cold stone of Uth" mentioned in an oath in *Helgakvitha Hundingsbana II*, 29. *Thjothmar's son*: the manuscript has simply "Thjothmar." Some editions change it as [fp. 467] here, some assume that Thjothmar is another name or an error for Thjothrek, and Finnur Jonsson not only retains Thjothmar here but changes Thjothrek to Thjothmar in stanza 5 to conform to it.]

[5. Regarding the death of Thjothrek's men cf. *Guthrunarkvitha II*, introductory prose, note. It was on these stanzas of *Guthrunarkvitha III* that the annotator based his introduction to *Guthrunarkvitha II*. The manuscript repeats the "thirty" in line 2, in defiance of metrical requirements.

6. In the manuscript this stanza follows stanza 7; many editions have made the transposition.

7. Who Saxi may be is not clear, but the stanza clearly points to the time when the ordeal by boiling water was still regarded as a foreign institution, and when a southern king (i. e., a Christian from some earlier-converted region) was necessary [fp. 467] to consecrate the kettle used in the test. The ordeal by boiling water followed closely the introduction of Christianity, which took place around the year 1000. Some editions make two stanzas out of stanza 7, and Müllenhoff contends that lines 1-2 do not constitute part of Guthrun's speech.]

[10. The word "requited" in line 4 is omitted in the manuscript, but it is clear that some such word was intended. The punishment of casting a culprit into a bog to be drowned was particularly reserved for women, and is not infrequently mentioned in the sagas.]

ODDRUNARGRATR

The Lament of Oddrun

INTRODUCTORY NOTE

The *Oddrunargratr* follows *Guthrunarkvitha   III* in   the *Codex Regius*; it is not quoted or mentioned elsewhere, except that the composer of the "short" Sigurth lay seems to have been familiar with it. The *Volsungasaga* says nothing of the story on which it is based, and mentions Oddrun only once, in the course of its paraphrase of Brynhild's prophecy from the "short" Sigurth lay. That the poem comes from the eleventh century is generally agreed; prior to the year 1000 there is no trace of the figure of Oddrun, Atli's sister, and yet the *Oddrunargratr* is almost certainly older than the "short" Sigurth lay, so that the last half of the eleventh century seems to be a fairly safe guess.

Where or how the figure of Oddrun entered the Sigurth-Atli cycle is uncertain. She does not appear in any of the extant German versions, and it is generally assumed that she was a creation of the North, though the poet refers to "old tales" concerning her. She does not directly affect the course of the story at all, though the poet has used effectively the episode of Gunnar's death, with the implication that Atli's vengeance on Gunnar and Hogni was due, at least in part, to his discovery of Gunnar's love affair with Oddrun. The material which forms the background of Oddrun's story belongs wholly to the German part of the legend (cf. introductory note to *Gripisspo*), and is paralleled with considerable closeness in the *Nibelungenlied*; only Oddrun herself and the subsidiary figures of Borgny and Vilmund are Northern additions. The geography, on the other hand, is so utterly chaotic as to indicate that the original localization of the Atli story had lost all trace of significance by the time this poem was composed.

In the manuscript the poem, or rather the brief introductory prose note, bears the heading "Of Borgny and Oddrun," but nearly all editions, following late paper manuscripts, have given the poem the title it bears here. Outside of a few apparently defective stanzas, and some confusing transpositions, the Poem has clearly been preserved in good condition, and the beginning and end are definitely marked.

Heithrek was the name of a king, whose daughter was called Borgny. Vilmund was the name of the man who was her lover. She could not give birth to a child until Oddrun, Atli's sister, had come to her; Oddrun had been beloved of Gunnar, son of Gjuki. About this story is the following poem.

1. I have heard it told | in olden tales
How a maiden came | to Morningland;
No one of all | on earth above
To Heithrek's daughter | help could give.

2. This Oddrun learned, | the sister of Atli,
That sore the maiden's | sickness was;
The bit-bearer forth | from his stall she brought,
And the saddle laid | on the steed so black.

3. She let the horse go | o'er the level ground,
Till she reached the hall | that loftily rose,
(And in she went | from the end of the hall;)
From the weary steed | the saddle she took;
Hear now the speech | that first she spake:

4. "What news on earth, | . . . . . .
Or what has happened | in Hunland now?"

A serving-maid spake:
"Here Borgny lies | in bitter pain,
Thy friend, and, Oddrun, | thy help would find."

Oddrun spake:
5. 'Who worked this woe | for the woman thus,
Or why so sudden | is Borgny sick?"

The serving-maid spake:
"Vilmund is he, | the heroes' friend,
Who wrapped the woman | in bedclothes warm,
(For winters five, | yet her father knew not)."

6. Then no more | they spake, methinks;
She went at the knees | of the woman to sit;
With magic Oddrun | and mightily Oddrun
Chanted for Borgny | potent charms.

7. At last were born | a boy and girl,
Son and daughter | of Hogni's slayer;
Then speech the woman | so weak began,
Nor said she aught | ere this she spake:

8. "So may the holy | ones thee help,
Frigg and Freyja | and favoring gods,
As thou hast saved me | from sorrow now."

Oddrun spake:
9. "I came not hither | to help thee thus
Because thou ever | my aid didst earn;
I fulfilled the oath | that of old I swore,
That aid to all | I should ever bring,
(When they shared the wealth | the warriors had)."

Borgny spake:
10. "Wild art thou, Oddrun, | and witless now,

That so in hatred | to me thou speakest;
I followed thee | where thou didst fare,
As we had been born | of brothers twain."

Oddrun spake:
11. "I remember the evil | one eve thou spakest,
When a draught I gave | to Gunnar then;
Thou didst say that never | such a deed
By maid was done | save by me alone."

12. Then the sorrowing woman | sat her down
To tell the grief | of her troubles great.

13. "Happy I grew | in the hero's hall
As the warriors wished, | and they loved me well;
Glad I was | of my father's gifts,
For winters five, | while my father lived.

14. "These were the words | the weary king,
Ere he died, | spake last of all:
He bade me with red gold | dowered to be,
And to Grimhild's son | in the South be wedded.

15. "But Brynhild the helm | he bade to wear,
A wish-maid bright | he said she should be;
For a nobler maid | would never be born
On earth, he said, | if death should spare her.

16. "At her weaving Brynhild | sat in her bower,
Lands and folk | alike she had;
The earth and heaven | high resounded
When Fafnir's slayer | the city saw.

17. "Then battle was fought | with the foreign swords,
And the city was broken | that Brynhild had;

Not long thereafter, | but all too soon,
Their evil wiles | full well she knew.

18. "Woeful for this | her vengeance was,
As so we learned | to our sorrow all;
In every land | shall all men hear
How herself at Sigurth's | side she slew.

19. "Love to Gunnar | then I gave,
To the breaker of rings, | as Brynhild might;
To Atli rings | so red they offered,
And mighty gifts | to my brother would give.

20. "Fifteen dwellings | fain would he give
For me, and the burden | that Grani bore;
But Atli said | he would never receive
Marriage gold | from Gjuki's son.

21. "Yet could we not | our love o'ercome,
And my head I laid | on the hero's shoulder;
Many there were | of kinsmen mine
Who said that together | us they had seen.

22. "Atli said | that never I
Would evil plan, | or ill deed do;
But none may this | of another think,
Or surely speak, | when love is shared.

23. "Soon his men | did Atli send,
In the murky wood | on me to spy;
Thither they came | where they should not come,
Where beneath one cover | close we lay.

24. "To the warriors ruddy | rings we offered,
That nought to Atli | e'er they should say;

But swiftly home | they hastened thence,
And eager all | to Atli told.

25. "But close from Guthrun | kept they hid
What first of all | she ought to have known.

.   .   .   .

.   .   .   .

26. "Great was the clatter | of gilded hoofs
When Gjuki's sons | through the gateway rode;
The heart they hewed | from Hogni then,
And the other they cast | in the serpents' cave.

27. "The hero wise | on his harp then smote,

.   .   .   .

For help from me | in his heart yet hoped
The high-born king, | might come to him.

28. "Alone was I gone | to Geirmund then,
The draught to mix | and ready to make;
Sudden I heard | from Hlesey clear
How in sorrow the strings | of the harp resounded.

29. "I bade the serving-maids | ready to be,
For I longed the hero's | life to save;
Across the sound | the boats we sailed,
Till we saw the whole | of Atli's home.

30. "Then crawling the evil | woman came,
Atli's mother-- | may she ever rot
And hard she bit | to Gunnar's heart,
So I could not help | the hero brave.

31. "Oft have I wondered | how after this,
Serpents'-bed goddess! | I still might live,

For well I loved | the warrior brave,
The giver of swords, | as my very self.

32. "Thou didst see and listen, | the while I said
The mighty grief | that was mine and theirs;
Each man lives | as his longing wills,--
Oddrun's lament | is ended now."

[*Prose.* Nothing further is known of *Heithrek, Borgny* or *Vilmund.* The annotator has added the name of Borgny's father, but otherwise his material comes from the poem itself. *Oddrun*, sister of Atli and Brynhild, here appears as proficient in birth. runes (cf. *Sigrdrifumol*, 8). Regarding her love for Gunnar, Guthrun's brother, and husband of her sister, Brynhild, cf. *Sigurtharkvitha en skamma*, 57 and note.

1. *Olden tales*: this may be merely a stock phrase, or it may really mean that the poet found his story in oral prose tradition. *Morningland*: the poem's geography is utterly obscure. "Morningland" is apparently identical with "Hunland" (stanza 4), and yet Oddrun is herself sister of the king of the Huns. Vigfusson tries to make "Mornaland" into "Morva land" and explain it as Moravia. Probably it means little more than a country lying vaguely in the East. With stanza 28 the confusion grows worse.]

[3. Line 3 (cf. *Völundarkvitha*, 17) or line 5 (cf. *Thrymskvitha*, 2), both quoted from older poems, is probably spurious; the manuscript marks line 3 as the beginning of a new stanza.

4. Line 1 in the original appears to have lost its second half. In line 2 the word rendered "has happened" is doubtful. The manuscript does not indicate the speaker of lines 3-4, and a few editors assign them to Borgny herself.

5. The manuscript does not indicate the speakers. *For the woman*: conjectural; the manuscript has instead: "What warrior now hath worked this woe?" The manuscript indicates line 3 as beginning a new stanza. Line 5, apparently modeled on line, 4 of stanza n, is probably spurious.]

[6. Charms: cf. *Sigrdrifumol*, 8.

7. *Hogni's slayer*: obviously Vilmund, but unless he was the one of Atli's followers who actually cut out Hogni's heart (cf. *Drap Niflunga*), there is nothing else to connect him with Hogni's death. Sijmons emends the line to read "Born of the sister | of Hogni's slayer.'"

8. Regarding *Frigg* as a goddess of healing cf. *Svipdagsmol*, 52, note. Regarding *Freyja* as the friend of lovers cf. *Grimnismol*, 14, note. A line is very possibly missing from this stanza.

9. The manuscript does not name the speaker. In line 2 the word rendered "earn" is omitted in the manuscript, but nearly all editions have supplied it. Line 5 is clearly either interpolated or out of place. It may be all that is left of a stanza which stood between stanzas 15 and 16, or it may belong in stanza 12.]

[10-20. In the manuscript the order is as follows: 12; 13; 14; 15, 3-4; 10; 11; 16; 17; 15; 19, 1-2; 19, 1-2; 19, 3-4; 20. The changes made here, following several of the editions, are: (a) the transposition of stanzas 10-11, which are clearly dialogue, out of the body of the lament to a position just before it; (b) the transposition of lines 1-2 of stanza 15 to their present position from the middle of stanza 19.

10. The manuscript does not name the speaker; cf. note on stanzas 10-20.

11. The manuscript does not name the speaker; cf. note on stanzas 10-20. The word rendered "evil" in line 1 is a conjectural addition. Apparently Borgny was present at Atli's court while the love affair between Oddrun and Gunnar was in progress, and criticised Oddrun for her part in it. *A draught*, etc.: apparently in reference to a secret meeting of the lovers.

12. In the manuscript this stanza follows stanza 9; cf. note on stanzas 10-20. No gap is indicated, but something has presumably been lost. Grundtvig supplies as a first line: "The maid her evil days remembered," and inserts as a second line line 5 of stanza 9.]

[13. The manuscript indicates line 3 as the beginning of a new stanza; many editions combine lines 1-2 with stanza 12 and lines 3-4 with lines 1-2 of stanza 14. *The hero*: Buthli, father of Oddrun, Atli, and Brynhild.

14. The manuscript indicates line 3, but not line 1, as the beginning of a new stanza; some editions combine lines 3-4 with lines 3-4 of stanza 15. Making Buthli plan the marriage of Oddrun and Gunnar may be a sheer invention of the poet, or may point to an otherwise lost version of the legend.

15. Lines 1-2 have here been transposed from the middle of stanza 19; cf. note on stanzas 10-20. *Wish-maid*: a Valkyrie, so called because the Valkyries fullfilled Othin's wish in choosing the slain heroes for Valhall. The reference to Brynhild as a Valkyrie by no means fits with the version of the story used in stanzas 16-17, and the poet seems to have attempted to combine the two contradictory traditions, cf. *Fafnismol*, note on stanza 44. In the manuscript stanzas 10-11 follow line 4 of stanza 15.]

[16. In stanzas 16-17 the underlying story seems to be the one used in *Sigurtharkvitha en skamma* (particularly stanzas 32-39), and referred to in *Guthrunarkvitha I*, 24, wherein Gunnar and Sigurth lay siege to Atli's city (it here appears as Brynhild's) and are bought off only by Atli's giving Brynhild to Gunnar as wife, winning her consent thereto by falsely representing to her that Gunnar is Sigurth. This version is, of course, utterly at variance with the one in which Sigurth wins Brynhild for Gunnar by riding through the ring of flames, and is probably more closely akin to the early German traditions. In the *Nibelungenlied* Brynhild appears as a queen ruling over lands and peoples. *Fafnir's slayer*: Sigurth.

17. Cf. note on preceding stanza.

19. Cf. *Sigurtharkvitha en skamma*, stanzas 64-70.

19. In the manuscript lines 1-2 of stanza 15 follow line 2, resulting in various conjectural combinations. The manuscript marks line 3 as beginning a new stanza. *Rings*, etc.: possibly, as [fp. 476] Gering maintains, payment offered by Gunnar and Hogni for Brynhild's death, but more probably, as in stanza 20, Gunnar's proffered "marriage gold" for the hand of Oddrun.]

[20. *Grani's burden*: the treasure won by Sigurth from Fafnir; cf. *Fafnismol*, concluding prose. The manuscript marks line 3 as beginning a new stanza, as also in stanzas 21 and 22.]

23. *Murky wood*: the forest which divided Atli's realm from that of the Gjukungs is in *Atlakvitha*, 3, called Myrkwood. This hardly accords with the extraordinary geography of stanzas 28-29, or with the journey described in *Guthrunarkvitha II*, 36.]

[24. In the manuscript lines 3 and 4 stand in reversed order.

25. No gap is indicated in the manuscript; some editors assume the loss not only of two lines, but of an additional stanza. Evidently *Guthrun*has already become Atli's wife.

26. If a stanza has been lost after stanza 25, it may well have told of Atli's treacherous invitation to the Gjukungs to visit him; cf. *Drap Niflunga*, which likewise tells of the slaying of *Hogni* and Gunnar (*the other*).

27. In the manuscript these three lines follow line 2 of stanza 28. No gap is indicated in the manuscript, In the *Volsungasaga* Guthrun gives her brother the harp, with which he puts the serpents to sleep. The episode is undoubtedly related to the famous thirtieth Aventiure {*sic* of the*Nibelungenlied*, in which Volker plays the followers of Gunther to sleep before the final battle.]}

[28. In the manuscript the three lines of stanza 27 follow line 2, and line 3 is marked as beginning a new stanza. *Geirmund*: nothing further is known of him, but he seems to be an ally or retainer of Atli, or possibly his brother. *Hlesey*: the poet's geography is here in very bad shape. Hlesey is (or may be) the Danish island of Läsö, in the Kattegat (cf. *Harbarthsljoth*, 37 and note), and thither he has suddenly transported not only Gunnar's death-place but Atli's whole dwelling (cf. stanza 29), despite his previous references to the ride to Hunland (stanzas 3-4) and the "murky wood" (stanza 23). Geirmund's home, where Oddrun has gone, is separated from Hlesey and Atli's dwelling by a sound (stanza 29). However, geographical accuracy is seldom to be looked for in heroic epic poetry.

29. Many editions combine this stanza with lines 3-4 of stanza 28. *The sound:* cf. note on stanza 28.

30. The manuscript marks line 3 as beginning a new stanza. *Atli's mother*: the *Volsungasaga* does not follow this version; Gunnar puts all the serpents but one to sleep with his harp playing, "but a mighty and evil adder crawled to him and drove his fangs into him till they reached his heart, and so he died." It is possible that "Atli" is a scribal error for a word meaning "of serpents."]

[31. *Serpents'-bed goddess*: woman (i. e., Borgny); "goddess of gold" was a frequent term for a woman, and gold was often called the "serpents' bed" (cf. *Guthrunarkvitha I*, 24 and note).

32. Some editions make line 4 a statement of the poet's, and not part of Oddrun's speech.]

ATLAKVITHA EN GRÖNLENZKA

The Greenland Lay of Atli

INTRODUCTORY NOTE

There are two Atli poems in the *Codex Regius*, the *Atlakvitha* (Lay of Atli) and the *Atlamol* (Ballad of Atli). The poems are not preserved or quoted in any other old manuscript, but they were extensively used by the compilers of the *Volsungasaga*. In the manuscript superscription to each of these poems appears the word "Greenland," which has given rise to a large amount of argument. The scribe was by no means infallible, and in this case his statement proves no more than that in the period round 1300 there was a tradition that these two poems originated in the Greenland settlement.

The two Atli poems deal with substantially the same material: the visit of the sons of Gjuki to Atli's court, their deaths, and the subsequent revenge of their sister, Guthrun, Atli's wife, on her husband. The shorter of the two, the *Atlakvitha*, tells the story with little elaboration; the *Atlamol*, with about the same narrative basis, adds many details, some of them apparently of the poet's invention, and with a romantic, not to say sentimental, quality quite lacking in the *Atlakvitha*. Both poems are sharply distinguished from the rest of the collection by their metrical form, which is the Malahattr (used irregularly also in the*Harbarthsljoth*), employed consistently and smoothly in the *Atlamol*, and with a considerable mixture of what appear to be Fornyrthislag lines (cf. Introduction) in the *Atlakvitha*.

It is altogether probable that both poems belong to the eleventh century, the shorter *Atlakvitha* being generally dated from the first quarter thereof, and the longer *Atlamol* some fifty years or more later. In each case the poet was apparently a Christian; in the *Atlamol* (stanza 82) Guthrun expresses her readiness to die and "go into another light," and in the *Atlakvitha* there is frequent use of mythological names (*e.g.*, Valhall, Hlithskjolf) with an evident lack of understanding of their relation to the older gods. These facts fit the theory of a Greenland origin exceedingly well, for the Greenland settlement grew rapidly after the first explorations of Eirik the Red, which were in 982-985, and its most flourishing period was in the eleventh century. The internal evidence, particularly in the case of the *Atlamol*, points likewise to an origin remote from Iceland, Norway, and the "Western Isles"; and the two poems are sufficiently alike so that, despite the efforts of Finnur Jonsson and others to separate them, assigning one to Greenland and the other to Norway or else where, it seems probable that the manuscript statement is correct in both instances, and that the two Atli poems did actually originate in Greenland. An interesting account of this Greenland settlement is given in William Hovgaard's *Voyages of the Norsemen to America*, published by the American-Scandinavian Foundation in 1914, and an extraordinarily vivid picture of the sufferings of the early settlers appears in Maurice Hewlett's *Thorgils*, taken from the *Floamannasaga*.

From the standpoint of narrative material there is little that is distinctively Norse in either the *Atlakvitha* or the *Atlamol*. The story is the one outlined in the prose *Drap Niflunga* (largely based on these two poems), representing almost exclusively the southern blending of the Attila and Burgundian legends (cf. introductory note to *Gripisspo*). In the *Atlakvitha*, indeed, the word "Burgundians" is actually used. Brynhild is not mentioned in either poem; Sigurth's name appears but once, in the *Atlamol*. Thus the material goes directly back to its South-Germanic origins, with little of the Northern making-over which resulted in such extensive changes in most parts of the Sigurth story. The general atmosphere, on the other hand, particularly in the *Atlamol*, is essentially Norse.

As has been said, the *Atlakvitha* is metrically in a chaotic state, the normal Malahattr lines being frequently interspersed with lines and even stanzas which apparently are of the older Fornyrthislag type. How much of this confusion is due to faulty transmission is uncertain, but it has been suggested that the composer of the *Atlakvitha* made over in Malahattr an older Atli poem in *Fornyrthislag*, and this suggestion has much to recommend it. That he worked on the basis of an older poem is, indeed, almost certain, for in oral prose tradition a far larger number of distinctively Norse traits would unquestionably have crept in than are found in the material of the *Atlakvitha*. As for the *Atlamol*, here again the poet seems to have used an older poem as his basis, possibly the *Atlakvitha* itself, although in that case he must have had other material as well, for there are frequent divergences in such matters as proper names. The translation of the *Atlakvitha* is rendered peculiarly difficult by the irregularity of the metre, by the evident faultiness of the transmission, and above all by the exceptionally large number of words found nowhere else in Old Norse, involving much guesswork as to their meanings. The notes do not attempt to indicate all the varying suggestions made by editors and commentators as to the reconstruction of defective stanzas and the probable meanings of obscure passages; in cases which are purely or largely guesswork the notes merely point out the uncertainty without cataloguing the proposed solutions.

Guthrun, Gjuki's daughter, avenged her brothers, as has become well known. She slew first Atli's sons, and thereafter she slew Atli, and burned the hall with his whole company. Concerning this was the following poem made:

1. Atli sent | of old to Gunnar
A keen-witted rider, | Knefröth did men call him;
To Gjuki's home came he | and to Gunnar's dwelling,
With benches round the hearth, | and to the beer so sweet.

2. Then the followers, hiding | their falseness, all drank
Their wine in the war-hall, | of the Huns' wrath wary;
And Knefröth spake loudly, | his words were crafty,
The hero from the south, | on the high bench sitting:

3. "Now Atli has sent me | his errand to ride,
On my bit-champing steed | through Myrkwood the secret,
To bid You, Gunnar, | to his benches to come,
With helms round the hearth, | and Atli's home seek.

4. "Shields shall ye choose there, | and shafts made of ash-wood,
Gold-adorned helmets, | and slaves out of Hunland,
Silver-gilt saddle-cloths, | shirts of bright scarlet,
With lances and spears too, | and bit-champing steeds.

5. "The field shall be given you | of wide Gnitaheith,
With loud-ringing lances, | and stems gold-o'er-laid,
Treasures full huge, | and the home of Danp,
And the mighty forest | that Myrkwood is called."

6. His head turned Gunnar, | and to Hogni he said:
"What thy counsel, young hero, | when such things we hear?
No gold do I know | on Gnitaheith lying
So fair that other | its equal we have not.

7. "We have seven halls, | each of swords is full,
(And all of gold | is the hilt of each;)
My steed is the swiftest, | my sword is sharpest,
My bows adorn benches, | my byrnies are golden,
My helm is the brightest | that came from Kjar's hall,
(Mine own is better | than all the Huns' treasure.)"

Hogni spake:
8. "What seeks she to say, | that she sends us a ring,
Woven with a wolf's hair? | methinks it gives warning;

In the red ring a hair | of the heath-dweller found I,
Wolf-like shall our road be | if we ride on this journey."

9. Not eager were his comrades, | nor the men of his kin,
The wise nor the wary, | nor the warriors bold.
But Gunnar spake forth | as befitted a king,
Noble in the beer-hall, | and bitter his scorn:

10. "Stand forth now, Fjornir! | and hither on the floor
The beakers all golden | shalt thou bring to the warriors.
.   .   .   .
.   .   .   .

11. "The wolves then shall rule | the wealth of the Niflungs,
Wolves aged and grey-hued, | if Gunnar is lost,
And black-coated bears | with rending teeth bite,
And make glad the dogs, | if Gunnar returns not."

12. A following gallant | fared forth with the ruler,
Yet they wept as their home | with the hero they left;
And the little heir | of Hogni called loudly:
"Go safe now, ye wise ones, | wherever ye will!"

13. Then let the bold heroes | their bit-champing horses
On the mountains gallop, | and through Myrkwood the secret;
All Hunland was shaken | where the hard-souled ones rode,
On the whip-fearers fared they | through fields that were green.

14. Then they saw Atli's halls, | and his watch-towers high,
On the walls so lofty | stood the warriors of Buthli;
The hall of the southrons | with seats was surrounded,
With targets bound | and shields full bright.

15. Mid weapons and lances | did Atli his wine
In the war-hall drink, | without were his watchmen,

For Gunnar they waited, | if forth he should go,
With their ringing spears | they would fight with the ruler.

16. This their sister saw, | as soon as her brothers
Had entered the hall,-- | little ale had she drunk:
"Betrayed art thou, Gunnar! | what guard hast thou, hero,
'Gainst the plots of the Huns? | from the hall flee swiftly!

17. "Brother, 'twere far better | to have come in byrnie,
With thy household helmed, | to see Atli's home,
And to sit in the saddle | all day 'neath the sun,
(That the sword-norns might weep | for the death-pale warriors,
And the Hunnish shield-maids | might shun not the sword,)
And send Atli himself | to the den of the snakes;
(Now the den of the snakes | for thee is destined.

Gunnar spake:
18. .   .   .   .
"Too late is it, sister, | to summon the Niflungs,
Long is it to come | to the throng of our comrades,
The heroes gallant, | from the hills of the Rhine."

*   *   *   *   *   *

19. Then Gunnar they seized, | and they set him in chains,
The Burgundians' king, | and fast they bound him.

20. Hogni slew seven | with sword so keen,
And an eighth he flung | in the fire hot;
A hero should fight | with his foemen thus,
As Hogni strove | in Gunnar's behalf.

21. .   .   .   .

.   .   .   .
The leader they asked | if his life he fain
With gold would buy, | the king of the Goths.

22. "First the heart of Hogni | shall ye lay in my hands,
All bloody from the breast | of the bold one cut
With ke-en-biting sword, | from the son of the king."

23. . . . .
They cut out the heart | from the breast of Hjalli,
On a platter they bore it, | and brought it to Gunnar.

24. Then Gunnar spake forth, | the lord of the folk:
"Here have I the heart | of Hjalli the craven,
Unlike to the heart | of Hogni the valiant,
For it trembles still | as it stands on the platter;
Twice more did it tremble | in the breast of the man.

25. Then Hogni laughed | when they cut out the heart
Of the living helm-hammerer; | tears he had not.
. . . .
On a platter they bore it, | and brought it to Gunnar.
26. Then Gunnar spake forth, | the spear of the Niflungs:
"Here have I the heart | of Hogni the valiant,
Unlike to the heart | of Hjalli the craven,
Little it trembles | as it lies on the platter,
Still less did it tremble | when it lay in his breast.

27. "So distant, Atli, | from all men's eyes,
Shalt thou be as thou | . . . . . from the gold.
. . . .
. . . .

28. "To no one save me | is the secret known
Of the Niflungs' hoard, | now Hogni is dead;
Of old there were two, | while we twain were alive,
Now is none but I, | for I only am living.

29. "The swift Rhine shall hold | the strife-gold of heroes,
That once was the gods', | the wealth of the Niflungs,
In the depths of the waters | the death-rings shall glitter,
And not shine on the hands | of the Hunnish men."

Atli spake:
30. "Ye shall bring the wagon, | for now is he bound."

*   *   *   *   *   *

31. On the long-maned Glaum | rode Atli the great,
About him were warriors | .   .   .   .   .
But Guthrun, akin | to the gods of slaughter,
Yielded not to her tears | in the hall of tumult.

Guthrun spake:
32. "It shall go with thee, Atli, | as with Gunnar thou heldest
The oaths ofttimes sworn, | and of old made firm,
By the sun in the south, | by Sigtyr's mountain,
By the horse of the rest-bed, | and the ring of Ull."

33. Then the champer of bits | drew the chieftain great,
The gold-guarder, down | to the place of death.
.   .   .   .

34. By the warriors' host | was the living hero
Cast in the den | where crawling about
Within were serpents, | but soon did Gunnar
With his hand in wrath | on the harp-strings smite;
The strings resounded,-- | so shall a hero,
A ring-breaker, gold | from his enemies guard.

35. Then Atli rode | on his earth-treading steed,
Seeking his home, | from the slaughter-place;
There was clatter of hoofs | of the steeds in the court,
And the clashing of arms | as they came from the field.

36. Out then came Guthrun | to meeting with Atli,
With a golden beaker | as gift to the monarch:
"Thou mayst eat now, chieftain, | within thy dwelling,
Blithely with Guthrun | young beasts fresh slaughtered."

37. The wine-heavy ale-cups | of Atli resounded,
When there in the hall | the Hunnish youths clamored,
And the warriors bearded, | the brave ones, entered.

38. Then in came the shining one, | .   .   .   .   .
　　.   .   .   .   . | and drink she bore them;
Unwilling and bitter | brought she food to the warrior,
Till in scorn to the white-faced | Atli did she speak:

39. "Thou giver of swords, | of thy sons the hearts
All heavy with blood | in honey thou hast eaten;
Thou shalt stomach, thou hero, | the flesh of the slain,
To eat at thy feast, | and to send to thy followers.

40. "Thou shalt never call | to thy knees again
Erp or Eitil, | when merry with ale;
Thou shalt never see | in their seats again
The sharers of gold | their lances shaping,
(Clipping the manes | or minding their steeds.)"

41. There was clamor on the benches, | and the cry of men,
The clashing of weapons, | and weeping of the Huns,
Save for Guthrun only, | she wept not ever
For her bear-fierce brothers, | or the boys so dear,
So young and so unhappy, | whom with Atli she had.

42. Gold did she scatter, | the swan-white one,
And rings of red gold | to the followers gave she;
The fate she let grow, | and the shining wealth go,
Nor spared she the treasure | of the temple itself.

43. Unwise then was Atli, | he had drunk to wildness,
No weapon did he have, | and of Guthrun bewared not;
Oft their play was better | when both in gladness
Each other embraced | among princes all.

44. With her sword she gave blood | for the bed to drink,
With her death-dealing hand, | and the hounds she loosed,
The thralls she awakened, | and a firebrand threw
In the door of the hall; | so vengeance she had.

45. To the flames she gave all | who yet were within,
And from Myrkheim had come | from the murder of Gunnar;
The timbers old fell, | the temple was in flames,
The dwelling of the Buthlungs, | and the shield-maids burned,
They were slain in the house, | in the hot flames they sank.

46. Now the tale is all told, | nor in later time
Will a woman in byrnie | avenge so her brothers;
The fair one to three | of the kings of the folk
Brought the doom of death | ere herself she died.

Still more is told in the Greenland ballad of Atli.

[*Prose.* On the marriage of Guthrun to Atli at the instigation of her brothers,
Gunnar and Hogni, and on the slaying of Atli and his two sons, Erp and Eitil,
cf. *Drap Niflunga* and note.

1. Line 1 apparently is in Fornyrthislag. *Knefröth* (the name is spelt in various
ways, and its meaning is uncertain): in the *Atlamol* (stanza 4) there are two
messengers, one named Vingi and the other unnamed; the annotator combines the
two versions in the *Drap Niflunga. Benches*, etc.: the adjective rendered "round
the hearth," which etymologically it ought to mean, is made obscure by its
application to "helmets" in stanzas 3 and 17.]

[2. *Falseness*: i.e., Gunnar's followers concealed their fear and hatred of the Huns
at the feast; but the word may mean "fear of treachery." *War-hall*: the word used
is "Valhall," the name of Othin's hall of slain warriors.

3. *Myrkwood the secret* (the adjective is literally "unknown") the which divided Atli's realm from that of the Gjukungs; cf. *Oddrunargratr*, 23 and note. *Around the hearth*: the adjective is the same one which is applied to "benches" in stanza 1 (cf. note); it may be an error here, or it may possibly have the force of "of your followers," i.e., Gunnar is to arm the men of his household (those who are round his hearth) for the journey.

4. *Slaves*, etc.: some editions have "swords in plenty." *Scarlet*: the word apparently means "slaughter-red," "blood-red," but it may mean something entirely different.]

[5. *Gnitaheith*: here the dragon Fafnir had his lair (cf. *Gripisspo*, 11). Sigurth doubtless owned it after Fafnir's death, and the Gjukungs after they had killed Sigurth. Possibly they had given it to Atli in recompense for the death of his sister, Brynhild, and he now offered to restore it to them, or--as seems more likely--the poet was not very clear about its ownership himself. *Stems*: i.e., the gilded stems of ships, carved like dragons,--an evident northern touch, if the word is correct, which is by no means certain . *Danp*: this name was early applied to a mythical Danish king (cf. *Rigsthula*, 49 and note) but it may have been fabricated by error out of the word "Danparstaþir" (the phrase here used is "staþi Danpar"), used in the *Hervararsaga* of a field of battle between the Goths and the Huns, and quite possibly referring to the region of the Dnieper. The name seems to have clung to the Atli tradition long after it had lost all definite significance. *Myrkwood*: cf. note on stanza 3.]

[7. The stanza is clearly in bad shape; the manuscript indicates line 5 as beginning a new stanza. In line 5 the manuscript has "and shield" after "helm." *Kjar*: Gering ingeniously identifies this Kjar with Kjar the father of Olrun, mentioned in the *Völundarkvitha*, introductory prose and stanza 2, on the basis of a genealogy in the *Flateyjarbok*, in which Authi, the grand father of Kjar (by no means certainly the same man) and Buthli, father of Atli, are mentioned as making a raiding voyage together. This identification, however, rests on slight evidence.

8. The manuscript does not name the speaker. One editor gives the first sentence to Gunnar. *She*, etc.: Guthrun, seeking to warn her brothers of Atli's treachery, sends them a ring with a wolf's hair as a sign of danger; in the *Atlamol* (stanza 4) she sends a message written in runes; cf.*Drap Niflunga. Heath-dweller*: wolf.]

[9. In line 1 the manuscript has "His comrades did not urge Gunnar," but the name, involving a metrical error, seems to have been inserted through a scribal blunder.

10. The manuscript indicates no lacuna, but probably two lines have dropped out, for the *Volsungasaga* paraphrase runs: "Give us to drink in great cups, for it may well be that this shall be our last feast." *Fjornir*: Gunnar's cup-bearer.

11. Bugge thinks this stanza is spoken by Gunnar's terrified followers; Grundtvig assigns it to Hogni. Apparently, however, Gunnar means that if he and his men are not valiant enough to make the journey and return safely, it matters little what may happen to them. *Niflungs*: regarding the application of this name to Gunnar's Burgundians cf. *Brot*, 17 and note. *Bears*: these "black" bears have been used as arguments against the Greenland origin of the poem. *And make glad the dogs*: i.e., by giving them corpses to eat, but the phrase in the original is more than doubtful.]

[12. Some editions in line 2 read "home of the Niflungs" instead of "their home," and others "home of the Huns," the manuscript reading being "home of the men." *Heir*: the *Atlamol* (stanza 28) names two sons of Hogni, Snævar and Solar, both of whom make the journey with their father and are killed.
The *Volsungasaga*, combining the two versions, says that Snævar and Solar went with their father, and implies that it was a third and still younger son who said: "Farewell, and have a good time" (thus literally).

11. *Myrkwood*: cf. stanza 3 and note; the journey is here made by land, whereas in the *Atlamol* it is made partly by boat; cf. *Atlamol*, 34 and note. *Whip-fearers*: horses, but there is some uncertainty as to the word.

13. In line 1 the manuscript has "land" instead of "halls," which involves a metrical error. *Watch-towers*: the word used is identical with the name of Othin's watch-tower, Hlithskjolf (cf. *Grimnismol*, introductory prose). *Buthli*: the manuscript has "Bikki," which has. led some editors to transfer this stanza to [fp. 488] the *Hamthesmol*, placing it between stanzas 16 and 17; it seems more likely, however, that "Bikki" was a scribal error for "Buthli." Regarding Bikki cf. *Sigurtharkvitha en skamma*, 63 and note. Line 4 is apparently in Fornyrthislag.]

[15. Line 1 in the manuscript is apparently incorrectly copied, and some editions omit "Mid weapons and lances" and assume a gap in either line 1 or line 3.

17. This may be the remains of two stanzas, the manuscript marks line 5 as beginning a new stanza. Editorial conjectures are [fp. 489] numerous and varied. *Household*: the phrase is the same "helms round the hearth" commented on in stanza 3. Some editions insert a conjectural line after line 3. *Sword-norns*, etc.: the line is exceedingly obscure, and the phrase rendered "sword-norns" may mean

"corpse-norns." Apparently it refers to the warrior-women of the Huns, the "shield-maids" of line 5 and of stanza 45. Roman writers refer to the warrior-women among the early Germanic tribes, and the tradition, closely allied to that of the Valkyries, attached itself readily to the ferocious Huns. *Den of snakes*: concerning the manner of Gunnar's death cf. *Drap Niflunga*.]

[18. The manuscript indicates no lacuna and does not name the speaker; perhaps a line similar to line 1 of stanza 24 (or 26) should be inserted here. *Rhine*: Gunnar's Burgundian home is here clearly localized. After this stanza it is probable that a passage describing the battle has been lost.

19. These two lines, apparently the remains of a full stanza, [fp. 490] may belong after stanza 20. *Burgundians' king*: the phrase may mean "Burgundians' men," i.e., they bound all the Burgundians who were left alive after the battle. This is the only place in the poems in which the name "Burgundian" appears; that the poet had no very clear conception of its meaning is indicated by the fact that in stanza 21 he calls Gunnar "king of the Goths."]

[20. Apparently a Fornyrthislag stanza, though most editions have attempted to expand the lines into Malahattr. The exploits of Hogni (Hagene), with the names of many of his victims, are told in the *Nibelungenlied*. *The fire*: in the Nibelungenlied Kriemhild has the hall set on fire, and the Burgundians fight amid the flames. Line 4 is clearly defective, and some editors regard the name "Gunnar" as all that is left of the first two lines of stanza 21.

21. Again apparently the remains of a Fornyrthislag stanza. Editors have attempted various combinations of the lines. *Gold*: presumably Sigurth's treasure.

22. The manuscript does not indicate the speaker; perhaps a first line similar to line 1 of stanza 24 should appear here. Some editors, however, assume that a line is missing after line 3. [fp. 491] Gunnar demands proof that Hogni is dead because, as stanza 29 shows, he is unwilling to die himself until he is assured that the secret of the treasure will perish with him. He did not, of course, intend that the heart should be cut from the living Hogni.]

[23. Most editions assume a gap (lines 1-2, 2-3 or 3-4). *Hjalli*: Atli's cook, killed to deceive Gunnar, as Atli hoped to wring the secret of the hoard from Hogni if Gunnar remained silent. In the *Atlamol* (stanzas 59-60) Atli's men prepare to kill Hjalli, but he is spared at Hogni's intercession.

25. *Helm-hammerer* (literally "helmet-smith"): warrior, i.e., Hogni. No gap indicated in the manuscript.]

[26. Line 1 may belong elsewhere (stanzas 18 or 22).

27. Apparently the remains of two Fornyrthislag lines; the manuscript combines them with lines 1-2 of stanza 28. Gunnar foretells Atli's speedy death.

28. Apparently in Fornyrthislag. The manuscript indicates line 3 as the beginning of a stanza, and many editions combine lines 3-4 with stanza 29. This stanza explains Gunnar's demand for Hogni's heart in stanza 22.

29. The manuscript marks line 3, and not line 1, as the beginning of a stanza. *Rhine*, etc.: the stanza shows the blending of [fp. 493] three different traditions with regard to the treasure: the German tradition of the gold of the Rhine (cf. *Völundarkvitha*, 16, and *Sigurtharkvitha en skamma*, 16), the tradition, likewise German, of the hoard of the Nibelungen (Niflungs), early blended with the first one, and finally the northern tradition of the theft of Andvari's treasure by Othin, Hönir, and Loki (cf. *Reginsmol*, 1-9).]

[30. Apparently all that is left of a full stanza. The manuscript does not name Atli as the speaker, and Grundtvig inserts: "Then Atli called, | the king of the Huns," as a first line. Some editors combine this line with the two lines of stanza 33. *Wagon*: in *Brot*, 16, Gunnar is led to his death in the serpents' den on horseback, not in a wagon.

31. The stanza in the original is hopelessly confused. *Glaum*: this horse of Atli's is mentioned by name elsewhere. *Long-maned*: uncertain. The manuscript indicates no gap, but something has evidently been lost. *Gods of slaughter*: perhaps the phrase, usually applied to Othin and the other gods, is here used simply to mean "heroes," i.e., Atli, Gunnar, and Hogni. Line 4 suggests Guthrun's tearlessness after Sigurth's death (cf. *Guthrunarkvitha II*, 11)]

[32. The manuscript does not indicate the speaker. *Sigtyr* ("Victory-God"): Othin; what particular mountain (if any) is meant is unknown. *Horse of the rest-bed*: probably this means "bedpost," i.e., the support of the marriage-bed. *Ull*: the archer god, cf. *Grimnismol*, 5 and note. Nothing is known of his ring.

33. Apparently the remains of a Fornyrthislag stanza. Some editors combine the two lines with the line here indicated as stanza 30. *Champer of bits*: horse. The manuscript indicates no gap.

54. Six Fornyrthislag lines which editors have tried to reconstruct in all sorts of ways. The manuscript marks line 5 as the beginning of a new stanza, Regarding the serpents' den, Gunnar's harp-playing, and the manner of his death, cf. *Drop*

Niflunga and *Oddrunargratr*, 27-30, and notes. In *Atlamol*, 62, Gunnar plays the harp with his feet, his hands being bound, and some editors change hand in line 4 to "foot." Lines 5-6 may be interpolated, or, as Bugge maintains, lines 1-4 may have been expanded out of two lines.]

[35. The manuscript marks line 3 as beginning a new stanza. Two (possibly three) of the lines appear to, be in Fornyrthislag. *Field*: so the manuscript, involving a metrical error; many editions have "wood."

36. *Young beasts*: Guthrun means Atli's sons, Erp and Eitil, but of course he thinks she refers to newly slaughtered beasts; cf.*Guthrunarkvitha II*, 41-45.

37. *Youths*: a conjectural addition. The brave ones is also conjectural, the manuscript having "each." No gap indicated in the manuscript; some editions insert as line 3 or line 4 a slightly altered version of line 2 of stanza 45.]

[38. No gap indicated in the manuscript, but the two fragments cannot be fitted together as one line. *The shining one*: Guthrun.

39. *Giver of swords*: generous prince, i.e., Atli. *Honey*: cf. *Guthrunarkvitha II*, 42. *To send to thy followers*: literally, "to send from thy high seat."

40. Apparently a Fornyrthislag stanza. *Merry with ale*: presumably this refers to Atli, but the manuscript reading makes it apply to the two boys. *Sharers of gold*: princes. Line 5 is either interpolated or all that is left of a separate stanza.

41. The text of the whole stanza has required a considerable amount of emendation. Lines 3-5 may have been expanded out of two lines, or line 5 may be an interpolation, possibly from stanza [fp. 497] 12 of the *Guthrunarhvot*. *Weapons*: the word literally means "good-weaving," and may refer to silken garments, but this hardly fits the noun here rendered "clashing." *Wept not*: cf. stanza 31 and note.]

[42. Line 1 appears to be in Fornyrthislag. Guthrun distributes Atli's treasures among his followers apparently to prevent their wrath at the slaying of Erp and Eitil from turning against her; Atli, as stanza 43 shows, is too drunk to realize or prevent what she is doing.

43. The second half of line 4 is apparently an error, but none of the editorial suggestions have improved it.

44. Guthrun allows the dogs and the house-thralls, who had no part in Gunnar's death, to escape before she burns the dwelling [fp. 498] with all who are left therein. In *Atlamol*, stanzas 83-84, Atli is slain by a son of Hogni (Hniflung?) with Guthrun's help.]

[45. Some editions transfer line 2 to stanza 37; others reject line 3 as interpolated. *Myrkheim* ("Dark-Home"): probably identical with Myrkwood; cf. stanza 3. *Temple*: probably both here and in stanza 42 the word means little more than the place where Atli's treasures were kept; the poet was by no means literal in his use of terms connected with the heathen religion. *Buthlungs*: sons of Buthli, i.e., Atli and his family. *Shield-maids*: cf. stanza 17 and note.

46. The entire stanza is very likely a later addition. *Three kings*: Atli and his two sons, Erp and Eitil.]

ATLAMOL EN GRÖNLENZKU

The Greenland Ballad of Atli

INTRODUCTORY NOTE

Many of the chief facts regarding the *Atlamol*, which follows the *Atlakvitha* in the *Codex Regius*, are outlined in the introductory note to the earlier Atli lay. That the superscription in the manuscript is correct, and that the poem was actually composed in Greenland, is generally accepted; the specific reference to polar bears (stanza 17), and the general color of the entire poem make this origin exceedingly likely. Most critics, again, agree in dating the poem nearer 1100 than 1050. As to its state of preservation there is some dispute, but, barring one or two possible gaps of some importance, and the usual number of passages in which the interpolation or omission of one or two lines may be suspected, the *Atlamol* has clearly come down to us in fairly good shape.

Throughout the poem the epic quality of the story itself is overshadowed by the romantically sentimental tendencies of the poet, and by his desire to adapt the narrative to the understanding of his fellow-Greenlanders. The substance of the poem is the same as that of the *Atlakvitha*; it tells of Atli's message to the sons of Gjuki, their journey to Atli's home, the slaying of Hogni and Gunnar, Guthrun's bitterness over the death of her brothers, and her bloody revenge on Atli. Thus in its bare out line the *Atlamol* represents simply the Frankish blending of the legends of the slaughter of the Burgundians and the death of Attila (cf. *Gripisspo*, introductory note). But here the resemblance ends. The poet has added characters, apparently of his own creation, for the sake of episodes which would appeal to both the men and the women of the Greenland settlement. Sea voyages take the place of journeys by land; Atli is reproached, not for cowardice in battle, but for weakness at the Thing or great council. The additions made by the poet are responsible for the *Atlamol's* being the longest of all the heroic poems in the Eddic collection, and they give it a kind of emotional vivid ness, but it has little of the compressed intensity of the older poems. Its greatest interest lies in its demonstration of the manner in which a story brought to the North from the South Germanic lands could be adapted to the understanding and tastes of its eleventh century hearers without any material change of the basic narrative.

In what form or forms the story of the Gjukungs and Atli reached the Greenland poet cannot be determined, but it seems likely that he was familiar with older poems on the subject, and possibly with the *Atlakvitha* itself. That the details which are peculiar to the *Atlamol*, such as the figures of Kostbera and Glaumvor, existed in earlier tradition seems doubtful, but the son of Hogni, who aids Guthrun in the slaying of Atli, appears, though under another name, in other late versions of the story, and it is impossible to say just how much the poet relied on his own imagination and how far he found suggestions and hints in the prose or verse stories of Atli with which he was familiar.

The poem is in Malahattr (cf. Introduction) throughout, the verse being far more regular than in the *Atlakvitha*. The compilers of the *Volsungasaga* evidently knew it in very much the form in which we now have it, for in the main it is paraphrased with great fidelity.

1. There are many who know | how of old did men
In counsel gather; | little good did they get;
In secret they plotted, | it was sore for them later,
And for Gjuki's sons, | whose trust they deceived.

2. Fate grew for the princes, | to death they were given;
Ill counsel was Atli's, | though keenness he had;
He felled his staunch bulwark, | his own sorrow fashioned,
Soon a message he sent | that his kinsmen should seek him.

450

3. Wise was the woman, | she fain would use wisdom,
She saw well what meant | all they said in secret;
From her heart it was hid | how help she might render,
The sea they should sail, | while herself she should go not.

4. Runes did she fashion, | but false Vingi made them,
The speeder of hatred, | ere to give them he sought;
Then soon fared the warriors | whom Atli had sent,
And to Limafjord came, | to the home of the kings.

5. They were kindly with ale, | and fires they kindled,
They thought not of craft | from the guests who had come;
The gifts did they take | that the noble one gave them,
On the pillars they hung them, | no fear did they harbor.

6. Forth did Kostbera, | wife of Hogni, then come,
Full kindly she was, | and she welcomed them both;
And glad too was Glaumvor, | the wife of Gunnar,
She knew well to care | for the needs of the guests.

7. Then Hogni they asked | if more eager he were,
Full clear was the guile, | if on guard they had been;
Then Gunnar made promise, | if Hogni would go,
And Hogni made answer | as the other counseled.

8. Then the famed ones brought mead, | and fair was the feast,
Full many were the horns, | till the men had drunk deep;
. . . .
Then the mates made ready | their beds for resting.

9. Wise was Kostbera, | and cunning in rune-craft,
The letters would she read | by the light of the fire;
But full quickly her tongue | to her palate clave,
So strange did they seem | that their meaning she saw not.

10. Full soon then his bed | came Hogni to seek,

. . . .

The clear-souled one dreamed, | and her dream she kept not,
To the warrior the wise one | spake when she wakened:

11. "Thou wouldst go hence, | Hogni, but heed my counsel,--
Known to few are the runes,-- | and put off thy faring;
I have read now the runes | that thy sister wrote,
And this time the bright one | did not bid thee to come.

12. "Full much do I wonder, | nor well can I see,
Why the woman wise | so wildly hath written;
But to me it seems | that the meaning beneath
Is that both shall be slain | if soon ye shall go.
But one rune she missed, | or else others have marred it."

Hogni spake:
13. "All women are fearful; | not so do I feel,
Ill I seek not to find | till I soon must avenge it;
The king now will give us | the glow-ruddy gold;
I never shall fear, | though of dangers I know."

Kostbera spake:
14. "In danger ye fare, | if forth ye go thither,
No welcoming friendly | this time shall ye find;
For I dreamed now, Hogni, | and nought will I hide,
Full evil thy faring, | if rightly I fear.

15. "Thy bed-covering saw I | in the flames burning,
And the fire burst high | through the walls of my home."
Hogni spake:
"Yon garment of linen | lies little of worth,
It will soon be burned, | so thou sawest the bed-cover."

Kostbera spake:
16. "A bear saw I enter, | the pillars he broke,

452

And he brandished his claws | so that craven we were;
With his mouth seized he many, | and nought was our might,
And loud was the tumult, ⌊not little it was."

Hogni spake:
17. "Now a storm is brewing, | and wild it grows swiftly,
A dream of an ice-bear | means a gale from the east."

Kostbera spake:
18. "An eagle I saw flying | from the end through the house,
Our fate must be bad, | for with blood he sprinkled us;

.   .   .   .

From the evil I fear | that 'twas Atli's spirit."

Hogni spake:
19. "They will slaughter soon, | and so blood do we see,
Oft oxen it means | when of eagles one dreams;
True is Atli's heart, | whatever thou dreamest."
Then silent they were, | and nought further they said.

20. The high-born ones wakened, | and like speech they had,
Then did Glaumvor tell | how in terror she dreamed,

.   .   .   .

.   .   .   .   . Gunnar | two roads they should go.

Glaumvor spake:
21. "A gallows saw I ready, | thou didst go to thy hanging,
Thy flesh serpents ate, | and yet living I found thee;

.   .   .   .

The gods' doom descended; | now say what it boded."

*   *   *   *   *   *

22. "A sword drawn bloody | from thy garments I saw,--
Such a dream is hard | o a husband to tell,--

A spear stood, methought, | through thy body thrust,
And at head and feet | the wolves were howling."

23. "The hounds are running, | loud their barking is heard,
Oft hounds' clamor follows | the flying of spears."

Glaumvor spake:
24. "A river the length | of the hall saw I run,
Full swiftly it roared, | o'er the benches it swept;
O'er the feet did it break | of ye brothers twain,
The water would yield not; | some meaning there was."

*   *   *   *   *   *

25. "I dreamed that by night | came dead women hither,
Sad were their garments, | and thee were they seeking;
They bade thee come swiftly | forth to their benches,
And nothing, methinks, | could the Norns avail thee. "

Gunnar spake:
26. "Too late is thy speaking, | for so is it settled
From the faring I turn not, | the going is fixed,
Though likely it is | that our lives shall be short."

27. Then bright shone the morning, | the men all were ready,
They said, and yet each | would the other hold back;
Five were the warriors, | and their followers all
But twice as many,-- | their minds knew not wisdom.

28. Snævar and Solar, | they were sons of Hogni,
Orkning was he called | who came with the others,
Blithe was the shield-tree, | the brother of Kostbera;
The fair-decked ones followed, | till the fjord divided them,
Full hard did they plead, | but the others would hear not.

29. Then did Glaumvor speak forth, | the wife of Gunnar,
To Vingi she said | that which wise to her seemed:
"I know not if well | thou requitest our welcome,
Full ill was thy coming | if evil shall follow."

30. Then did Vingi swear, | and full glib was his speech,
. . . .
"May giants now take me | if lies I have told ye,
And the gallows if hostile | thought did I have."

31. Then did Bera speak forth, | and fair was her thought,
. . . .
"May ye sail now happy, | and victory have,
To fare as I bid ye, | may nought your way bar."

32. Then Hogni made answer,-- | dear held he his kin,-
"Take courage, ye wise ones, | whatsoever may come;
Though many may speak, | yet is evil oft mighty,
And words avail little | to lead one homeward."

33. They tenderly looked | till each turned on his way,
Then with changing fate | were their farings divided.

34. Full stoutly they rowed, | and the keel clove asunder,
Their backs strained at the oars, | and their strength was fierce;
The oar-loops were burst, | the thole-pins, were broken,
Nor the ship made they fast | ere from her they fared.

35. Not long was it after-- | the end must I tell--
That the home they beheld | that Buthli once had;
Loud the gates resounded | when Hogni smote them;
Vingi spake then a word | that were better unsaid:

36. "Go ye far from the house, | for false is its entrance,
Soon shall I burn you, | ye are swiftly smitten;

I bade ye come fairly, | but falseness was under,
Now bide ye afar | while your gallows I fashion."

37. Then Hogni made answer, | his heart yielded little,
And nought did he fear | that his fate held in store:
"Seek not to affright us, | thou shalt seldom succeed;
If thy words are more, | then the worse grows thy fate."

38. Then Vingi did they smite, | and they sent him to hell,
With their axes they clove him | while the death rattle came.

39. Atli summoned his men, | in mail-coats they hastened,
All ready they came, | and between was the courtyard.

* * * * * *

40. Then came they to words, | and full wrathful they were:
"Long since did we plan | how soon we might slay you."

Hogni spake:
41. "Little it matters | if long ye have planned it;
For unarmed do ye wait, | and one have we felled,
We smote him to hell, | of your host was he once."

42. Then wild was their anger | when all heard his words;
Their fingers were swift | on their bowstrings to seize,
Full sharply they shot, | by their shields were they guarded.

43. In the house came the word | how the heroes with out
Fought in front of the hall; | they heard a thrall tell it;
Grim then was Guthrun, | the grief when she heard,
With necklaces fair, | and she flung them all from her,
(The silver she hurled | so the rings burst asunder.)

44. Then out did she go, | she flung open the doors,
All fearless she went, | and the guests did she welcome;

To the Niflungs she went-- | her last greeting it was,--
In her speech truth was clear, | and much would she speak.

45. "For your safety I sought | that at home ye should stay;
None escapes his fate, | so ye hither must fare."
Full wisely she spake, | if yet peace they might win,
But to nought would they hearken, | and "No" said they all.

46. Then the high-born one saw | that hard was their battle,
In fierceness of heart | she flung off her mantle;
Her naked sword grasped she | her kin's lives to guard,
Not gentle her hands | in the hewing of battle.

47. Then the daughter of Gjuki | two warriors smote down,
Atli's brother she slew, | and forth then they bore him;
(So fiercely she fought | that his feet she clove off;)
Another she smote | so that never he stood,
To hell did she send him,-- | her hands trembled never.

48. Full wide was the fame | of the battle they fought,
'Twas the greatest of deeds | of the sons of Gjuki;
Men say that the Niflungs, | while themselves they were living,
With their swords fought mightily, | mail-coats they sundered,
And helms did they hew, | as their hearts were fearless.

49. All the morning they fought | until midday shone,
(All the dusk as well | and the dawning of day,)
When the battle was ended, | the field flowed with blood;
Ere they fell, eighteen | of their foemen were slain,
By the two sons of Bera | and her brother as well.

50. Then the warrior spake, | and wild was his anger:
"This is evil to see, | and thy doing is all;
Once we were thirty, | we thanes, keen for battle,
Now eleven are left, | and great is our lack.

51. "There were five of us brothers | when Buthli we lost,
Now Hel has the half, | and two smitten lie here;
A great kinship had I,-- | the truth may I hide not,--
From a wife bringing slaughter | small joy could I win.

52. We lay seldom together | since to me thou wast given,
Now my kin all are gone, | of my gold am I robbed;
Nay, and worst, thou didst send | my sister to hell."

Guthrun spake:
53. "Hear me now, Atli! | the first evil was thine;
My mother didst thou take, | and for gold didst murder her,
My sister's daughter | thou didst starve in a prison.
A jest does it seem | that thy sorrow thou tellest,
And good do I find it | that grief to thee comes."

Atli spake:
54. "Go now, ye warriors, | and make greater the grief
Of the woman so fair, | for fain would I see it;
So fierce be thy warring | that Guthrun shall weep,
I would gladly behold | her happiness lost.

55. "Seize ye now Hogni, | and with knives shall ye hew him,
His heart shall ye cut out, | this haste ye to do;
And grim-hearted Gunnar | shall ye bind on the gallows,
Swift shall ye do it, | to serpents now cast him."

Hogni spake:
56. "Do now as thou wilt, | for glad I await it,
Brave shalt thou find me, | I have faced worse before;
We held thee at bay | while whole we were fighting,
Now with wounds are we spent, | so thy will canst thou work."

57. Then did Beiti speak, | he was Atli's steward:
"Let us seize now Hjalli, | and Hogni spare we!

Let us fell the sluggard, | he is fit for death,
He has lived too long, | and lazy men call him."

58. Afraid was the pot-watcher, | he fled here and yon,
And crazed with his terror | he climbed in the corners:
"Ill for me is this fighting, | if I pay for your fierceness,
And sad is the day | to die leaving my swine
And all the fair victuals | that of old did I have."

59. They seized Buthli's cook, | and they came with the knife,
The frightened thrall howled | ere the edge did he feel;
He was willing, he cried, | to dung well the court yard,
Do the basest of work, | if spare him they would;
Full happy were Hjalli | if his life he might have.

60. Then fain was Hogni-- | there are few would do thus--
To beg for the slave | that safe hence he should go;
"I would find it far better | this knife-play to feel,
Why must we all hark | to this howling longer?"

61. Then the brave one they seized; | to the warriors bold
No chance was there left | to delay his fate longer;
Loud did Hogni laugh, | all the sons of day heard him,
So valiant he was | that well he could suffer.

* * * * * *

62. A harp Gunnar seized, | with his toes he smote it
So well did he strike | that the women all wept,
And the men, when clear | they heard it, lamented;
Full noble was his song, | the rafters burst asunder.

63. Then the heroes died | ere the day was yet come;
Their fame did they leave | ever lofty to live.

· · · · · · · · · · · ·

64. Full mighty seemed Atli | as o'er them he stood,
The wise one he blamed, | and his words reproached her:
"It is morning, Guthrun; | now thy dear ones dost miss,
But the blame is part thine | that thus it has chanced."

Guthrun spake:
65. "Thou art joyous, Atli, | for of evil thou tellest,
But sorrow is thine | if thou mightest all see;
Thy heritage heavy | here can I tell thee,
Sorrow never thou losest | unless I shall die."

Atli spake:
66. "Not free of guilt am I; | a way shall I find
That is better by far,-- | oft the fairest we shunned;--
With slaves I console thee, | with gems fair to see,
And with silver snow-white, | as thyself thou shalt choose."

Guthrun spake:
67. "No hope shall this give thee, | thy gifts I shall take not,
Requital I spurned | when my sorrows were smaller;
Once grim did I seem, | but now greater my grimness,
There was nought seemed too hard | while Hogni was living.

68. "Our childhood did we have | in a single house,
We played many a game, | in the grove did we grow;
Then did Grimhild give us | gold and necklaces,
Thou shalt ne'er make amends | for my brother's murder,
Nor ever shalt win me | to think it was well.

69. "But the fierceness of men | rules the fate of women,
The tree-top bows low | if bereft of its leaves,
The tree bends over | if the roots are cleft under it;
Now mayest thou, Atli, | o'er all things here rule."

70. Full heedless the warrior | was that he trusted her,
So clear was her guile | if on guard he had been;

But crafty was Guthrun, | with cunning she spake,
Her glance she made pleasant, | with two shields she played.

71. The beer then she brought | for her brothers' death feast,
And a feast Atli made | for his followers dead
No more did they speak, | the mead was made ready,
Soon the men were gathered | with mighty uproar.

72. Thus bitterly planned she, | and Buthli's race threatened,
And terrible vengeance | on her husband would take;
The little ones called she, | on a block she laid them;
Afraid were the proud ones, | but their tears did not fall;
To their mother's arms went they, | and asked what she would.

Guthrun spake:
73. "Nay, ask me no more! | You both shall I murder,
For long have I wished | your lives to steal from you.

The boys spake:
"Slay thy boys as thou wilt, | for no one may bar it,
Short the angry one's peace | if all thou shalt do."

74. Then the grim one slew both | of the brothers young,
Full hard was her deed | when their heads she smote off;
Fain was Atli to know | whither now they were gone,
The boys from their sport, | for nowhere he spied them.

Guthrun spake:
75. "My fate shall I seek, | all to Atli saying,
The daughter of Grimhild | the deed from thee hides not;
No joy thou hast, Atli, | if all thou shalt hear,
Great sorrow didst wake | when my brothers thou slewest.

76. 'I have seldom slept | since the hour they were slain,
Baleful were my threats, | now I bid thee recall them;

461

Thou didst say it was morning,-- | too well I remember,--
Now is evening come, | and this question thou askest.

77. "Now both of thy sons | thou hast lost .   .   .   .
       .   .   .   .   . | as thou never shouldst do;
The skulls of thy boys | thou as beer-cups didst have,
And the draught that I made thee | was mixed with their blood.

78. 'I cut out their hearts, | on a spit I cooked them,
I came to thee with them, | and calf's flesh I called them;
Alone didst thou eat them, | nor any didst leave,
Thou didst greedily bite, | and thy teeth were busy.

79. "Of thy sons now thou knowest; | few suffer more sorrow;
My guilt have I told, | fame it never shall give me."

Atli spake:
80. "Grim wast thou, Guthrun, | in so grievous a deed,
My draught with the blood | of thy boys to mingle;
Thou hast slain thine own kin, | most ill it be seemed thee,
And little for me | twixt my sorrows thou leavest."

Guthrun spake:
81. "Still more would I seek | to slay thee thyself,
Enough ill comes seldom | to such as thou art;
Thou didst folly of old, | such that no one shall find
In the whole world of men | a match for such madness.
Now this that of late | we learned hast thou added,
Great evil hast grasped, | and thine own death feast made."

Atli spake:
82. "With fire shall they burn thee, | and first shall they stone thee,
So then hast thou earned | what thou ever hast sought for."

Guthrun spake:
"Such woes for thyself | shalt thou say in the morning,
From a finer death I | to another light fare."

83. Together they sat | and full grim were their thoughts,
Unfriendly their words, | and no joy either found;
In Hniflung grew hatred, | great plans did he have,
To Guthrun his anger | against Atli was told.

84. To her heart came ever | the fate of Hogni,
She told him 'twere well | if he vengeance should win;
So was Atli slain,-- | 'twas not slow to await,--
Hogni's son slew him, | and Guthrun herself.

85. Then the warrior spake, | as from slumber he wakened,
Soon he knew for his wounds | would the bandage do nought:
"Now the truth shalt thou say: | who has slain Buthli's son?
Full sore am I smitten, | nor hope can I see."

Guthrun spake:
86. "Ne'er her deed from thee hides | the daughter of Grimhild,
I own to the guilt | that is ending thy life,
And the son of Hogni; | 'tis so thy wounds bleed."

Atli spake:
"To murder hast thou fared, | though foul it must seem;
Ill thy friend to betray | who trusted thee well.

87. "Not glad went I hence | thy hand to seek, Guthrun,
In thy widowhood famed, | but haughty men found thee;
My belief did not lie, | as now we have learned;
I brought thee home hither, | and a host of men with us.

88. "Most noble was all | when of old we journeyed,
Great honor did we have | of heroes full worthy;

Of cattle had we plenty, | and greatly we prospered,
Mighty was our wealth, | and many received it.

89. "To the famed one as bride-gift | I gave jewels fair,
I gave thirty slaves, | and handmaidens seven;
There was honor in such gifts, | yet the silver was greater.

90. "But all to thee was | as if nought it were worth,
While the land lay before thee | that Buthli had left me;
Thou in secret didst work | so the treasure I won not;
My mother full oft | to sit weeping didst make,
No wedded joy found I | in fullness of heart."

Guthrun spake:
91. "Thou liest now, Atli, | though little I heed it;
If I seldom was kindly, | full cruel wast thou;
Ye brothers fought young, | quarrels brought you to battle,
And half went to hell | of the sons of thy house,
And all was destroyed | that should e'er have done good.

92. "My two brothers and I | were bold in our thoughts,
From the land we went forth, | with Sigurth we fared;
Full swiftly we sailed, | each one steering his ship,
So our fate sought we e'er | till we came to the East.

93. "First the king did we slay, | and the land we seized,
The princes did us service, | for such was their fear;
From the forest we called | them we fain would have guiltless,
And rich made we many | who of all were bereft.

94. "Slain was the Hun-king, | soon happiness vanished,
In her grief the widow | so young sat weeping;
Yet worse seemed the sorrow | to seek Atli's house,
A hero was my husband, | and hard was his loss.

95. "From the Thing thou camst never, | for thus have we heard,
Having won in thy quarrels, | or warriors smitten;
Full yielding thou wast, | never firm was thy will,
In silence didst suffer, | .   .   .   .   .

Atli spake:
96. "Thou liest now, Guthrun, | but little of good
Will it bring to either, | for all have we lost;
But, Guthrun, yet once | be thou kindly of will,
For the honor of both, | when forth I am home."

Guthrun spake:
97. "A ship will I buy, | and a bright-hued coffin,
I will wax well the shroud | to wind round thy body,
For all will I care | as if dear were we ever."

98. Then did Atli die, | and his heirs' grief doubled;
The high-born one did | as to him she had promised;
Then sought Guthrun the wise | to go to her death,
But for days did she wait, | and 'twas long ere she died.

99. Full happy shall he be | who such offspring has,
Or children so gallant, | as Gjuki begot;
Forever shall live, | and in lands far and wide,
Their valor heroic | wherever men hear it.

[1. *Men*: Atli and his advisers, with whom he planned the death of the sons
of *Gjuki*, Gunnar and Hogni. The poet's reference to the story as well known
explains the abruptness of his introduction, without the mention of Atli's name,
and his reference to Guthrun in stanza 3 simply as "the woman" ("husfreyja,"
goddess of the house).

2. *Princes*: Atli, Gunnar, and Hogni. *Bulwark*: Atli's slaying [fp. 501] of his wife's
brothers, who were ready to support and defend him in his greatness, was the
cause of his own death.]

[3. *The woman*: Guthrun, concerning whose marriage to Atli cf. *Guthrunarkvitha II. The sea*: a late and essentially Greenland variation of the geography of the Atli story. Even the *Atlakvitha*, perhaps half a century earlier, separates Atli's land from that of the Gjukungs only by a forest.

4. *Runes*: on the two versions of Guthrun's warning, and also on the name of the messenger (here Vingi), cf. *Drap Niflunga* and note.*Limafjord*: probably the Limfjord of northern Jutland, an important point in the wars of the eleventh century. The name was derived from "Eylimafjorþ," i.e., Eylimi's fjord. The poet may really have thought that the kingdom of the Burgundians was in Jutland, or he may simply have taken a well-known name for the sake of vividness.]

[5. Some editors assume a gap after this stanza.

6. Some editions place this stanza between stanzas 7 and 8. *Kostbera* ("The Giver of Food") and *Glaumvor* ("The Merry"): presumably creations of the poet. *Both*: Atli's two emissaries, Vingi and the one here unnamed (Knefröth?).

7. It is altogether probable that a stanza has been lost between stanzas 6 and 7, in which Gunnar is first invited, and replies doubtfully. *Made promise*: many editions emend the text to read "promised the journey." The text of line 4 is obscure; the manuscript reads "nitti" ("refused"), which many editors have changed to "hlitti," which means exactly the opposite. 8. No gap is indicated in the manuscript; Bugge adds (line [fp. 503] 3): "Then the warriors rose, | and to slumber made ready." The manuscript indicates line 4 as beginning a new stanza, and some editions make a separate stanza out of lines 1-2. Others suggest the loss of a line after line 4.]

[9. The manuscript does not indicate line 1 as the beginning of a stanza; cf. note on stanza 8.

10. Some editions combine this stanza with lines 1-2 of stanza 11. The manuscript indicates no gap. Grundtvig adds (line 2) "But sleep to the woman | so wise came little."

11. Some editions make a separate stanza out of lines 1-2, or combine them with stanza 10, and combine lines 3-4 with stanza [fp. 504]12 (either lines 1-4 or 1-2). The manuscript marks line 3 as beginning a new stanza.]

[12. Line 5 may be spurious, or else all that is left of a lost stanza. The manuscript marks it as the beginning of a new stanza, which, as the text stands, is clearly impossible.

13. The manuscript, followed by some editions, has "Hogni spake" in the middle of line 1. *Ill*: the manuscript and many editions have "this."*The king*: Atli.

14. The manuscript does not indicate the speakers in this dialogue between Kostbera and Hogni (stanzas 14-19). Two line, may possibly have been lost after line 2, filling out stanza 14 and [fp. 505] making stanza 15 (then consisting of lines 3-4 of stanza 14 and lines 1-2 of stanza 15) the account of Kostbera's first dream. The manuscript marks line 3 as beginning a new stanza. In any case, the lost lines cannot materially have altered the meaning.]

[15. *Saw I*: the manuscript here, as also in stanzas 16, 18, 2r, 22, and 24, has "methought," which involves a metrical error. Some editors regard lines 3-4 as the remains of a four-line stanza. Regarding Kostbera's warning dreams, and Hogni's matter-of-fact interpretations of them, cf.*Guthrunarkvitha II*, 39-44.

16. The meaning of the first half of line 3 in the original is obscure.]

[17. Two lines may have been lost after line 2, but the *Volsungasaga* paraphrase gives no clue. *Ice-bear*: polar bears, common in Greenland, are very rarely found in Iceland, and never in Norway, a fact which substantiates the manuscript's reference to Greenland as the home of the poem.

18. The manuscript indicates no gap, but most editors assume the loss of a line after line 1 or 2; Grundtvig adds, after line 1: "Black were his feathers, | with blood was he covered." *Atli's spirit*: the poet's folk-lore seems here a bit weak. Presumably he means such a female following-spirit ("fylgja") as appears in *Helgakvitha Hjorvarthssonar*, prose following stanza 34 (cf. note thereon), but the word he uses, "hamr" (masculine) means "skin," "shape." He may, however, imply that Atli had assumed the shape of an eagle for this occasion.

19. The manuscript indicates line 4 as beginning a new stanza.]

[20. The manuscript indicates no gap, but none of the many attempted emendations have made sense out of the words as they stand. The proper location for' the missing words is sheer guesswork. *Two roads*: probably the meaning is that their way (i.e., their success) would be doubtful.

21. The manuscript does not indicate the speakers in this dialogue (stanzas 21-26). No gap is indicated after line 2. Most editors assume the loss of two lines or of a full stanza after [fp. 508] stanza 21 giving Gunnar's interpretation of Glaumvor's dream, but the *Volsungasaga* gives no clue, as it does not mention this first dream at all. Grundtvig suggests as Gunnar's answer: "Banners are gleaming, | since of

gallows didst dream, / And wealth it must mean | that thou serpents didst watch." *Gods' doom*: an odd, and apparently mistaken, use of the phrase "ragna rök" (cf. *Voluspo*, introductory note).]

[25. Perhaps two lines have been lost after line 2. Possibly the concluding phrase of line 2 should be "bloody spears," as in the *Volsungasaga*paraphrase.

24. Again Gunnar's interpretation is missing, and most editors either assume a gap or construct two Malahattr lines (out of the *Volsungasaga*prose paraphrase, which runs: "The grain shall [fp. 509] flow, since thou hast dreamed of rivers, and when we go to the fields, often the chaff rises above our feet."]

[25. The meaning of line 4 is uncertain, but apparently it refers to the guardian spirits or lesser Norns (cf. *Fafnismol*, 12-13 and notes).

26. Possibly a line has been lost from this stanza.

27. *Five*: Gunnar, Hogni, and the three mentioned in Stanza 28.

28. Perhaps a line has been lost before line 1; Grundtvig supplies: "Gunnar and Hogni, the heirs twain of Gjuki." *Snævar* (the manuscript here has "Snevar"), *Solar* and *Orkning* [fp. 510] appear only in this poem and in the prose narratives based on it. Lines 2-3 may have been expanded out of one line, or possibly line 3 is spurious. The manuscript indicates line 4 as beginning a new stanza, and many editions make a separate stanza out of lines 4-5, many of them assuming the loss of two lines. *Shield-tree*: warrior (Orkning), here identified as Kostbera's brother. *Fair-decked ones*: women, i.e., Glaumvor and Kostbera. *Fjord*: perhaps specifically the *Limafjord* mentioned in stanza 4.]

[30. The manuscript indicates no gap. Grundtvig inserts (line 2): "The evil was clear when his words he uttered."

31. *Bera*: Kostbera; the first element in compound feminine [fp. 511] proper names was not infrequently omitted; cf. Hild for Brynhild (*Helreith Brynhildar*, 6). The manuscript indicates no gap; Grundtvig inserts (line 2): "And clear was her cry to her kinsmen dear."]

[32. Hogni's method of cheering his wife and sister-in-law is somewhat unusual, for the meaning of lines 3-4 is that good wishes and blessings are of little use in warding off danger.

33. Perhaps two lines have been lost after line 2; Grundtvig supplies: "Then weeping did | Glaumvor go to her rest-bed, / And sadly did Bera | her spinning wheel seek."

34. *Keel*, etc.: in the *Nibelungenlied*, and presumably in the older German tradition, Hagene breaks his oar steering the Burgundians across the Danube (stanza 1564), and, after all have landed, splinters the boat (stanza 1581) in order that there may be no retreating. The poet here seems to have confused the story, [fp. 512] connecting the breaking of the ship's keel with the violence of the rowing, but echoing the older legend in the last line, wherein the ship is allowed to drift away after the, travellers have landed. *Oar-loops*: the thongs by which the oars in a Norse boat were made fast to the *thole-pins*, the combination taking the place of the modern oarlock.]

[35. The manuscript indicates line 4 as beginning a new stanza, and many editions combine it with stanza 36, some of them assuming the loss of a line from stanza 35. In the *Volsungasaga* paraphrase the second half of line 4 is made a part of Vingi's speech: "Better had ye left this undone."

36. Cf. note on preceding stanza; the manuscript does not indicate line I as beginning a stanza. Line 3 may be spurious.

37. In the *Volsungasaga* paraphrase the second half of line 1 and the first half of line 2 are included in Hogni's speech.]

[38. Possibly two lines have been lost after line 2.

39. It is probable that a considerable passage has been lost between stanzas 39 and 40, for the *Volsungasaga* paraphrase includes a dialogue at this point. The manuscript indicates no gap, and most editions combine stanzas 39 and 40 as a single stanza. The prose passage, indicating the substance of what, if any thing, is lost, runs as follows: "'Be welcome among us, and give me that store of gold which is ours by right, the gold that Sigurth had, and that now belongs to Guthrun.' Gunnar said: 'Never shalt thou get that gold, and men of might shalt thou find here, ere we give up our lives, if it is battle thou dost offer us; in truth it seems that thou hast prepared this feast in kingly fashion, [fp. 514] and with little grudging toward eagle and wolf.'" The demand for the treasure likewise appears in the Nibelungenlied.]

[40. These two lines, which most editions combine with stanza 39, may be the first or last two of a four-line stanza. The *Volsungasaga* gives Atli's speech very much as it appears here.

41. The manuscript does not indicate the speaker; Grundtvig adds as a first line: "Then Hogni laughed loud where the slain Vingi lay." Many editors assume the loss of a line somewhere in the stanza. *Unarmed*: Hogni does not see Atli's armed followers, who are on the other side of the courtyard (stanza 39). One: Vingi.

42. Most editors assume the loss of one line, after either line 1 or line 3.

45. The manuscript reading of lines 1-2, involving a metrical error, is: "In the house came the word | of the warring without, / Loud in front of the hall | they heard a thrall shouting." Some editors assume a gap of two lines after line [fp. 515] 2, the missing passage giving the words of the thrall. The manuscript marks line 3 as the beginning of a stanza, and many editions make a separate stanza of lines 3-5, same of them assuming the loss of a line after line 3. With the stanza as here given, line 5 may well be spurious.]

[44. *Niflungs*: regarding the application of this term to the Burgundians cf. *Atlakvitha*, 11, and *Brot*, 17, and notes. The manuscript here spells the name with an initial N, as elsewhere, but in stanza 83 the son of Hogni appears with the name "Hniflung." In consequence, some editors change the form in this stanza to "Hniflungs," while others omit the initial H in both cases. I have followed the manuscript, though admittedly its spelling is illogical.]

[46. The warlike deeds of Guthrun represent an odd transformation of the German tradition. Kriemhild, although she did no actual fighting in the *Nibelungenlied*, was famed from early times for her cruelty and fierceness of heart, and this seems to have inspired the poet of the *Atlamol* to make his Guthrun into a warrior outdoing Brynhild herself. Kriemhild's ferocity of course, was directed against Gunther and especially Hagene, for whose slaying she rather than Etzel was responsible; here, on the other hand, Guthrun's is devoted to the defense of her brothers.

47. Line 3 is very likely an interpolation. The manuscript marks line 4 as the beginning of a new stanza, and some editions make a separate stanza of lines 4-5. *Atli's brother*: doubtless a reminiscence of the early tradition represented in the *Nibelungenlied* by the slaying of Etzel's brother, Blœdelin (the historical Bleda), by Dancwart.]

[48. Line 3 may well be spurious, for it implies that Gunnar and Hogni were killed in battle, whereas they were taken prisoners. Some editors, in an effort to smooth out the inconsistency, change "themselves" in this line to "sound." Line 5 has also been questioned as possibly interpolated. *Niflungs*: on the spelling of this name in the manuscript and the various editions cf. note on stanza 44.

470

49. Line 2 is probably an interpolation, and the original apparently lacks a word. There is some obscurity as to the exact meaning of lines 4-5. *The two sons of Bera*: Snævar and Solar; *her brother* is Orkning; cf. stanza 28.

50. *The warrior*: Atli. *Thirty*: perhaps an echo of the "thirty warriors" of Thjothrek (cf. *Guthrunarkvitha III*, 5). Subtracting the eighteen killed by Snævar, Solar and Orkning (stanza 49), and Vingi, killed by the whole company (stanza [fp. 518] 38), we have eleven left, as Atli says, but this does not allow much for the exploits of Gunnar and Hogni, who, by this reckoning, seem to have killed nobody. The explanation probably is that lines 4-5 of stanza 49 are in bad shape.]

[51. *Five brothers*: the *Volsungasaga* speaks of four (not five) sons of Buthli, but names only Atli. Regarding the death of the first two brothers cf. stanza 91 and note. The manuscript marks line 3 as beginning a stanza, and many editions combine lines 3-4 with stanza 52. Some insert lines 2-3 of stanza 52 ahead of lines 3-4 of stanza 51.

52. Possibly a line has been lost from this stanza. The manuscript marks line 3 as beginning a new stanza, which is impossible unless something has been lost. *Gold*: the meaning of this half line is somewhat doubtful, but apparently Atli refers to Sigurth's treasure, which should have been his as Brynhild's brother. *Sister*: Brynhild; regarding Guthrun's indirect responsibility for Brynhild's death cf. *Gripisspo*, 45 and note.]

[53. The manuscript does not name the speaker. *The Volsungasaga* gives the speech, in somewhat altered form, to Hogni. "Why speakest thou so? Thou wast the first to break peace; thou didst take my kinswoman and starved her in a prison, and murdered her and took her wealth; that was not kinglike; and laughable does it seem to me that thou talkest of thy sorrow, and good shall I find it that all goes ill with thee." This presumably represents the correct form of the stanza, for nowhere else is it intimated that Atli killed Guthrun's mother, Grimhild, nor is the niece elsewhere mentioned. Some editions make a separate stanza of lines 4-5, Grundtvig adding a line after line 3 and two more after line 5. Other editors are doubtful about the authenticity of either line 3 or line 5.

54. The manuscript does not indicate the speaker.]

[56. The text of the first half of line 3 is somewhat uncertain, but the general meaning of it is clear enough.

57. Beiti: not elsewhere mentioned. The *Atlakvitha* version of this episode (stanzas 23-25) does not mention Beiti, and in the *Volsungasaga* the advice to cut

out Hjalli's heart instead of Hogni's is given by an unnamed "counsellor of Atli." In the *Atlakvitha* Hjalli is actually killed; the *Volsungasaga* combines the two versions by having Hjalli first let off at Hogni's intercession and then seized a second time and killed, thus introducing the *Atlakvitha* episode of the quaking heart (stanza 24). The text of the first half of line 3 is obscure, and there are many and widely varying suggestions as to the word here rendered "sluggard."

58. Some editions mark line 5 as probably interpolated.]

[59. *Cook*: the original word is doubtful. The *Volsungasaga* does not paraphrase lines 3-5; the passage may be a later addition, and line 5 is almost certainly so.

61. It is probable that a stanza describing the casting of Gunnar into the serpents' den has been lost after this stanza. *Sons of day*: the phrase means no more than "men."]

[67. Regarding Gunnar's harp-playing, and his death, cf. *Oddrunargratr*, 27-30 and notes, and *Atlakvitha*, 34. *Toes* (literally "sole-twigs"): the *Volsungasaga* explains that Gunnar's hands were bound. *Rafters*: thus literally, and probably correctly; Gering has an ingenious but unlikely theory that the word means "harp."

63. There is some doubt as to the exact meaning of line 2. After this line two lines may have! been lost; Grundtvig adds: "Few braver shall ever | be found on the earth, / Or loftier men | in the world ever give."

64. *Wise one*: Guthrun. The manuscript marks line 3 as beginning a new stanza.]

[65. The manuscript does not indicate the speaker.

66. The manuscript does not name the speaker. The negative in the first half of line 1 is uncertain, and most editions make the clause read "Of this guilt I can free myself." *The fairest*, etc.: i. e., I have often failed to do the wise thing.

67. The manuscript does not indicate the speaker. *Requital*, etc.: it is not clear just to what Guthrun refers; perhaps she is thinking of Sigurth's death, or possibly the poet had in mind his reference to the slaying of her mother in stanza 53.]

[68. Line 5 is very probably a later addition, though some editors question line 3 instead.

69. Guthrun suddenly changes her tone in order to make Atli believe that she is submissive to his will, and thus to gain time for her vengeance. Line 2 in the original is thoroughly obscure; it runs literally: "On the knee goes the fist if the twigs are taken off." Perhaps the word meaning "fist" may also have meant "tree-top," as Gering suggests, or perhaps the line is an illogical blending of the ideas contained in lines 1 and 3.

70. The manuscript indicates line 3 as the beginning of a new stanza, *Two shields*, etc.: i. e., Guthrun concealed her hostility (symbolized by a red shield, cf. *Helgakvitha Hundingsbana* I, 34) by a show of friendliness (a white shield).]

[71. Many editions make a separate stanza of lines 1-2, some of them suggesting the loss of two lines, and combine lines 5-4 with lines 1-2 of stanza 72, The manuscript marks both lines 1 and 3 as beginning stanzas.

72. The manuscript marks line 3 as beginning a new stanza; some editions make a separate stanza of lines 3-5, while others combine them with lines 1-2 of stanza 73. Line 2 in the original is clearly defective, the verb being omitted. The meaning of line 3 is uncertain; the *Volsungasaga* paraphrase has: "At evening she took the sons of King Atli (Erp and Eitil) where they were playing with a block of wood." Probably the text of the line as we have it is faulty. Lines 4-5 may possibly have been expanded out of a single line, or line 5 may be spurious.]

[73. The manuscript does not name the speakers. It indicates line 3 as beginning a new stanza, in which it is followed by many editions. The *Volsungasaga* paraphrases line 4 thus: "But it is shameful for thee to do this." Either the text of the line has been changed or the *Volsungasaga* compilers misunderstood it. *The angry one*: Atli.

74. The manuscript indicates line 3 as beginning a new stanza.

75. The manuscript does not name the speaker.]

[76. *Morning*: Guthrun refers to Atli's taunt in stanza 64.

77. The manuscript indicates no gap (lines 1-2), and most editions make a single line, despite the defective meter: "Thy sons hast thou lost | as thou never shouldst lose them." The second part of line 2 is in the original identical with the second half of line 3 of stanza 80, and may perhaps have been inserted here by mistake. *Skulls*: it is possible that line 3 was borrowed from a poem belonging to the Völund tradition (cf. *Völundarkvitha*, 25 and 37), and the idea doubtless came from some such source, but probably the poet inserted it in a line of his own

composition to give an added touch of horror. The *Volsungasaga* follows the *Atlamol* in including this incident.]

[78. Some editions add lines 5-4 to stanza 79; Finnur Jonsson marks them as probably spurious.

79. Perhaps these two lines should form part of stanza 78, or perhaps they, rather than lines 3-4 of stanza 78, are a later addition. A gap of two lines after line 1 has also been conjectured.

80. The manuscript does not indicate the speaker.

81. The manuscript does not indicate the speaker. Lines 1-2 may be the remains of a separate stanza; Grundtvig adds: "Thou wast foolish, Atli, | when wise thou didst feel, / Ever the whole | of thy race did I hate." The Volsungasaga paraphrase, however, indicates no gap. Many editions make a separate stanza of lines 3-6, which, in the *Volsungasaga*, are paraphrased as a speech of Atli's. Lines 5-6 may be spurious.]

[82. The manuscript does not indicate the speakers. Many editions make two separate stanzas of the four lines. *Another light:* a fairly clear indication of the influence of Christianity; cf. Introductory Note.

83. The manuscript marks line 3 as the beginning of a new stanza. *Hniflung*: the *Volsungasaga* says that "Hogni had a son who was called Hniflung," but the name appears to be nothing more than the familiar "Niflung" applied in general to the sons of Gjuki and their people. On the spelling cf. note on stanza 44. [fp. 530] This son of Hogni appears in later versions of the story. In the *Thithrekssaga* he is called Aldrian, and is begotten by Hogni the night before his death. Aldrian grows up and finally shuts Attila in a cave where he starves to death. The poet here has incorporated the idea, which finds no parallel in the *Atlakvitha*, without troubling himself to straighten out the chronology.]

[84. Line 4 may be in Fornyrthislag, and from another poem.

85. The manuscript marks line 3 as beginning a new stanza.

The *Volsungasaga* makes line 2 part of Atli's speech.

86. The manuscript does not name the speakers. It marks line 4 as the beginning of a new stanza, and many editions follow this arrangement, in most cases making

a stanza of lines 4-5 and line 1 of stanza 87. However, line 1 may well have been interpolated here from stanza 75. Grundtvig adds after line 3: "His father he avenged, and his kinsmen fully." Some editors assume the loss of one or two lines after line 5.]

[87. The manuscript marks line 2 as beginning a new stanza, and some editions make a stanza out of lines 2-4 and line 1 of stanza 88.

88. The manuscript marks line 2 as the beginning of a stanza, and many editions make a stanza out of lines 2-4, or combine them with stanza 89. Some question the genuineness of line 4. 89. Many editions assume a gap of one line after line 3; [fp. 532] Grundtvig adds: "Bit-champing horses and wheel-wagons bright." Line 4 may be spurious. *Greater*: i. e., the silver which Atli gave Guthrun was of greater value even than the honor of receiving such royal gifts. Line 4 may be spurious.]

[90. Some editions mark line 3 as spurious or defective. The manuscript marks line 4 as the beginning of a new stanza. *The land*, etc.: there is much obscurity as to the significance of this line. Some editors omit or question "me," in which case Atli is apparently reproaching Guthrun for having incited him to fight with his brothers to win for himself the whole of Buthli's land. In stanza 91 Guthrun denies that she was to blame for Atli's quarrels with his brothers.
The *Volsungasaga* reading supports this interpretation. The historical Attila did actually have his brother, Bleda, killed in order to have the sole rule. *The treasure*: Sigurth's hoard, which Atli claimed as the brother of Brynhild and husband of Guthrun, Sigurth's widow, but which Gunnar and Hogni kept for themselves, with, as Atli here charges, Guthrun's connivance. *My mother*: the only other reference to Atli's mother is in *Oddrunargratr*, 30, wherein she appears as the adder who stings Gunnar to death, and in the prose passages based on that stanza.]

[91. The manuscript does not indicate the speaker. It marks both lines 4 and 5 as beginning new stanzas, but line 5 is presumably an interpolation. The text of the second half of line 2 is obscure, and many emendations have been suggested. *Ye brothers*: cf. note on stanza go.*Half*: i. e., two of Atli's brothers were killed, the other two dying in the battle with Gunnar and Hogni; cf. stanza 51.

92. *From the land*: this maritime expedition of Guthrun and her two brothers, Gunnar and Hogni (the poet seems to know nothing of her half-brother, Gotthorm), with Sigurth seems to have been a pure. invention of the poet's, inserted for the benefit of his Greenland hearers. Nothing further is reported concerning it.

93. *The forest*: i. e., men who were outlawed in the conquered land were restored to their rights--another purely Norse touch.]

[94. *Hun-king*: Sigurth, though most illogically so called; cf. *Sigurtharkvitha en skamma*, 4 and note. The Volsungasaga paraphrase of line 2 is so remote as to be puzzling: "It was little to bear the name of widow." Perhaps, however, the word "not" fell out between "was" and "little."

95. *Thing*, etc.: here the poet makes Atli into a typical Norse land-owner, going to the "Thing," or general law council, to settle his disputes. Even the compilers of the *Volsungasaga* could not accept this, and in their paraphrase changed "Thing" to "battle." The text of the second half of line 2 is uncertain. The manuscript leaves a blank to indicate the gap in-line 4; Grundtvig adds: "as beseems not a king."]

[94. *Hun-king*: Sigurth, though most illogically so called; cf. *Sigurtharkvitha en skamma*, 4 and note. The Volsungasaga paraphrase of line 2 is so remote as to be puzzling: "It was little to bear the name of widow." Perhaps, however, the word "not" fell out between "was" and "little."

95. *Thing*, etc.: here the poet makes Atli into a typical Norse land-owner, going to the "Thing," or general law council, to settle his disputes. Even the compilers of the *Volsungasaga* could not accept this, and in their paraphrase changed "Thing" to "battle." The text of the second half of line 2 is uncertain. The manuscript leaves a blank to indicate the gap in-line 4; Grundtvig adds: "as beseems not a king."]

[97. The manuscript does not indicate the speaker. Many editors assume a gap either before or after line 1. *A ship*: the burial of Norse chiefs in ships was of frequent occurrence, but the Greenland poet's application of the custom to Atli is some what grotesque.

98. *Heirs*, etc.: merely a stock phrase, here quite meaningless, as Atli's heirs had all been killed. *Long*: cf. *Guthrunarhvot*, introductory prose.]

GUTHRUNARHVOT

Guthrun's Inciting

INTRODUCTORY NOTE

The two concluding poems in the *Codex Regius*, the *Guthrunarhvot* (*Guthrun's Inciting*) and the *Hamthesmol* (*The Ballad of Hamther*), belong to a narrative cycle connected with those of Sigurth, the Burgundians, and Atli (cf. *Gripisspo*, introductory note) by only the slenderest of threads. Of the three early historical kings who gradually assumed a dominant place in Germanic legend, Ermanarich, king of the East Goths in the middle of the fourth century, was actually the least important, even though Jordanes, the sixth century author of *De Rebus Getecis*, compared him to Alexander the Great. Memories of his cruelty and of his tragic death, however, persisted along with the real glories of Theoderich, a century and a half later, and of the conquests of Attila, whose lifetime approximately bridged the gap between Ermanarich's death and Theoderich's birth.

Chief among the popular tales of Ermanarich's cruelty was one concerning the death of a certain Sunilda or Sanielh, whom, according to Jordanes, he caused to be torn asunder by wild horses because of her husband's treachery. Her brothers, Sarus and Ammius, seeking to avenge her, wounded but failed to kill Ermanarich. In this story is the root of the two Norse poems included in the *Codex Regius*. Sunilda easily became the wife as well as the victim of the tyrant, and, by the process of legend-blending so frequently observed, the story was connected with the more famous one of the Nibelungs by making her the daughter of Sigurth and Guthrun. To account for her brothers, a third husband had to be found for Guthrun; the Sarus and Ammius of Jordanes are obviously the Sorli and Hamther, sons of Guthrun and Jonak, of the Norse poems. The blending of the Sigurth and Ermanarich legends

477

probably, though not certainly, took place before the story reached the North, in other words before the end of the eighth century.

Regarding the exact status of the *Guthrunarhvot* and the *Hamthesmol* there has been a great deal of discussion. That they are closely related is obvious; indeed the first parts of the two poems are nearly identical in content and occasionally so in actual diction. The annotator, in his concluding prose note, refers to the second poem as the "old" ballad of Hamther, wherefore it has been assumed by some critics that the composer of the *Guthrunarhvot* used the *Hamthesmol*, approximately as it now stands, as the source of part of his material. The extant *Hamthesmol*, however, is almost certainly a patchwork; part of it is in *Fornyrthislag* (cf. Introduction), including most of the stanzas paralleled in the *Guthrunarhvot*, and likewise the stanza followed directly by the reference to the "old" ballad, while the rest is in Malahattr. The most reasonable theory, therefore, is that there existed an old ballad of Hamther, all in Fornyrthislag, from which the composer of the *Guthrunarhvot* borrowed a few stanzas as the introduction for his poem, and which the composer of the extant, or "new," *Hamthesmol* likewise used, though far more clumsily.

The title "Guthrunarhvot," which appears in the *Codex Regius*, really applies only to stanzas 1-8, all presumably borrowed from the "old" ballad of Hamther. The rest of the poem is simply another Guthrun lament, following the tradition exemplified by the first and second Guthrun lays; it is possible, indeed, that it is made up of fragments of two separate laments, one (stanzas 9-18) involving the story of Svanhild's death, and the other (stanzas 19-21) coming from an otherwise lost version of the story in which Guthrun closely follows Sigurth and Brynhild in death. In any event the present title is really a misnomer; the poet, who presumably was an eleventh century Icelander, used the episode of Guthrun's inciting her sons to vengeance for the slaying of Svanhild simply as an introduction to his main subject, the last lament of the unhappy queen.

The text of the poem in *Regius* is by no means in good shape, and editorial emendations have been many and varied, particularly in interchanging lines between the *Guthrunarhvot* and the *Hamthesmol*. The *Volsungasaga* paraphrases the poem with such fidelity as to prove that it lay before the compilers of the saga approximately in its present form.

Guthrun went forth to the sea after she had slain Atli. She went out into the sea and fain would drown herself, but she could not sink. The waves bore her across the fjord to the land of King Jonak; he took her as wife; their sons were Sorli and Erp and Hamther. There was brought up Svanhild, Sigurth's daughter; she was married to the mighty Jormunrek. With him was Bikki, who counselled that Randver, the king's son, should have her. This Bikki told to the king. The king had Randver hanged, and Svanhild trodden to death under horses' feet. And when Guthrun learned this, she spake with her sons.

1. A word-strife I learned, | most woeful of all,
A speech from the fullness | of sorrow spoken,
When fierce of heart | her sons to the fight
Did Guthrun whet | with words full grim.

2. "Why sit ye idle, | why sleep out your lives,
Why grieve ye not | in gladness to speak?
Since Jormunrek | your sister young
Beneath the hoofs | of horses hath trodden,
(White and black | on the battle-way,
Gray, road-wonted, | the steeds of the Goths.)

3. "Not like are ye | to Gunnar of yore,
Nor have ye hearts | such as Hogni's was;
Vengeance for her | ye soon would have
If brave ye were | as my brothers of old,
Or hard your hearts | as the Hunnish kings'."

4. Then Hamther spake, | the high of heart:
"Little the deed | of Hogni didst love,
When Sigurth they wakened | from his sleep;
Thy bed-covers white | were red with blood
Of thy husband, drenched | with gore from his heart.

5. "Bloody revenge | didst have for thy brothers,
Evil and sore, | when thy sons didst slay;
Else yet might we all | on Jormunrek
Together our sister's | slaying avenge.

6. .   .   .   .
The gear of the Hunnish | kings now give us!
Thou hast whetted us so | to the battle of swords."

7. Laughing did Guthrun | go to her chamber,
The helms of the kings | from the cupboards she took,
And mail-coats broad, | to her sons she bore them;
On their horses' backs | the heroes leaped.

8. Then Hamther spake, | the high of heart:
"Homeward no more | his mother to see
Comes the spear-god, | fallen mid Gothic folk;

One death-draught thou | for us all shalt drink,
For Svanhild then | and thy sons as well."

9. Weeping Guthrun, | Gjuki's daughter,
Went sadly before | the gate to sit,
And with tear-stained cheeks | to tell the tale
Of her mighty griefs, | so many in kind.

10. "Three home-fires knew I, | three hearths I knew,
Home was I brought | by husbands three;
But Sigurth only | of all was dear,
He whom my brothers | brought to his death.

11. "A greater sorrow | I saw not nor knew,
Yet more it seemed | I must suffer yet
When the princes great | to Atli gave me.

12. "The brave boys I summoned | to secret speech;
For my woes requital | I might not win
Till off the heads | of the Hniflungs I hewed.

13. "To the sea I went, | my heart full sore
For the Norns, whose wrath | I would now escape;
But the lofty billows | bore me undrowned,
Till to land I came, | so I longer must live.

14. "Then to the bed-- | of old was it better!--
Of a king of the folk | a third time I came;
Boys I bore | his heirs to be,
Heirs so young, | the sons of Jonak.

15. "But round Svanhild | handmaidens sat,
She was dearest ever | of all my children;
So did Svanhild | seem in my hall
As the ray of the sun | is fair to see.

16. "Gold I gave her | and garments bright,
Ere I let her go | to the Gothic folk;
Of my heavy woes | the hardest it was
When Svanhild's tresses | fair were trodden
In the mire by hoofs | of horses wild.

17. "The sorest it was | when Sigurth mine
On his couch, of victory | robbed, they killed;
And grimmest of all | when to Gunnar's heart
There crept the bright-hued | crawling snakes.

18. "And keenest of all | when they cut the heart
From the living breast | of the king so brave;
Many woes I remember, | .   .   .   .   .

.   .   .   .

19. "Bridle, Sigurth, | thy steed so black,
Hither let run | thy swift-faring horse;
Here there sits not | son or daughter
Who yet to Guthrun | gifts shall give.

20. "Remember, Sigurth, | what once we said,
When together both | on the bed we sat,
That mightily thou | to me wouldst come
From hell and I | from earth to thee.

21. "Pile ye up, jarls, | the pyre of oak,
Make it the highest | a hero e'er had;
Let the fire burn | my grief-filled breast,
My sore-pressed heart, | till my sorrows melt."

22. May nobles all | less sorrow know,
And less the woes | of women become,
Since the tale of this | lament is told.

[*Prose*. In the manuscript the prose is headed "Of Guthrun," the title "Guthrunarhvot" preceding stanza 1. The prose introduction is used both by Snorri (*Skaldskaparmal*, chapter 42) and in the *Volsungasaga*. It would be interesting to know on what the annotator based this note, for neither Bikki nor Randver is mentioned by name in either the *Guthrunarhvot* or the *Hamthesmol*. On the prose notes in general, cf. *Reginsmol*, introductory note. *Guthrun*: on the slaying of Atli by his wife, Guthrun, Sigurth's widow, cf. *Atlamol*, 83-86 and notes. *Jonak*: a Northern addition to the legend, introduced to account for Svanhild's half-brothers; the name is apparently of Slavic origin. *Sorli*, *Erp*, and *Hamther*: Sorli and Hamther are the Sarus and Ammius of the Jordanes story (cf. introductory note). The *Volsungasaga* follows this note in making Erp likewise a son of Guthrun, but in the *Hamthesmol* he is a son of Jonak by another wife. *Svanhild*: cf. *Sigurtharkvitha en skamma*, 54 and note.*Jormunrek* (Ermanarich): cf. introductory note. *Bikki*: the Sifka or Sibicho of the Gothic legends of Ermanarich, whose evil counsel always brings trouble. *Randver*: in the *Volsungasaga* Jormunrek sends his son Randver with Bikki to seek Svanhild's hand. On the voyage home Bikki says to Randver: "It were right for you to have so fair a wife, and not such an old man." Randver was much pleased with this advice, "and he spake to her with gladness, and she to him." Thus the story becomes near of kin to those of Tristan and Iseult and Paolo and Francesca. According to the *Volsungasaga*, Bikki told Ermanarich that a guilty love existed between his son and his young wife, and presumably the annotator here meant as much by his vague "this."]

[1. The poet's introduction of himself in this stanza is a fairly certain indication of the relative lateness of the poem.

2. *Idle*: a guess; a word is obviously missing in the original. The manuscript marks line 5 as beginning a new stanza, and lines 5-6 may well have been inserted from another part of the "old" *Hamthesmol* (cf. *Hamthesmol*, 3).

3. *Gunnar* and *Hogni*: cf. *Drap Niflunga*. Line 5 may be interpolated. *Hunnish*: here used, as often, merely as a generic term for all South Germanic peoples; the reference is to the Burgundian Gunnar and Hogni.

4. *Hamther*: some editions spell the name "Hamthir." *Sigurth*, etc.: cf. *Sigurtharkvitha en skamma*, 21-24, and *Brot*, concluding prose. This stanza has been subjected to many conjectural re-arrangements, [fp. 539] some editors adding two or three lines from the *Hamthesmol*.]

[5. *Bloody*: a guess; a word in the original is clearly missing, and the same is true of all in line 3. *Thy sons*: i.e., by killing her sons Erp and Eitil (cf. Atlamol, 72-74)

Guthrun deprived Hamther, Sorli, and the second Erp of valuable allies in avenging Svanhild's death.

6. The manuscript indicates no gap, but most editors assume the loss of one, two or even more lines before the two here given.

7. The manuscript indicates line 4 as beginning a new stanza.

8. Line 1, identical with line 1 of stanza 4, may be interpolated [fp. 541] here. *Spear-god*: warrior, i.e., Hamther himself. With this stanza the introductory *hvot* ("inciting") ends, and stanza 9 introduces the lament which forms the real body of the poem.]

[11. Line 1 in the original is of uncertain meaning. Many editors assume the loss of a line after line 1, and some completely reconstruct line 1 on the basis of a hypothetical second line. *Princes*: Gunnar and Hogni.

12. Some editors assume the loss of one line, or more, before line 1. *Hniflungs*: Erp and Eitil, the sons of Guthrun and Atli. On the application of the name Niflung (or, as later spelt, [fp. 542] Hniflung) to the descendants of Gjuki, Guthrun's father, cf. *Brot*, 17, note.]

[13. *Norns*: the fates; cf. *Voluspo*, 8 and note.

14. The manuscript omits the first half of line 4.

16. Some editors assume a gap of two lines after line 2, and make a separate stanza of lines 3-5; Gering adds a sixth line of his own coining, while Grundtvig inserts one between lines 3 and 4. The manuscript indicates line 5 as beginning a new stanza.

17. The manuscript does not indicate line I as beginning a stanza (cf. note on stanza 16). Stanzas 17 and 18 are very likely [fp. 543] later interpolations, although the compilers of the *Volsungasaga* knew them as they stand here. The whole passage depends on the shades of difference in the meanings of the various superlatives: *harþastr*, "hardest"; *sárastr*, "sorest"; *grimmastr*, "grimmest," and *hvassastr*, "keenest." *Snakes*: cf. *Drap Niflunga*.]

[18. *The king*: Hogni; cf. *Atlakvitha*, 25. The manuscript marks line 3 as beginning a new stanza. Most editors agree that there is a more or less extensive gap after stanza 19, and some of them contend that the original ending of the poem is lost, stanzas 19-21 coming from a different poem, probably a lament closely following Sigurth's death.

19. The manuscript does not indicate line 1 as beginning a stanza, and it immediately follows the fragmentary line 3 of stanza 18. The resemblance between stanzas 19-21 and stanzas 64-69 of *Sigurtharkvitha en skamma* suggests that, in some other wise lost version of the story, Guthrun, like Brynhild, sought to die soon after Sigurth's death. *Thy steed*: Guthrun's appeal to the dead Sigurth to ride back to earth to meet her is reminiscent of the episode related in *Helgakvitha Hundingsbana II*, 39-48 The promise mentioned in stanza 20 is spoken of elsewhere only in the *Volsungasaga* paraphrase of this passage.]

[21. Perhaps something has been lost between stanzas 20 and 21, or possibly stanza 21, while belonging originally to the same poem as stanzas 19 and 20, did not directly follow them. *Sore-pressed*: a guess; a word seems to have been omitted in the original.

22. Words of the poet's, like stanza 1, and perhaps constituting a later addition. Many editors assume the loss of a line after line 3. The meaning, of course, is that the poet hopes the story of Guthrun's woes will make all other troubles seem light by comparison.]

HAMTHESMOL

The Ballad of Hamther

INTRODUCTORY NOTE

The Hamthesmol, the concluding poem in the *Codex Regius*, is on the whole the worst preserved of all the poems in the collection. The origin of the story, the relation of the *Hamthesmol* to the *Guthrunarhvot*, and of both poems to the hypothetical "old" *Hamthesmol*, are outlined in the introductory note to the *Guthrunarhvot*. The *Hamthesmol* as we have it is certainly not the "old" poem of that name; indeed it is so pronounced a patch work that it can hardly be regarded as a coherent poem at all. Some of the stanzas are in Fornyrthislag, some are in Malahattr, one (stanza 29) appears to be in Ljothahattr, and in many cases the words can be adapted to any known metrical form only by liberal emendation. That any one should have deliberately com posed such a poem seems quite incredible, and it is far more likely that some eleventh century narrator constructed a poem about the death of Hamther and Sorli by piecing together various fragments, and possibly adding a number of Malahattr stanzas of his own.

It has been argued, and with apparently sound logic, that our extant *Hamthesmol* originated in Greenland, along with the *Atlamol*. In any case, it can hardly have been put together before the latter part of the eleventh century, although the "old" *Humthesmol* undoubtedly long antedates this period. Many editors have attempted to pick out the parts of the extant poem which were borrowed from this older lay, but the condition of the text is such that it is by no means clear even what stanzas are in Fornyrthislag and what in Malahattr. Many editors, likewise, indicate gaps and omissions, but it seems doubtful whether the extant *Hamthesmol* ever had a really consecutive quality, its component fragments having apparently been strung together with little regard for continuity. The notes indicate some of the more important editorial suggestions, but make no attempt to cover all of them, and the metrical form of the translation is often based on mere guesswork as to the character of the original lines and stanzas. Despite the chaotic state of the text, however, the underlying narrative is reasonably clear, and the story can be followed with no great difficulty.

---

1. Great the evils | once that grew,
With the dawning sad | of the sorrow of elves;
In early mom | awake for men
The evils that grief | to each shall bring.

2. Not now, nor yet | of yesterday was it,
Long the time | that since hath lapsed,
So that little there is | that is half as old,
Since Guthrun, daughter | of Gjuki, whetted
Her sons so young | to Svanhild's vengeance.

3. "The sister ye had | was Svanhild called,
And her did Jormunrek | trample with horses,
White and black | on the battle-way,
Gray, road-wonted, | the steeds of the Goths.

4. "Little the kings | of the folk are ye like,
For now ye are living | alone of my race.

5. "Lonely am I | as the forest aspen,
Of kindred bare | as the fir of its boughs,
My joys are all lost | as the leaves of the tree
When the scather of twigs | from the warm day turns."

6. Then Hamther spake forth, | the high of heart:
"Small praise didst thou, Guthrun, | to Hogni's deed give
When they wakened thy Sigurth | from out of his sleep,
Thou didst sit on the bed | while his slayers laughed.

7. "Thy bed-covers white | with blood were red
From his wounds, and with gore | of thy husband were wet;
So Sigurth was slain, | by his corpse didst thou sit,
And of gladness didst think not: | 'twas Gunnar's doing.

8. "Thou wouldst strike at Atli | by the slaying of Erp
And the killing of Eitil; | thine own grief was worse;
So should each one wield | the wound-biting sword
That another it slays | but smites not himself."

9. Then did Sorli speak out, | for wise was he ever:
"With my mother I never | a quarrel will make;
Full little in speaking | methinks ye both lack;
What askest thou, Guthrun, | that will give thee no tears?

10. "For thy brothers dost weep, | and thy boys so sweet,
Thy kinsmen in birth | on the battlefield slain;
Now, Guthrun, as; well | for us both shalt thou weep,
We sit doomed on our steeds, | and far hence shall we die."

11. Then the fame-glad one-- | on the steps she was--
The slender-fingered, | spake with her son:
"Ye shall danger have | if counsel ye heed not;
By two heroes alone | shall two hundred of Goths
Be bound or be slain | in the lofty-walled burg."

12. From the courtyard they fared, | and fury they breathed;
The youths swiftly went | o'er the mountain wet,
On their Hunnish steeds, | death's vengeance to have.

13. On the way they found | the man so wise;

. . . .

"What help from the weakling | brown may we have?"

14. So answered them | their half-brother then:
"So well may I | my kinsmen aid
As help one foot | from the other has."

15. "How may afoot | its fellow aid,
Or a flesh-grown hand | another help?"

16. Then Erp spake forth, | his words were few,
As haughty he sat | on his horse's back:
"To the timid 'tis ill | the way to tell."
A bastard they | the bold one called.

17. From their sheaths they drew | their shining swords,
Their blades, to the giantess | joy to give;
By a third they lessened | the might that was theirs,
The fighter young | to earth they felled.

18. Their cloaks they shook, | their swords they sheathed,
The high-born men | wrapped their mantles close.

19. On their road they fared | and an ill way found,
And their sister's son | on a tree they saw,
On the wind-cold wolf-tree | west of the hall,
And cranes'-bait crawled; | none would care to linger.

20. In the hall was din, | the men drank deep,
And the horses' hoofs | could no one hear,
Till the warrior hardy | sounded his horn.

21. Men came and the tale | to Jormunrek told
How warriors helmed | without they beheld:

489

"Take counsel wise, | for brave ones are come,
Of mighty men | thou the sister didst murder."

22. Then Jormunrek laughed, | his hand laid on his beard,
His arms, for with wine | he was warlike, he called for;
He shook his brown locks, | on his white shield he looked,
And raised high the cup | of gold in his hand.

23. "Happy, methinks, | were I to behold
Hamther and Sorli | here in my hall;
The men would I bind | with strings of bows,
And Gjuki's heirs | on the gallows hang."

24. In the hall was clamor, | the cups were shattered,
Men stood in blood | from the breasts of the Goths,

25. Then did Hamther speak forth, | the haughty of heart:
"Thou soughtest, Jormunrek, | us to see,
Sons of one mother | seeking thy dwelling;
Thou seest thy hands, | thy feet thou beholdest,
Jormunrek, flung | in the fire so hot."

26. Then roared the king, | of the race of the gods,
Bold in his armor, | as roars a bear:
"Stone ye the men | that steel will bite not,
Sword nor spear, | the sons of Jonak."

Sorli spake:
27. "Ill didst win, brother, | when the bag thou didst open,
Oft from that bag | came baleful counsel;
Heart hast thou, Hamther, | if knowledge thou hadst!
A man without wisdom | is lacking in much "

Hamther spake:
28. "His head were now off | if Erp were living,
The brother so keen | whom we killed on our road,

The warrior noble,-- | 'twas the Norns that drove me
The hero to slay | who in fight should be holy.

29. "In fashion of wolves | it befits us not
Amongst ourselves to strive,
Like the hounds of the Norns, | that nourished were
In greed mid wastes so grim.

30. "We have greatly fought, | o'er the Goths do we stand
By our blades laid low, | like eagles on branches;
Great our fame though we die | today or tomorrow;
None outlives the night | when the Norris have spoken."

31. Then Sorli beside | the gable sank,
And Hamther fell | at the back of the house.

This is called the old ballad of Hamther.

[1. This stanza looks like a later interpolation from a totally unrelated
source. *Sorrow of elves*: the sun; cf. *Alvissmol*, 16 and note.

2. Some editors regard lines 1-2 as interpolated, while others question line
3. *Guthrun*, etc.: regarding the marriage of Jonak and Guthrun (daughter of Gjuki,
sister of Gunnar and Hogni, and widow first of Sigurth and then of Atli), and the
sons of this marriage, Hamther and Sorli (but not Erp), cf. *Guthrunarhvot*,
introductory prose and note.

3. *Svanhild* and *Jormunrek*: regarding the manner in which Jormunrek
(Ermanarich) married Svanhild, daughter of Sigurth and Guthrun, and afterwards
had her trodden to death by horses, cf. *Guthrunarhvot*, introductory note. Lines 3-
4 are identical with lines 5-6 of *Guthrunarhvot*, 2.

4. These two lines may be all that is left of a four-line stanza. [fp. 567] The
manuscript and many editions combine them with stanza 5, while a few place
them after stanza 5 as a separate stanza, reversing the order of the two lines. *Kings
of the folk*: Guthrun's brothers, Gunnar and Hogni, slain by Atli.]

[5. Cf. note on stanza 4; the manuscript does not indicate line i as beginning a
stanza. *Scather of twigs*: poetic circumlocution for the wind (cf.*Skaldskaparmal*,

chapter 27), though some editors think the phrase here means the sun. Some editors assume a more or less extensive gap between stanzas 5 and 6.

6. Lines 1-3 are nearly identical with lines 1-3 of *Guthrunarhvot*, 4. On the death of *Sigurth* cf. *Sigurtharkvitha en skamma*, 21-24, and *Brot*, concluding prose. The word thy in line 3 is omitted in the original.

7. Lines 1-2 are nearly identical with lines 4-5 of *Guthrunarhvot*, 4. The manuscript, followed by many editions, indicates line 3 and not line 1 as beginning a stanza.]

[8. Some editors regard this stanza as interpolated. *Erp* and *Eitil*: regarding Guthrun's slaying of her sons by Atli, cf. *Atlamol*, 72-75. The Erp here referred to is not to be confused with the Erp, son of Jonak, who appears in stanza 13. The whole of stanza 8 is in doubtful shape, and many emendations have been suggested.

10. Some editors assign this speech to Hamther. *Brothers*: Gunnar and Hogni. *Boys*: Erp and Eitil.]

[11. In the manuscript this stanza follows stanza 21, and some editors take the word here rendered "fame-glad one" (hróþrgoþ) to be a proper name (Jormunrek's mother or his concubine). The *Volsungasaga*, however, indicates that Guthrun at this point "had so fashioned their war-gear that iron would not bite into it, and she bade them to have nought to do with stones or other heavy things, and told them that it would be ill for them if they did not do as she said." The substance of this counsel may well have been conveyed in a passage lost after line 3, though the manuscript indicates no gap. It is by being stoned that Hamther and Sorli are killed (stanza 26). On the other hand, the second part of line 3 may possibly mean "if silent ye are not," in which case the advice relates to Hamther's speech to Jormunrek and Sorli's reproach to him thereupon (stanzas 25 and 27). *Steps*: the word in the original is doubtful. Line 3 is thoroughly obscure. Some editors make a separate stanza of lines 3-5, while others question line 5.

12. Many editors assume the loss of a line after line 1. In several editions lines 2-3 are placed after line 2 of stanza 18. *Hunnish*: the word meant little more than "German"; cf. *Guthrunarhvot*, 3 and note.]

[13. In the manuscript these two lines follow stanza 16; some editors insert them in place of lines 2-3 of stanza 11. The manuscript indicates no gap. *The man so wise*: Erp, here represented as a son of Jonak but not of Guthrun, and hence a half-brother of Hamther and Sorli. There is nothing further to indicate whether or not

492

he was born out of wedlock, as intimated in stanza 16. Some editors assign line 3 to Hamther, and some to Sorli.

14. The stanza is obviously defective. Many editors add Erp's name in line 1, and insert between lines 2 and 1 a line based on stanza 15 and the *Volsungasaga* paraphrase: "As a flesh grown hand | another helps." In the *Volsungasaga*, after Erp's death, Hamther stumbles and saves himself from falling with his hand, whereupon he says: "Erp spake truly; I had fallen had I not braced myself with my hand." Soon thereafter Sorli has a like experience, one foot slipping but the other saving him from a fall. "Then they said that they had done ill to Erp, their brother."

15. Many editions attach these two lines to stanza 14, while a few assume the loss of two lines.

16. In the manuscript this stanza stands between stanzas 12 and 13. Some editors make line 4 a part of Erp's speech.]

[17. The manuscript does not indicate line 1 as beginning a stanza. *The giantess*: presumably the reference is to Hel, goddess of the dead, but the phrase is doubtful.

18. In the manuscript these two lines are followed by stanza 19 with no indication of a break. Some editions insert here lines 2-3 of stanza 12, while others assume the loss of two or more lines.

19. Cf. note on stanza 18. *Ill way*: very likely the road leading through the gate of Jormunrek's town at which Svanhild was trampled to death. *Sister's son*: many editors change the text to read "stepson," for the reference is certainly to Randver, son of Jormunrek, hanged by his father on Bikki's advice (cf. *Guthrunarhvot*, introductory note). *Wolf-tree*: the gallows, the wolf being symbolical of outlaws. *Cranes'-bait*: presumably either snakes or worms, but the passage is doubtful.]

[20. Many editors assume the loss of a line after line 3. *The warrior*: presumably a warder or watchman, but the reference may be to Hamther himself.

21. The word here rendered men (line 1) is missing in the original, involving a metrical error, and various words have been suggested.

22. Line 2 in the original is thoroughly obscure; some editors directly reverse the meaning here indicated by giving the line a negative force, while others

completely alter the phrase rendered "his arms he called for" into one meaning "he stroked his cheeks."

23. *Gjuki's heirs*: the original has "the well-born of Gjuki," and some editors have changed the proper name to Guthrun, but the phrase apparently refers to Hamther and Sorli as Gjuki's grandsons. In the manuscript this stanza is followed by stanza 11, [fp. 553] and such editors as have retained this arrangement have had to resort to varied and complex explanations to account for it.]

[24. Editors have made various efforts to reconstruct a four line stanza out of these two lines, in some cases with the help of lines borrowed from the puzzling stanza 11 (cf. note on stanza 23). Line 2 in the original is doubtful.

25, Some editors mark line 1 as an interpolation. The manuscript marks line 4 as beginning a new stanza. As in the story told by Jordanes, Hamther and Sorli succeed in wounding Jormunrek (here they cut off his hands and feet), but do not kill him. 26. The manuscript marks line 3, and not line I, as beginning a stanza. *Of the race of the gods*: the reference here is apparently to Jormunrek, but in the *Volsungasaga* the advice to kill Hamther and Sorli with stones, since iron will not wound them (cf. note on stanza 11), Comes from Othin, who enters the hall as an old man with one eye.]

[27. in the manuscript this stanza is introduced by the same line as stanza 25: "Then did Hamther speak forth, the haughty of heart," but the speaker in this case must be Sorli and not Hamther. Some editors, however, give lines 1-2 to Hamther and lines 3-4 to Sorli. *Bag*: i.e., Hamther's mouth; cf. note on stanza 11. The manuscript indicates line 3 as beginning a new stanza.

28. Most editors regard stanzas 28-30 as a speech by Hamther, but the manuscript does not indicate the speaker, and some editors assign one or two of the stanzas to Sorli. Lines 1-2 are quoted in the *Volsungasaga*. The manuscript does not indicate line I as beginning a stanza. *Erp*: Hamther means that while the two brothers had succeeded only in wounding Jormunrek, Erp, if he had been with them, would have killed him. Lines 3-4 may be a later interpolation. *Norns*: the fates; the word used in the original means the goddesses of ill fortune.]

[29. This is almost certainly an interpolated Ijothahattr stanza, though some editors have tried to expand it into the Fornyrthislag form. *Hounds of the Norns*: wolves.

30, Some editors assume a gap after this stanza.

31. Apparently a fragment of a stanza from the "old" *Hamthesmol* to which the annotator's concluding prose note refers. Some editors assume the loss of two lines after line 2.

Prose. Regarding the "old" *Hamthesmol*, cf. *Guthrunarhvot*, introductory note.]

PRONOUNCING INDEX OF PROPER NAMES

Introductory Note

The pronunciations indicated in the following index are in many cases, at best, mere approximations, and in some cases the pronunciation of the Old Norse is itself more or less conjectural. For the sake of clarity it has seemed advisable to keep the number of phonetic symbols as small as possible, even though the result is occasional failure to distinguish between closely related sounds. In every in stance the object has been to provide the reader with a clearly comprehensible and approximately correct pronunciation, for which reason, particularly in such matters as division of syllables, etymology has frequently been disregarded for the sake of phonetic clearness. For example, when a root syllable ends in a long (double) consonant, the division has arbitrarily been made so as to indicate the sounding of both elements (e. g., Am-ma, not Amm-a).

As many proper names occur in the notes but not in the text, and as frequently the more important incidents connected with the names are outlined in notes which would not be indicated by textual references alone, the page numbers include all appearances of proper names in the notes as well as in the text.

The following general rules govern the application of the phonetic symbols used in the index, and also indicate the approximate pronunciation of the unmarked vowels and consonants.

VOWELS. The vowels are pronounced approximately as follows:

a -- as in "alone"   o -- as in "on"
â -- as in "father"   ô -- as in "old"

e -- as in "men"

ê -- as *a* in "fate"

i -- as in "is"

î -- as in "machine"

û -- as *ou* in "wound"

y -- as *i* in "is" *

ÿ -- as *ee* in "free" *

æ -- as *e* in "men"

<u>æ</u> -- as *a* in "fate"

ö -- as in German "öffnen"

ö -- as in German "schön"

<u>ö</u> -- as *aw* in "law"

u -- as *ou* in "would"

ei -- as *ey* in "they"

ey -- as in "they"

au -- as *ou* in "out"

ai -- as *i* in "fine"

[* Both with a slight sound of German ü.]

No attempt has been made to differentiate between the short open "o" and the short closed "o," which for speakers of English closely resemble one another.

CONSONANTS. The consonants are pronounced approximately as in English, with the following special points to be noted:

G is always hard, as in "get," never soft, as in "gem;" following "n" it has the same sound as in "sing."

J is pronounced as y in "young."

Th following a vowel is soft, as in "with;" at the beginning of a word or following a consonant it is hard, as in "thin."

The long (doubled) consonants should be pronounced as in Italian, both elements being distinctly sounded; e. g., "Am-ma."

S is always hard, as in "so," "this," never soft, as in "as."

H enters into combinations with various following consonants; with "v" the sound is approximately that of *wh* in "what"; with "l" "r" and "n" it produces sounds which have no exact English equivalents, but which can be approximated by pronouncing the consonants with a marked initial breathing.

ACCENTS. The accented syllable in each name is indicated by the acute accent ('). In many names, however, and particularly in compounds, there is both a primary and a secondary, accent, and where this is the case the primary, stress is indicated by a double acute accent (") and the secondary one by a single acute accent ('). To avoid possible confusion with the long vowel marks used in Old Norse texts, the accents are placed, not over the vowels, but after the accented syllables.

PRONOUNCING INDEX

Æg'-ir, *the sea-god.*
Æk'-in, *a rive.*
Af'-i, *Grandfather.*
Ag'-nar, *a warrior.*
Ag'-nar, *brother of Geirröth.*
Ag'-nar, *son of Geirröth.*
Âi, *a dwarf.*
Âi, *Great-Grandfather.*
Alf, *a dwarf.*
Alf, *husband of Hjordis.*
Alf, *slayer of Helgi.*
Alf, *son of Dag.*
Alf, *son of Hring.*
Alf, *son of Hunding.*
Alf, *son of Ulf.*
Alf'-heim, *home of the elves.*
Alf'-hild, *wife of Hjorvarth.*
Alf'-roth-ul, *the sun.*
Al'-grön, *an island.*
Âl'-i, *a warrior.*
Alm'-veig, *wife of Halfdan.*
Â'-lof, *daughter of Franmar.*
Al'-svith, *a giant.*
Al'-svith, *a horse.*
Al'-thjöf, *a dwarf.*
Al'-vald-i, *a giant.*
Al'-vis, *a dwarf.*
Al"-vîss-möl.
Âm, *son of Dag.*
Am'-bött, *daughter of Thræll.*
Am'-ma, *Grandmother.*
Ân, *a dwarf.*
And'-hrim-nir, *a cook.*
And"-var-a-naut', *a ring.*
And'-var-i, *a dwarf.*
An'-gan-tӯr, *a berserker.*
An'-gan-tӯr, *a warrior.*

Ang'-eyj-a, *mother of Heimdall.*
Angr'-both-a, *a giantess.*
Arf'-i, *son of Jarl.*
Ar"-in-nef'-ja, *daughter of Thrœll.*
Arn'-grîm, *father of the berserkers.*
Âr'-vak, *a horse.*
As"-a-thôr', *Thor,.*
As'-garth, *home of the gods.*
Ask, *Ash.*
Âs'-laug, *daughter of Brynhild.*
Âs'-mund, *a giant* (?).
Ath'-al, *son of Jarl.*
At'-la, *mother of Heimdall.*
At"-la-kvith'-a, *the Lay of Atli.*
At"-la-môl', *the Ballad of Atli.*
At'-li, *Attila.*
At'-li, *son of Hring.*
At'-li, *son of Ithmund.*
At'-rîth, *Othin.*
Aur'-both-a, *a giantess.*
Aur'-both-a, *Mengloth's handmaid.*
Aur'-gelm-ir, *Ymir.*
Aur'-vang, *a dwarf.*
Austr'-i, *a dwarf.*
Auth, *mother of Harald Battle-Tooth.*
Auth'-a, *sister of Agnar.*
Auth'-i, *son of Halfdan the Old.*

Baldr, *a god* .
Baldrs Draurnar, *Baldr's Dreams.*
Bâl'-eyg, *Othin.*
Bar'-i, *a dwarf.*
Barn, *son of Jarl.*
Bar'-ri, *a berserker.*
Bar'-ri, *a forest,* ixg.
Beit'-i, *Atli's steward.*
Bekk'-hild, *sister of Brynhild.*
Bel'-i, *a giant.*
Ber'-a, *Kostbera.*

Ber'-gel-mir, *a giant.*
Best'-la, *Othin's mother.*
Beyl'-a, *servant of Freyr.*
Bif'-lind-i, *Othin.*
Bif'-rost, *the rainbow bridge .*
Bî'-fur, *a dwarf.*
Bik'-ki, *follower of Jormunrek .*
Bîl'-eyg, *Othin.*
Bil'-ling, *a giant (?).*
Bil'-rost, *the rainbow bridge.*
Bil'-skirn-ir, *Thor's dwelling.*
Bjort, *Mengloth's handmaid.*
Blâin, *Ymir (?).*
Bleik, *Mengloth's handmaid.*
Blind, *follower of Hunding.*
Blîth, *Mengloth's handmaid.*
Bod'-di, *son of Karl.*
Bộ'-fur, *a dwarf.*
Bolm, *an island.*
Bol'-thorn, *Othin's grandfather.*
Bol'-verk, *Othin.*
Bom'-bur, *a dwarf.*
Bond'-i, *son of Karl.*
Borg'-ar, *brother of Borghild (?).*
Borg'-hild, *mother of Helgi.*
Borg'-nÿ, *daughter of Heithrek, .*
Both'-vild, *daughter of Nithuth.*
Brag'-a-lund, *a forest.*
Brag'-i, *a god .*
Brag'-i, *brother of Sigrun.*
Brag'-i Bod'-da-son, *a skald.*
Brâ'-lund, *birthplace of Helgi.*
Brâm'-i, *a berserker.*
Brand'-ey, *an island.*
Bratt'-skegg, *son of Karl.*
Brâ'-voll, *a field.*
Breith, *son of Karl.*
Breith'-a-blik, *Baldr's home.*
Brim'-ir, *a giant.*

Brim'-ir, *a sword.*
Bris'-ings, *the dwarfs* .
Brodd, *follower of Hrolf.*
Brot af Sig"-urth-ar-kvith'-u, *Fragment of a Sigurth Lay* .
Brun"-a-vâg'-ar, *a harbor.*
Brûth, *daughter of Karl.*
Bryn'-hild, *wife of Gunnar.*
Bû'-i, *a berserker.*
Bû'-i, *son of Karl.*
Bund"-in-skeg'-gi, *son of Karl.*
Bur, *father of Othin.*
Bur, *son of Jarl.*
Buth'-Ii, *father of Atli.*
Buth'-lungs, *descendants of Buthli.*
Bygg'-vir, *Freyr's servant* .
Bӱ'-leist (or Bӱ'-leipt), *brother of Loki.*

Dag, *a god (Day)*
Dag, *brother of Sigrun* .
Dag, *husband of Thora.*
Dâin, *a dwarf.*
Dâin, *a hart.*
Dâin, *an elf.*
Dan, *a king.*
Dan'-a, *daughter of Danp.*
Danp, *a king.*
Del'-ling, *father of Day.*
Digr'-ald-i, *son of Thrœll.*
Dog'-ling, *Delling.*
Dög'-lings, *descendants of Dag.*
Dolg'-thras-ir, *a dwarf.*
Dôr'-i, *a dwarf.*
Drâp Nifl'-ung-a, *the Slaying of the Niflungs.*
Draup'-nir, *a dwarf.*
Draup'-nir, *a ring.*
Dreng, *son of Karl.*
Drott, *son of Thrœll.*
Drumb, *son of Thrœll.*
Drumb'-a, *daughter of Thrœll.*

Dûf, *a dwarf.*
Dun'-eyr, *a hart.*
Dur'-in, *a dwarf.*
Dval'-in, *a dwarf .*
Dval'-in, *a hart.*
Dyr'-a-thrôr, *a hart.*

Ed'-da, *Great-Grandmother.*
Egg'-thêr, *the giants' watchman.*
Eg'-il, *brother of Völund, .*
Eg'-il, *father of Thjalfi (?).*
Eg"-ils-sag'-a, *the Saga of Egil.*
Eik"-in-skjald'-i, *a dwarf.*
Eik"-in-tjas'-na, *daughter of Thrœll.*
Eik'-thyrn-ir, *a hart.*
Eir, *Mengloth's handmaid.*
Eist'-la, *mother of Heimdall.*
Eit'-il, *son of Atli.*
Eld'-hrim-nir, *a kettle.*
Eld'-ir, *Ægir's servant.*
El"-i-vâg'-ar, *the Milky Way (?).*
Emb'-la, *Elm.*
Ern'-a, *Wife of Jarl.*
Erp, *son of Atli.*
Erp, *son of Jonak.*
Ey'-fur-a, *mother of the berserkers.*
Eyj'-olf, *son of Hunding.*
Ey'-lim-i, *father of Hjordis.*
Ey'-lim-i, *father of Svava .*
Ey'-môth, *Atli's emissary.*
Ey'-mund, *king of Holmgarth.*
Eyr'-gjaf-a, *mother of Heimdall.*

Fâf'-nir, *brother of Regin.*
Fâf"-nis-môl', *the Ballad of Fafnir.*
Fal'-hôfn-ir, *a horse.*
Far'-baut-i, *father of Loki.*
Farm'-a-tÿr, *Othin.*
Fath'-ir, *Father.*

Feim'-a, *daughter of Karl.*
Feng, *Othin.*
Fen'-ja, *a giantess.*
Fenr'-ir, *a wolf,* - .
Fen'-sal-ir, *Frigg's hall.*
Fil'-i, *a dwarf.*
Fim'-a-feng, *Ægir's servant.*
Fim'-bul-thul, *a river.*
Fith, *a dwarf.*
Fit'-jung, *Earth.*
Fjal'-ar, *a cock.*
Fjal'-ar, *a dwarf.*
Fjal'-ar, *Suttung (?).*
Fjal'-ar, *Utgartha-Loki.*
Fjol'-kald, *Svifdag's grandfather.*
Fjol'-nir, *Othin.*
Fjol"-svinns-môl' *the Ballad of Fjolsvith* .
Fjol'-svith, *Mengloth's watchman* .
Fjol'-svith, *Othin.*
Fjol'-var, *a giant (?).*
Fjôn, *an island.*
Fjorg'-yn, *Jorth.*
Fjorg'-yn, *Othin.*
Fjorm, *a river.*
Fjorn'-ir, *Gunnar's cupbearer.*
Fjors'-ungs, *the fishes (?).*
Fjôsn'-ir, *son of Thrœll.*
Fjot'-ur-lund, *a forest.*
Fljôth, *daughter of Karl.*
Folk'-vang, *Freyja's home.*
For'-set-i, *a god.*
Fôst"-brœth-ra-sag'-a, *the Saga of the Foster-Brothers.*
Frâ Dauth'-a Sinf'-jotl-a, *Of Sinfjotli's Death.*
Frægg, *a dwarf.*
Frân'-ang, *a waterfall.*
Frân'-mar, *Sigrlin's foster father.*
Frâr, *a dwarf.*
Frath'-mar, *son of Dag.*
Frek'-a-stein, *a battlefield* .

Frek'-i, *a Wolf*.
Frek'-i, *son of Dag*.
Frey'-ja, *a goddess*.
Freyr, *a god*.
Fri'-aut, *daughter of Hildigun*.
Frigg, *a goddess*.
Frith, *Mengloth's handmaid*.
Frost'-i, *a dwarf*.
Frôth'-i, *a Danish king*.
Frôth'-i, *father of Hledis*.
Frôth'-i, *father of Kari (?)*.
Ful'-la, *Frigg's handmaid*.
Ful'-nir, *son of Thrall*.
Fund'-in, *a dwarf*.

Gagn'-râth, *Othin*.
Gand'-alf, *a dwarf*.
Gang, *brother of Thjazi*.
Gang'-ler-i, *King Gylfi*.
Gang'-ler-i, *Othin*.
Garm, *a hound* .
Gast'-ropn-ir, *Mengloth's dwelling*.
Gaut, *Othin*.
Gef'-jun, *a goddess*.
Geir'-mund, *kinsman of Atli*.
Geir'-on-ul, *a Valkyrie*.
Geir'-röth, *a king*.
Geir'-skog-ul, *a Valkyrie*.
Geir'-vim-ul, *a river*.
Geit'-ir, *Gripir's servant*.
Ger'-i, *a hound*.
Ger'-i, *a wolf*.
Gerth, *daughter of Gymir*.
Gîf, *a hound*.
Gim'-lê, *a mountain*.
Gin'-nar, *a dwarf*.
Gin"-nung-a-gap', *Yawning Gap*.
Gip'-ul, *a river*.
Gîsl, *a horse*.

Gjaf'-laug, *Gjuki's sister.*
Gjal"-lar-horn', *Heimdall's horn.*
Gjol, *a river.*
Gjolp, *mother of Heimdall.*
Gjûk'-i, *father of Gunnar.*
Gjûk'-i, *son of Hogni.*
Gjûk'-ungs, *Gjuki's sons.*
Glap'-svith, *Othin.*
Glas'-ir, *a forest.*
Glath, *a horse.*
Glaths'-heim, *Othin's dwelling.*
Glaum, *Atli's horse.*
Glaum'-vor, *wife of Gunnar.*
Gleip'-nir, *a chain.*
Gler, *a horse.*
Glit'-nîr, *Forseti's dwelling.*
Glô'-in, *a dwarf.*
Gnip"-a-hel'-lir, *a cave.*
Gnip'-a-lund, *a forest.*
Gnit'-a-heith, *Fafnir's mountain.*
Gô'-in, *a serpent.*
Gol, *a Valkyrie.*
Gol"-lin-kamb'-i, *a cock.*
Goll'-nir, *a giant (?).*
Goll'-rond, *daughter of Gjuki.*
Goll'-topp, *a horse.*
Goll'-veig, *a Wane.*
Gom'-ul, *a river.*
Gond'-lir, *Othin,*
Gond'-ul, *a Valkyrie.*
Gop'-ul, *a river.*
Gorm (the Old), *King of Denmark.*
Goth'-mund, *son of Granmar.*
Got'-thorm, *slayer of Sigurth.*
Grâ'-bak, *a serpent.*
Graf'-vit-nir, *a serpent.*
Graf'-vol-luth, *a serpent.*
Gram, *Sigurth's sword.*
Gran'-i, *Sigurth's horse.*

Gran'-mar, *father of Hothbrodd.*
Greip, *mother of Heimdall.*
Gret'-tir, *a hero.*
Gret"-tis-sag'-a, *the Saga of Grettir.*
Grîm, *follower of Hrolf.*
Grîm, *Othin.*
Grîm'-hild, *wife of Gjuki.*
Grîm'-nir, *Othin.*
Grim"-nis-môl, *the Ballad of Grimnir.*
Grip'-ir, *Sigurth's uncle .*
Grip"-is-spô', *Gripir's Prophecy.*
Grô'-a, *mother of Svipdag.*
Grôth, *a river.*
Grot"-ta-songr', *the Song of Grotti.*
Grot'-ti, *a mill.*
Grô"-u-galdr', *Groa's Spel.*
Gull'-fax-i, *a horse.*
Gull"-in-tan'-ni, *Heimdall.*
Gung'-nir, *a spear.*
Gun'-nar, *brother of Borghild (?).*
Gun'-nar, *follower of Hrolf.*
Gun'-nar, *son of Gjuki.*
Gunn'-loth, *daughter of Suttung.*
Gunn'-thor-in, *a river.*
Gunn'-thrô, *a river.*
Gust, *Andvari (?).*
Guth, *a Valkyrie.*
Guth'-rûn, *wife of Sigurth.*
Guth"-rûn-ar-hvot', *Guthrun's Inciting.*
Guth"-rûn-ar-kvith'-a I (en-Fyrst'-a), *the First Lay of Guthrun.*
Guth"-rûn-ar-kvith'-a II (On'-nur, en Forn'-a), *the Second (Old) Lay of Guthrun.*
Guth"-rûn-ar-kvith'-a III (Thrith'-ja), *the Third Lay of Guthrun.*
Gylf"-a-gin'-ning, *the Deceiving of Gylfi.*
Gyl'-lir, *a horse.*
Gym'-ir, *Ægir.*
Gym'-ir, *a giant .*
Gyrth, *son of Dag.*

Had'-ding, *a Danish king*.
Had"-ding-ja-skat'-i, *Haddings'-Hero (Helgi)*.
Had'-dings, *berserkers*.
Hæm'-ing, *son of Hunding*.
Hag'-al, *Helgi's foster-father*.
Hak'-i, *son of Hvethna*.
Hal, *son of Karl*.
Hâlf, *King of Horthaland*.
Half'-dan, *father of Kara*.
Half'-dan (the Old), *a Danish king*.
Hâlfs'-sag-a, *the Saga of Half*.
Ham'-al, *son of Hagal*.
Ham'-thêr, *son of Jonak* .
Ham"-thês-môl', *the Ballad of Hamther*.
Ha'-mund, *son of Sigmund*.
Han'-nar, *a dwarf*.
Hâr, *Othin*.
Har'-ald (Battle-Tooth), *son of Hrörek*.
Har'-ald (Blue-Tooth), *King of Denmark*.
Hâr'-barth, *Othin*.
Hâr"-barths-ljôth', *the Poem of Harbarth*.
Hat'-a-fjord, *a fjord*.
Hat'-i, *a giant*.
Hat'-i, *a wolf*.
Haug'-spor-i, *a dwarf*.
Heer'-fath-er, *Othin* .
Heim'-dall, *a god*.
Heim'-ir, *Brynhild's foster-father*.
Heith, *daughter of Hrimnir*.
Heith, *Gollweg (?)*
Heith'-draup-nir, *Mimir (?)*.
Heith'-rek, *father of Borgny*.
Heith'-rûn, *a goat*.
Hel, *goddess of the dead*.
Hel'-blind-i, *Othin*.
Helg"-a-kvith'-a Hjor"-varths-son'-ar, *the Lay of Helgi the Son of Hjorvarth*.
Helg"-a-kvith'-a Hund"-ings ban'-a I (en Fyr'-ri), *the First Lay of Helgi Hundingsbane*.

Helg"-a-kvith'-a Hund"-ings ban'-a II (On'-nur), *the Second Lay of Helgi Hundingsbane.*
Helg'-i (Had"-ding-ja-skat'-i), *Helgi the Haddings-Hero.*
Helg'-i, *Hialmgunnar (?).*
Helg'-i, *son of Hjorvarth, .*
Helg'-i, *son of Sigmund .*
Hel'-reith Bryn'-hild-ar, *Brynhild's Hell-Ride.*
Hept"-i-fil'-i, *a dwarf.*
Her'-borg, *queen of the Huns.*
Her'-fjot-ur, *a Valkyrie.*
Her'-jan, *Othin.*
Herk'-ja, *Atli's servant.*
Her'-môth, *son of Othin.*
Hers'-ir, *father of Erna.*
Her'-teit, *Othin.*
Her"-var-ar-sag'-a, *the Saga of Hervor.*
Her'-varth, *a berserker.*
Her'-varth, *son of Hunding.*
Her'-vor, *a swan-maiden.*
Heth'-in, *brother of Helgi.*
Heth'-ins-ey, *an island.*
Hild, *a Valkyrie.*
Hild, *Brynhild.*
Hild, *mother of King Half.*
Hild-i-gun, *daughter of Sækonung.*
Hild"-i-svîn'-i, *a boar.*
Hild-olf, *a warrior.*
Him'-in-bjorg, *Heimdall's dwelling.*
Him"-in-vang'-ar, *Heaven's Field.*
Hind-ar-fjoll, *Brynhild's mountain.*
Hjal'-li, *Atli's cook.*
Hjalm'-ar, *a warrior.*
Hjalm'-ber-i, *Othin.*
Hjalm'-gun-nar, *a Gothic king.*
Hjalp'-rek, *father of Alf.*
Hjor'-dîs, *mother of Sigurth .*
Hjor'-leif, *father of King Half.*
Hjor'-leif, *followier of Helgi.*
Hjor'-varth, *a berserker.*

Hjor'-varth, *father of Helgi,.*
Hjor'-varth, *father of Hvethna.*
Hjor'-varth, *son of Hunding.*
Hlath'-guth, *a swan-maiden.*
Hlê'-barth, *a giant.*
Hlê'-bjorg, *a mountain.*
Hlê'-dîs, *mother of Ottar.*
Hlêr, *Ægir.*
Hlês'-ey, *an island.*
Hlê-vang, *a dwarf.*
Hlîf, *Mengloth's handmaid.*
Hlîf-thras-a, *Mengloth's handmaid.*
Hlîn, *Frigg.*
Hlîth'-skjolf, *Othin's seat.*
Hlokk, *a Valkyrie.*
Hlôr'-rith-i, *Thor.*
Hloth'-varth, *follower of Helgi.*
Hloth'-vêr, *a Frankish king.*
Hloth'-vêr, *father of Htrvor.*
Hloth'-yn, *Jorth.*
Hlym'-dal-ir, *Brynhild's home.*
Hnifl'-ung, *son of Hogni.*
Hnifl'-ungs, *the people of Gjuki (Nibelungs).*
Hnik'-ar, *Othin.*
Hnik'-uth, *Othin.*
Hǫ'-alf, *a Danish king.*
Hǫ'-alf, *King Half of Horthaland.*
Hǫ'-brôk, *a hawk.*
Hodd'-mim-ir, *Mimir.*
Hodd'-rof-nir, *Mimir (?)*
Hog'-ni, *brother of Sigar.*
Hog'-ni, *father of Sigrun.*
Hog'-ni, *son of Gjuki.*
Hǫk'-on, *father of Thora.*
Hol, *a river.*
Holm'-garth, *Russia.*
Holth, *son of Karl.*
Hön'-ir, *a god.*
Hǫr, *a dwarf.*

Hôr, *Othin* .
Horn; *a river.*
Horn'-bor-i, *a dwarf.*
Horth'-a-land, *Half's kingdom.*
Hörv'-ir, *follower of Hrolf.*
Hos'-vir, *son of Thræll.*
Hoth, *slayer of Baldr* .
Hoth'-brodd, *son of Granmar* .
Hô'-tûn, *Helgi's home.*
Hôv"-a-môl'- *the Ballad of the High One.*
Hô'-varth, *son of Hunding.*
Hræ'-svelg, *an eagle.*
Hran'-i, *a berserker.*
Hrauth'-ung, *ancestor of Hjordis.*
Hrauth'-ung, *father of Geirröth.*
Hreim, *son of Thrall.*
Hreith'-mar, *father of Regin.*
Hrim'-fax-i, *a horse.*
Hrim'-gerth, *a giantess* .
Hrim"-gerth-a-môl', *the Ballad of Hrimgerth.*
Hrîm'-grim-nir, *a giant.*
Hrim'-nir, *a giant.*
Hring, *a warrior.*
Hring'-stath-ir, *Ringsted.*
Hring'-stoth, *Ringsted (?).*
Hrist, *a Valkyrie.*
Hrîth, *a river.*
Hrô'-ar, *brother of Borghild (?).*
Hrolf (the Old), *King of Gautland.*
Hrol'-laug, *a warrior.*
Hrô'-mund, *a warrior.*
Hrô'-mund-ar Sag'-a Greips'-son-ar, *the Saga of Hromund Greipsion.*
Hron, *a river.*
Hrôpt, *Othin.*
Hrôpt'-a-tÿr, *Othin.*
Hrö'-rek, *King of Denmark.*
Hross'-thjôf, *son of Hrimnir.*
Hrôth, *a giant.*
Hrôth'-mar, *lover of Sigrlin.*

Hrôth'-vit-nir, *Fenrir.*
Hrot'-ti, *a sword.*
Hrung'-nir, *a giant* .
Hrym, *a giant.*
Hug'-in, *a raven.*
Hum'-lung, *son of Hjorvarth.*
Hund'-ing, *enemy of Sigmund.*
Hund'-land, *Hunding's kingdom.*
Hver'-gel-mir, *a spring.*
Hveth'-na, *mother of Haki.*
Hym'-ir, *a giant.*
Hym"-is-kvith'-a, *the Lay of Hymir.*
Hym'-ling, *son of Hjorvarth.*
Hynd'-la, *a giantess.*
Hynd"-lu-ljôth', *the Poem of Hyndla.*

If'-ing, *a river.*
Im, *son of Vafthruthnir.*
Imth, *a giant.*
Imth, *mother of Heimdall.*
Ing'-un, *sister of Njorth (?).*
Ing'-un-ar – Freyr, *Freyr.*
In'-stein, *father of Ottar.*
Îr'-i, *a dwarf.*
Îs'-Olf, *son of Olmoth.*
Îs'-ung, *a warrior.*
Ith'-a-voll, *meeting-place of the gods.*
Îth'-i, *brother of Thjazi.*
Ith'-mund, *follower of Hjorvarth.*
Îth'-un, *a goddess.*
Î'-vald-i, *a dwarf.*
I'-var, *King of Sweden.*

Jafn'-hôr, *Othin.*
Jalk, *Othin.*
Jar'-i, *a dwarf.*
Jar'-iz-leif, *Atli's emissary.*
Jar'-iz-skâr, *Atli's emissary.*
Jarl, *son of Rig.*

Jarn'-sax-a, *a giantess*.
Jarn'-sax-a, *mother of Heimdall*.
Jof'-ur-rnar, *son of Dag*.
Jôn-ak, *father of Hamther*.
Jor'-mun-rek, *Ermanarich*.
Jorth, *Earth*.
Jôth, *son of Jarl*.
Jot'-un-heim, *the world of the giants*.

Kâr'-a, *daughter of Hafdan*.
Kâr'-i, *ancestor of Ketil*.
Karl, *son of Rig*.
Kâr"-u-jôth', *the Poem of Kara*.
Kef'-sir, *son of Thrœll*.
Ker'-laug, *a river*.
Ket'-il Horth'-a = Kâr'-i, *husband of Hildigun*
Kîl'-i, *a dwarf*.
Kjal'-ar, *Othin*.
Kjâr, *father of Olrun*.
Kleg'-gi, *son of Thrœll*.
Klûr, *son of Thrœll*.
Klypp, *father of Ketil*.
Knê'-fröth, *Atli's messenger*.
Kolg'-a, *daughter of Ægir*.
Kon, *son of Rig*.
Kormt, *a river*.
Kost'-ber-a, *wife of Hogni*.
Kumb'-a, *daughter of Thrœll*.
Kund, *son of Jarl*.

Lǽ'-gjarn, *Loki*.
Lǽ'-rith, *Yggdrasil*.
Lǽv'-a-tein, *a sword*.
Lauf'-ey, *mother of Loki*.
Leg'-gjald-i, *son of Thrœll*.
Leipt, *a river*.
Leir'-brim-ir, *Ymir (?)*.
Lêtt'-fet-i, *a horse*.
Lîf, *mother of the new race*.

Lîf-thras-ir, *father of the new race.*
Lim'-a-fjord, *a fjord.*
Lit, *a dwarf.*
Ljôth'-a-tal, *the List of Charms.*
Lodd"-fâf-nir, *a singer.*
Lodd"-fâf-nis-môl', *the Ballad of Loddfafnir.*
Lof'-ar, *a dwarf.*
Lofn'-heith, *daughter of Hreithmar.*
Log'-a-fjoll, *a mountain.*
Lok"-a-sen'-na, *Loki's Wrangling.*
Lok'-i, *a god.*
Lôn'-i, *a dwarf.*
Lopt, *Loki.*
Loth'-in, *a giant.*
Lôth'-ur, *Loki.*
Lût, *son of Thræll.*
Lyf'-ja-berg, *a mountain.*
Lyng'-heith, *daughter of Hreithmar.*
Lyng'-vi, *son of Hunding.*
Lÿr, *Mengloth's hall.*

Mag'-ni, *son of Thor.*
Mân'-i, *Moon.*
Meil'-i, *brother of Thor.*
Mêln'-ir, *a horse.*
Men'-gloth, *beloved of Svipdag.*
Men'-ja, *a giantess.*
Mim (or Mim'-ir), *a water-spirit.*
Mîm'-a-meith, *Yggdrasil.*
Mîm'-ir, *brother of Regin.*
Mist, *a Valkyrie.*
Mith'-garth, *the world of men.*
Mith"-garths-orm', *a serpent.*
Mith'-vit-nir, *a giant.*
Mjoll'-nir, *Thor's hammer.*
Mjoth'-vit-nir, *a dwarf.*
Mog, *son of Jarl.*
Mog'-thras-ir, *a giant (?).*
Mô'-in, *a serpent.*

Mô"-ins-heim'-ar, *a battlefield*.
Morn'-a-land, *an eastern country*.
Môth'-i, *son of Thor*.
Môth'-ir, *mother of Jarl* .
Môt'-sog-nir, *a dwarf*.
Mund"-il-fer'-i, *father of Sol*.
Mun'-in, *a raven*.
Mû'-spell, *father of the fire-dwellers*.
Mû'-spells-heim, *home of the fire-dwellers*.
Mÿln'-ir, *a horse*.
Myrk'-heirn, *Myrkwood (Atli's land)*.
Myrk'-wood, *a forest in Atli's land* .
Myrk'-wood, *a forest in Hothbrodd's land*.
Myrk'-wood, *a forest in Muspellsheim*.
Myrk'-wood, *a forest in Nithuth's land*.

Nab'-bi, *a dwarf*.
Nagl'-far, *a ship*.
Nâin, *a dwarf*.
Nal, *Laufey*.
Nâl'-i, *a dwarf*.
Nan'-na, *daughter of Nokkvi*.
Nan'-na, *wife of Baldr*.
Nâr, *a dwarf*.
Narf'-i, *Nor*.
Narf'-i, *son of Loki*.
Nâ'-strond, *Corpse-Strand*.
Nep, *father of Nanna*.
Ner'-i, *a giant (?)*.
Nifl'-heirn, *the world of the dead*.
Nifl'-hel, *land of the dead*.
Nifl'-ungs, *the people of Gjuki (Nibelungs)*.
Nîp'-ing, *a dwarf*.
Nith, *son of Jarl*.
Nith'-a-fjoll, *a mountain*.
Nîth"-a-vel'-lir, *home of the dwarfs*.
Nith'-hogg, *a dragon*.
Nith'-i, *a dwarf*.
Nith'-jung, *son of Jarl*.

Nith'-uth, *king of the Njars,.*
Njâls'-sag-a, the Saga of Njal.
Njars, *the people of Nithuth .*
Njorth, *a Wane.*
Nô'-a-tûn, *home of Njorth.*
Nokk'-vi, *father of Nanna.*
Non, *a river.*
Nor (or Norv'-i), *father of Not.*
Nôr'-i, *a dwarf.*
Norn"-a-gests-thâttr', *the Story of Nornagest.*
North'-ri, *a dwarf.*
Not, *a river.*
Nôt, *Night.*
Nÿ'-i, *a dwarf.*
Nÿr, *a dwarf.*
Nÿ'-râth, *a dwarf.*
Nyt, *a river.*

Odd'-rûn, *sister of Atli.*
Odd"-rûn-ar-grâtr', *the Lament of Oddrun.*
Ofn'-ir, *a serpent.*
Ofn'-ir, *Othin.*
Ô'-in, *father of Andvari.*
Ökk"-vin-kalf'-a, *daughter of Thrœll.*
Ô'-köl-nir, *a volcano (?).*
Ol'-môth, *father of Isolf.*
Ol'-rûn, *a swan-maiden.*
Ôm'-i, *Othin.*
Ôn'-ar, *a dwarf.*
Ôr'-i, *a dwarf.*
Ork'-ning, *brother of Kostbera.*
Ormt, *a river.*
Orv'-and-il, *husband of Groa.*
Orv'-ar = Odd, *a warrior.*
Orv'-ar = Odds'-sag-a, *the Saga of Orvar-Odd.*
Orv'-a-sund, *a bay.*
Ôsk'-i, *Othin.*
Ô'-skôp-nir, *an island.*
Ôs'-olf, *son of Olmoth.*

Ôth, *husband of Freyja.*
Ôth'-in, *chief of the gods.*
Oth'-lings, *a mythical race.*
Ôth'-rör-ir, *a goblet.*
Ôtr, *brother of Regin.*
Ôt'-tar, *a warrior.*

Ræv'-il, *a sea-king.*
Rag'-nar Loth'-brôk, *a Danish king.*
Rand'-grîth, *a Valkyrie.*
Rand'-vêr, *son of Jormunrek.*
Rand'-vêr, *son of Rathbarth.*
Ran'-i, *Othin.*
Rat'-a-tosk, *a squirrel.*
Râth'-barth, *a Russian king.*
Râth'-grîth, *a Valkyrie.*
Râths'-ey, *an island.*
Râth'-svith, *a dwarf.*
Rat'-i, *a gimlet.*
Reg'-in, *a dwarf.*
Reg'-in, *son of Hreithmar.*
Reg'-in-leif, *a Valkyrie.*
Reg"-ins-môl', *the Ballad of Regin.*
Reif'-nir, *a berserker.*
Rîg, *Heimdall (?).*
Rîgs'-thul-a, *the Song of Rig.*
Rîn, *a river.*
Rind, *mother of Vali.*
Rin'-nand-i, *a river.*
Rist'-il, *daughter of Karl.*
Rith'-il, *a sword.*
Rog'-a-land, *Norway.*
Rog'-heim, *Home of Battle.*
Rôn, *wife of Ægir.*
Rosk'-va, *sister of Thjalfi.*
Roth'-uls-fjoll, *a mountain.*
Roth'-uls-voll, *a field.*
Ruth, *a river.*

Sǽ'-far-i, *father of Ulf.*
Sǽ'-hrim-nir, *a boar.*
Sæk'-in, *a river.*
Sǽ'-kon-ung, *father of Hildigun.*
Sǽ'-morn, *a river.*
Sǽ'-reith, *wife of Hjorvarth.*
Sǽ'-var-stath, *an island.*
Sâg'-a, *a goddess.*
Sal'-gof-nir, *a cock.*
Sâms'-ey, *an island.*
Sann'-get-al, *Othin.*
Sath, *Othin.*
Sax'-i, *a southern king.*
Segg, *son of Karl.*
Sess'-rym-nir, *Freyja's hall.*
Sev'-a-fjoll, *Sigrun's home.*
Sif, *Thor's wife.*
Sig'-ar, *a Danish king.*
Sig'-ar, *brother of Hogni.*
Sig'-ar, *father of Siggeir.*
Sig'-ar, *Helgi's messenger.*
Sig'-ars-holm, *an island.*
Sig'-ars-voll, *a battlefield.*
Sig'-fath-er, *Othin.*
Sig'-geir, *husband of Signy.*
Sig'-mund, *son of Sigurth.*
Sig'-mund, *son of Volsung.*
Sig'-nÿ, *sister of Sigmund .*
Sigr'-drif-a, *Brynhild.*
Sigr"-drif-u-môl', *the Ballad of the Victory-Bringer.*
Sigr'-lin, *wife of Hjorvarth.*
Sig'-rûn, *wife of Helgi.*
Sig'-trygg, *a king.*
Sig'-tÿr, *Othin.*
Sig'-urth, *son of Sigmund.*
Sig"-urth-a-kvith'-a en Skam'-ma, *the Short Lay of Sigurth.*
Sig'-urth Ring, *son of Randver.*
Sig'-yn, *wife of Loki.*
Silf'-rin-topp, *a horse.*

Sind'-ri, *a dwarf.*
Sin'-flot-li, *son of Sigmund*
Sin'-ir, *a horse.*
Sin'-mor-a, *a giantess .*
Sin'-rjôth, *wife of Hjorvarth.*
Sith, *a river.*
Sith'-gran-i, *Othin.*
Sith'-hott, *Othin.*
Sith'-skegg, *Othin.*
Skâf'-ith, *a dwarf.*
Skâld"-skap-ar-mâl, *the Treatise on Poetics.*
Skat'-a-lund, *a forest.*
Skath'-i, *a goddess.*
Skegg'-jold, *a Valkyrie.*
Skeith'-brim-ir, *a horse.*
Skek'-kil, *father of Skurhild.*
Skelf'-ir, *a king.*
Skilf'-ing, *Othin.*
Skilf'-ings, *descendants of Skelfir.*
Skin'-fax-i, *a horse.*
Skirf'-ir, *a dwarf.*
Skirn'-ir, *Freyr's servant.*
Skirn"-is-môl', *the Ballad of Skirnir.*
Skîth'-blath-nir, *a ship.*
Skjold, *a Danish king.*
Skjöld"-ung-a-sag'-a, *the Saga of the Skjoldungs.*
Skjold'-ungs, *descendants of Skjold.*
Skog'-ul, *a Valkyrie.*
Skoll, *a wolf.*
Skor'-u-strond, *home of Varin.*
Skrÿm'-ir, *a giant.*
Skuld, *a Norn.*
Skuld, *a Valkyrie.*
Skûr'-hild, *daughter of Skekkil.*
Slag'-fith, *brother of Völund.*
Sleip'-nir, *Othin's horse.*
Slîth, *a river.*
Smith, *son of Karl.*
Snæ'-fjoll, *a mountain.*

Snæv'-ar, *son of Hogni*.
Snör, wife of Karl.
Snöt, *daughter of Karl*.
Sogn, *a bay*.
Sôg'-u-nes, *a cape*.
Sökk'-mîm-ir, *a giant*.
Sökk'-va-bekk, *Saga's dwelling*.
Sôl, *Sun*.
Sôl'-ar, *son of Hogni*.
Sôl'-bjart, *father of Svipdag*.
Sôl'-blind-i, *a dwarf*.
Sô'-fjoll, *a mountain*.
Sôl'-heim-ar, *Hothbrodd's home*.
Sorl'-i, *son of Jonak*.
Spar'-ins-heith, *Sparin's Heath*.
Spor'-vit-nir, *a horse*.
Sprak'-ki, *daughter of Karl*.
Sprund, *daughter of Karl*.
Stafns'-nes, *a cape*.
Stark'-ath, *son of Granmar*.
Stor'-verk, *father of Starkath*.
Strond, *a river*.
Styr'-kleif-ar, *a battlefield*.
Sun, *son of Jarl*.
Surt, *a giant*.
Suth'-ri, *a dwarf*.
Sut'-tung, *a giant*.
Svaf'-nir, *a king*.
Svaf'-nir, *a serpent*.
Svaf'-nir, *Othin*.
Svafr'-thor-in, *Mengloth's grandfather*.
Sval'-in, *a shield*.
Svan, *father of Sæfari*.
Svan'-hild, *daughter of Sigurth*.
Svan'-ni, *daughter of Karl*.
Svâr'-ang, *a giant*.
Svar'-in, *a hill*.
Svar'-ri, *daughter of Karl*.
Svart"-alf-a-heim', *the world of the dark elves*.

Svart'-hofth-i, *a magician.*
Svath"-il-far'-i, *a stallion.*
Svâv'-a, *daughter of Eylimi.*
Svâv'-a, *wife of Sækonung.*
Svâv'-a-land, *Svatnir's country.*
Svegg'-juth, *a horse.*
Svein, *son of Jarl.*
Sver"-ris-sag'-a, *the Saga of Sverrir.*
Svip'-al, *Othin.*
Svip'-dag, *son of Solbjart .*
Svip"-dags-môl', *the Ballad of Svipdag.*
Svip'-uth, *a horse.*
Svith'-rir, *Othin.*
Svith'-ur, *Othin.*
Svî'-ur, *a dwarf.*
Svol, *a river.*
Svôs'-uth, *father of Summer.*
Sylg, *a river.*

Thakk'-râth, *Nithuth's thrall.*
Thegn, *son of Karl.*
Thekk, *a dwarf.*
Thekk, *Othin.*
Thîr, *wife of Thræll.*
Thith"-reks-sag'-a, *the Saga of Theoderich.*
Thjalf'-i, *Thor's servant.*
Thjaz'-i, *a giant.*
Thjôth'-mar, *father of Thjothrek.*
Thjôth'-num-a, *a river.*
Thjôth'-rek, *Theoderich .*
Thjôth'-rör-ir, *a dwarf.*
Thjôth'-var-a, *Mengloth's handmaid.*
Thjôth'-vit-nir, *Skoll.*
Thol, *a river.*
Tholl'-ey, *an island.*
Thôr, *a god.*
Thôr'-a, *daughter of Hokon.*
Thôr'-a, *wife of Dag.*
Thôr'-in, *a dwarf.*

Thôr'-ir, *follower of Hrolf.*
Thôrs'-nes, *a cape.*
Thræll, *son of Rig.*
Thrâin, *a dwarf.*
Thrith'-i, *Othin.*
Thrôr, *a dwarf.*
Thrôr, *Othin.*
Thrûth, *a Valkyrie.*
Thrûth, *daughter of Thor.*
Thrûth'-gel-mir, *a giant.*
Thrûth'-heim, *Thor's home.*
Thrym, *a giant.*
Thrym'-gjol, *a gate.*
Thrym'-heim, *Thjazi's home.*
Thryms'-kvith-a, *the Lay of Thrym.*
Thund, *a river.*
Thund, *Othin.*
Thuth, *Othin.*
Thyn, *a river.*
Tind, *a berserker.*
Tot"-rug-hyp'-ja, *daughter of Thræll.*
Tron"-u-bein'-a, *daughter of Thræll.*
Tron'-u-eyr, *Crane-Strand.*
Tveg'-gi, *Othin.*
Tÿr, *a god.*
Tyrf'-ing, *a berserker.*

Ulf, *follower of Hrolf.*
Ulf, *son of Sefari.*
Ulf'-dal-ir, *Völund's home.*
Ulf'-rûn, *mother of Heimdall.*
Ulf'-sjâr, *a lake.*
Ull, *a god.*
Un"-a-vâg'-ar, *a harbor.*
Un'-i, *a dwarf.*
Urth, *a Norn.*
Ût'-garth-a = Lok'-i, *a giant.*
Uth, *daughter of Ægir.*
Uth, *Othin.*

Vaf'-thrûth-nir, *a giant.*
Vaf"-thrûth-nis-môl', *the Ballad of Vafthruthnir.*
Vak, *Othin.*
Vâl'-a-skjolf, *Othin's home.*
Val'-bjorg, *Grimhild's land.*
Vald'-ar, *a Danish king.*
Val'-fath-er, *Othin.*
Val'-grind, *a gate.*
Val'-hall, *Othin's hall.*
Vâl'-i, a god.
Vâl'-i, *son of Loki.*
Val'-land, *Slaughter-Land.*
Val'-tam, *father of Vegtam.*
Vam, *a river.*
Van'-a-heim, *home of the Wanes.*
Vand'-ils-vê, *a shrine.*
Van'-ir, *the Wanes.*
Var, *a dwarf.*
Var'-in, *a Norwegian king (?).*
Var'-ins-fjord, *a bay.*
Vâr'-kald, *father of Findkald.*
Vath'-gel-mir, *a river.*
Vê, *brother of Othin.*
Veg'-dras-il, *a dwarf.*
Veg'-svin, *a river.*
Veg'-tam, *Othin*
Veg"-tams-kvith'-a, *the Lay of Vegtam.*
Vel"-ents-sag'-a, *the Saga of Velent.*
Ver'-a-tÿr, *Othin.*
Ver'-land, *Land of Men.*
Verth'-and-i, *a Norn.*
Vestr'-i, *a dwarf.*
Vestr'-sal-ir, *Rind's home.*
Vethr'-fol-nir, *a hawk.*
Vê'-ur, *Thor*
Vif, *daughter of Karl.*
Vîg'-blær, *Helgi's horse.*
Vîg'-dal-ir, *Battle-Dale.*
Vigg, *a dwarf.*

Vig'-rîth, *a field.*
Vil'-i, *brother of Othin.*
Vil'-meith, *a dwarf (?).*
Vil'-mund, *lover of Borgny.*
Vin, *a river.*
Vin'-bjorg, *Grimbild's land.*
Vind'-alf, *a dwarf.*
Vind'-heim, *Wind-Home.*
Vind'-kald, *Svipdag.*
Vind'-ljôn-i, *Vindsval.*
Vind'-sval, *father of Winter.*
Ving'-i, *Atli's messenger.*
Ving'-nir, *Thor.*
Ving'-skorn-ir, *a horse.*
Ving'-thôr, *Thor.*
Vin'-ô, *a river.*
Virf'-ir, *a dwarf.*
Vit, *a dwarf.*
Vith, *a river.*
Vith'-ar, *a god.*
Vith'-ga, *son of Völund.*
Vith'-i, *Vithar's land.*
Vith'-of-nir, *a cock.*
Vith'-olf, *a dwarf (?).*
Vith'-rir, *Othin.*
Vith'-ur, *Othin.*
Vôf'-uth, *Othin.*
Vols'-ung, *father of Sigmund.*
Vols"-ung-a-sag'-a, *the Saga of the Volsungs.*
Vols'-ungs, *descendants of Volsung*
Vö'-und, *a smith.*
Vö"-und-ar-kvith'-a, *the Lay of Völund.*
Vol"-u-spô', *the Wise-Woman's Prophecy.*
Vôn, *a river.*
Vond, *a river.*
Vôr, *a goddess.*

Y'-dal-ir, *Ull's home.*
Ygg, *Othin.*

Ygg'-dras-il, *the world-ash*.
Ylf'-ings, *a Danish race*.
Ylg, *a river*.
Ym'-ir, *a giant*.
Yng (or Yng'-vi), *son of Halfdan the Old*.
Yng"-ling-a-sag'-a, *the Saga of the Ynglings*.
Yng'-lings, *descendants of Yng*.
Yng'-vi, *a dwarf*.
Yng'-vi, *son of Hring*.
Yng'-vi, *Ynq*.
Ys'-ja, *daughter of Thræll*.

Made in the USA
Lexington, KY
02 February 2014